Pre-Publication Quotes

"In *Parts Psychology*, Dr. Jay Noricks presents a bold, yet very natural theory of psychodynamics in crystal clear prose that draws the reader along with the insistency of a good mystery novel. This is not surprising because each of us presents a sort of mystery acted out by our *parts* (subpersonalities) pursuing their own concerns and relationships with other parts and persons. In Noricks' theory, parts consist of bundles of memories organized into hierarchies based on level of associated pain or pleasure. The therapist attempts to help the client follow an affect bridge (free association from an emotion) to discover and name his/her parts and interview each to discover its most painful memories. Then each part is given methods to unburden itself of troublesome memories. The most painful memories are treated first. The influence of dysfunctional memories is dissipated by inserting them into fantasies that remove them from concern, typically by washing them out, burning them up, or shutting them away. Noricks' approach is based in ethnology and cognitive anthropology as well as personality theory. The narrative quality of his theory of parts helps us to see the therapeutic value of folktales and other folk narratives that work collective cures by speaking to the troubled parts and separation anxieties of entire cultures. His theory of therapy helps us to see that the process of maturation as a human being involves recognizing one's own parts and promoting one or more of them to the role of in-house therapist. I strongly recommend this book to anyone seeking a better balance and synergy in the dynamics of their own personality."
—Gary B. Palmer, PhD, Author, *Toward a Theory of Cultural Linguistics*
University of Nevada, Las Vegas

"This fascinating book describes Dr. Noricks' creative strategies for treating such issues as anxiety, depression, jealousy, grief and loss, and others. Appealing to therapists and clients alike, these are intimate and compelling accounts of emotional pain and trauma and of successful healing. Clients love the way this approach to therapy really works."
—Carol L. Cathey, MPH; MS, MFT

"Dr. Noricks has written a lucid exposition of parts psychology, arguing that each of us maintains a variety of subpersonalities which can function to help or hinder the attainment of our goals. By using case histories drawn from his own practice, he demonstrates the manner in which his approach deals with troubling issues like jealousy, anger, hatred, depression, and addiction and results in psychological healing. Therapists will find this book provocative and instructive, and the general public will find it intriguing and helpful."
—Thomas W Hill, PhD, Professor Emeritus and former Head of the Department of Sociology, Anthropology, and Criminology, University of Northern Iowa

"[Dr. Noricks'] form of clinical observing and reporting is a fine teaching method. It brings the reader right into the process of parts work. I was deeply engaged in it. I was understanding how the patient was empowered to bring her true self into identifying, controlling, and managing the sources of her extreme feelings and her patterns of thought that might otherwise be taken as character traits."
—Louis W Tinnin, MD
Emeritus Professor
West Virginia University

"Dr. Noricks has given us a wonderful book, which allows the reader to learn about both Parts Psychology and Internal Family Systems and their application in treatment. A masterful clinician, Dr Noricks' approach is a very readable and clear theoretical account backed up by lively case examples. It is a must read for all students and seasoned clinicians who wish to understand their clients more fully and assist in their continued growth by helping them deal with their *parts*."
—Paula Howie, ATR-BC, LPC
Associate Professorial Lecturer, George Washington University
Past President, American Art Therapy Association

Parts Psychology

A Trauma-Based, Self-State Therapy for Emotional
Healing in Counseling and Psychotherapy:
Case Studies in Normal Dissociation

Jay Noricks PhD

New University Press

Los Angeles

Publisher's Note:

This book is intended for the entertainment of its readers. It is not a self-help book. In addition to entertainment, the book also suggests new ways for experienced therapists, skilled in the stabilization of emotional overwhelm, to consider expanding their approaches. The book is not intended as advice for novice therapists. Clients who desire expert assistance in psychotherapy should consult a competent, licensed mental health care professional.

Cover by Dany BenDavid and Chay Samson

For information about permission to reproduce selections from this book, write to:
Permissions
New University Press
12405 Venice Blvd Suite 330
Los Angeles, CA 90066

You may also contact the publisher at
NewUniversityPress.com

ISBN: 978-0-9829219-8-2

Library of Congress Control Number: 2010915312

To my wife, Dina Noricks, who was an active collaborator at the inception of this book and a constant support during its writing. And to my daughters Darcy Miyuki Eleni Noricks and Siena Rose Holland, and my son Jacob Takeo Noricks, all of whom make me very proud.

Table of Contents

Foreword

This book offers a field map to the inner worlds of psychotherapy patients. Our guide, Dr. Jay Noricks, began his training in the field of anthropology at the University of Pennsylvania at a time when anthropology emphasized the importance of good ethnography (cultural description) as the foundation for good culture theory. His doctoral dissertation was an ethnography of the culture of a remote Polynesian island. Good ethnography meant describing behavior in terms of the concepts and standards of the people who carried out the behavior. This sort of description was called *Cognitive Anthropology* or *Ethnoscience.* It was about understanding the observed phenomena from the point of view of the people who lived the phenomena.

When Jay left academic anthropology for a career in psychotherapy, he applied his ethnographic view to his work with his clients. He wanted to understand them from the framework of how their minds were organized without making assumptions ahead of time about that organization. He hoped to understand the concepts and structures that were behind the way they organized their approach to living in their world. He found the tools he needed in the emerging field of *Parts Psychology.*

This approach holds that the mind's underlying concepts and structures contain states of being that are dissociated residuals of challenging experiences or activated intrinsic survival structures. Such states originate in the efforts of body and mind to manage a challenge or survive a threat. Once activated these structures can persist and influence for good or bad the person's behavior in the face of later challenges. Together these structures influence the person's approach to living in the world.

Clinicians have labeled these structures in a variety of ways: parts, self states, ego states, subpersonalities, or alter personalities. Jay learned a lot from the techniques of clinicians doing parts therapy but especially those treating *dissociative identity disorder (DID)* with its many alter personalities. He concluded that the alter personalities of DID differed only in degree from non-DID structures. Jay has come to believe that everyone has an internal world of subpersonalities and that these parts are the same mental structures as DID alter personalities.

He asserts that not only are parts normal but that they are permanent. This puts him on the side of a growing number of therapists treating dissociative disorders who reject the earlier treatment goal of fusion of the personality structures into a single self. Jay holds that the treatment goal should be the achievement of integrated functioning among normally dissociated parts. He believes that the unity of self is an illusion. That is, the familiar *I* and *me* is merely a conventional way of speaking that does not represent the actual organization of our minds. The personality is not unitary. Instead, the natural condition of the human personality is one of multiplicity.

I have seen how Jay's goal for psychotherapy –integrated functioning of parts – helps to make it possible to treat dissociative patients in a time-limited outpatient program. Jay's influence came from his keynote presentations in 2005 and 2007 to the annual conference on *Treating Trauma and Dissociation* sponsored by West Virginia University and Intensive Trauma Therapy Inc., Morgantown, West Virginia (http//:www.traumatherapy.us). His concepts made it possible to develop methods for unburdening the dissociated parts responsible for a trauma victim's pessimistic worldview, which we understand as *victim mythology*. The two treatment tasks of bringing closure to traumatic memories and reversing traumatic dissociation had been achieved in the ITT marathon treatment but the third task of resolving victim mythology still required long term psychotherapy. A different approach was suggested when the component attitudes of victim mythology were understood as outdated trauma burdens carried by dissociated subpersonalities. These burdens included victim entitlement, secrecy, shame, guilt, distrust, absolute safety, and despair, all of which could now be dispelled in the light of present-day reality through dialogue between the patient's self and the parts.

I know that Jay and the other proponents of Parts Psychology face a universal human resistance to the idea of parts. It evokes the images of many people in one body or multiple minds in a single brain, or maybe multiple souls. Since we all did have a dual brain with independent cerebral hemispheres during our first three years before the connecting neurons of the corpus callosum matured, perhaps we just cannot get over the shame of it and do not want to think about it. For whatever reason there seems to be an obligatory illusion of mental unity that we hold to and defend.

If this is the reader's first encounter with Parts Psychology there may be initial surprise with Jay's rejection of single-mindedness but the reader will find Jay's exposition to be persuasive, straightforward, and easy to grasp.

Louis W. Tinnin, MD
Professor Emeritus
West Virginia University

Preface

There are 15 chapters in this book. Thirteen of them form its core. These 13 chapters describe the in-depth success stories of 12 previously troubled psychotherapy clients. The stories represent a blend between psychological case reports and anthropological cultural narratives. Narrative description is the focus of the book. Theory is minimal except in the first and last chapters. Taking the time to describe the inner worlds of troubled clients is consistent with an anthropological approach to understanding whole cultures. It is consistent with the way I approached writing up the results of my fieldwork on a tiny island in Polynesia. My first publications aimed at describing and understanding the way my anthropological consultants understood their world: a Polynesian-English dictionary, a paper on the local meaning of *crazy*, and a description of a method for eliciting native-speaker models of thinking.[1] Only later did I write more theoretical papers.[2] Now, having changed careers from anthropology to psychotherapy, I follow a similar path of emphasizing description before theory. The book contains both, but the theory is dependent upon the description.

This book aims for two audiences. The first is the general reader with an interest in psychology, especially those with interests in the organization of mind and the process of psychotherapy. My hope is that readers will find the inner worlds described here, and the therapeutic changes made through work with these worlds, just as fascinating as I found them. The idea that we all have multiple personalities—but not a disorder of personalities—may at first be shocking. But the evidence for this normal multiplicity among relatively ordinary people is so powerful that even the most skeptical of readers may change their minds before finishing the book. Many readers may discover some of their own parts as they read the stories in the core chapters.

The second audience is the experienced, professional psychotherapist or counselor. Therapists are always looking for new and better ways to help their clients. This book provides a complete description of how to do therapy in a new way. My hope for professionals is that that they will find something they can use in their own work. First in Chapter 1, which provides an overview of the model, and then through commentary embedded in the narratives of Chapters 2 through 14, I try to make clear in step-by-step fashion how *Parts Psychology* works. A careful reading of the introduction, the commentary on the narratives, and the concluding chapter should answer most technical questions professionals might pose if they decide to add Parts Psychology to their treatment frameworks.

I have organized the book with a view toward entertaining as well as teaching. The entertainment emphasis is inherent in storytelling. From tiny islands isolated in the South Pacific to booming metropolises on the continents, humans love the telling of stories. This book tells stories about the intimate details of people's lives, especially the details of the problems they face in the living of those lives. All core chapters present narratives of the successes ordinary people found in overcoming ordinary problems. Of course, some problems are less ordinary than others, but none of them are of the more serious psychotic and dissociative issues that land people in mental wards. We all have some understanding of jealousy, anger, procrastination, food issues, sexual desire, and most other problems described in the narrative chapters. Some readers may have less familiarity with a few issues, such as sexual swinging and porn addictions, but even these are well known through widespread media outlets.

In deciding which stories to include in the book, one determinant was variety. A second was complexity. I wanted to include a variety of problems and a range of complexity in order to illustrate the wide applicability of Parts Psychology. Each of the 13 narrative chapters presents a distinctly different set of therapeutic issues. Chapters 2 and 3, on jealousy and rage, present the least complex narratives in the book. Chapter 4 on work performance, while dealing with mundane issues, describes a significantly more complex inner world. Sex and love, perennial human interest topics, are represented in Chapters 5, 6, and 7 as problems of sexual desire, sexual swinging, and letting go of love after a breakup. Chapters 8 (binge eating) and 12 (bulimia) present healing stories involving food issues. Both narratives illustrate the complexity of internal systems produced by child abuse. Chapter 9 (grief and depression) represents the mid-range in treatment complexity, while Chapter 10, *Body and Beauty*, continues the story of one client's longer-term therapy begun in chapter 4. Chapter 11 illustrates that addiction to pornography can be easily treated with Parts Psychology; but the case becomes a complex matter when healing the porn problem leads to low sex drive. Chapter 13 (lifetime depression) is complex primarily because healing the depression also required withdrawal from psychoactive therapeutic drugs. The final narrative chapter (Chapter 14, *Scaredy Cat and the Monster*) addresses the notions of symbol and metaphor in doing parts work.

Most chapters illustrate that seemingly intractable problems can resolve themselves through Parts Psychology in short-term therapy. This is especially evident in Chapter 2, which contains the stories of two women with extreme jealousy issues that healed in just five and six sessions. Most clients can finish their work within 20-24 sessions, which is still short-term therapy of five or six months with once-a-week meetings. However, it is also possible to do effective longer term work with the model. Chapters 4, 10, and 14 all represent work with a single client lasting about two years.

Of course, some problems take many years to resolve, such *as dissociative identity disorder (DID)*, previously labeled *multiple personality disorder (MPD)*. In writing this book I have been careful to exclude the narratives of clients who are diagnosable with DID or even *DDNOS (dissociative disorder not otherwise specified)*. My purpose in excluding dissociative disorders is simply to avoid confusion. Otherwise it might be less clear that it is normal for people to have hidden parts of themselves. The clients whose worlds I describe here are similar to hundreds of other clients whose inner worlds we explored in doing the therapy of Parts Psychology. Over the last 10 years I have worked with more than 30 cases of DID and my caseload has included, at any given time, three to six clients with this diagnosis. Parts Psychology is effective in work with these persons, too; however, long-term therapy is the rule for them. There are no DID, DDNOS, or other clients with dissociative disorders described in this book.

Acknowledgements

My first expression of gratitude goes to the 12 clients who graciously agreed to allow me to tell their stories in the 13 narrative chapters. They asked only that their identities be concealed. Each of them read their own narrative and agreed that they would not be recognized in the descriptions. Several others also gave their permission to include their stories but space limitations prevented their inclusion in the final version of the book. Their stories were nevertheless important in conceptualizing the book.

In alphabetical order, all of the following read one or more chapters and provided helpful comments during the writing of the book: Sherri Conley, Linda Gantt, Ken Heck, Jeffrey Kottler, Hugh Marr, Darcy Noricks, Darciann Samples, Diane Standley, John Swetnam, Louis Tinnin, Joanne Urioste, and Richard Vande Voort. Darcy Noricks, Darciann Samples, and Joanne Urioste provided additional help through detailed commentary and editing of large portions of the book. Darciann Samples urged me to write a summary chapter of the book based upon my embedded commentary in the narrative chapters. She also did the final proofreading of the book. Drawing upon her own excerpts from the narrative chapters, Darcy Noricks actually wrote the first draft of Chapter 15, Summary and Conclusion.

The inspiration for writing this book came from Louis Tinnin, MD, who twice invited me to make Keynote presentations at his and Linda Gantt's annual conference on *Treating Trauma and Dissociation,* sponsored by West Virginia University and Intensive Trauma Therapy Inc. We had met online in a discussion group on the treatment of dissociative disorders. When Lou invited me to present two Keynotes, I found it necessary to systematize my thoughts. Once I began doing this, I discovered that I needed case studies to substantiate the model. These studies form the core of the book.

Chapter 1
The Parts Psychology Treatment Model

Parts Psychology is both a way of doing psychotherapy and a way of understanding the mind. It approaches the therapy of troubled individuals by suggesting that the normal personality is not unitary; instead, the normal sense we have of being a unitary *I* or *me* is an illusion. It seems to be a necessary illusion, but still an illusion. The actuality is that the self is an agglomeration of many selves, and whichever self speaks as the I on any given occasion may be different from the self or group of selves that speaks as the I on another occasion.

We recognize our natural multiplicity in the ordinary language we use to express ourselves. A frustrated employee might say, "A part of me wants to tell my boss to go to hell, but the rational part of me says I need this job." Someone with marital issues might say, "A part of me wants to leave, but another part is afraid to be alone." A friend with an addiction might say, "I can go for a few days without using, but then a part of me takes over and I find myself getting high all over again." These *parts* are the focus of Parts Psychology. Calling them parts is consistent with our everyday language, but the professional literature provides many other terms as well, including *subpersonalities, sides, subselves, internal self states,* and *ego states.* When these parts are extreme and capable of taking full control of the person, as in the case of *multiple personality disorder* (now renamed *dissociative identity disorder),* they are called *alters* or *alter personalities.* This book does not describe any cases of multiple personality disorder. Each of the extended case descriptions that make up the body of the book is a study of the inner world of a person with normal personality structure.

The idea that the normal personality consists of parts is not a new one. Morton Prince, a 19th and early 20th century pioneer in the study of multiple personality disorder, also explored the natural divisions of the normal personality. He called these normal parts *sides.* He made the point that the sides of normal personalities are not very different from the alters of multiple personality disorder.[3] We now know that the difference is that alter personalities can completely take control of a person and the person retains no memory for the episode once the alter personality has relinquished control.[4] However, with normal persons, parts blend with the self without taking complete control and the person remembers the behavior influenced by the part. Generally, a person is unaware of a part's blending, and whether the person is feeling anger, sadness, joy or some other emotion, the blending is so seamless that the person owns the experience entirely. She would say, for example, "I am angry," without any sense that the anger originated with a blended subpersonality.

Following the early appearance of ideas about the natural multiplicity of the self,[5] there was a long period of neglect as Sigmund Freud's psychoanalytic framework overwhelmed psychology's treatment programs. Modern psychology is only now beginning to focus on what some scholars understood a century ago about the organization of the mind. Parts Psychology recognizes the importance of the previous generation of scholars but takes the knowledge of our divided minds a step further. What is new, and even startling for some, is that we can help people artificially separate their parts from the self in the therapy room and actually engage in conversations with these parts. In this way, because we are working directly with the parts of the self that are most problematic, therapy becomes much more efficient. Healing moves at a much faster pace.

Two other models of psychotherapy heavily influence Parts Psychology as presented in this book. The first is the *Ego State* therapy of John and Helen Watkins.[6] The second is Richard C. Schwartz's *Internal Family Systems* therapy.[7] These two approaches are similar in that subpersonalities are accepted as important and natural elements of the mind and are not interpreted in terms of the older, grand theories of psychodynamic writers.[8] Both accept subpersonalities as "part persons" with a sense of self, a sense of purpose, and a way of perceiving the world that is unique to each part. Both approaches work with the individual parts that carry the problems in order to alleviate the distress of the whole person. The differences are minor. The Watkinses work almost exclusively through hypnosis while Schwartz emphasizes work with the fully aware person. Another difference is that Schwartz encourages the therapist to work through the self, coaching its interaction with subpersonalities. The Watkinses, on the other hand, emphasize direct interaction between therapist and parts while the client is in a state of hypnotic trance. As an apparent consequence of bypassing the fully aware person in working with parts, the Watkinses do not directly acknowledge the presence of a self that is different from parts.

Most of the interventions I emphasize in Parts Psychology are also found in the work of either or both of the above writers, but there are some important differences. I have borrowed the most important of these interventions from the work of Richard C Schwartz. This is the concept of *unburdening*.[9] It involves the use of symbolic visualizations to release the problem emotions and beliefs the client brings to therapy. I have added to the unburdening intervention the use of a measuring tool to determine the degree to which a part has completely unburdened itself through a given intervention. I have also extended the concept of unburdening beyond work with negative emotions to include work with positive emotions or sensations, such as love and sexual arousal. Like Schwartz, I find that formal hypnosis is unnecessary in work with clients' internal worlds. I did not use formal hypnosis with any of the case descriptions presented in this book, although when clients concentrate on internal parts their appearance is sometimes trance-like.

Another difference from other approaches is that I emphasize that parts appear in our lives naturally, as the result of a universal, developmental process. When we need to adjust to something new in our lives, whether it is something in our own development, such as puberty, or something in our external environment, such as the way we are parented, additional subpersonalities spontaneously appear, enabling us to adjust to our changed situations. Thus, as we grow and develop, new parts appear whenever our existing parts cannot easily deal with a new challenge. Parts Psychology holds that subpersonalities are the natural building blocks of the mind, and without their development, we would lack the essential human flexibility that has allowed us to adjust to virtually every social and physical environment our planet has to offer.

A second difference lies in my emphasis upon painful life experiences as the basis for the development of most subpersonalities and for the later negative consequences that bring our clients to therapy. This emphasis means that healing has to do with neutralizing the negative energy (e.g., anger, anxiety) that is attached to the remembered experiences. The result of this neutralizing, usually through unburdening, is that the experiences will no longer negatively impact our clients' lives. Internal parts develop in response to our need to adjust to our life circumstances and, once created, these parts specialize in containing the memories that have some similarity to the original experiences that brought the parts into being. When the way our parts influence us becomes less helpful and more damaging to the way we function, it is essential to help them become more centered and flexible in their roles. Flexibility follows from neutralizing some or all of the emotional content of a part's set of memories, beginning with the earliest memories recorded in the memory set. The original painful events, sometimes so painful they should be called *traumas,* are the most important concerns of therapy. Until the memories of the original events are neutralized, many later painful events cannot be fully processed.

There are a few exceptions to the rule that subpersonalities appear in our lives in response to painful life experiences. Parts can also appear as the result of our experience of positive but novel life events. For example, a female client developed a new part at the age of ten when she met a boy who became a friend and who introduced her to his world of video and computer games. This fun-loving part became an important aspect of the client's life, expanding its original function of adjusting to her new friend to many other situations where a joyful and energetic approach to life was appropriate. With such positively functioning subpersonalities, there is no need for therapeutic intervention. In another case, discussed later in Chapter 4, the client developed a part who took joy in helping others. In childhood, this was an endearing trait. In adulthood, however, this trait worked against her in the workplace, where the time she spent helping coworkers meant she was not finishing her own assigned tasks. In this case, change was necessary. The positive energy attached to the helper part's early experiences had to be neutralized before the part could become flexible enough to know when to give priority to the client's own needs over the needs of others.

Case Example

In the following example, I sketch the inner world of a normal person with a small number of subpersonalities. My purpose is to give the reader a sense of how internal parts can be organized in a normally functioning person. I address many other questions raised by the case example in later chapters of the book. In this case, all of the client's parts have names, although they evidently did not have names before we did the work to differentiate them from the self. I later learned that, on their own, the parts chose names as we sought them out and interviewed them.

Madeline, the client, is a successful, 40-year-old professional woman with no outstanding psychological issues. She is a normal high-functioning person. She is the district sales manager for a multinational corporation. Madeline did not come to me for therapy for specific issues; instead, she wanted to get a better understanding of *who* she was. She said that she had read about the idea that everyone had internal subpersonalities, and if that were true, she wanted to know about hers. Except for helping Madeline differentiate her parts, I did no other therapeutic interventions with her. All she wanted to accomplish was to become acquainted with her internal world. We did the work without formal hypnosis. Simple absorption techniques were all that was necessary. An example of such a technique is, "Focus upon that feeling and ask it to give you a picture of itself." I describe additional techniques later in this chapter.

Madeline has five internal parts, an unusually small number. Possibly, the small number is due to the relative absence of significant trauma in Madeline's early life. There is a child, an adolescent, and three adults. The child is *Bunny* who presents herself as a six-year-old girl. Madeline believes that Bunny's internal image probably represents what she herself looked like as a child. Bunny is playful, relates well to Madeline's children, and loves animals. She often gives Madeline dreams because, she says, she does not have the vocabulary to communicate like a grownup. She claims to have the ability to retrieve all of Madeline's memories, including everything Madeline has ever read. Bunny was the second of Madeline's internal parts to develop, appearing at the age of four when Madeline felt shut out from her grieving parents after her younger brother died. Incidentally, Bunny does not view Madeline's mother as her own mother, although she sees Madeline's father as her father. The closest Bunny has to a mother is *Vivian*, the system's internal manager. The two of them relate to each other, Madeline says, like a mother and daughter.

The adolescent is *Suzanne*. She presents herself as 14 years old. She developed during Madeline's tumultuous teenage years slightly before Vivian became active and began evolving toward her eventual role as the system manager. However, unlike Vivian, Suzanne did not rebel against the mother. Instead, she passively endured. She wanted to be pretty and desirable, while her mother regularly told her she was ugly and undesirable. The internal image Madeline has of Suzanne is that of a beautiful teenager with only a slight resemblance to Madeline. Suzanne is a romantic, given to reading romance novels. Among her functions are ensuring Madeline's appropriate dress and social etiquette. Suzanne is quite vain.

The three adults are Vivian, aged 44, the internal manager; *Janice*, aged 33, the worker and taskmaster; and *Sally*, aged 34, the worrier. Janice and Sally's ages are approximate; they do not claim an exact age. Vivian says she first appeared in Madeline's life at about 10 years of age but did not become active until slightly after Suzanne, the adolescent, appeared, perhaps at 14 or 15. Vivian developed in response to the need to stand up to a dominating mother. The teenage years were difficult, full of the mother's verbal, and occasionally physical, abuse. It was the time when Vivian was most angry, and led to her becoming the system's anger manager. The mother sometimes called Madeline a devil. That was Vivian, expressing herself through Madeline, while accepting the mother's label for her. Vivian, who Madeline perceives as classically beautiful, also functions as Madeline's primary sexual part, although all the adult parts can be sexual at times. Vivian is the primary protector of Bunny, the six-year-old. Because Vivian views Bunny as too young to be involved in sexual activities, she ensures that the child is absent whenever Madeline and her husband engage in lovemaking. Like Bunny, Vivian does not view Madeline's mother as *her* mother, and like Bunny, Vivian views Madeline's father as *her* father.

The second adult is Janice. She is the only subpersonality to have developed during Madeline's adulthood. She presents herself internally as plain looking, but with no resemblance to Madeline. She does not view Madeline's family members as her own. She first appeared when Madeline was 28 and beginning a new career. The new career was demanding and required a steep learning curve of Madeline. Janice was the part who brought the necessary energy and drive to succeed. She is a worker, an organizer, and a taskmaster, with few interests other than doing what is expected of her. She provides a focus on practical matters while excluding concerns that might interfere with task completion. Domestically, she is also the *duty sex* part, available to Madeline's husband when Madeline is uninterested in sex.

The third adult is Sally. She was actually the first of Madeline's parts to develop. She first appeared when Madeline was two years old in response to the birth of Madeline's younger brother, the same brother whose death led indirectly to the appearance of Bunny two years later. The new child was sickly and generally secluded. Sally was anxious about him, reflecting her parents' anxiety about their son's health. In physical appearance, Sally presents herself as Madeline appeared in her 30s, before she lost weight and toned her body. According to Madeline, Sally says she is roughly 34 years old. She had aged along with Madeline until Vivian, who replaced her as the system manager, became dominant during Madeline's program of diet and exercise a few years previously. As the system manager, Sally was anxious and depressed, but as her leadership gave way to that of Vivian, Madeline lost about 60 pounds and became an avid cyclist. Vivian's replacement of Sally as internal manager symbolizes Madeline's shift from an anxious depression-based view of the world to a positive action-based view. With Vivian in control of her internal world, Madeline stayed in a program of physical conditioning, maintained her competence at work, and refused to be submissive in social relationships. Sally, although no longer depressed, continues to amplify negative energy in the form of anxiety. She is a frequent worrier, anxious about the possibility of any significant disruption in Madeline's life. Sally, the worrier, and Janice, the worker, often combine their efforts in order to bring to Madeline's attention whatever problem Sally has seen on the horizon. Sally views Madeline's mother and father as her own.

Four years after Madeline differentiated her internal parts, she describes her internal world as stable. She says that because of her awareness of her internal family her life is fuller and richer now than it ever was before. She feels a sense of being centered and knows exactly what she wants from life. In technical language, Madeline achieved *increased integrative functioning* through working with her parts. She frequently consults with her parts and listens to what they have to say. When she experiences a strong negative emotion, she often seeks out the part who is expressing the emotion so that she can deal with it appropriately. Madeline does not experience a confusion of identity when a part blends with her. She maintains executive control across all situations. She does not experience "a disruption in the usually integrated functions of consciousness, memory, identity, or perception of the environment" which is characteristic of persons with dissociative disorders.[10] Moments of distress for Madeline are not clinically significant; they are in proportion to the situation. Overall, as the result of her work with Parts Psychology, Madeline continues to experience an enhanced positive functioning.

The Basic Treatment Plan

The procedures for healing through work with the inner world are straightforward. First, find the part that carries the problem behavior, while remaining aware that sometimes more than a single part may be involved. Second, elicit the problem memories held by the part. Third, neutralize the energy attached to the problem memories. Finally, help the now flexible part adjust to a newly defined role when necessary. Sometimes, adjustments have to be made to the basic plan. I describe the most common of these adjustments through the case descriptions that follow this chapter. The following sections sketch the most important elements of the basic treatment plan.

SUD and SUE Scales

In doing Parts Psychology, we will normally collect a set of significant memories from a newly differentiated part, including, whenever possible, its earliest painful memories. These are the memories that must be neutralized if the part is to be flexible enough to change the way it functions. As these memories are collected, it is important to get a sense of how disturbing they are to the client. The measure to do this is called a *SUD* scale, for *Subjective Units of Disturbance*.[11] The therapist asks the client to ask the part how disturbing the memory is on a scale from zero to 10, where zero represents neutrality and 10 represents the most disturbing level a memory can reach. For example, a part created to handle the pain of physical punishment might rate its earliest remembered beating as a 10 on the SUD scale, but might rate a later, similar beating as a level five on the SUD scale. In working with troubled parts, we want to reduce the disturbances to a zero on the SUD scale whenever possible.

Sometimes, as with the case of the helper part mentioned above, a different kind of scale is needed because the memories are not disturbing. In such cases, I use a *SUE* scale, for *Subjective Units of Energy*. Generally, these memories are positive, but occasionally a client cannot characterize an event as either positive or negative, just as containing a lot of energy. Thus, a 0-10 SUE scale measures the energy invested in an experience when that energy is not negative. The therapy described in Chapter 4 includes interventions that neutralize the energy attached to a client's early positive experiences of helping others. The purpose of that therapy was to free the part from its intense desire to please others even to the client's own detriment.

Locating Parts

Finding a problem part can be easily accomplished by roughly 90 percent of clients. Suppose the problem is excessive anger. I might ask the client to think about a person or event that causes the client to become aware of irritation or anger. Next, I would ask the client to focus on the emotion or its associated body sensations. Then I would ask the client to speak inwardly to the emotion, asking it "to give you a picture, an internal image of itself." The client can make the request of its internal part while speaking aloud or, as most do, by speaking silently, subvocally, to the emotion or sensation. In the great majority of cases, there is an immediate response as the client notices an internal image of the part. The most frequent response is an image of the client as viewed in present time, sometimes dressed as she is in the therapy room, but more often with a different set of clothing, and perhaps with an expression on her face that is consistent with the emotional state we are working with, e.g., a frown. Another frequent response is an image of the client at an earlier age, ranging from a few years distant to a picture from childhood. Less frequently, the client will visualize a person with no physical similarity to her at all. Still less frequently, the internal image may be that of an animal, such as a lion or a fox, a cartoon figure, or a symbol such as a triangle or a fog. The particular costume worn by the part, i.e., the image visualized by the client, is much less important than the content of the part's memories.

A variety of other techniques helps a person to visualize a part. When the direct approach above does not produce a viable image, my favorite next attempt is the following guided imagery. I ask my client to focus on the experienced emotion or sensation and then to imagine the presence of two harmless fishermen who hold between them a tightly stretched magical fishing net, magical because it can pass through the body without harm. I suggest that the client imagine the fishermen walking past her on either side of her holding the net between them. As they walk past her, the net passes easily through her body, but snags on and wraps around the part (i.e., the negative emotion or body sensation). Then, as the visualized fishermen continue walking past the client, the net pulls the part out of her body. When she visualizes the part emerging from her body in the net, I suggest that she place it gently into a nearby room, and then look into the room and describe what she sees there. The visualized image is the part we are looking for.

Sometimes, when freestanding parts cannot easily be located, it is useful to find them as they appear in significant memories. Often, when a client recalls a memory, she may be able to visualize herself in the memory as if she were standing outside the memory scene rather than experiencing it from within. If so, the therapist can guide the client in interacting with that memory self. It may or may not have additional memories or knowledge of the client's life outside the memory scene.

A few clients cannot visualize their subpersonalities but still manage to do excellent parts work. Of these, most connect to their internal parts through body sensations. For example, a male client experienced parts sensations at various locations in his body. There were parts who spoke from the left, right, and back of his head; another manifested a sensation between his eyes and yet another from the area of the heart. These sensations appeared to be permanent connections between the client and his parts, and he communicated with them just as well as those who have internal images upon which to focus.

Still another technique for locating parts builds upon earlier success. Once the client has developed the skill to maintain an internal dialog with a given part, I might ask this part to assist me in finding others. Suppose, for example, the client had managed to develop a relationship with a task-oriented worker part, but an anger-carrying part had not yet shown itself. In such a case, if anger was an issue, I might suggest to the client that he ask the worker part if it knew an angry part. If so, the next step would be to request that the worker part bring the angry part onto the client's internal screen. If this internal bridging is successful, therapist and client can then proceed with interviewing the new part in the usual manner.

Unfortunately, not all clients are able to develop and maintain an internal image or other means of consistently connecting with an internal part. I find that perhaps 10 percent of my clients are unable to do parts work of any sort. This does not include those clients who can do parts work but choose not to do so. For most of these latter clients, talking with an aspect of self as if it were a person raises the fear that they might be mentally ill, or might become so through this work. Although such fears are groundless, it is better to turn to more traditional helping approaches than to force the parts approach on the unwilling client.

Memory Sets

The primary content of a subpersonality is its memory set. This set of memories provides the distinctive perspective the part brings to the larger self. Most often, these memories consist of a series of negatively experienced events with a common theme. For example, the theme might be improper favoritism and the memory set might contain all of the experiences that support a client's view that a parent unduly favored a sibling in childhood. The memory set might also contain memories of teachers favoring another child over the client, or of an employer promoting a less talented worker ahead of the client. Typically, other experiences that might cast doubt on the perception of favoritism are either not included in the memory set, or are discounted as exceptions and explained away by special circumstances.

The earliest painful memory, the one that most likely brought about the existence of the subpersonality, deserves special attention. If an intervention aimed at reducing the negative energy carried by the part is to be successful, this earliest memory must be reduced to neutrality. Otherwise, later memories cannot be successfully desensitized. The earliest memory will continue to amplify its negative energy onto the later ones, preventing their desensitization. Additionally, current life experiences will continue to trigger the early memory and create additional distress in the present.

It is sometimes possible to collect a part's entire set of significant memories, both positive and negative. The part is the judge of what is significant. Sometimes, however, there are too many memories to make the task of recording them practical. In such cases, a representative sample is sufficient, ranging throughout the historical period in which the part actively functioned. In most cases, a relatively small number of memories, five to eight experiences, will capture the essence of a part's role. During the processing of these memories, other memories will spontaneously appear, enabling the part to process its entire memory set.

There is a finite number of significant memories in the memory set. Additionally, a group of memories with a similar theme can be represented by a single memory that includes all of the major issues, such as fear, anger, and abandonment that appear repetitively over time. For example, a person may have experienced chronic abuse over many years but the part who encapsulates the abuse memories in its content may include in its memory set only the most painful ones. When the client processes these more powerful memories, he may not consciously register the processing of the less painful memories. Yet, at the conclusion of work, the less powerful memories do not register distress for the part.

The therapist can sometimes safely elicit the full memory set before processing the content. However, my experience suggests that the client is emotionally safer when the therapist helps her process painful memories as they are elicited. Otherwise, she may be overwhelmed later by the emotions she accessed during the session but did not process to neutrality. For example, a depressed client who experienced the loss of both parents during childhood might experience a deeper depression in the following days if the therapist does not help her to deal with her unresolved grief before ending the session. Similarly, a man whose extreme anger is fueled by his memories of physical abuse throughout childhood should work through major abuse memories as they appear in session rather than wait until the next therapy session. Otherwise, he may find himself overreacting to minor provocations for the next few days. A useful guide to working with these volatile cases is to collect only the number of memories that can be successfully processed during the same session. In those cases where it proves impossible to complete the processing of painful memories prior to ending the session, the therapist should help the client place the unresolved material in temporary storage until the following session. I describe techniques for doing so in the text.

Keeping in mind these cautions, there can be benefits to working with the entire memory set. When therapist and client together examine the full content of a part's memory set, they can more easily see what should be unburdened and what should be left untouched. Selective unburdening is invaluable for work with certain kinds of problems. For example, many men with pornography addictions have a part that includes within its memory set both normal sexual encounters, as well as problematic pornographic encounters. In such cases, the therapist would want to desensitize the pornographic memories while leaving intact the energies of sexual memories that are not a problem for the client.

The Affect Bridge

In locating a part's earliest memory, it is sometimes sufficient simply to coach the client to ask the part to recall it. At other times, however, the part's recall may be aided through an *affect bridge,* a technique developed by John Watkins which, with its companion *somatic bridge,* is widely utilized in Watkins and Watkins' Ego State therapy.[12] With this technique, the therapist asks the client to speak to the part they are working with and to ask it to connect to the emotion it feels when they discuss a current problem issue. Then, let the part's mind search back across time for the earliest memory that somehow connects to the emotion it feels in the present. The therapist might also ask for a somatic bridge by asking the client to focus on a body sensation, such as tightness in the chest, a knot in the stomach, etc., and search for the earliest memory of that sensation. These techniques do not always reach the *earliest* relevant memory but the memories that *are* located are always significant. The therapist may repeat the request using the last memory located and, with that as an anchor, bridge to still earlier memories. I use both of these techniques frequently in doing Parts Psychology.

Unburdening

Unburdening is a technique developed by Richard C. Schwartz,[13] which enables internal parts to discard the accumulated loads of distress they have acquired in their history of protecting the self. The content of a part's burden consists primarily of negative energies such as guilt, fear, humiliation, anger, sadness, etc. that are attached to its accumulated memories. A part is unburdened of these noxious emotions as the therapist guides the client in working with his internal parts. The tools for unburdening are visualization and imagination. The client visualizes the part giving up its burden through some sort of symbolic action. Once the part agrees to relinquish its burden, the therapist might ask the client whether the part would like to give it up to wind, water, fire, or something else.[14] Depending upon the part's response, the client might visualize wind blowing the burden away, water dissolving it, or fire burning it up. Other symbolic actions that parts have chosen include throwing the burden over a cliff, flushing it down the toilet, burying it in a deep hole, and using various means of smashing it into nothingness. Once unburdened, the part becomes flexible and centered while giving up its extreme beliefs and behaviors. The client can now move forward with more positive integrated functioning.

I illustrate below three metaphors for unburdening. The precise language for any given intervention will vary according to the context. These examples address negative emotions, but the procedure is the same when addressing positive emotions that require unburdening. Sometimes the client will listen and repeat the words to the subpersonality and sometimes he will simply allow my words to pass through to the subpersonality. Occasionally, when my client has difficulty in reproducing the language or imagery, I will intentionally speak directly to the subpersonality.

Visualize the part standing in a waterfall and notice how sometimes there are drops of water and sometimes mist and sometimes a powerful pouring of water. Let the water flow over, around and through her. Notice how the part's hair is plastered to her head and her clothes stick to her skin. Ask her to locate where it is within her that she stores the problem memory and then ask her to feel the water dissolving the pain and negative emotions connected to the memory.

Notice how the negative emotions dissolve in the water as the water washes them out of her. You may even notice how the water around her is discolored as the dissolved negative emotions are washed away. As the water continues to wash away her anger [or fear, sadness, etc.] you may notice how it gradually becomes clear again as the memory is washed clean.

Visualize a bonfire for the part and ask him to stand in front of it. Then ask him to locate where it is within him that he stores the painful memories. Now ask him to reach inside of himself and lift out the negative emotions [or negative energy] and throw them into the fire. As the fire touches them, you can see them burst into flame. Ask him to go back for more and keep repeating the action until all of the negative emotions and sensations that were attached to the memories are entirely consumed in the fire.

Visualize the part standing in an open field and bring up a powerful wind to blow over, around, and through her. Ask her to locate where it is within her that she stores the memory and ask her to feel the wind scouring the memories and washing them clean of fear and anger [or sadness, shame, etc.]. As the wind breaks up the fear and anger into tiny particles, you may notice that as the wind blows away from her it is darker because it is blowing away the particles of those emotions like dust or sand. Let the wind continue to blow until the memory is just a neutral memory with no particular emotion attached to it.

Using guided imagery is not new in psychotherapy. What is new is the use of these techniques in a context where subpersonalities are explicitly recognized. The therapist focuses the intervention on an internal part with whom the client maintains contact as opposed to asking the client to experience directly the imagined wind, water, fire, etc. The powerful results of unburdening are the direct consequence of working with the specific subpersonality that actually carries the painful emotions in its memory set. A therapist may achieve some limited success through working just with the client without a direct connection to an internal part. However, the work with internal parts is the source of the dramatic results I describe in this book.

Much of the time, the initial intervention does not fully unburden the part, although the part may communicate that the visualization was successful. This is where the therapist makes use of the SUD and SUE scales. The therapist coaches the observing self (i.e., the client) to ask the part how disturbing the targeted experience is now on the 0-10 SUD scale. If we are working with positive emotion, the therapist asks for a measure of the remaining energy on the SUE scale. Typically, the initial unburdening intervention succeeds in reducing the level of distress from, for example, 10 to six, eight to five, or seven to two. Repetition of the intervention leads to additional unburdening. After the initial unburdening, the therapist coaches the client to ask the part what is the most disturbing aspect of the remaining burden. The unburdening then focuses specifically on that disturbing element. Suppose, for instance, that we were trying to unburden the part who carried the disappointment of a mother's lack of attention while growing up. Assuming that the initial intervention reduced the SUD level to a three, we might then ask what made it a three rather than a zero. The response might be, "Because it's wrong!" We could then ask the part to focus on that wrongness as we repeated the unburdening metaphor. The intervention might require three or four repetitions before the unburdening is complete.

A good example of unburdening positive energy using a SUE scale comes from a case of marriage counseling. My client, the wife, wanted to hurt a romantic rival in some way. She had followed her around the city for hours. She had twice verbally confronted her. The rival obtained a restraining order against my client to keep her at a safe distance. Unfortunately, my client's jealous and vengeful part, overwhelmed by powerful emotions, led her to stalk the other woman anyway. Because my client recognized that she was putting herself in danger of further legal problems, she agreed to work with her inner world. In working with the vengeful part, we discovered that she acquired her earliest memory at her fourth birthday party where she received a sandbox as one of her birthday gifts. A neighborhood boy insisted upon "messing with" her sandbox in spite of her demands that he stay out of it. Finally, exasperated, she hit the boy in the head with a rock. He ran home, bleeding and crying. As my client relates the incident, she got in trouble for injuring the boy, but she got her sandbox to herself. For the vengeful part, this experience was satisfying to a SUE level of 10. It seems that just as she viewed the sandbox as her property and did not want to share it, she also viewed her husband as her property and was unwilling to share him. In a single intervention of unburdening, however, she was able to reduce the energy level of the sandbox memory to zero. She accomplished this through the symbolic action of visualizing the part detaching the positive energy from the memory and throwing it into a fire. The consequence was that she was able to stop stalking her rival. Later, there were a few other positive memories that required unburdening, but the procedure was the same.

Generally, there are just two reasons for why a part cannot unburden itself completely. First, a manager part, especially an angry part, might believe that it needs the negative energy amplified by a burdened part to fuel its own drive. It fears that if the first part is unburdened it will not be able to carry out its agenda without the agitation produced by the distressed part. The second reason is the presence of another part, usually a younger one with an earlier memory, who is amplifying its pain to the degree that the targeted part is experiencing the pain as its own. In either case, the task is to find the blocking part, develop a cooperative relationship with it, and then either unburden it or gain its permission to continue the work with the first part. The focus of therapy then returns to the original part in distress.

Unburdening may also stall when the part feels it has not yet been sufficiently heard or understood. The client may report something like "She [the part] wants you to know it wasn't her fault." In such cases, it is helpful to halt the direct attempts to unburden the problem emotions and to take time just to listen to the part's story. Once a part has told its story, it is usually ready to return to the work of direct unburdening.

Other Interventions

Unburdening is the most dramatic intervention for bringing about immediate therapeutic change. There are a few other interventions that are useful at times. For example, listening to a part's story, mentioned above, helps to reduce the negative energy attached to a part's memory set. Such narrative processing of life events is one aspect of nearly all psychotherapies.

What is new here is that the therapist coaches the client to elicit the narrative directly from the subpersonality who carries the memories. There is something about this direct connection between subpersonality and client that increases his ability to release negative energies as the part tells its story.

Another intervention, one with a long and venerable history, involves changing the way the client remembers a traumatic event. This sort of intervention can be traced to the 19th century work of Pierre Janet who succeeded in healing distressed clients through revisiting the original trauma memory during hypnosis and changing the remembered outcome with hypnotic suggestion.[15] In Parts Psychology, similar but less dramatic memory interventions can be helpful in the healing process, but without the use of formal hypnosis. For example, a child part visualized by the client as trapped in the memory of her parents' fighting can sometimes be encouraged to tell her parents to stop the fighting and go to their rooms. If the child part is unable to act in this way, the client can imagine herself going into the remembered scene to demand an end to the fighting. Finally, if neither the child part nor the client can imagine herself standing up to the parents, the therapist can ask the client to visualize the therapist going into the scene and bringing about appropriate changes.[16] Another client, dealing with the effects of childhood physical abuse, might imagine his adult self entering the remembered scene of a severe beating and ordering the abuser to cease his or her activity. The result of such interventions can be the immediate reduction, or even cessation, of distress for the part still trapped in the painful scene. For the client it means that current events will no longer trigger the targeted memory. That memory will then no longer amplify emotional pain into the life of the client.

Another way to work with traumatic memories is to remove the part from the memory scene. In most cases, this results in an immediate diminution in the part's distress. Carrying out the intervention can be quite simple. The therapist could suggest that the client visualize taking the part's hand and stepping out of the scene and into another, more comfortable scene. For this purpose, the client can create an internal safe place, perhaps a combination of a playroom and family room for both child and adult parts. While such a safe place is imaginary to the client, it is real to internal parts, as is the relief parts feel when going there.

Still another valuable intervention brings about a dialog between polarized subpersonalities. For example, one part may push the client to take a stronger stand with real world adversaries, while a second part argues that greater success will come from a gentler approach. The result for the client can be a vacillation between positions, never knowing what is best, with a resultant anxiety over decisions previously made and a dread of making future decisions. An example could be the pressures felt when friends or relatives make unreasonable requests of the client. In such cases, the therapist can help to bring about a reduction in anxiety and self-blame by brokering an exchange of views between the extreme parts. Once the client visualizes the opposing parts, she can encourage them to understand each other's position and to work together as a team for the welfare of the client. Parts often take extreme positions because they are afraid that if they give in to the other part, all will be lost and the client will be damaged in some permanent way. By encouraging a dialog between parts, the client can bring about a cooperative working relationship between formerly polarized parts, combining the skills of both subpersonalities. The client thus acquires greater flexibility in the outside world, drawing upon the resources of either part depending upon what will work best in a particular situation.

Normal and Abnormal

One possible criticism of Parts Psychology might be that the inner worlds of subpersonalities illustrated throughout this book are abnormal worlds, and the persons whose stories are told here could be suffering from dissociative identity disorder or lesser degrees of dissociative problems. In dissociative identity disorder, painful memories are separated (dissociated) from the observing self and sequestered within the boundaries of alter personalities who have the ability to switch into control of the client for varying periods of time. When such powerful alter personalities take control, the client typically has no memory for what transpires during the period of control. The presence of these subpersonalities is the most well known aspect of dissociative identity disorder. It is one major purpose of this book, however, to argue that having subpersonalities is not abnormal. What is abnormal is the autonomous ability of some subpersonalities to take full control of the person and to leave the person with amnesia when the part gives up its control. It is not abnormal, however, for subpersonalities to influence a person from within and thus bring about shifts in moods and attitudes. This is normal functioning. In order to assure readers that the case descriptions that follow this chapter are descriptions of dissociatively normal people, I have taken pains to choose for this book, with the exception of Chapter 13, only those clients whose scores are less than average on the Dissociative Experiences Scale, the most widely used measure of dissociation.

The Dissociative Experiences Scale

The *Dissociative Experiences Scale (DES)* is a 28-item questionnaire that measures the degree of dissociation a person experiences in everyday life.[17] Dissociation includes common experiences such as losing track of time and place while driving, or having your mind wander while someone is talking to you. It also refers to more problematic symptoms, such as having the sense that you are observing yourself from outside your body, or having the sense that the world is not real. Dissociation also includes the separation of painful memories from the person and the sequestering them in the memory sets of the alter personalities found in dissociative identity disorder. This process may leave the person with few memories of some significant life events. Although the dissociation of painful memories into alter personalities is best known in dissociative identity disorder, the process is not in itself pathological. It fact, it is the normal process by which people put aside their problematic experiences and resume normal activities, for example, after a death in the family or a disappointment at school or work. Such memories are collected in the memory sets of normal parts (subpersonalities). Dissociation is the process that brings about new subpersonalities, whether in the normal person or in the case of dissociative identity disorder, whenever the new experiences are sufficiently novel or too painful to handle by existing parts. The difference between normal and abnormal dissociation is in the degree of amnesia. With dissociative identity disorder, it may be impossible to access dissociated memories without an alter personality taking control of the person. The normal person can generally gain access to partially dissociated memories through concentration and discussion.

The average DES score is 10.[18] Persons diagnosed with posttraumatic stress disorder typically score in the high teens or 20s. More severe dissociative disorders, including dissociative identity disorder, become increasingly likely as scores approach 30 and higher.[19] With one exception, I have intentionally limited the case descriptions in this book to persons who score the average or less than the average of 10 on the DES scale. My intent is to ensure that the case descriptions represent people with normal degrees of dissociation. Thus, the ability to go inside and work with subpersonalities is a normal ability and not an abnormal one. I do not include any cases of clients with dissociative disorders. At the beginning of the description of each case study, I include the DES score of the person in the study.

Chapter 2
Extreme Jealousy

The experience of extreme jealousy is a common problem in psychotherapy. Fortunately, it is also easily treated. Surprisingly, perhaps, the most common cause of problem jealousy is the experience of relationship loss during childhood. The loss may be due to the death of a close friend or relative, or it may be due to loss through a family's move to another location. Divorce that involves the resultant absence of one or the other parent is another example of such traumatic loss. Two other sources for adult problem jealousy are more obvious. Children raised in a family where questions of parental infidelity become an issue affecting the entire family may also experience problem jealousy in their own relationships. Finally, problem jealousy in adult relationships may be due to an unfortunate personal history of romantic partners' infidelity. Combinations of these three sources of extreme jealousy can also occur, leading to greater or lesser expressions of the problem.

Anger inevitably accompanies the experience of jealousy, but the expression of extreme anger may not be limited to incidents of jealousy. Consequently, the treatment of overwhelming anger may require additional work beyond the treatment of jealousy alone. An illustration of this appears in the first case description below, where the client required another session of work just on anger even after her problem jealousy had been resolved. In the two cases of problem jealousy described in this chapter, resolution of the issues happened quickly. Both clients had other issues they might have worked on, and other subpersonalities whose content they might have explored. However, they were pleased with the quick results in therapy for their major issues. They were excited about moving on with their lives once they had removed the major obstacles to positive functioning. Jealousy and anger had blocked their achievement of happiness for so long that they now experienced bursts of positive energy they wanted to put to good use outside the therapy room. They were not particularly interested in further insight into their internal worlds. They focused instead upon their new enjoyment of their external worlds.

Sharon

Sharon was a 34-year-old married professional who came to therapy with a problem of excessive jealousy. Her score on the Dissociative Experiences Scale was a modest 5.0, a low average in comparison with the norm of 10.0. Her first words in our initial session identified her greatest problem as her frequent outbursts of anger at her husband. She screamed at him, demanded he account for all time away from her, accused him of infidelity, and found herself enraged over the smallest issues. She got upset when he talked to another woman, even a fellow employee or a member of his staff. She was irritated even if he glanced at a passing woman when they were out together. She had been jealous of this, her second husband, throughout the five years of their marriage. Additionally, her outbursts had increased since the death of her father three years ago. This increase is consistent with a view of jealousy that views it as one result of previous losses.

When asked to focus on her feeling of jealousy and to request that feeling to provide a picture of itself, Sharon saw an internal image of herself at her present age, with messy hair and no makeup, wearing a pink t-shirt and shorts. When Sharon got the part's attention by speaking subvocally to the image and asking it to look her way, the visualized part answered that her name was also *Sharon*. She was not quite sure, however, how she and the observing Sharon were related to each other. To distinguish the part from Sharon, we called her *Sharon 34*. Referring to a part by its presenting age is helpful in keeping track of the many subpersonalities with the same name. She accepted Sharon's explanation of internal parts and acknowledged that she was the jealous part. In an occasional twist found in parts work, we learned that although she presented herself as age 34, she felt like she was just eight years old. Her felt age makes more sense when we learn that her earliest memory was of being eight years old as she waited for her father to come home. She waited for him and watched through the living room window for him to appear. This experience repeated itself frequently. Sometimes he did not come home all night. Emotionally, she appeared to be stuck in childhood. Other memories she held included hearing her mother scream at her father after he came home drunk, and of her mother leaving home for hours, or even overnight, following parental arguments. It was common for her to see her father drunk and asleep at the kitchen table. Sometimes neighborhood cops brought him home too drunk to drive. She constantly worried that he would die in an accident while driving in an inebriated state. Interestingly, Sharon 34 had narrative memories only from about age eight through her early 20s. Sharon was married to her first husband during her early 20s and to her second husband beginning in her late 20s. Sharon 34 had no specific memories of the second husband or later life history. Having a set of memories that is limited to certain age ranges is common among subpersonalities.

All of the preceding information appeared in our first session. In the second session, because the first jealous part had no knowledge of the second husband, I asked Sharon to focus specifically on her current jealousy of her husband and to ask that feeling to provide a picture of itself. The internal image she produced was that of a younger version of Sharon, about age 21, wearing a different t-shirt and shorts, and with a different hairstyle. With the permission of the part, we called her *Sharon 21*. Her memories began at age 17 and continued through the present. Her earliest memories were of feeling panicky and pacing the floor as she waited for her boyfriend to pick her up for dates. This boyfriend became her first husband. He was late frequently, both as boyfriend and as husband. Other memories Sharon 21 carried were of her frequent crying as she longed to marry her reluctant boyfriend, and of getting married while sporting a black eye, given to her by the boyfriend. She also remembered being home alone while her husband went out with people from work and, later, going through the divorce process. Finally, she remembered how her ex-husband stalked her for a time, following the divorce. Not all of Sharon 21's memories were negative. She also had the powerful positive memories of meeting Sharon's second husband and marrying him. These memories did not require unburdening. Still later memories, merging with current concerns, had to do with her jealous fears involving her second husband, such as imagining the women in his office thrilling to what she considered his attractive French accent.

As Sharon spoke during this second session, she noticed she was feeling angry but was not sure if the anger originated with Sharon 21. We bridged to the angry part by asking Sharon 21 to locate the angry part and bring it onto Sharon's internal mental screen. The image Sharon reported was that of a blob, beige in color and featureless. *The Blob* did not immediately know Sharon, but after an explanation of internal parts, the new subpersonality indicated that, while she did not know her age, she felt like a female teenager. Her earliest memories were of her father coming home drunk and engaging in screaming arguments with her mother. Later memories were of moving in with the boyfriend who would become her first husband, but worrying about whether her mother would be safe alone with her father. She also remembered phone calls from her mother reporting that her father was drinking and not going to work. Another small set of memories involved being married, upset, and angry with no one to talk to about her husband or her father. The Blob acknowledged that she sometimes screamed at the current husband, but she indicated that she was also angry with Sharon because Sharon was so quick to attack her husband.

In our third session, we began the unburdening using a wind metaphor, with Sharon visualizing wind blowing away the negative emotions carried by Sharon 34. We worked first with her earliest memories, those of staring out the window and waiting for her father to come home. From there, we moved on to unburdening her later painful memories. After completion of the unburdening work with Sharon 34, this part reported that she now felt herself to be age 34 and not eight as she originally felt. As a final touch, Sharon visualized an internal family room, a safe place, and moved Sharon 34 there, where other parts would later join her.

Sharon 21 was next, and she quickly unburdened her painful experiences through a water metaphor as Sharon visualized her standing in a mountain waterfall with the water washing away her negative emotions. Sharon said that at the conclusion of the intervention Sharon 34 exclaimed, "I'm free!" Her appearance also changed somewhat, morphing from dry to wet hair and aging from 21 to her late 20s. Sharon then visualized her joining Sharon 34 in the family room.

The third unburdening involved The Blob, who chose a wind metaphor for her relief. She stood in an open field as Sharon imagined the wind blowing over, around, and through her. The wind carried away as dark particles the negative emotions of the painful events that had continued to haunt her.

The Blob also changed her appearance during the course of the unburdening. She now appeared as Sharon remembered herself as a teenager, but with shorter hair and wearing "a little skirt and a t-shirt." She, too, joined the other parts in the internal family room.

Among the hundreds of clients with whose internal systems of parts I have worked, Sharon responded to the unburdening therapy more quickly than others did. Unburdening frequently takes weeks, and often requires that we unburden individual memories one at a time. Sharon, however, unburdened entire memory sets without flinching. From the beginning, she was focused and intent on getting the job done. She knew she had a problem and she wanted to fix it. She trusted me to help her to do that. She accepted the approach without question and quickly and efficiently worked with her parts to heal them. We had now brought major relief to the problem of jealousy, but two more sessions were necessary to deal with the additional problem of rage.

Near the end of the third session, following the unburdening of the three parts we had found so far, we found a fourth part whose functions included household organization and the expression of anger, especially when Sharon was under stress and household chores were piling up. Sharon found this part by thinking about the previous evening when her husband announced that his boss had invited them to his house. Sharon's response was to "freak out" over all her household chores yet undone. By connecting to her stress over unfinished laundry and then asking that stressed out feeling to show itself, Sharon discovered the new part. She viewed it internally as an image of herself at her current age and with her current hairstyle, but wearing household work clothes and visibly angry. This new part was comfortable with being referred to as *Sharon Homemaker*. Her role in Sharon's life included making lists of chores needing attention, and crossing them off the list as they are accomplished. Sharon said that this part of her also demanded that household chores be done in a particular way. A memory from six years earlier was of Sharon Homemaker's anger over the way her husband had vacuumed the carpet—so she vacuumed it again herself. Her husband's vacuuming disturbed her then to only a SUD level of two. The earliest memory this part could identify had to do with jealousy. Seven years previously when she and her current husband first moved in together,

Sharon found a love letter from her husband's previous girlfriend. The event disturbed her to a level eight on the 0-10 SUD scale. The collection of this information brought us to the end of the session. We planned to continue to explore the homemaker part and do an initial unburdening in the next session.

At the beginning of the fourth session, we checked on the three parts we had unburdened to this point. All was well, according to Sharon, except that she had experienced some distressing thoughts about her husband interacting with his female staff in the office. Simply thinking about such normal interaction was distressing, though not nearly as distressing as it had been when she first came to therapy. We would check on this distress again, after we worked with the new part.

We continued to explore the memories of Sharon Homemaker. She carried the burden of the death of Sharon's father six years previously. Among her other memories were the positive experiences of introducing her new husband to her parents and then, four years before our sessions, the birth of Sharon's daughter. Neither of these experiences needed unburdening. Near the end of the session, with a focus on the memories of the father dying, the love letter from the husband's old girlfriend, and the husband's vacuuming, we unburdened Sharon Homemaker of her accumulated load of painful affect. Utilizing a water metaphor, Sharon visualized the part swimming in a gentle sea as the water dissolved her burden of grief, jealousy, anger, and other pain.

In the fifth and final session two weeks later, we worked again with Sharon Homemaker. Although there were no incidents of jealousy between sessions, there was rage. Sharon said that two nights prior to our session she had screamed uncontrollably at her husband for 30 minutes for his failure to bring in the trashcans. Everything else in her life was good now, with no excessive jealousy. She just wanted to stop her angry outbursts. Further questioning revealed that Sharon Homemaker had still earlier memories, so far unreported. These memories began by the age of seven and lasted at least through the age of 12. They were all about the constant screaming between her mother and father about many different things, but especially regarding household duties and chores. I suggested to Sharon Homemaker that her anger toward her husband about doing chores was not really her own but her parents', and that she could give it back to them. The unburdening involved the symbolic return of her anger to her parents. She expressed immediate relief after she visualized herself handing her anger back to them. With her anger gone, she felt the fear it had blocked. This was the fear that one or the other of them would leave her if they divorced. The final unburdening involved the use of a wind metaphor to blow away Sharon's burden of fear and hurt attached to those many years of painfully watching her parents screaming at each other. Sharon Homemaker then accepted her redefined role of dealing calmly and efficiently with practical matters. Sharon's report at six months follow-up was that she remained free of her excessive jealousy and of her angry outbursts.

Samantha

Samantha was 24 years old, married, and struggling somewhat with the question of parenthood versus career. However, her primary reason for coming to therapy was her concern with her extreme experiences of jealousy and anger toward her husband. Her score on the Dissociative Experiences Scale was 7.5, an average tendency toward dissociation in comparison with the norm of 10. Her first comments in the therapy room were about her fears of abandonment. She connected those fears to her parents' sudden divorce when she was a teenager. They came home from a walk one evening, with her mother sobbing, and told Samantha they were divorcing. Her father had decided to resume his old love affair with his high school girlfriend. Now, every couple of weeks, Samantha's husband did something, such as going golfing in the afternoon without telling her that triggered her fear that he, too, will suddenly leave her. "I try to be a perfect wife," she said, "so he won't leave me. My fear controls me since I became a wife." Her fear lead her to feel intense anger, and sometimes jealousy, so great that she felt she had to isolate herself from her husband for a few hours lest she lash out against him and cause him to leave her for expressing her fearsome rage.

Samantha had other concerns she wanted to address in therapy, such as her fear of beginning professional life as a new college graduate, but her fear and anger about possible abandonment represented her core issues. The anger was overwhelming and gave her such a burst of unpleasant energy that she had to find ways to dissipate it. Often she cleaned house for hours or went to the gym for heavy physical workouts.

I introduced Parts Psychology in the first session, and Samantha was fascinated by the idea that the personality might be naturally divided into discrete subpersonalities with whom she could consciously interact. I asked her to think about what made her angry, and to focus upon a particular memory of this. "I get angry when he chooses someone over me," she said, such as his brother or someone from work. When asked to do so, she remembered and re-experienced some of the intense anger she felt on a recent day when she learned that her husband had been released early from work and, rather than come home right away, he played golf with his coworkers. I asked her to focus on her anger and to speak to it, asking that emotion to give Samantha an internal image of itself. The response was immediate.

Samantha suddenly found herself visualizing a female in her teens with long dark hair, dressed in black or dark colors, "Gothic looking," and very intense. Samantha described her as "pacing, and wanting to throw things." In appearance she was similar to Samantha, but without her "exact face." This internal image responded quickly as Samantha asked the questions I coached her to ask. Yes, she knew Samantha, and called her "my sister." She knew John, Samantha's husband, but did not know the two were married. Samantha said that the part thought of John as "somebody trying to hurt me [i.e., Samantha]." The part's name was *Rachel* and she thought her age was 17.

Rachel's earliest memory went back to about age three, when her father sent her (Samantha, as Rachel) to her room. She had wanted more of the snack they were having. When her father said no, Samantha cried. Her tears angered her father who yelled at her and sent her to her room. Rachel said this incident still bothered her at a level seven on the 0-10 SUD (Subjective Units of Disturbance) scale. It seems clear that this punishment for the display of tears at an early age laid the foundation for Samantha's adult fear of expressing her emotions.

At the beginning of our second session, Samantha reported that during her week of journaling she had discovered an additional 13 subpersonalities, all with personal names and ranging in age from five to 40. We now had 14 parts, 12 of them female and two of them male. Samantha said that her parts were adamant in claiming that, prior to revealing themselves to her, they already had their present visual forms. Most of these internal pictures had little resemblance to Samantha. Their names were also theirs before Samantha differentiated them. Two of the teenagers, Rachel and *Tessa,* would be the focus of our therapy. Among the roles Samantha attributed to other parts were playful child, cynic, romantic, artist, and homemaker. Samantha ended her therapy before we worked with these others.

In her journal, Samantha described Rachel, whom we had met the week before, as *the protector*. She viewed Rachel as having "a strong personality" and "a fiery temper." She was "rebellious and intimidating" while also being "blunt but loving." Her energy level was high and intense. Her role in Samantha's life was to experience and remember "all the punishments, anger, resentments, betrayals and hurtful" events.

In her journal entry for Tessa, Samantha described her as 13 years old and lacking in self-confidence. She believed that Tessa hated herself and was "awkward, gawky, and unattractive." She wore "unfashionable clothes." She had "blond hair, braces and zits." According to Samantha, Tessa "felt like an outsider" but worked hard "to correct her shortcomings, but because of a lack of guidance, she often took the least efficient path and blamed herself for less than desirable results." On a positive note, Tessa was also "very funny and clever, but only a few close people knew this side."

After reviewing Samantha's discovery of her additional parts, we discussed the possibility of doing healing work with the Rachel subpersonality. Rebellious Rachel was skeptical about change but agreed to try the unburdening technique for relief of some of her trauma load. She understood that use of the technique would involve reviewing her memories, and that we would begin this in our next session.

In the third session, Rachel talked about the emotional burden of growing up with her father. As noted above, she remembered being sent to her room at age three as punishment for her display of tears. As she went through grade school, she tried to stand up for herself in disagreements with her father. She would ask him how doing something she did not want to do would help her when she did not understand why she should do it, but he took her questions as defiance and demanded complete obedience. He was domineering most of the time and he switched into this attitude quickly when questioned. Rachel absorbed Samantha's frequent spankings, the reasons for which were often unclear. She knew she was too small to protect herself and that she had no choice but to endure her father's domination. Over time, she became more and more angry, and more and more rebellious. In her teenage years, she tried to avoid even being in the same room with her father. She remembered a lot of humiliation from this time. "Eventually," she said, "I was angry all the time."

Among Rachel's early memories were the responses from her father when she came home unhappy from painful experiences with her classmates in grade school. Her father would send her to her room and not allow her to come down until she had "a smile on my face." The anger she felt now for her father sending her to her room rather than just listening to her problems angered her to a level eight on the 0-10 SUD scale.

During grade school and much of middle school, it was the Tessa part who protected Samantha through encapsulating and dissociating her internal low self-esteem while expressing her outward devotion to pleasing her friends. In this way, she secured Samantha's acceptance by others. Sometimes, however, when Samantha's situation became too difficult for Tessa to handle, Rachel intervened. Samantha viewed herself as physically flawed and in a lesser class of person than her friends, whom she viewed as "very beautiful." On Samantha's behalf, Tessa tried to maintain her connection with friends by being "the nice one." One day a friend named Rachel began teasing Samantha, who was being particularly nice in her Tessa role. The friend Rachel got "more and more mean," and among other things called Samantha "weak." Finally, it was too much for Samantha's internal Rachel to bear. She surprised everybody by taking executive control of Samantha and punching friend Rachel in the face. It was a powerful moment, and one that helped define internal Rachel's role. On a 0-10 point SUE (Subjective Units of Energy) scale, this moment ranked at a level nine for positive energy. It seemed to be the incident where Rachel found a personal name for herself. By taking the name of her oppressor, internal Rachel felt she equalized Samantha's relationship with friend Rachel.

During those times of difficulty with her classmates at school and lack of support at home, Samantha "wasn't around very much," she said. Instead, it was Tessa who presented Samantha's outward demeanor. Tessa was there to experience the low self-esteem that she based in her perceived lack of physical attractiveness. Tessa believed that she should protect Samantha from her classmates' rejection. Consequently, she took executive control from Samantha in order to bear her burden. Rachel said that when Samantha was herself, she would often get herself into trouble by trying to figure things out on her own. Because of this, Rachel and Tessa worked together to protect her. At first Tessa would take over, but that often led to more trouble for Samantha, and so Rachel would come to the rescue. Samantha observed that during this process of alternating control of her, she would "watch and remember," often experiencing sadness because she felt she was a prisoner of her own parts. It wasn't that she was aware of her parts at that time. Rather, now that she *was* aware, she could explain the time in her life when she was more of an observer than a participant. She said that when Rachel and Tessa took control of her as a child, "I felt like what I was doing wasn't entirely me. I felt like I was in a glass cage." Eventually, after her father divorced her mother and Samantha felt safer at home, Rachel and Tessa "let me out more and more."

The manner in which Rachel and Tessa previously took control of Samantha is similar to how alter personalities in dissociative identity disorder (multiple personality disorder) sometimes alternate in taking executive control of consciousness. A significant difference, however, is that Samantha remained aware, or coconscious, of her protector-influenced behavior and of the consequences of that behavior. Her sense of not being fully in control of herself was an accurate one. Her internal parts were blended with her so strongly that she actually was not a free agent acting on her own behalf for much of this period of her life.

A particularly memorable experience with her father happened when Samantha was 16 and her father was teaching her to drive. Rachel blended with Samantha during the lessons. She "wasn't getting it." She made a wrong turn and failed to make it into a gas station as her father directed. Her father thought Samantha purposely ignored his instruction. He humiliated her, cursing her as a "fucking bitch," and made her get into the back seat of the car while he drove home. She cried the entire night. Her father would not permit her to explain that it was an accident. Rachel wanted to attack him physically, but she knew she could not face him in that way. The best she could do was to encapsulate the memory and partially dissociate it from Samantha's consciousness. This experience remained at a level 10 disturbance on the SUD scale for Rachel.

Much of Rachel's current concerns related to Samantha's fears about her husband, John. When he failed to come home at the expected time, Rachel went into a rage or panic that Samantha suppressed. Samantha chose instead to isolate herself from her husband rather than risk a blowup fueled by Rachel's powerful emotions.

Collecting a part's significant memories, as we did with Rachel, serves several purposes. It permits the part to develop its own personal narrative, in itself a centering exercise. The set of experiences recalled by a part also enables both therapist and client to gain insight into the part's larger functioning in the internal system. Finally, the set of memories provides the raw material for processing that will bring about successful change. The most important of these memories are the earliest. They are the foundation memories for the development of the part. In Rachel's case, we had actually elicited the most important foundation memory in our first session. That was the memory of Samantha's father sending her to her room at age three for crying when her father limited her snacks. Rachel evidently came into being to help Samantha deal with this early demand that she control her emotions. For Rachel, this memory remained a level seven SUD scale disturbance.

Near the end of the third session, we unburdened Rachel's memory for Samantha's experience at age three. After Samantha visualized the wind blowing away the negative emotions from her memory ("like dust particles in a windstorm"), Rachel reported that she had a better understanding of the event, and she could forgive her father for his action. The initial unburdening brought the experience to a level one disturbance; a single repetition of the intervention brought the level to zero. Rachel indicated that it was "scary" to give up this last small part of the burden. She no longer felt badly about the incident; however, she did feel more vulnerable. The vulnerability seemed to have to do with giving up a bit of her armor, the anger she continued to feel for the forced suppression of her emotions. Regarding her forgiveness of her father, it is important to note that while forgiveness is often the result of an unburdening, it is not necessary for healing.

Upon her return a week later for our fourth session, Samantha reported that she had already noticed that her negative emotions had subsided somewhat. However, she also experienced a small amount of jealousy, mostly relating to the good times her husband had enjoyed visiting with his brother. Because Rachel seemed to be the key player in Samantha's expression of jealousy and rage, we continued to focus upon Rachel's memories. We had done the first unburdening in the previous session, and now it was important to discover whether we had all the information we needed to do the next unburdenings.

At the beginning of the session, Samantha described her response, as expressed by Rachel, to a recent incident involving her husband. John had flown to Chicago for a company function and, while there, he went out with the single men to a strip club. When he told Samantha of his actions upon his return home, Rachel was overwhelmed with rage. Samantha said that the part was so enraged that she felt flames coming off her face. According to Samantha, this was the first time in recent memory that Rachel had taken complete executive control of her. With Rachel in control, Samantha felt disconnected from her rage, becoming an observer of herself again, rather than being the agent of action. This is the sort of control by a part that unburdening aims to relieve.

For Samantha, there was an exact parallel between the memory of her husband's actions and that her father's actions in his divorce of her mother. In the lead-up to the divorce, Samantha's father had secretly contacted both his college girlfriend and his high school girlfriend. He took Samantha's mother to a strip club one time, and then went out on his own to explore his "mid-life crisis." Eventually, after her father renewed his relationship with his high school girlfriend, he told Samantha's mother he wanted a divorce. Samantha's mother was devastated. She had been unaware of her husband's lone activities, believing that she and he were working through temporary marital difficulties. Samantha's father, incidentally, did marry his high school girlfriend, but also divorced her when, says Samantha, she gained weight and became "too fat" for him.

Another group of Rachel's memories had to do with how her father punished Samantha and her sister when they fought with each other. The father would require that the sisters make up by kissing each other on the lips.

Samantha found these experiences awkward and humiliating. They were disturbing at a level ten on the SUD scale. A subset of level 10 anger experiences had to do with Samantha's disagreements with her father. It was never okay for Samantha to differ with her father. He was relentless in his pursuit of dominance over her. He would not stop his verbal assaults of her until she finally gave in and accepted his position and control.

In the final third of this fourth session, we did extensive work with unburdening Rachel. We began with the level 10 experience of her father teaching her how to drive and then continued the work with her other painful memories. The symbolic scene for the unburdening of Rachel's rage was one of fire. Samantha imagined a bonfire with Rachel standing next to it. As Samantha visualized holding her hand, Rachel would reach into her own body, lift out the painful memories, and throw them into the fire. As each memory emerged, the attached painful feelings would burst into flame and turn into ash. She would retain the memories but not the emotions. In each case, the initial unburdening reduced the SUD level to a two or three, requiring repetition of the intervention before moving on to the next memory group. A final check of the SUD level for the teaching-how-to-drive event, the kissing-her-sister punishments, and the verbal assaults for domination showed that each had been reduced to zero at the end of the session. We would check these SUD levels again in our next session.

Two weeks later at our fifth session, Rachel maintained a zero level of disturbance for the kissing–her–sister punishment and for her father's over-riding demands that Samantha give up all disagreements with him. The painful experience of being taught to drive registered at a level one. The follow-up was almost perfect. I expected that the level one disturbance for learning to drive would slide to zero again as we unburdened other subpersonalities.

We turned next to Tessa, Rachel's longtime internal nemesis. As with Rachel, we wanted to collect a set of memories so that we could better understand Tessa's essence. First, we wanted to check whether Tessa had also been present for the painful driving lesson. She had, and the SUD level was three, suggesting that the level one disturbance still experienced by Rachel was due to her picking up Tessa's amplification of her own distress.

Tessa's earliest memory of being active in Samantha's life dated to Samantha's age nine, when the family moved and Samantha enrolled in a new school that drew upon a higher socioeconomic class of students. Prior to this, Tessa was merely an observer as Samantha moved through the early grades with her friends. The fourth grade was different because Samantha now found herself among a new set of classmates, girls who looked different from and were noticeably wealthier than her previous classmates. She discovered that she, too, was different from her new classmates; she was taller with crooked teeth and she felt unattractive when she compared herself to them.

On the second day of classes of her fourth grade, she joined the rest of her class on a field trip. All the other children already had partners except one: the existing class "outcast". Partnering up with the class outcast set the tone for the remainder of this school year and the years to come. She failed to connect with the larger community of schoolchildren. Her life became progressively worse. She could not overcome her isolation during the years of grade school through middle school. Tessa rated her distress at a level six for the beginning of the fourth grade and a level 10 when things were at their worst.

By age 12 in the seventh grade, Tessa remembered, Samantha succeeded in making friends with the popular group of girls but she did not fully trust them. Within two years, in the ninth grade, her friends had started smoking and drinking. They knew about these things and about sex, too, while Samantha was still anchored in a more conservative childhood. Again, she felt left out and she carried around a sense of being "less than" her peers. That was when she shut down and became a shy listener in groups. Over time, her friends learned that they could "walk all over" her, and they did so. Samantha did not know she could do anything about it. Tessa handled it by never taking offense and by always being "as nice as she could be." These memories disturbed Tessa at a level eight on the SUD scale.

"The lowest time in my life," Samantha said, "was in the seventh grade." She was tall and ungainly with severe acne. The braces that would correct her crooked teeth would not come until the eighth grade. She tried out for the choir, thinking that she had a "pretty good voice." Unfortunately, during her solo she saw some of her friends laughing at her. She was devastated.

She was not accepted for the choir, but what caused her the greatest distress was her friends' laughter. Tessa, who handled the low self-esteem, accepted their judgment that Samantha lacked talent. It was still disturbing to Tessa at a level 10. Rachel's attitude, on the other hand, was one of anger toward Tessa "for letting them keep Samantha down" for so long.

In the ninth grade, with her braces off, the acne gone, and with long blond hair, Samantha tried out for and made the dance team at school. She was, however, the least accomplished member of the team. Her coach would sometimes demean her and try to embarrass her in front of other team members, making her an example of how not to perform. This was disturbing to Tessa at a level nine.

In the 10th grade, Samantha became a cheerleader. Life was better. Tessa would "let Samantha out" when she felt it was safe. Through it all, the successes and the inevitable failures, Tessa carried with her an underlying sense of worthlessness, a level 10 negative burden. Even now, she still had the fear that if something good happened to Samantha, something else would take it away.

Recently, Samantha had been taking dancing lessons, but with any hint of criticism from any source, Tessa would step in and overwhelm her with sadness and hopelessness. Samantha would hear Tessa's voice: "Don't do it; quit; give it up!" Happiness made Tessa uncomfortable. Samantha wanted it but Tessa was afraid of it, afraid to embrace it lest the fall be too great when disappointment came. Samantha was fatigued by this constant battle with Tessa.

In our sixth session two weeks later, Samantha reported that Tessa was excited about the unburdening work planned for the day. She was ready to let Samantha "move forward and experience life." The entire session was devoted to unburdening Tessa through a swimming-in-the-ocean metaphor, so that as she flopped about in the water, the water saturated Tessa and dissolved the accumulated burden she carried of a lifetime of painful events.

As Tessa experienced the process of unburdening, she expressed concern about her role once the intervention was complete. We told her that it was best to decide upon this role after the unburdening was complete, and that the role was to be decided by a discussion between the two of them. After about five minutes of silence in the therapy room as Tessa processed her memories, and as these memories flashed through Samantha's mind, Samantha said, "Okay." It was done.

In doing unburdenings it is important to use the previously collected SUD scores to verify that the unburdening is, indeed, complete. Most of the time, following the initial report of completion, there will be some remaining negative energy that requires additional attention. The fourth grade move to a new school and consequent disconnection between Samantha and her classmates was no longer bothersome. The age 12 and later experiences when her friends would say negative things about her was also a zero disturbance. She was still bothered by the memories of letting her friends walk all over her, but another 30 seconds of Samantha visualizing Tessa swimming in a calm sea and allowing the water to fully dissolve the remaining negative emotions attached to those memories. Being "ugly' in the seventh grade was no longer disturbing to Samantha, and she said she could almost laugh about it. She could empathize with what so many teenagers must be going through. The tryout for choir with her solo was no longer disturbing. The coach's demeaning comments on her dance skills were not significant. Instead, said Samantha, she now understood why someone would hurt someone else—because of their own pain. The sense of worthlessness she experienced in the 10th grade and later, still contained some negative associations, but a quick dunk in the symbolic ocean dissipated this final portion of Tessa's burden. Just to be sure that we had succeeded in completely unburdening Tessa, we asked her to review (at the speed of thought) her entire life history. After about one minute of silence, Samantha reported that Tessa's history was clear of negative energy. The experience of learning to drive became a zero on the SUD scale for Tessa and also for Rachel, as predicted.

The final step for Tessa was to acquire a new role. Together, she and Samantha chose her new role to be that of coaching Samantha in maintaining high self-esteem. Such a complete reversal of a part's role is not unusual.

In concluding the session, Samantha said that Tessa's physical image of herself had changed in the course of the unburdening. Tessa allowed what both she and Samantha called her "physical deformities"—acne, braces, glasses, awkward body, anything she did not like about herself—to dissolve during her ocean swim. Samantha said, "I watched her go through each memory. As each one's associated interpretations and thoughts dissolved, that left just the actual stories. I didn't hate myself or judge myself anymore."

The sixth session was our last. In the week following this session, Samantha took a full-time job with time demands that made it unlikely that therapy could resume in the near future. However, she had made tremendous progress in just six sessions. Samantha had other things she might have worked on, and perhaps she will later. For now, however, the changes she made through her work with the subpersonalities, Rachel and Tessa, gave her a new foundation for moving out into the career mainstream. She no longer felt extreme jealousy when her husband was interacting with others.

Chapter 3
Rage with Sexual Aversion

This chapter addresses the treatment of rage. However, rage rarely stands alone among a person's life problems. In this case, rage coexisted with the client's aversion to sexuality, but almost incidentally. Healing the sexual aversion was a byproduct of healing the rage. Only some of the experiences connected to the overdevelopment of the raging part had to do with sexuality. Most of the client's foundation experiences for rage had to do with abandonment issues, parental quarrelling, and mistreatment by peers.

Tina was 30 years old and the mother of one when she first came to therapy. She was an assistant manager in the accounting department of a major casino. Her score on the Dissociative Experiences Scale was an average 9.6 in comparison to the norm of 10.0, suggesting that the inner world we would explore was not the product of major trauma. Only as scores approach 30.0 does a red flag appear, suggesting a possible dissociative disorder. Petite and vivacious, Tina explained that she had to control her anger if she was to continue in her career path. She had recently been passed over for a major promotion, an opening for which she felt she was by far the most qualified candidate. She believed that her supervisor unfairly promoted others based on how much they "stroked his ego." Women who flirted with him were especially likely to do well in their careers. When Tina asked for an explanation for why she had not been promoted, the supervisor scolded her for "not knowing [her] place." She had barely been able to contain her rage. She quickly removed herself from this dangerous situation. She knew that if she had cursed him as she felt driven to do, she would have been fired. This incident was her incentive for coming to therapy.

Tina acknowledged her rage as a life-long problem. Many of those closest to her had experienced her out-of-control anger first-hand. While she wanted to save her job, Tina also wanted to improve her relationship with her fiancé, who was the most frequent target of her screaming, cursing, and breaking of objects. Another concern was the potential effect of her expressions of rage on her six-year-old son. She was not sure how she might be harming him, but she knew that it was not healthy to expose him to her outbursts.

Her fiancé, Robert, was the father of her son. Tina and Robert had lived together for eight years. Although Robert had proposed marriage many times, Tina consistently refused him because of his excessive jealousy of her. She said that she had not been interested in any other man since they had been together, yet he regularly accused her of flirting and more with other men. She might marry him if he agreed to work on his excessive jealousy with a therapist.

Another issue Tina wanted to address in therapy was her lack of interest in sexual activities. Once involved in lovemaking with Robert she could enjoy sex and even occasionally reach orgasm, but most of the time she had no interest at all in sexuality. In fact, said Tina, "Sex is gross." She described herself as having been promiscuous for a period during her teens, but it was not because she liked sex; it was because she was drawn to the "closeness" she felt with her partners during the lovemaking.

Tina's personal history suggested some possible sources for her aversion to sex and possibly also for her rage. For example, she remembered with disgust that her father and mother would engage in lovemaking with her in the room when she was seven. Additionally, her stepfather, whom her mother married when Tina was 11, often made sexually inappropriate comments about her as she grew up. He would try to touch her and wanted to kiss her on the lips. Tina had a powerful memory of her stepfather kissing her on the mouth when she was 11 years old. She could still remember with anger and disgust the taste of his saliva.

A Joyful Part

Near the end of our first session, I introduced Tina to the idea of working with her internal parts. With little time left, however, I chose not to differentiate a part who might leave Tina with a surge of negative emotion before she left for the day. For that reason, I asked her to identify something that caused her joy. She remembered the joy she felt when her son was a baby. I asked her to focus on this joyful feeling and to ask it to provide an image of itself. Tina visualized herself a few years younger, somewhat heavier, and with a smile on her face. When she spoke inwardly to this image, she was surprised that the part responded. It knew who Tina was and said, "You're me." When asked for her name, the part responded with *Simone,* which is Tina's middle name and the name she had used most of her life as her primary name. Tina was also surprised to learn that the part's memories began just six years previously with the birth of her son. The part had no autobiographical memories before that event. As we ended the session, Tina was impressed with her ability to talk with another aspect of herself. She looked forward to working with parts in dealing with her therapeutic issues.

Angry Teenager

At our second session, Tina was ready to embrace Parts Psychology in doing therapy for her anger problem. When asked to focus upon a recent moment of anger, she thought of the favoritism shown by her boss. An even more powerful moment was the comment by Robert after their recent lovemaking when he said, "You just lay there like a dead fish." When she focused upon the anger she felt about Robert's comment and asked that emotion to provide a picture of itself, Tina found herself internally visualizing a picture of her own face, but younger than her current age, with "messy, dark hair, big eyes, and enraged." The part acknowledged Tina and called her Simone, her childhood name. She acknowledged that she was "the angry part." She said that she did not have a name of her own. Tina said that she seemed to be a teenager and asked if we could call her *Teenager.* The part accepted this name. Teenager did not want to change; she wanted to continue to be free to express her rage when she felt the situation warranted it. When Tina pointed out to Teenager that her rage was sometimes self destructive, her response was an ambiguous, "Oh, well, whatever!"

Tina remembered that as a teenager she often expressed her anger as rage. Consistent with this, the Teenager part began to provide Tina with incidents from her memory set. For example, Tina remembered that in high school when she had tried out for the track team, she made a couple of false starts out of the sprinters' blocks. When her coach wouldn't permit her to try again as he did male athletes, Tina threw her shoes at him and cursed him, leading her to be dismissed from the team. The memory was disturbing to Teenager at a level eight on the SUD (Subjective Units of Disturbance) scale, and a positive three on the SUE (Subjective Units of Energy) scale. In the eighth grade, Tina had a best friend but made new friends with two other girls. Her best friend grew jealous of the new friends and said some uncomplimentary things about Tina. Tina found out about the comments. She telephoned her best friend and cursed her, calling her, among other things, "You fucking slut!" because, "She talked shit about me!" Teenager scaled the incident as a two on the negative SUD scale but a three on the positive SUE scale. As the session ended, Tina said that she had the sense that Teenager was protecting someone. "As a kid I used to get hurt a lot," she explained. Maybe she had "a hurt child part somewhere inside."

In session three, Tina returned to the theme of the previous session. She talked about being picked on because she was darker skinned than other kids in her neighborhood. "I wore thick glasses and was olive skinned. They called me "four-eyes" and said I used a tanning machine. Tina remembered an incident from the eighth grade. "This big blonde girl, a lot bigger than me, teased me," said Tina, "I went off on her!" By that, Tina meant she cursed the girl extensively, calling her a number of names, and warned her to be careful how she talked to her. Tina believed that her childhood experiences of being viewed as "less than" others followed her into adulthood. For example, Robert's mother was highly critical of her, and Tina felt the same pain she felt as a teenager. "We moved from Chicago to San Francisco to get away from her." When Tina consulted within, she found that it was Teenager's memories she had been recalling. Teenager also acknowledged that she was the one who was angry with Robert's mother. Her earliest memories were of being teased by her peers and feeling isolated at home. Her parents didn't pay much attention to her and the kids at school teased her because she wore glasses, was sometimes awkward, and tanned too deeply in comparison with her classmates.

Many of Teenager's memories had to do with the stepfather. As Tina grew older and began to acquire some money of her own, she learned to hide it from him. When Tina graduated high school, her stepmother had given her a number of small, cash gifts in colorful boxes she was to open on consecutive weekends. When Tina discovered that some of the money was missing she screamed, cursed, and accused her stepfather of taking the money. "He was a drug addict," she explained. The incident was disturbing only to a level one or two, but it contained positive energy in the form of rage at a level eight. In another incident after high school, Teenager remembered that Tina's tips from her waitressing job were missing one morning. She screamed, cursed and blamed the stepfather. The satisfaction of her rage was pleasing to her at a level eight on the SUE scale, and not at all disturbing.

More recent incidents when Teenager influenced Tina to express rage included confronting a competitive friend during a training program, confronting Robert when he called her a *bitch*, and tailgating, flashing her lights, and *flipping off* a driver who cut her off on the expressway. The SUD scores for these experiences were low for Teenager, only a one or two, but the positive SUE score for her actions registered at levels five or six. Like disturbing memories, the positive experiences of feeling the power of rage must also be unburdened if the angry part is to become a cooperative team player in the internal system.

A Little Girl Part

Late in the session, Tina commented that she was now aware that Teenager was protecting a little girl, a suspicion she had expressed in an earlier session. When she asked Teenager for an image of the little girl, Tina found herself visualizing a girl of about eight years old with her hair in pigtails and wearing a flowery dress. When asked if she knew Tina, the new part identified her as *Simone* (Tina's middle name) and said that she, the little girl, was "the younger version" of Simone. When asked for her own name, the little girl said it was *Sally*, a name she had just then picked for herself. Sally knew of other parts. She knew Teenager, Simone, and "a lot of others." Her earliest memory was of going fishing with her father when she was four years old. At the same age, she also remembered burning herself with hot water while her father was at work. She remembered screaming for her father. The incident was disturbing to a level seven on the SUD scale.

In our fourth session, we returned to work with Sally, but not until Tina had passed along some information about how she managed to keep Teenager in check during the week. Tina revealed that she was really "pissed off" at the people with whom she interacted at interdepartmental meetings. "I smiled and acted calm," she said, but "I felt anger in my chest and knew Teenager wanted to come out." Teenager restrained herself, however, and held her feelings for later expression in the therapy office. Then she said, "Those fucking bitches! They're conniving, sneaky, and dishonest!" Having expressed herself, Teenager was then happy to turn over the topic of the session to Sally, the little girl she protected so fiercely.

It turned out that Sally considered herself six years old rather than the eight years old Tina originally perceived her to be. The next memory she shared was that of being sick with chicken pox and not wanting to go to the doctor. Her father was driving her there and he only laughed when Sally, in an effort to prevent the trip, tried to push his hand away from the stick shift. The SUD level for this incident was a five.

Tina and Sally were unsure of Tina's age at the time of the next memories, but Tina placed them between ages seven and nine. The first three all involved her parents' fighting. In the first, Tina played "patty cakes" on the wall to divert herself from her parents' loud argument, but her father yelled at her to stop hitting the wall. The SUD level was eight. In the next memory, Tina's father was yelling at her mother about his son from his previous marriage, blaming her mother because the boy was diagnosed with bipolar disorder. Her father believed the illness resulted from his falling down a set of stairs while under the mother's care. Standing outside their room, Tina remembered hearing the sound of her father hitting her mother. The SUD level was 10. In the third memory, Tina's father was confronting her mother as he looked at the telephone bill. There were long-distance charges for calls between their phone in Chicago and another phone in Peoria. He demanded to know with whom the mother had been talking. The name of the man in Peoria was that of her eventual stepfather. The SUD level was eight for Sally.

In the final incident from Sally's memory set, Tina's mother was having "phone sex" with Tina's stepfather. Neither Tina nor Sally could place the event in relation to whether Tina's mother was still married to the father, divorced, or remarried. The memory remained disturbing to Tina at a level 10. For six-year-old Sally, the incident rated an eight on the SUD scale, and for Teenager it was a level seven. This sort of spread of ratings for different parts in relation to a single incident is not uncommon. Because each subpersonality's experience is somewhat different from that of other subpersonalities, the level of disturbance is also somewhat different. What is unusual here is that Tina's rating is greater than either of the two parts. Since the self experiences events only as different parts present them, there had to be another, as yet unknown, part who was amplifying its distress through the self. We did not explore the question further at this time because it seemed more important to begin the unburdening of Sally in order to make inroads in the problem rages experienced by Tina.

Before beginning the unburdening of Sally, we asked permission to do so from Teenager, her protector. Although skeptical of the process Teenager grudgingly granted permission to proceed. For the three memories we had time to unburden during this session, Tina and Sally chose a tropical rain as the symbolic means of ridding Sally of the negative energy. Tina visualized Sally standing in the open during the downpour, with the warm rain flowing over, around and through her. Sally's job was to focus on the stored memory of her scalding with hot water at age four as the rain dissolved the attached negative energy. As each lowered level of distress was reached, we asked Sally to identify what continued to bother her. This provided the focus for continued unburdening. The first effort lowered the SUD rating from seven to three, a number that represented Sally's distress that her father wasn't there when she needed him. A second visualization of the cleansing by tropical rain brought the remaining disturbance down to a level one, which Sally related to the hurt she felt over her mother scolding her for turning on the hot water. A final visualization of the tropical rain intervention brought the SUD level to zero. Teenager, who was the source of the rage we wanted to diminish, admitted to being "a little bit" impressed by the alleviation of Sally's pain. Near the end of the session, the chicken pox memory yielded quickly to a zero SUD rating with just a single use of the tropical rain visualization, and the "patty cakes" memory took two efforts. The first brought the SUD level from eight to three as Sally continued to be hurt about the father's anger with her; the repetition of the intervention brought the memory to a zero rating.

At the beginning of our fifth session, Tina passed along the information that Robert had commented on her being "less sensitive, not as angry" during the week, which she took to mean that our work was already yielding positive results. Tina also reported that during the week she had a dream that she had spent a day with her "in-laws." She had not seen nor spoken with her "mother-in-law" in two years. She said that "In the past, I would have been silent and gritting my teeth," but in the dream "the day was actually pleasant." Tina believed that this dream indicated she was becoming more centered and less tense. We returned then to the unburdening of six-year-old Sally.

We began with the unburdening of Sally's memory of her father hitting her mother, which had spontaneously fallen from a SUD level of 10 to five, apparently as the result of our previous work with Sally. This time we used a waterfall as the symbolic means of releasing the negative energy. After the first immersion in the visualized waterfall, Sally reported the SUD level had reduced to a level of two, which she attributed to the sounds of her mother screaming as she was hit by her father. Sally could feel the fear in her chest. Tina asked me then if she should unburden the fear she felt in her own chest. I replied that if we take care of Sally's fear, her own fear would take care of itself. The second visualized immersion in the waterfall reduced the SUD level to zero for both Sally and Tina.

Like the previous memory, the memory of the fight between her parents over her mother's long-distance phone calls had also spontaneously reduced some of its negative energy. It was now a level four. Again, we used the waterfall intervention but encountered significant problems of concentration due to interference from Teenager. She was upset that we had ignored her by failing to ask for her permission before resuming our work with Sally. After apologizing to Teenager and again getting her permission to continue the work, the SUD level for the problem memory reduced quickly to zero.

Another Little Girl

This brought us to Sally's memory of her mother's phone sex with her stepfather. Because Tina's SUD level was greater than either Sally's or Teenager's, we decided to search for the suspected subpersonality who was amplifying its distress onto Tina. When Tina focused inwardly on the negative feelings associated with remembering her mother's phone sex, she asked the part amplifying those feelings to give her an image of itself. What came to her mind was an image of herself as a child, but "younger and chubbier" than Sally. Her name was *Dinah*, and she said that she knew Tina, but as Simone. Dinah did not know, however, that she was a part of Tina, who quickly explained their relationship. Dinah's earliest memory no longer disturbed her, she said, but it involved her mother's anger when she and a friend got themselves dirty while playing near the trash dumpster.

We were near the end of the session when Tina said that she was feeling afraid. When she checked with Dinah, she found that the child part was crying with fear of the next memory about which she expected us to ask. The end of a session is not a good time to bring up disturbing material and so Tina, who did not know the content of the memory, visualized the child placing the memory into a time-locked safe until our next session. She then placed all three of the young parts we had worked with that day, Dinah, Sally, and Teenager, in a visualized internal safe room to be sure there would be calm as she left the therapy office.

Before returning to our work with Dinah in session six, Tina described what she considered a setback in her efforts to gain control of her anger. After work one evening as they prepared for bed, Robert noticed that Tina wore her panties inside out. He was convinced she had had sex with some-one else that day. He demanded that she take off her panties so that he could check them. In a rage, Tina complied with Robert's demands, but then dressed again and tried to leave the house. He blocked her exit, refusing to allow her to leave the house. Tina said she "went off on him," and cursed him repeatedly during a three-hour rage. "How could he think I had sex with someone?" she asked, "I don't even like sex!"

When we returned to work with Dinah, we found that she claimed her age to be three years old. Her earliest memory dated also to age three, but she may have been four at the time of the distressing experiences she re-called at the end of the previous session. The incidents involved a neighbor boy who was one or two years older than Dinah. Without providing details, Tina said that "stuff happened" in the boy's grandparents' bedroom and "in one other place." Dinah felt fear and disgust to a level 10. For the unburden-ing of these memories, Tina visualized herself carrying the child to a magical healing pool behind a waterfall and immersing her in the pool as the water cleansed the memories of their associated fear and disgust. The first effort reduced Dinah's burden to a level two or three, which had to do with kiss-ing, both by the neighbor boy and later, when Tina's stepfather kissed her on the mouth. Once these thoughts were expressed, a second immersion in the magical waters reduced the level of distress to zero.

In working with the child part Dinah, I coached Tina to do the unburdenings immediately after the collection of each of the memories rather than collect her full memory set. My sense was that cooperation from Teenager was tenuous. Collecting a part's entire memory set can be disturbing to the inner world and I did not want us to end the session with newly recalled memories left unresolved. By unburdening them as they surfaced, I wanted to limit the degree to which Teenager and other parts might be disturbed by recall of the painful material. Surprisingly, three-year-old Dinah's memory set included a range of experiences occurring as late as Tina's age 17. All of these negative memories related to sexuality in some way. Thus, the perspective of a very young and sexually distressed child part significantly colored Tina's adult experience of sexuality. Unburdening Dinah's memories led to significant changes in Tina's adult sexual functioning.

Dinah's next memories related to experiences when Tina was age 11 and beginning puberty. Her stepfather wanted to look under her shirt to "check" to see if she needed a bra. Tina reported Dinah's SUD level simply as "a lot." Once again, Tina transported the child part to the magical healing pool. She was not immediately successful in unburdening the child because, she said, "Teenager is distracting me." However, once she asked for Teenager's permission to continue, the level of distress quickly resolved to the necessary zero. The next two memories were also quickly unburdened to a level zero in the healing pool. The first incident was disturbing to a level seven and occurred at a party when Tina was 12. Her stepfather playfully put a long, inflated balloon down the front of his pants, simulating a penis. The second concern was actually a series of memories involving Tina's need, at around the ages of 16 and 17, to block her stepfather's attempts to peek into her room and catch her unaware while she was dressing.

In our final work with Dinah during this session, Tina placed her in a playroom of her own. She then brought wind into the room to unburden her of the level 10 distress connected to listening to her mother having phone sex with her eventual stepfather. The memory yielded its burden easily to a zero rating. We planned to return to our interrupted work with Sally and the Teenager in our next session.

Healing the Teenager Part

Unfortunately, current events in Tina's life prevented immediate resumption of the work with her inner world in session seven. Robert's jealousy of Tina had overcome him the night before and forced an argument that continued, after a period of sleep, into the morning of our session. Tina was quite upset and again asserted that she could not stay with her fiancé unless he could gain control of his irrational jealousy. There were two positive notes to the week's happenings. The first was that Tina did not *go off* on Robert during the argument. Instead, when it was late and she had lost her patience for more argument, she simply told him that he "couldn't get through" to her that night and she had to sleep, which she did. The second piece of good news was that during their sexual activities during the week, Tina found herself enjoying sex. This was a major change for her; the connection to unburdening of her early negative sexual experiences was obvious.

At the beginning of our eighth session, we had a short discussion of appropriate discipline for Tina's son. Tina described how Robert would threaten to put their six-year-old into the closet with the "monsters." The boy was terrified, grabbing onto anything he could reach to prevent his father from carrying him to the closet. Tina believed that this could damage her son. I agreed! This is the sort of trauma that leads to the adult problems that are the focus of work in Parts Psychology. Tina pledged to stop Robert from using such threats in disciplining the boy.

We returned then to our work with Teenager, the angry part. First, we checked the levels of current distress felt by Tina, six-year-old Sally, and Teenager for the memory of the mother's phone sex with the step-father-to-be. Their distress levels now measured four, three, and five respectively. Working with the hypothesis that the levels of distress experienced by both Tina and Sally were reflections of Teenagers level five, we decided to work exclusively with her. Using the imagery of unloading her distress into a bonfire Teenager quickly reduced the SUD level to one, which she attributed to her disgust with the mother's moaning on the phone in front of young Tina and her sister. A repeat of the bonfire imagery reduced the SUD level to zero. When we checked with Sally and Tina their levels were also at zero.

Our last two interventions in the session were with Sally and Teenager. Sally had a remnant level one disturbance for the memory of her father hitting her mother as they argued. It yielded quickly to a bonfire intervention. Teenager still held a level three of positive energy on the SUE scale for the middle school memory of going off on the big blonde girl. This, too, quickly became a zero as Teenager symbolically tossed her positive energy into the flames of the bonfire.

In session nine, Tina reported that she and Robert had had sex four times in the last week and that she enjoyed it. This compared to their usual average of once or twice a month for the last few years. Unfortunately, Robert complained about Tina not agreeing to a fifth event of lovemaking and, in anger, called her a "tease." This set off Teenager who "came out" and cursed him soundly for not recognizing Tina's progress. She also accused him of shutting off Tina's spontaneity, saying she should be able to be playful and flirty without Robert demanding she have sex with him. Healing this temporary breach of the peace was easily accomplished. Tina had previously told Robert about the existence of her Teenager part. On this occasion, she told him Teenager was angry. Robert wisely apologized directly to Teenager, who gave up her anger immediately.

It was evident that the relationship between Tina and Robert had evolved in a positive way. Tina had shared with him some of her work with her inner parts so that he now was able to speak directly to Teenager to bring her back to a centered place. Additionally, Tina's anger was no longer overwhelming rage; instead, it was more contained and more subject to modification in a short period of time.

When asked about memories that still bothered her, Teenager instead provided a significant memory that rated a level 10 on the positive SUE scale. The setting was a family gathering for the Thanksgiving holiday when Tina was in her senior year of high school. Tina recalled, "My mother bought a box of wine and I drank a lot. I was mocking and making fun of my mother and stepfather. People laughed at them. I liked it that everybody was laughing at them." Tina went on to say that Teenager is naturally mean. "When I get drunk she comes out and is mean to people." She added that Teenager comes out also when she is with her sisters and all of them poke fun at each other and other people as well. Teenager had no interest in giving up the positive experience of making fun of other people.

The next session was our tenth, and we decided to use it to assess how much more work Tina needed to do in order to achieve her stated goals. We began by checking with Teenager to see what degree of disturbance this part still felt for the incident involving the coach at whom she threw her shoes. Teenager indicated the level of disturbance for this event remained a level three, but so did the level of positive energy for her felt rage. Another early incident, the one where she had called her friend a "slut" did not disturb her at all, but also measured a level three of positive energy.

When Tina asked if Teenager was ready to unburden the negative and positive energies still connected to these memories, Teenager indicated that she did not wish to do so. She believed that if she did the unburdening she would no longer be able to protect Tina. At this point, I coached Tina in negotiating further unburdening with Teenager. Tina pointed out the level of disturbance for the coach incident had diminished from a level eight to a level three, but she was still able to protect Tina. She pointed out also how much wiser Teenager was being with Robert in deciding when to come out and protect Tina. With these points made by Tina, Teenager agreed to do further unburdening.

Using a bonfire intervention, Teenager quickly unburdened the level three positive energy connected to the memory of calling her friend a *slut*. However, when Tina tried to guide Teenager in unburdening the remainder of energy connected to the coach incident, she ran into difficulty. She found herself unable to maintain her focus for the unburdening. When I suggested she check with Teenager to see if the problem originated with her, Tina confirmed that it did. Tina asked Teenager the preferred question for these sorts of situation: "What are you afraid will happen if you unburden?" Teenager told Tina that it wasn't that she was afraid; rather, it was that she thought Tina still needed protection. There will be situations in the future, said Teenager, when Tina will need to be able to speak out, as she did with the coach, and she needed to retain that ability. Teenager was concerned that the work we were doing would lead to the loss of her "bravery." She didn't want Tina to be so nice that people would take advantage of her. I suggested that Teenager do a temporary unburdening, putting the energy for the coach incident into a container separate from her, so that we could test her reactions. Teenager agreed to this, placing the positive and negative energy for the incident at different ends of an imaginary cylinder. That left ratings at a level zero for Teenager. Next, I asked Tina how we might test Teenager's ability to respond. Tina suggested calling her a "fucking bitch," and so I did. Tina said that Teenager's response was, "Nice try, asshole!" I suggested that Teenager's response was appropriate. She knew it was just a test and so she responded in a joking way, but with enough of an edge to communicate that she could be serious if she needed to be. With the test successfully accomplished, Teenager permitted the remaining energy for the coach incident to be permanently unburdened to a bonfire.

Although Tina and Teenager were making progress with Teenager's anger there was an incident during the week that indicated there was still more work to do. Tina had given Robert a Father's Day card with a gift certificate for 100 dollars. He questioned Tina regarding the source of the money. Tina said, "I got really mad because I could have gone shopping with that money." Tina was still angry the next day. However, Robert apologized directly to Teenager, and Tina found that within five minutes she was no longer angry. Robert had also made Tina aware that she was "a different person" when Teenager was present. "I have different facial expressions and a different posture."

The day before our session was Father's Day. Tina called her father, "for the first time," she said. He wasn't home and so she left a message. Later her father called her back and thanked her. He told her he was sad. He also asked for her sister's phone number, who later confirmed that he had called her, too, leaving "a sad message" on her answering machine. Tina recalled that she smiled when her sister told her of the message left by their father. Teenager acknowledged that it was she who smiled. She did so because she was pleased that the father felt bad about not having much contact with his daughters. She wanted him to suffer because when he left the mother when Tina was 10 he hurt the three- and six-year-old parts. The father's leaving was still disturbing to Teenager to a level 10.

In response to Tina's question, Teenager said there was also a 10-year-old part created when the father left. She was "off to the side, a good student." Tina visualized the new part as "taller than Sally, with dark black hair, and wearing lime green shorts, a grey t-shirt, and dirty sneakers." The father's departure disturbed her to a level 10 on the SUD scale. She did not have a name of her own but would like to have one. She chose *Paula* for herself.

At the beginning of our eleventh session, Tina talked of her anger during the week. She was pleased to say that although she was angry with Robert, she did not scream at him. She just "refused to talk to him for 24 hours." For Tina, this was a significant improvement. The situation that provoked Tina's anger was Robert's desire for sexual intimacy at a time when she was exhausted following two consecutive 12-hour workdays. The cold silence with which she treated him kept him at arm's length. "He had to kiss my ass before I'd talk to him," she said.

A Timid 10-year-Old

When we returned to Paula, the newly discovered 10-year-old subpersonality, we found that this shy part was uncomfortable with the positive attention Tina was giving her. After some reassurances, however, that she was indeed worthy of attention, she was cooperative and wanted to help Tina. She affirmed that she felt like she was 10 years old and that this was the age when the father left and moved into an apartment. His leaving continued to disturb her to a level 10 on the SUD scale. She also revealed for Tina, who had some difficulty recalling her age when the events occurred, that Tina was 11 when the mother married the stepfather. The disturbing kiss by the stepfather was also at age 11, but it now bothered Paula only to a level four, an indication that the work we had done had already been helpful to her.

Paula agreed to give up her sadness over the father leaving. We used a wind intervention in which Tina visualized Paula standing between two posts in an open field with wind rushing between the posts as Paula experienced the wind "blowing over, around, and through her." Tina visualized Paula letting her sadness be carried away by the wind. When Tina said, "Okay," that the intervention was complete, we checked Paula for remaining distress. She provided a SUD rating for the memory at a level two. What continued to bother her was a related memory from this period. Tina had fractured her ankle and home alone. The absence of her father made her feel particularly lonely. She added that, on other occasions, she would fake illness so that her mother would give her attention. After Paula expressed her thoughts, a repetition of the wind intervention reduced the SUD level to zero. With the unburdening complete, we checked Paula's distress for the stepfather-kissing incident and found it to have spontaneously reduced to a level two. A quick return to the wind intervention reduced this incident to zero distress.

Thinking of the loneliness she felt after her father moved out, Tina explained that this was the time when her depression established itself. Paula carried the sadness and loneliness. She was lonely and lacked attention at home, and shy and unpopular at school. However, life changed in middle school. "I started cheerleading in the seventh grade, and that brought me out of my shyness." "Then," she went on, "in the eighth grade I started hanging out with a tougher crowd. That's when Teenager appeared."

Paula shared two other low-level memories of her sad and lonely years. In grade school, there was a time when she was unable to stop crying. For hours, she could not stop the tears from flowing. Her mother's response was to say to her, "You're crazy!" Paula could not remember why she was crying, only that she could not stop. "Nobody paid attention to me," she said. "Nobody cared that I was crying." This memory disturbed Paula to a level five, but she quickly unburdened it with a wind intervention. The other memory had to do with a fight with her sister when they were children. Tina's grandmother hit Tina (as Paula) over the head with a spatula and punished her by making her stay in her grandmother's room, crying and feeling sad and lonely, while her sister was allowed to go out and play. Paula unburdened without a problem the level three disturbance of this memory, using another wind intervention.

At the end of the session, Tina realized that it was also Paula who carried her depression in the present. She realized that it was Paula who had influenced her to go to bed on the previous Sunday when Teenager was angry with Robert. As she thought more about it, Tina added that she used to become ill after a fight with someone, both as a child and as an adult. "I got sick when I was depressed. I got attention from my mother and so I looked forward to getting sick." We intended to do more work with Paula's depression at our next session. We also planned to get back to our unfinished unburdening work with Teenager.

Ending Therapy

Because of an increased work schedule, Tina did not return for our twelfth session until four weeks later. It was our final session. Work pressure continued to be high for Tina, but more importantly for her, there had been no significant problems during the month she was absent. She continued to enjoy sex with Robert several times a week, and she did not "go off" now when she was angry. She decided that she did not need to do more work with 10-year-old Paula on depression. Fortunately, because of our work with Paula, we could now complete our unburdening work with Teenager, who, although she no longer went into a raging mode, did punish Robert with long periods of silence when they had a disagreement.

Teenager's unburdening work went quickly with the use of a fire pit intervention. Tina visualized Teenager standing next to a pit in the ground full of burning coals as she reached into herself, lifted out, and threw into the pit the negative emotions connected to six specific memories we had previously collected. Five of the six memories already had reduced levels of distress as the result of the work we had done with the Paula part. As each package of emotion reached the coals, it burst into flame and totally incinerated itself. The first three packages were memories relating to the stepfather; the fourth was her anger about a friend who competed with her in a training course and later "came on" to her fiancé. The fifth was that of Robert calling her a "bitch," while the sixth was the potentially dangerous road rage incident where she followed, tailgated, cursed and made obscene gestures at a man who had flashed a light in her face on the city street. The work went quickly in unburdening these memories. Teenager felt that her burden of negative energy was greatly alleviated.

However, even with this work accomplished, Teenager found that she was still deeply troubled by Robert's jealousy of her and his lack of trust of her. Tina observed, "He has a little boy part who thinks I'm a whore, who says, 'Don't believe her, she's lying!'" Interestingly, Robert accepted that Tina had internal subpersonalities and had learned to recognize when Teenager blended with Tina. He had also shared, during an intimate moment of peace; that while he trusted her much of the time, he had the "little boy part" to which Tina referred. Teenager's anger over Robert's continued jealousy measured an eight on the SUD scale. She agreed to use the fire pit to unburden her present irritation with him. Tina said that as Teenager released this continuing irritation and frustration to the fire, countless incidents of Robert's jealousy and mistrust flashed through her mind. The first effort at unburdening past incidents of jealousy reduced the SUD score only to a level three, "because there's nothing I can say or do; it's annoying; it never stops." One repetition of the intervention reduced the remaining distress to zero. At the conclusion of this work, with Teenager in a calm state, Tina recognized that this unburdening only related to the incidents of the past. She understood that there would be more incidents in the future. Tina convinced Teenager to try a new strategy with her fiancé's jealousy. She would work to be a friend to the "little boy voice" in the fiancé's head by speaking directly to him, talking softly to him, and soothing him, rather than confronting him with anger. As we concluded the session, Tina also said she would continue to try to convince Robert to do his own therapy on his lack of trust and his jealousy. If he did so, she would consent to marry him.

When Tina left therapy, she felt that she had made major life changes. She no longer screamed, cursed and threw things when Robert acted inappropriately. She was prepared to relate to him in a softer way. She no longer experienced road rage. At work, while the politics of promotion irritated her, she was unwilling to compromise her values by flirting with her boss in order to advance. She accepted that she might advance less quickly than others as a consequence. She had learned to enjoy sex with Robert and understood that she had little control over his insecurity and jealousy. She viewed the problem as his rather than hers. At three months follow up, she was doing well with the control of her anger. Robert's jealous behavior continued to irritate, but she was hopeful that he would eventually do the therapy he needed to do.

Chapter 4
Career Loss, Procrastination and Helping Too Much

In the case described, below specific goals were at first quite broad. Georgia, my client, knew that she was anxious most of the time, especially at work, and that her work activities had been unsatisfactory for both her and her employers for some time. We let her full set of issues and concerns develop over the course of therapy. While the problems we worked on were those of everyday life, the inner world she presented was anything but ordinary. Georgia is unusual in that she visualizes all of her parts as active drawings or paintings from animated films she has seen in the past. She is a big fan of Walt Disney films. Many persons visualize a part occasionally as a cartoon figure, but Georgia is the rare person whose entire cast of internal characters consists of drawings or animated film characters. It is noteworthy that, throughout her life, Georgia's favorite leisure activity has been to lose herself in animated film, computer games of the *Dungeons and Dragons* sort, and science fiction and fantasy novels.

Georgia was a divorced, 41 year old licensed attorney and mother of one who came to therapy for help with dealing with work stress and its associated anxiety. She was unemployed, but found work quickly, soon after we began our work in therapy. Her score on the Dissociative Experiences Scale was an average 6.7, an early suggestion that her childhood was not trauma laden.

Georgia had given up, at least temporarily, any plans to continue her career as an attorney. The workload was both exhausting and anxiety producing. A year previously, she was fired for not billing enough hours, in spite of working evenings and weekends. The problem was that she spent too much time doing nonbillable activities, such as helping other staff with their computer problems. She also felt a need to make her work near perfect, and so she spent extra time on document drafts that did not require such painstaking perfection, especially since they would be amended significantly before reaching a final stage. Because her perfectionism negatively influenced her output of work, Georgia spent many evening and weekend hours completing the tasks she was expected to finish during the normal workday.

Ultimately, the stress of meeting requirements for billable hours proved too great for her; consequently, she chose to do what she thought would be less demanding work as a paralegal. Unfortunately, her problems continued, and she found herself once again working additional evening and weekend hours in order to complete her assigned work. Two months before entering therapy, she was fired again. She then chose to seek work as a legal secretary, hoping to work an ordinary day from nine to five, with weekends off.

Beginning Parts Therapy

During our first session, Georgia talked of the continuing anxiety she suffered throughout her workdays, regardless of what kind of work she might be doing. A Parts Psychology approach assumes that such pervasive anxiety would have its origin in earlier life experiences, especially in childhood. Consequently, I helped Georgia begin to locate those experiences through an affect bridge. The technique is simple. I asked her to focus on her anxiety and while staying connected to it, to let her mind float back through time, bridging to the earliest memories she had which somehow connected to the anxiety. The bridge helped her connect to an incident she experienced in the third grade when her teacher sent her on an errand to another teacher's classroom. She found herself petrified when she reached this classroom and could not force herself to knock on the door and enter the second teacher's room. She had to return to her own room with her errand unaccomplished. Even now, some 33 years later, she was still bothered somewhat by the memory of this embarrassing experience of failure. On a SUD (Subjective Units of Disturbance) scale from zero to 10, she gave herself a score of three for current anxiety when thinking of the incident, and a score of eight or nine for her current negative judgment of herself in relation to this early incident. "What's wrong with me?" she asked. "That's ridiculous!" We would use this memory as a means of beginning our work with internal parts.

In the second session, Georgia reported that she had read the material I had given her on how the mind is naturally organized into parts. She indicated that she was comfortable with the idea, although she did not know what working with parts might entail. She already had some familiarity with the idea of internal parts through a previous client who had referred Georgia to me.

At the beginning of the session, Georgia stated a specific goal she wanted to reach. She wanted to overcome her ever-present tendency to procrastinate in getting things done in her private life. On weekends, for example, in spite of a high level of anxiety about tasks to be done and errands to be run, she often "didn't do anything at all." She could not relax because of the anxiety she felt about what she needed to do, but she did not do the things she needed to do either. The result was that she returned to work tired and unrested, with an additional load of anxiety and frustration because of the "wasted" weekend.

We began to search for Georgia's internal parts in the second half of the session by again focusing on her anxiety. Her remembered anxiety from the incident in the third grade was still evident. She reported feeling a similar anxiety when she thought about coming to our first therapy session a week previously. She experienced the same sort of anxiety when she recalled traveling to her recent job interviews. I asked Georgia to focus on the anxiety that she had located in her stomach and to ask it to give her a picture of itself. The first internal image Georgia found was one she described as a picture of her "shrunken stomach." This part did not otherwise want to show itself, but it acknowledged that it was the part who was anxious about the job interviews, and it was the part who was afraid to open the teacher's door in the third grade. It also indicated that there was another part present at the third grade incident, one more embarrassed than fearful. When asked to do so, the first part agreed to connect Georgia to the second part. We were at the end of the session and there was only time for Georgia to report an image of "a big, black blob" and to say "hello" to this new part. Neither of these first appearances of internal parts is atypical. When a client asks a part associated with a body sensation to show itself, it is not unusual for her to report an image of the body part where she feels the sensation. The presence of some sort of blob is also fairly common. The therapist can either ask for further personalization of the part or simply wait for the part to do so on its own. I chose to do the latter. When first introducing parts work to a new client, I am less concerned with imagery or conversation content than with developing the continuing ability to communicate with her inner world.

In our third session, we looked again for parts associated with the anxiety of job interviews. I coached Georgia through the interaction with the part she discovered when she focused on her felt anxiety. Georgia spoke silently to the part and reported the responses to me. The part did not show itself to Georgia, and so she continued to speak to it by addressing her own sensation of anxiety. The part indicated that it was nine years old, but did not respond to the questions of whether it had a name or wanted one. Its rather odd response to the question of whether it would like to have the name, *Rumplestiltskin*, was to provide a picture of the world in which it sees itself: "an underwater view, in dark water, with a flow like a tide." Its answer regarding whether it would like to give up its anxiety was, "No." Asked if it was afraid that it would disappear if it gave up its anxiety, there was no immediate response, but Georgia reported that the part seemed to be confused. As I continued to coach her, Georgia explained to the part how it had helped her by holding within itself the negative emotions of Georgia's memories. She thanked the part for providing the help that allowed her to grow safely into adulthood. Given that the part had successfully accomplished its purpose, Georgia again asked if it would like to give up its burden. This time the part agreed. Georgia would help the part to release its burden of fear of opening the teacher's door in the third grade. The symbolic release would happen as the current in the water around the part carried away its burden. As Georgia visualized the scene, she was able to see the part for the first time as it hung onto a rock in the water and allowed the waves to wash over it. "I think she's letting it go," Georgia said. A moment later, the burden was gone. As we ended the session, Georgia said of the part, "As she hung onto the rocks I could see her arms, so she's a little girl, maybe a mermaid, but still kinda hiding."

Rumplestiltskin is a name I suggest fairly often when a part is shy or otherwise reluctant to participate. It is a name that only a rare part wants, and frequently the suggestion serves to give the part more energy in the interview. Often a sense of humor aids the interview process. The most frequent reason a part does not wish to give up its negative emotion is that it identifies so strongly with the emotion that it fears it might disappear if the emotion is unburdened. Thus, the next question I asked of the part related to this fear. When the part did not respond because of its confusion, I decided to go to the next step of explaining its function in the larger self-system, the sequestering of negative emotion so that the self is not overwhelmed. Thanking a part generally leads to greater cooperation in therapy because the part feels appreciated, even if it does not understand the reason for the thanks. In this case, both the thanks and the explanation of function seem to have been what the part needed to agree to unburden itself.

The Eye and Other Parts

In the fourth session, Georgia reported that the sense of relief she experienced at the end of the session continued during the past week. However, she also felt a lot of anger. She found herself yelling at bad drivers and noticed that she was frequently angry with herself at other times.

Early in the session, Georgia mentioned that she had stubbed her toe during the week, and she went on to say that as a child she thought of herself as clumsy. She recalled that she often bumped into things from the fifth or sixth grade, when she grew a lot, through junior high and high school. Her family sarcastically called her *Grace* well into her 30s. However, now she knew that she was not particularly clumsy; her accidents were due to rushing too much. This discussion about being clumsy turned out to be relevant when we returned to work with the blob who had appeared in the second session.

We returned to Georgia's memory of being afraid to enter a third grade classroom. This permitted us to find again the girl in the water who we would use to connect to the blob. Georgia simply asked the girl to connect us to the blob. When the blob appeared, it immediately changed into a closed eye with long eyelashes. *The Eye* reported that the incident in the third grade did not disturb it. Apparently, this incident was not even included in The Eye's set of memories. Instead, its earliest disturbing memory was of an incident in a restaurant during junior high school. When Georgia got up to get more napkins for her table, she bumped into a group of highchairs and produced a loud clatter, loud enough so that everybody in the restaurant looked at her. She rated her embarrassment for this incident at a level eight on the SUD scale. The Eye readily agreed to give up this embarrassment. We began with a wind intervention where we asked The Eye to let the wind blow away her embarrassment. This brought the SUD level down to a three. We then repeated the intervention as the part focused especially on its feelings of having all eyes upon her. Notice the *eyes*, which seem to be the source of The Eye costume worn by this part. Adding blowing water to the wind intervention lowered the SUD level to its final zero.

Another memory carried by The Eye was a *chicken fight* in junior high school among members of the swim team. The chicken, Georgia explained, was the person who stood in the water and carried a second person on his or her shoulders while engaged in a contest to see who could cause the other team to fall over into the water. Georgia was one chicken, and she had a crush on the boy who was the chicken on another team. She said to him that their chicken had nice legs. Unfortunately, the boy had no clue that Georgia was flirting with him; this caused Georgia embarrassment. The Eye was willing to unburden this embarrassment, but when we began the symbolic unburdening through an imagined hurricane, The Eye balked, saying it was afraid the hurricane would be too strong. This sudden fear, not previously evident and appearing only when the part had begun the intervention, was a sign that another part was blending with The Eye. When I asked Georgia to focus on the fear and ask for a picture of itself, she shortly reported an image of the edge of a chasm, but no further clues as to the identity of the fearful part. We would try again in our next session to identify it. The power of the imagery and other internal work was clear when, at the end of the session, Georgia reported that her arms were shaking during the session when The Eye struggled with its fear.

In session six, we returned immediately to the fear, because we couldn't otherwise proceed with unburdening The Eye. Georgia focused on the anxiety she felt in her stomach and asked the fearful part to show itself. There was no response. We then tried a different visualization technique. I asked Georgia to imagine reaching into her own body (eyes closed), lifting out the fear, and placing it into a nearby room. She did so but found that the room was completely dark. When I suggested she add light, Georgia could see the surface of the ocean or lake where the little girl resided. The young part did not show herself, but she did acknowledge that it was her fear that blocked The Eye from unburdening the chicken fight memory.

The little girl, still unseen, reported that an early memory of hers was that of riding in an aerial tram at a theme park. (Note the connection here with the earlier picture of fear as represented by a chasm). She was terrified and shivered uncontrollably as she scrunched into a corner of the tram. Her experience of this fear was at a level 10 on the SUD scale. Georgia said that she could now visualize the tram. The little girl was like a fairy, hiding in a corner. She agreed to unburden her fear through letting the wind blow it away. She quickly reduced her SUD level to a two, but could do no more because she felt the tram rocking in the wind and this was causing further fear. Georgia visualized the tram moving to its stable destination and, once there, the unburdening was easily completed.

The part now showed herself as *Tinker Bell*, from the Walt Disney movie, *Peter Pan*. She said that she might have earlier memories but they were not about fear. She knew who Georgia was, referring to her as *The Boss*. Tinker Bell gave permission then to complete the unburdening of The Eye for the playing-chicken incident, which Georgia quickly accomplished. At this point, it was unclear as to whether the little girl in the water from our first intervention was the same as the Tinker Bell part, or whether they were separate but somehow connected to each other. As we concluded the session, Georgia said that she had the sense that Tinker Bell was "somewhere around three or four years of age." At the end of the session, another memory surfaced: the experience of being fired as an attorney, about which Georgia was still angry. We would come back to this in a later session.

The Problem of Running Late

In session seven, we worked with a current issue precipitated by Georgia's distress over being late to our meeting. When she focused inward upon this distress and asked it to provide an image of itself, she saw the hilt of a sword. We called this part *The Sword*. It reported its earliest memory to be "a vague general feeling of running around, being late." When asked the meaning of the sword as a symbol for itself, the part communicated that it is more dangerous than other parts. The sword is for attacking rather than defending. When it feels the stress that comes with being late, it wants to strike out at others.

In the remainder of this session, we collected a set of troubling memories that formed the foundation for the stress Georgia felt when she was running late. The first memory came from the beginning of the 10th grade of high school when Georgia was unable to open her locker. Throughout the school day, she had to carry a large stack of books from class to class. "The books piled up almost to my face as I held them," Georgia said. Between classes, she would rush to her locker to try again to open it, and then rush again to the next class carrying her stack of books. She experienced considerable embarrassment this day, and felt that all the other kids were staring at her. No one else was carrying a pile of books. The Sword reported its level of distress over this incident to be a level six on the SUD scale.

On the weekend following the locker incident, Georgia sprained her ankle and had to use a cane to help her get around between classes in the next week. She could use her locker now and could carry her books in a backpack, but the slow pace of walking, even with the help of the cane, meant that she was constantly in danger of being late to the next class. She had no time to stop by her locker and leave some of her books there. Again, she felt embarrassment and anxiety because, "I stood out when I wanted to fit in." The part's SUD level for this incident was a seven.

The next incident happened in Georgia's first year of law school during moot court competition when she had advanced to the final. The afternoon before the evening final, she stopped off at home and fell asleep, awakening with just barely enough time to travel the four blocks back to school. When she rushed into the room, she sat next to the opposing counsel, the wrong seat. Although she moved on to her own seat, she says, "I never got myself together well enough to do well in the argument." The Sword part continued to experience this incident as a level nine of distress.

A series of events led to the level nine distress she also felt for the next significant memory. In Georgia's first court appearance as an attorney, she was to argue a discovery motion. Everything was rushed. She learned only that morning that her boss wanted her in court in just a few hours. When she arrived, she was delayed because she parked in the wrong parking garage. Then she found that her boss had directed her to the wrong floor of the courthouse. When she found the correct floor and room, she was already late and the session had already begun. She lost the argument for the motion and left the courtroom, angry with herself for being late and unprepared, and angry with her boss for giving poor directions and for providing insufficient information regarding the motion.

In session eight, we unburdened The Sword of the negative energy attached to the memories of lateness, using a fire intervention in which Georgia imagined The Sword bathed in fire. At the end of the intervention, Georgia reported that The Sword had changed its appearance somewhat, becoming bright and shiny. This sort of change in appearance is common following an unburdening. With child parts, sad faces frequently become all smiles, and they can't wait to go out to play.

The Problem of Procrastination

Shortly after completing the intervention, Georgia reported another set of memories not yet unburdened. All of them had to do with running late because of her procrastination. These memories carried by The Sword were quickly unburdened, but it was immediately clear that procrastination was a character trait involving another part. By asking The Sword to connect us to the procrastinating part, we were soon working with the new entity.

Georgia described a brighter spot in her inner vision with triangular shaped eyes showing through. The part was startled and surprised when Georgia addressed it. When she asked if it had a name she saw the face of a dragon. She asked if she should call it *Dragon*. It responded that it should be called *Mister Dragon,* with the emphasis on *Mister.* Mister Dragon initially reported his first memory as dating to grade school "when I was playing in the woods with my brothers and sisters. We're supposed to go inside when it gets dark, but I don't want to. Somebody will say we should head in, and I keep saying it's not dark yet. We stay out until we hear Mother calling from the carport. We're kind of in trouble, but not really. And somebody ratted me out. So we went over the rule again, that when it starts to get dark, we are to come in." The incident was a zero on the SUD scale. Georgia reported that it was funny to think about it. Incidents that do not register on the SUD scale are not uncommon, but the most frequent earliest memory is one of distress. As it turns out there was a memory prior to this one and it was somewhat disturbing. Generally, memories that are not disturbing do not require unburdening; however, as we will see below in working with a different dragon, it is sometimes important to unburden the positive energy of some memories.

Mister Dragon's earlier memory rated only a two on the SUD scale. In this memory, Georgia was watching television when her mother called downstairs to tell her to turn off the television and do her chores. She continued to watch her show because she wanted to see its conclusion. Her mother called again and Georgia continued to watch her show. Finally, her mother called down again but with an irritated edge to her voice and Georgia reluctantly turned off the television and began her assigned chore of cleaning the bathroom.

Another level two SUD score dated to Georgia's junior high years. She had always had difficulty getting out of bed for school in the mornings; her father had to call her to get up almost every day. On one morning, he lost his patience and simply turned on her light and pulled off her covers, exposing her to the winter cold.

Procrastination led to another difficult experience during Georgia's late 20s. She had put off doing her taxes until the last minute and found herself at the post office at midnight in a long line of cars, all waiting to turn in their tax envelopes. There was no good reason for her to be late. Her form was a *short-form 1040EZ* and she would get money back, but she "just couldn't get around to" completing it. This memory rated as a level five disturbance.

Mister Dragon's final memory related to Georgia's need to get her application for the bar exam in the mail by the deadline. The memory bothered Mister Dragon at a level nine. On the final day, Georgia had completed everything in the application except for the notarizing of two forms. Finding an available notary was an anxiety-producing experience, causing her to scurry about to a number of places. She ended the afternoon standing in line at the post office in order to get her envelope postmarked by the deadline. In the next session, we would work on unburdening Mister Dragon of the procrastination problem.

At the beginning of the ninth session, we began the unburdening. We started by helping Mister Dragon give up to the wind his procrastination of chores. The procrastination energy for staying in bed when Georgia should be up and getting ready for the day was found in Mister Dragon's stomach. He vomited it up in his own fiery breath and then dissolved it in water.

Next, he unburdened the procrastination of chores from all of his memories from the earliest to the latest. Finally, Georgia guided him in unburdening the procrastination in her professional life by dissolving it in the water of a lake.

Near the end of the session, Georgia negotiated a new role for Mister Dragon. He would specialize in making wise judgments as to when to take care of pending matters, and he would supply the energy to motivate Georgia to follow through on her tasks.

An interesting phenomenon had occurred during the unburdening of Mister Dragon. He reported that whenever he was temporarily stuck in unburdening his negative energies he got help from another dragon, one he identified as a female "wind dragon" with a powerful breath. She would blow away any remaining negativity when he was having difficulty letting go of it. He said that she was a helper, sometimes too much of a helper. "All she does is help other people," he said, "but she doesn't take the time to do things for herself. Sometimes she needs to learn to say no."

The Problem of Helping Too Much

When the new part presented herself to Georgia, she said her name was *White Dragon*. She reported her first memory as dating to age four or five when she had fun helping the family clean up their newly acquired first house. "It was a terrible mess," said Georgia. "We all pitched in and cleaned it." The SUD score for this memory was a zero because White Dragon experienced it as a *fun* activity. Later, we would find it important to unburden this positive energy in the same way that we unburdened negative energy. The memory is an important one in theoretical terms, because it illustrates that not all parts are created in painful experiences. Occasionally, parts are a response to energetic but positive experiences.

White Dragon's more painful experiences derive from the time when Georgia was in grade school. In doing class work, Georgia was always the first one to finish.Her teachers, wanting to keep her busy, would regularly ask her to help the slower kids. While she liked helping others, doing so with kids she did not know very well meant that she did not get to work with her friends. White Dragon rated these experiences at a level four on the SUD scale.

At the beginning of session 10, Georgia reported success in her job search. She had begun a temporary assignment as a legal secretary. The position could become permanent if they liked her work. They might also ask her to do some paralegal work as well.

In this session, we collected a rather full set of memories from White Dragon. Her next significant memories involved the chore of cleaning bathrooms in the family's first house. This task was assigned to Georgia who, with White Dragon's help, never found it to be a problem. Eventually, however, this chore fell to her younger sister. The problem was that her sister, unlike Georgia, was paid for doing the chore. This difference in treatment disturbed White Dragon to a level six on the SUD scale.

Another memory with a similar theme had to do with Georgia's use of the family car as a teenager. When, at age 16, she got her driver's license, her mother made a deal with her. In return for picking up her siblings at school or for taking them to doctors' appointments, Georgia could use the car on weekends. Georgia was not disturbed by the arrangement, and was happy to be able to use the family car. However, after Georgia went off to college, her younger brother was permitted to drive the same car to school and use it on weekends, but he was not required to run errands in return for its use. As with the case of the bathroom chores, Georgia was later disturbed by the difference in the way her mother treated her and a sibling. White Dragon rated the disturbance at a level two.

For her next significant memory, White Dragon took Georgia back to the time when she was in junior high school. Between Georgia's seventh and eighth grades, the family moved into a new house. All members of the family worked together in clearing the overgrown landscape left by the prior residents. For White Dragon, this was a level seven positive experience on the *SUE* (Subjective Units of Energy). This scale measures positive energy or energy that is not negative. Another positive experience, registering a nine on the SUE scale, involved Georgia's swim team. The girls swam year-round. Georgia and three other girls voluntarily formed a subgroup within the 13-14 year old age group, running errands for the coach, doing cheers for the other kids, and ensuring that the younger members of the team kept warm. "We were almost like assistant coaches," Georgia says.

White Dragon's next significant memory came from Georgia's adult years. As an attorney, Georgia found herself swamped with work and in need of help from someone who could do more of her less complex work. She was assigned a paralegal with no experience. She spent a great deal of time training her, both because she needed help and because she knew what it was like to be thrown into a job she didn't understand. This training took a lot of time away from her own work. Once she had trained her paralegal, however, her boss reassigned the employee elsewhere, leaving Georgia with little benefit and considerable lost time from her own work. Georgia said that during this period she also answered many questions from secretaries while training them to understand and utilize the computer system. She could not bill anyone for this time away from her own legal work and found herself in a vulnerable situation with her bosses. White Dragon nevertheless rated these experiences as a level nine on a positive SUE scale. When asked, however, White Dragon also acknowledged a negative level five on the SUD scale. The approaching end of the session prevented further investigation of this odd divided rating of the experience.

By the time we met for session eleven, I had thought more about Georgia's experiences of helping other workers at her own expense, and more about White Dragon's dual ratings of those experiences as both positive and negative. It seemed to me worth investigating the question of whether a negative SUD rating alongside a positive SUE rating might be due to amplification onto White Dragon of the distress of a different, as yet unidentified, subpersonality. The same part might also have been responsible for the earlier negative ratings we had encountered for some of White Dragon's helper experiences. Consequently, I suggested that Georgia ask White Dragon directly whether the level five negative rating for helping coworkers was her own feeling, or could it be an amplification from another part. She quickly responded that the negative rating was not hers. All of her helping actions were positive only. The next step was obvious. We asked White Dragon if she could find the part with the negative rating and bring it into Georgia's visualization field.

Georgia found herself with the image of a manta ray, flapping its "wings" as it swam in the ocean. In response to Georgia's questions, it indicated that it could "hear" her and that it knew who she was. However, it gave no response to the questions about whether it knew it was a part of Georgia or whether it knew about the helping experiences under discussion. Because we were having communication difficulties, we asked White Dragon if she could help. She responded that a manta ray was not the part's true form, and it was using that form to hide. Georgia assured the manta ray that there was no need to hide and that we wanted to call upon its wisdom. Georgia then requested that it provide an image of itself in its *true form*. The manta ray then transformed itself into the image of a giant sea turtle, swimming underwater. It could now communicate more clearly.

It reported its name to be *Sunny*, and that its true form to be a female giant sea turtle. Sunny indicated that she knew Georgia and thought of her as the big boss. She acknowledged that she had a problem with the helping experiences in the law office. They disturbed her to a level six. Note here the slight difference in Sunny's report of a negative level six versus White Dragon's negative level five. While it could be normal testing variation, it is also consistent with a filtering effect. When the self or a part reports on a SUD level amplified from elsewhere, it is usually diminished somewhat from the level experienced by the part who carries the experience.

Sunny reported her earliest memory to be from a time prior to law school when, just out of college, Georgia worked as a project administrator for a national construction firm. For a week when she should have been preparing for an upcoming audit, Georgia spent considerable time helpfully answering questions from engineers in another state. The result was that in order to be ready for her audit she had to "pull an all-nighter," foregoing sleep to meet all her own requirements. Sunny says that what Georgia should have done was to cut off communication with the engineers for the week, until after she had finished her own audit preparations. Sunny found this experience to be disturbing to a SUD level of seven.

We were at the end of the session, and so we did not collect additional memories. Based upon what we knew so far, however, Sunny is a relatively new part in Georgia's life. Apparently, Georgia's friendly and helpful nature did not become a problem for her until she became gainfully employed, a situation where she was held responsible for producing work that was measurable against her own job description. Not only was Sunny a relatively new part in Georgia's life, but she was a part who expressed herself in a timid and fearful way, clearly dominated by the more powerful manager, White Dragon. It was evident that we needed to find a way for Sunny and White Dragon to work together. There was an obvious downside for Georgia if either of these subpersonalities dominated her personality. If her helpful part was allowed free reign, she would have trouble keeping a job. If her self-interested part were to be fully in control, Georgia would suffer socially, risking ostracism for not being a team player. We would need to find a way for these two parts to work together.

At the beginning of session twelve, Georgia reported that she had made a good step during the week by turning down extra work from an attorney who was not one of her direct bosses. When Georgia searched inside for the part responsible for this important step, she could not at first locate her. Eventually, however, the helpful White Dragon identified Sunny, the giant sea turtle, as the responsible party. Asked why she did not acknowledge her responsibility for the boundary setting action, Sunny replied that she was afraid she might be in trouble for doing so. This reluctance to take action and to take credit for the action was characteristic of this aspect of Georgia. Typical activities of Georgia's childhood, her helping behaviors, were some-times no longer adaptive in her professional life. Her propensity to help others, and to put aside her own needs to do so, was symbolically represented by the dominance of the White Dragon and her intimidation of Sunny. Sunny represented Georgia's desire to put herself first, at least in the professional arena.

When asked why she didn't object to Sunny's boundary setting, White Dragon said that her first impulse was to help the troublesome attorney, but she didn't really like her because of the way she tried to use all of the secre-tarial staff for her own purposes, regardless of their workloads. Thus, it was not difficult for her to step aside and allow Sunny to say no to work that would divert Georgia from her assigned tasks.

Now that Sunny and White Dragon were cooperating in finding a work-able solution to the problem of helping others versus helping Georgia, the question was whether any further action was required. Often it is enough of an intervention when we are able to bring two formerly polarized parts into a continuing dialog. In discussing the matter, however, Georgia felt that while she had made some progress, she was still too strongly tempted to help others when she should be taking care of herself. It would not have taken much, she said, for her to have helped the intruding attorney. Were it not for previous discussions among the secretarial staff about how this attorney selfishly used everyone around her, Georgia might not have been able to say no when the attorney approached her. Georgia chose to do significant unburdening work with White Dragon in order to make a more dramatic change in her attitude toward placing others' needs ahead of her own.

In principle, the unburdening work with White Dragon would be the same as with other parts. The difference would be in the nature of the energy we would be unburdening. Just as the negative energy attached to a problem behavior requires the unburdening of underlying memories in order to free the person to be more flexible, so too does the positive energy attached to some memories require unburdening. In this case, the positive experiences of helping others in childhood were the foundation for Georgia's excess in helping others to her own detriment. Subjectively speaking, the positive energies attached to her helping memories were not a burden at all, but a pleasure. Georgia recognized that she would be letting go of subjectively positive experiences in order to change her external behavior, but she felt the sacrifice was necessary. She decided to neutralize the positive energy of some, but not all, of her helping behaviors. We would focus upon the earliest, and therefore most important, memories.

The interventions proceeded almost without problems. White Dragon quickly released to a wind metaphor the age-four memories of helping to clean up the new house, and in the process remembered that some of that work was not pleasant. Young Georgia grew tired during the work and her little body could not sustain the effort to do all the necessary cleaning. Regarding the positive memories of helping slower kids in grade school, some of the energy was easily unburdened to wind but some was not. When White Dragon reported to Georgia that she was having trouble letting go of the positive energy, Georgia reminded White Dragon that she was a helper and that right now it was Georgia who needed her help. That reminder was all it took for White Dragon to release to the wind the remainder of the positive energy still attached to the grade school helping memories. Georgia then agreed that before doing additional work on being less helpful, she would observe herself for a time in order to gauge how well White Dragon and Sunny were working together.

The Problem of Meeting Deadlines

Session 13 brought a new problem to our attention. Although White Dragon and Sunny seemed to be cooperating well, Georgia still stressed over not getting enough work finished during the course of the day. The problem revealed itself on the previous Friday (our sessions were on Wednesdays) when, unexpectedly, a different boss gave Georgia new documents to complete, as well as additional work. None of this work was on Georgia's list of things to do. She experienced significant anxiety about not accomplishing what she had planned. She was fearful of not meeting the deadline her first boss had given her and resentful of her apparent need to work overtime while other staff members went home.

In seeking out the internal source for Georgia's negative emotions, we first called upon White Dragon and Sunny for their views. White Dragon acknowledged her presence at the scene, but Sunny, again fearful of "getting in trouble," responded to questions only after considerable coaxing. Sunny indicated that she was the resentful part who tried to help Georgia on Friday by setting work boundaries, but she was unable to get White Dragon to slow down. Although White Dragon agreed that she was the part who wanted to help everyone, she denied feeling anxiety over the boss's deadline. I asked Georgia to focus just on her anxiety about the deadline and to search internally for a part connected to that anxiety. She quickly reported the image of a coiled snake, hissing, with tongue waving, and resembling an image from an American flag. Both White Dragon and Sunny thought that this was the source of the anxiety. Before we could address the snake image, Georgia said, "Oh, I don't like snakes!" This strong reaction signaled the presence of an additional part because the self does not on its own present strong emotions. We were able to calm Georgia for the interview with The Snake by asking the unidentified part simply to step back. The *step back* technique is useful in many contexts. In this case, Georgia addressed her feeling of dislike for snakes in making her request.

During the interview, as I coached Georgia through a set of standard interview questions, the snake image indicated that it knew who Georgia was:

Scaredy Cat, a part we had yet to meet, and possibly the part who said that it did not like snakes. Evidently, The Snake could not view Georgia clearly; instead, it confused her with this new part. Without an image of Scaredy Cat, Georgia nevertheless asked it to *step aside* from her so that The Snake could perceive her more clearly. She then proceeded to orient The Snake to herself as the self, with The Snake as a part of her. The Snake also revealed that it had a name of its own but chose not to share it.

We were at the end of the session, and Georgia had time only to observe how distressing it was to be so anxious about meeting deadlines and to ask The Snake if it would step back from her at work when she asked it to do so. The part indicated that it would "think about" the request. In our next session, we planned to continue our interview with The Snake, and perhaps to look for the part who was afraid of it.

At the beginning of session 14, Georgia reported that she had asked The Snake to step back on several occasions during the workweek, and each time she felt some relief from performance stress. When asked, The Snake still would not reveal its name, but did indicate that it was male.

Curiously, as Georgia tried to communicate with The Snake, holding in her mind an image of him in the lush forest environment of her imagination, she reported the presence of a door "off to the right" of her visual field. Then she reported that The Snake had just lunged at the door. When questioned, The Snake said there was a monster behind the door, and that he and *The Monster* got along fine as long as each of them stayed on their own side of the door. The Monster, said The Snake, had a "really big human jaw and big teeth." Further, The Monster didn't like Georgia. "It likes to hurt things, anything it can. That's why it has to stay behind the door." Georgia's questions led The Snake to share additional information. He believed that The Monster was put into a cage behind the door so that it wouldn't hurt things. He did not know for how long The Monster had been locked up. It had never hurt The Snake because The Snake could fight back, but it had hurt Scaredy Cat. And no, it had not hurt anyone Georgia had met so far in her internal journeys.

With a highly imaginative person like Georgia who has such a well developed inner world, it becomes obvious that much of the imagery and reported conflict must be understood as metaphor. Many of us probably have monsters of some sort lurking in our unconscious minds, but we do not all visualize them and their fellow participants with such vivid imagery. We had yet to meet The Monster or Scaredy Cat but we would. However, in doing the work of Parts Psychology it seems best to stay with a single problem until it is resolved rather than be distracted by other fascinating hints along the way. Thus, we returned to interviewing The Snake with our standard set of questions without further investigation of the two unknown parts.

Georgia asked The Snake to connect to the stress she had been feeling in the office the past week and to bridge back to its earliest memories that connected somehow to that stress. The Snake provided her with images of her parents arguing at a time when she was "just barely out of the crib, a toddler, before I was four." Further introspection led Georgia to say that her impression was that she was two years old. We were at the end of another session, and so we planned further interviews with The Snake regarding its early memories.

Following Georgia's description of her current work relationships and how they had improved, session 15 was devoted to the collection of more of The Snake's memories. The first memory was one of discomfort as Georgia remembered her mother trying to get her to take an adult vitamin pill in the third or fourth grade at age eight or nine. The pill was too large for Georgia to swallow. She couldn't remember whether she had actually swallowed the pill, but she did remember her mother's anxiety and frustration. The school bus was due to arrive, and Georgia had to swallow the pill and then get to the bus stop before the bus left her behind. Additionally, it was upsetting to Georgia that her mother was frustrated over her inability to accomplish what should have been a simple task, that of swallowing a vitamin pill. The Snake rated the incident as a four on the SUD scale.

The Snake's next memory had to do with the breakage of an object that belonged to Georgia's mother. One of Georgia's siblings had broken the object and had clumsily pushed it under a low table, barely out of sight. Her mother had discovered it while sweeping. She made Georgia and her three siblings line up in a row in the living room and demanded to know who had broken the object and how it had happened. None of the siblings admitted to the deed. The mother was seemingly more disturbed by the hiding of the broken object than by its actual breakage. She threatened that if no one admitted to the crime she would punish all of them. Finally, to end the interrogation, and so that her mother wouldn't be so upset, Georgia volunteered that she had broken the object and hidden it. After Georgia falsely claimed responsibility for the act, the sibling who actually did it finally confessed. The incident was disturbing to The Snake at a level eight on the SUD scale, primarily because Georgia couldn't stand the rising anxiety of waiting for the culprit to admit to the act before her mother's patience ran out and all of them would be punished.

In high school, Georgia had a summer job as a file clerk. The workday ended at five o'clock. Another of The Snake's memories had to do with getting work done by the five o'clock deadline. Her boss had sent Georgia with a letter for typing by the firm's typists, but they told her she had arrived too late. She was five minutes too late to meet their cutoff time of 4:30 for accepting new work. Georgia was upset that the clerks would not accept the work and upset that she would upset her boss. She cried in the elevator on the way back to her boss. The incident was disturbing to a SUD level of seven because she had to tell her boss that she couldn't get her assigned job done. As it turned out, when she returned to her boss, her boss called the typists and berated them for being unprofessional; she then sent Georgia back to them with the letter. Georgia waited while the letter was typed. In our next session, we planned to unburden The Snake of his distress about meeting deadlines, either explicitly stated or internally experienced (as in the case of mother's deadline before punishing all the children).

In session 16, we gave all of our attention to helping The Snake to unburden his memory set, beginning with the vitamin pill incident. The Snake chose a fire symbol for the unburdening, permitting his ball of bad feelings to be consumed by fire. By the time we moved on to Georgia's memory of falsely confessing to breaking her mother's object, the SUD level had already fallen from eight to four. This is an instance of a common result of working with earlier memories. In this case and many others, a generalization effect from the unburdening of earlier memories reduces the SUD level of later memories without any conscious focusing upon them. We continued to use the fire symbol in unburdening The Snake. The broken object memory quickly reduced to a SUD of one and then to zero. The summer job incident was a level two when we reached it, and quickly reduced to less than one, and then to zero.

At this point, The Snake finally revealed his name to be *Sandy*. He did not explain why he had held it back until now. We asked Sandy to check his memory set between high school and the present for any other unburdening needs. He reported that there were a couple of incidents when Georgia was in college when she worked all night to finish term papers, papers that were not well done because of the pressure of the deadline. Sandy quickly unburdened the term paper stress (level five) to fire. There were two other memories. One involved finishing an academic paper at the last possible moment in order to be permitted to walk in the law school graduation ceremony (a SUD level of seven), and the other involved working in her professional life as an attorney when she actually missed a deadline (a SUD level of six). These memories were unburdened quickly to fire.

With Sandy's deadline-related stress now unburdened, we could turn our attention to Georgia's next concern. We planned to check on the new cooperative relationship between Sunny and White Dragon, to ensure that there were no problems there. We would also consider whether it was a good time to meet Scaredy Cat or the Monster.

In session 17, Georgia reported that her work life had shown no problems recently in helping others to her own detriment. We decided to check in again later with the two formerly polarized parts, Sunny and White Dragon, regarding further progress. In her family relationships, Georgia had also noticed a pleasant change. Whereas previously she was fiercely independent and insisted that she be the helper to family members, she said that she now found it easier to accept proffered help from her mother in organizing her life events and activities.

The Problem of Being Timid

We decided to look for the Scaredy Cat part next because of the previous report that The Monster had hurt it. We would wait before trying to approach The Monster until we had more information. We asked Sandy The Snake to help us find Scaredy Cat. I call this kind of work, where we use a known part to bring out an unknown part, *internal bridging*. It makes use of

the internal knowledge within a system even where the client has no conscious knowledge of the part we are seeking.

When Georgia brought Sandy onto her internal screen, she said that he
was "feeling feisty," meaning that he was more energetic than usual. She
said, "He likes to use the energy to wrap himself around trees and find out
what is going on in the forest." In this remark, Georgia was passing on what
Sandy communicated to her. She explained that what he meant was that he
liked to observe what was happening among other members of the internal
system of parts. She asked him to bridge to Scaredy Cat. After about one
minute of silence as she focused internally, Georgia said, "He's gonna see if
he can get her to come out." After another two minutes she said, "I think
Scaredy Cat has come out, but it is just a shape, and I'm asking Sandy to
help me see what she looks like." Then, "She's hiding inside a wicker basket
with a lid on top. She pushed off the lid from inside, and now I can see her
looking over the rim of the basket. She's an Easter Bunny!" Surprising us,
Scaredy Cat wasn't a cat at all, but a child's stuffed toy rabbit. It is interesting to see here how Georgia's internal world continues to unfold itself,
having its own, unpredictable dynamics.

We proceeded with the standard set of interview questions. Yes, the part
knew Georgia. She was *the one in charge.* She did not know Georgia's name,
however. After Georgia introduced herself, Scaredy Cat said that her own
name was *Fluffy. Scaredy Cat* is what The Snake calls her, and she thinks The
Monster also calls her that, but it doesn't talk to her so she is not sure." Yes,
The Monster hurt her but, "She doesn't want to tell me what The Monster
did to her. She just keeps showing me the wound, an open sore within the
fur on her body." We will keep in mind that this wound is metaphorical and
that eventually we will learn the source of this psychic damage.

We moved on to ask Fluffy about her earliest memory. Georgia reported
the following: "She's showing me my bedroom. I must have been in the
fourth or fifth grade when I started sleeping in that room. I'm crying and
upset. I'm mad at my mother about something, but I can't tell about what."
The experience was disturbing to Fluffy at a SUD level of four.

We were at the end of the session then, and it was time for Georgia to return fully to the present in my office. From the moment I asked her to disen-
gage from her internal world and to return to my office in the present, about

a minute and a half had passed. She was clearly in a kind of trance state, but at the same time, she was fully connected to my coaching and to me. For most clients, the process of switching between talking directly with me and working with the inner world took no more than a few seconds. For Georgia, however, it was a deeper experience. As we ended the session, Georgia exclaimed, "I just realized what is in the background as I come back from deep work—it's the dark shapes from the Disney movie, *Alice in Wonderland*, and the feeling I get with Alice wandering around in the forest."

At the beginning of session 18, Georgia followed up on her discovery at the end of the previous session. "Now I know the place I go to [to work with parts] is Alice's *Wonderland*, but I usually just think of it as *my lake*. The colors are vivid, and the scene is beautiful."

Georgia also reported a small setback to her progress in controlling her free overtime. She had stayed late on two evenings, about three hours on each occasion. Such late hours had previously caused her to give up her career as an attorney. She had a legitimate reason for staying late—getting the last of a backlog out of the way—but in her new way of thinking the reason wasn't good enough. We would later do more work to address the issue. For now, though, we would continue to get to know the latest member of her internal cast of characters, Fluffy the Easter Bunny.

Fluffy's next reported memories were of living in a small Southern town from the fourth to the sixth grade in school. One particular incident had to do with the mother's tiredness from driving the four children long distances to reach each of the appointments for their medical and dental needs. Frustrated after one day of taking care of their needs, and frustrated as well with their incessant quarreling with each other, the mother required them each to take positions facing the wall in her bedroom where they couldn't see each other. They were to keep quiet while she took a nap. This punishment disturbed Fluffy to a level eight on the SUD scale.

In the next memory, Georgia, then in the eighth grade and in another new city, was permitted to fly back to visit friends in a third city where the family had lived for several years. She attended a junior high school dance there among her old group of friends. Near the end of the evening, a boy for whom Georgia had carried a torch for some time asked her to dance a slow dance. At the end of the song, there was a sudden ending to the slow music and an abrupt beginning to a fast rock and roll song. The abrupt loss of her partner's embrace was unsettling to Georgia who had been enjoying herself immensely. Fluffy rated this disturbance at a seven on the SUD scale.

There were two other memories Georgia described before the end of the session; both involved the feeling of being distanced from relatives or friends through their disapproval of her words or actions. In both incidents, Georgia was surprised to learn she was not as close to them as she thought she was. In one, a family friend who had long been a part of Georgia's life refused to give her the birthday gift of birthstone earrings she brought on behalf of Georgia's mother; instead, she told her that it was up to her mother to do that. In the other memory, Georgia was embarrassed and felt out of place when, as the family representative to a relative's wedding, she asked when would be the champagne toast. Her grandmother and uncles, it turned out, were teetotalers and shocked at Georgia's question. Both memories were level five disturbances for Fluffy. In the following session, I wanted to check with Georgia as to whether she had a sense of what theme might connect Fluffy's memories.

In session 19, I asked Georgia to ask Fluffy, the Scaredy Cat, how old she was. In this, I was indirectly trying to discover what theme, or themes, might connect her memories. The symbol of an Easter Bunny, as well as her earliest reported memories, suggested a child subpersonality, but her memory set now included incidents from Georgia's teenage years and possibly later. By their nature, subpersonalities specialize in certain kinds of memories, and I was somewhat puzzled by the range of memories we had so far collected.

Georgia reported that Fluffy was confused by the question about her age. With coaxing, she was able to say that she was not an old person, and she didn't feel like an adult. She decided that she was a child, not a teenager. She didn't like teenagers. "They're difficult," she said. "You never know what they are thinking, and they change their minds a lot." They are "unpredictable," and "They can be very mean."

I asked Georgia to reflect on the set of memories we had collected to this point, and to consider what might be the theme that connected them. After a few moments of contemplation, she said that the theme seemed to be "separation." There was separation from her siblings so that her mother could take a nap and separation from her dance partner after a slow dance. There was also a separation from her mother's friend because she seemed to be not as close as Georgia thought they were, and there was a definite sense of being separate and different from her relatives at the wedding.

Returning to collect more of Fluffy's memory set, Georgia recalled that shortly after her family had moved back to an eastern city from the south, she and her siblings went to a pool party at the club to which they formerly belonged. During much of the evening, a particular topic of conversation among Georgia and her friends was how much they had all changed during Georgia's three-year absence. While these recollections were not disturbing to Georgia, they were significant, with an energy level of about three on the non-negative SUE scale. The changes she and her friends noticed could also be seen as a kind of separation or distancing between them.

Three more memories filled out Fluffy's memory set. The first had to do with going away to college. Her father drove Georgia there and spent a couple of days helping her settle in. Parting from her mother was disturbing to a level seven, especially because her mother gave her a hurried goodbye following a couple of days during which she seemed to be angry with her. Georgia had the sense that her mother might miss her less than the other members of her family would. The second memory was that of saying goodbye to her father after he dropped her off for college. Her father was somewhat emotional as he left, unusual for him, and Fluffy rated this parting as a level eight on the SUD scale. The third memory remained the most disturbing for Georgia. Fluffy rated it at the maximum of 10 on the SUD scale and Georgia said that even now, nearly 20 years later, she still felt some pain. The event was the breakup with her long-term boyfriend. She had met him during her freshman year of college and dated him for five years. They graduated college and entered graduate school together. However, Georgia didn't like the graduate school program and moved back near her parents to begin her professional career (becoming an attorney came later). As she continued a long-distance relationship with her boyfriend, she became more and more disenchanted with his apparent lack of long-term career goals. Eventually, on a weekend trip to visit him, she ended the relationship in spite of her love for him because of her discomfort with his lack of plans for the future.

In session 20, we worked on Georgia's internal world only during the last 15 minutes. We first processed some current events. The previous week had been a difficult one. Georgia was limping due to an infection in her foot; she had broken up with her current boyfriend; and she had decided to leave her job. Although we did not discuss it, the last two issues seemed related to the theme of separation on which we had worked during the previous two sessions. Both decisions seemed appropriate. Her boyfriend had said once again that he wanted a vacation from their relationship (the third time), and Georgia decided that enough was enough. She had patiently waited for him to work through whatever he needed to work through before returning to her on previous occasions. Now, however, it seemed unfair and insulting to ask her once more to wait for him to decide whether he wanted to be with her. Consequently, she told him that rather than a vacation she wanted a permanent break from him.

In the decision regarding work, Georgia had waited for her temporary assignment to turn into a permanent one. She had worked for her employers for 14 weeks and felt it was enough time for them to decide whether they liked her work well enough to make her a permanent employee with benefits. She was now doing almost 100 percent paralegal work and billing a reasonable number of hours. To make it worse, her employers had just hired two permanent workers, one a paralegal like herself but in a different specialty area, and the other another secretary. Evidently, she decided, they intended to keep her low pay status indefinitely. She would go back to her hiring agency and ask for another assignment, one where she had a better chance of becoming a permanent employee. It was probably not a coincidence that the issue of boundaries, including work boundaries, on which we had been working in therapy, coincided with Georgia's taking steps to ensure that both her personal and professional boundaries were appropriate. Georgia also decided that she might be getting close to deciding to work again as an attorney, especially since she seemed to have under control her propensity for overtime work. She was working just an extra hour per day, half of which was the half hour she needed at the end of each day to prepare her desk for the following workday.

During the last quarter of the hour, we began the formal unburdening of Fluffy, the stuffed Easter Bunny, who was eager to proceed. During the symbolic unburdening with wind, in a scene we often used, Fluffy playfully changed the imagery. A typical wind unburdening involves Georgia imagining her part standing in an open field between two posts that are connected by a bar that the part grasps as the wind rushes between the posts. Fluffy chose to hang from the bar upside down with her knees hung over the bar as the wind carried away her negative energy. The memory was that of being isolated from her siblings, facing the wall, as her mother took a nap. Fluffy enjoyed the process, Georgia said, and was eager to do more.

Session 21 would be our last for about five weeks because of certain matters unrelated to therapy. Consequently, I wanted to do the work of unburdening Fluffy without introducing any new material. That was not to be, however. Of all my clients, Georgia required the greatest amount of time to connect to her world of internal images; she was also the client who most clearly went into a voluntary trance as she did so. When she tried to reconnect with Fluffy there was a long period of silence, about three minutes, before she responded to my prompt to say, "Fluffy hasn't come out, but there's something else here. Looks like the sculpture, *The Thinker*, but he's in a boat rowing toward me with his back to me. But he's not making any progress; he's not getting any closer to me." When prompted to ask this part the usual initial interview questions, Georgia reported that he did not respond and that she thought he was somehow unable to respond. I suggested that Georgia find her internal helper part, White Dragon, to see whether she might have any ideas about this phenomenon. White Dragon said there was "a darkness in him," and wanted Georgia to walk away with her. White Dragon also said, "There's a poison inside him, some kind of disease eating away at him, from the inside." Georgia went on to say that she thought there was someone stopping him from responding, and that White Dragon thought that someone was controlling him "like a puppet." We seemed stalled in getting useful information quickly, so I suggested that we put aside this interesting development until we had more time to deal with it. Instead, we should return to work with Fluffy as planned.

After thanking both The Thinker and White Dragon for their appearances and their help, Georgia led White Dragon back to the topic of working with Fluffy. With eyes closed as usual during parts work, Georgia next reported, "White Dragon and I went back to the edge of the lake. We are standing in the water waiting to see if Fluffy will come out." Then, "Fluffy has come out now. She's been in her basket. Things weren't calm enough for her to come out before." With Fluffy present and willing to proceed with the unburdening, we began to unburden the incident involving separation from Georgia's dance partner, discussed previously. "We're on the shore of the lake and the wind is picking up and blowing all through her fur, and the wind is swirling and swirling. It almost feels like it's going to lift us up." Georgia continued: "The wind carries away the burden as a darker color in the wind. It almost looks like smoke, going higher and higher, and then it dies down and stops." The level of disturbance had been reduced to zero.

We next turned to unburdening the incidents involving champagne at the wedding and the birthstone birthday gift, once again using the metaphor of blowing wind. "It starts to grow all around us. It's even harder this time. It's almost pounding there's so much wind. It's blowing all around Fluffy, in a spiral, and it's getting darker as it goes up, taking away the pain. Fluffy doesn't want it to go away entirely because it makes her a cool hat. I tell her we can make her a hat like that but out of different stuff. It moves on and the darkness disappears way up high. It's calming down. And Fluffy has a new hat—it's black and made out of straw. It's like one I bought two weeks ago. She likes that. Now we have matching hats." The level of disturbance for these two painful incidents had reached zero. Regarding how Fluffy got her hat, Georgia reported that, "She says she just imagined it and it was there."

This work left us at the end of the session, with plans to meet again in five weeks. At this point we were left with two mysteries yet unsolved. The first was that of the monster behind the door. The second was that of The Thinker who appeared in this session. The Thinker might or might not be another part, or it could be just a metaphorical vehicle of another part. At times like this, therapy acquires an additional energy: the drive to solve the mysteries and puzzles uncovered in doing the primary work. However, in Georgia's case, we would be taking a five-week break and she had already made significant progress. It was possible that Georgia would decide she had achieved good-enough functioning and that she didn't really need to solve the mysteries. She was the boss and the therapist needed to adjust to her decisions, with curiosity sometimes unsated.

Postscript

We did not return to the mystery of The Thinker, although we did explore the problem of the monster behind the door. It turned out that the story of The Monster and his relationship to Fluffy the Easter Bunny involved a crucial incident in Georgia's life history, one with a tremendous impact on Georgia's life course. That story appears as the final narrative chapter in this book.

Georgia maintained her gains in decreasing her voluntary overtime work during the five weeks of our break. During this time, she also accepted the firm's offer of a permanent position as a paralegal. At our first meeting after the break, she said that she was leaving work daily by 6:30 and had a goal of leaving at 6:00. Then, just two weeks later, and without further attention to the problem in session, she managed a further reduction in her voluntary overtime work; she was leaving work by 5:20 every day. Possibly, this additional change related to Georgia's reading of a draft of this chapter between sessions. It may be that reading her own story of therapy helped her to solidify her gains and give her a stronger sense of ownership of them. After a few months more, Georgia was leaving work at 5:00 sharp, the same time as other employees. She proudly reported that, on a few afternoons, she had clocked out from work at 4:58 or 4:59. She found that she could no longer relate to the internal pressures that previously kept her at work long after other employees had gone home.

Chapter 5
Low Sexual Desire

This case is unusual because resolution of the problem was achieved almost entirely through negotiation among parts to bring about internal reorganization rather than through extensive unburdening of painful memories. In many systems, parts agree to reorganize and adjust the way they work on behalf of the self once they understand their contribution to the problem. However, such agreements are seldom sufficient to bring about the desired change. In spite of their good intentions, parts are often unable to keep their agreements when something triggers the painful memories of their origins. In such cases, they revert to the defensive positions that created the therapeutic problems. Before such parts have the ability to change the way they function, some unburdening of the emotional load they carry must generally be achieved. However, in this case only a single unburdening of excessive emotional energy was necessary. The client accomplished the remainder of the work through direct negotiation with the parts of her who were blocking what she wanted to achieve.

Katie was a 26-year-old medical technician whose work supported the family during her husband's last year of college as he prepared for entry into medical school. With the average score on the Dissociative Experiences Scale at 10, her score of 3.0 is low; consequently, the internal parts with which we would work are not likely to have been the result of pathological dissociation.

Marital Issues

Katie and her husband, Aaron, came to therapy to work out certain marital issues, chief among them being their sexual relationship. Other issues included Katie's discomfort with her mother-in-law's visits and Aaron's resentment that Katie's mother didn't give them greater financial support—they had previously lived rent-free in a house belonging to the mother for six months at the beginning of their marriage. Katie and Aaron had been together almost four years and married for three. For most of their married life, Katie showed little interest in sexuality. Aaron complained that they engaged in sexual activities only about three times a month, while he preferred "eight or nine times a week." Katie didn't dispute Aaron's numbers but suggested that his expectations were too high. Once or twice a week should be sufficient, she believed.

Aaron said that their marriage had been awkward since he learned how unhappy Katie was. His relationship with her felt more like that of a roommate than that of a wife or lover. Feeling neglected and unappreciated, Aaron suggested that Katie was more affectionate with the dog than with him. He admitted that he felt "standoffish" because of Katie's dissatisfaction, but except for sex his expectations for personal happiness were low. He didn't really know, he said, what happiness felt like.

A part of their stalemate had to do with their differing life goals. Aaron held steadfast to his goal of becoming a medical doctor. He saw the future of his family as living a sophisticated urban life, socially and materially rewarding, centered on his career. Katie, however, had a different dream. She wanted children as soon as possible, and a lifestyle centered around horses. She had grown up in a rodeo family. She and her siblings all had horses of their own. Her family followed the rodeo circuit and some of them competed in rodeo events. At a minimum, she hoped that her family with Aaron would include horses for their children and frequent interactions with the rodeo life. Aaron didn't object to Katie's involvement with horses but said that she would have to do it on her own. He didn't like to get dirty and didn't want to spend time caring for horses.

After four sessions with Katie and Aaron as a couple, they agreed that they could not see their current relationship continuing into the future as it was. They had mostly incompatible life goals and their personal relationship was strained by the lack of physical intimacy between them. Katie viewed having sexual relations with Aaron as part of her humdrum duties as a wife, just a part of the larger set of chores she had to deal with. Understandably, perhaps, Aaron was disappointed with *duty sex*. He wanted Katie to desire him as he did her.

Aaron was unwilling to give much energy to improving their relationship since, for him, the bedrock problem was Katie's lack of sexual desire and her refusal to have sex with him more frequently. Katie, however, proved willing to invest a greater effort in the relationship. Not only was she unwilling to give up too quickly on making her marriage work, she also reasoned that her low sexual desire might negatively impact any future marriage she might have if she divorced Aaron. She chose to work on the problem of sexual desire in individual therapy.

Individual Therapy

In our first individual session, Katie spoke about her lack of sexual passion for Aaron, and, because of that, her doubts about whether she loved him. Since their marriage, Katie had developed the pattern of having sexual relations with Aaron just "to get him off my back." Sexual intercourse was limited to *the missionary position*, and oral sex involved only her giving, and never receiving, although she said Aaron also liked to give. She was starved for intimacy since Aaron was not affectionate with her even at home. For him, hugging and cuddling were associated with *unmanliness*. Although Aaron could clearly benefit from additional therapy, that was not an option. Whatever work would be done to improve the marriage would have to done, initially at least, by Katie. Both partners appeared to have ideas about sexuality and intimacy that worked against developing a fulfilling sexual relationship.

Before her marriage to Aaron, Katie thought sex would be *a sacred bonding moment*. She thought she experienced that a couple of times before their wedding, but never after that. She met Aaron at the beginning of her freshman year of college and began having sex with him in the following January. They married in June of that same year. Between January and June, as the wedding approached, Katie noticed her feelings changing. She had begun to doubt her love for Aaron as her lust diminished. In April and the first part of May, she had ceased sexual relations with him so that she could be "a good little girl and not have sex before marriage, and be ready for it in the Church's eyes." Nevertheless, she gave in to Aaron's insistence by the end of May and began having the passionless sex that would mark most of the years of their marriage.

In Katie's family of origin, her father was physically and emotionally abusive but it was through him that horses and rodeo participation became the family's passion. Ultimately, her departure from this lifestyle was a reaction to her father. Her parents divorced when she was fifteen and she chose to live with her father so that she could continue to participate in rodeos. Living with him proved too much for her, however, and she returned to live with her mother to get away from his continuing emotional abuse. Within the year, her father had sold her horse, "illegally," she said. At 17, to spite her father, she married man 10 years older than him and moved to another state. She quickly learned that her hasty action was a mistake. The man was as abusive as her father had been and demanded that she be entirely domestic and subordinate to him. Katie would take care of all traditional female tasks, provide sex when her husband demanded it, and otherwise wait at home until he returned from work. It was during this brief marriage that she learned to provide dutiful sex, passionless and submissive. She left her husband within a year and returned to her home state.

Prior to her first marriage, and following her parents' divorce, Katie had had brief relationships with several boyfriends. Sex with them was generally unpleasant or unsatisfying. She engaged in sexual relations simply because that was what her boyfriends wanted to do. The pattern of brief, submissive connections with boyfriends together with unsatisfying sexual experiences continued after her divorce. By the age of 19, she had sworn off sex altogether. She was 20 when she met Aaron in her freshman year of college.

Although Katie had resumed sexual relations with Aaron before their official wedding date, the way she experienced sex changed permanently on their wedding night and during their honeymoon. Sex during the honeymoon, said Katie, was "atrocious." She now gained no satisfaction whatsoever. Sex with Aaron was grudgingly given with a *get-it-over-with* attitude. The next three years were a blur for Katie. What she remembered was her obsession with becoming pregnant, in spite of her agreement with Aaron to wait until better economic times before having children. By the time the couple came to see me they were both resentful of the other and not willing to accommodate to the other's wishes. Katie was resentful of Aaron for not making her a mother, resentful for her choice to quit college while he focused on his medical school preparations, and resentful of his failure to show the sort of affection and caring she needed.

Katiebug and Other Parts

In our second individual session, we searched for those of Katie's sub-personalities with some interest in sexuality. We began with her memory of feeling sexually attracted to Aaron at the beginning of their relationship. It was a time when, in addition to starting college, she worked as a horse trainer, an activity that brought her great pleasure. In addition, she liked it that Aaron's family was heavily involved in the practice of religion. Thinking back, she remembered feeling joyful and excited. When asked to focus on her remembered excitement and joy, she quickly visualized a younger version of herself. This part, or subpersonality, was 18 years old, was "skinnier" than she is now, and wore a cowboy hat, jeans, and boots. Her jeans were muddy. This part was coconscious with Katie in that she was fully aware of Katie's current life. Her name was *Katiebug*. She had had sex with Aaron early in their relationship, but "not for a long time now." She had also had sex with Katie's second boyfriend, but with no one else. It is quite common for parts to have knowledge of a person's life experiences but to claim participation in only some of them. Katiebug was aware of Katie's entire stream of experiences since the age of six, but participated only in those that had to do with joyful sex, the rodeo life, and other activities that had to do with dogs and horses. Katiebug's earliest memory dated to being six years old and going on a family horseback ride, with all family members on their own horses and the family dog running alongside.

Katie said that Katiebug had all the memories of the dogs and horses that she had, but the Parts Psychology approach hypothesizes that memory works the other way around; Katiebug would hold the memories and Katie would have access to them when Katiebug was present. In answer to our questions, Katiebug indicated that she knew that she was a part and she knew of other internal parts as well. She named three others: *Ham, The Church One,* and *The City One.* She agreed to bring The Church One onto Katie's mental screen. Katiebug admitted that she and The Church One had been blocking Katie from sex with Aaron because, said Katiebug, she had to protect herself from Aaron's "promising things he won't live up to," such as letting her come out and play at rodeos and horseback riding.

Katie described The Church One as "thirtyish in age," wearing a simple dress, "not as skinny as" Katiebug, and having "shorter, straight hair." She was a *Plain Jane* in appearance. Her name was *Katie Ann*. Her earliest memory was of getting in trouble in Sunday School at age eight. Katie Ann acknowledged having had sex with husband, Aaron. She said she has sex with him when she feels close to him, but that it had been about a year now since that happened. She did not have sex with Aaron before marriage. "That's not what I do," Katie reported Katie Ann as saying. Katie also said that Katie Ann's greatest desire was "to be a mom." She had been present on Katie's wedding night and honeymoon, but in a negative way. Additionally, "She was punishing me," said Katie, by not permitting her to enjoy sex during the three months between the civil ceremony and the Temple wedding. After the church ceremony, Katie Ann participated in enjoyable sex with Aaron "for a couple of months." In response to our question, Katie Ann acknowledged that she knew the part who dutifully had sex with Aaron without joy, and she agreed to bring her into Katie's internal vision.

The *duty sex* part appeared to Katie as "frumpy," wearing a baggy sweatshirt and jeans. Her name was *Wife*. She was overweight, wore no makeup, and had a "typical housewife look." Her earliest memory was that of making the bed at the apartment she shared with her first husband when she was 17.

We were at the end of a session that had been quite productive in identifying some of the key subpersonalities in the problem of Katie's low sex drive. Her system of parts was well developed, with considerable awareness among parts of other parts and a fair amount of communication between them. Because it was such a well-developed system, we were able to bridge between parts to other parts by simply asking to speak to someone else. This contrasts to a sometimes-painstaking approach in which parts are identified one at a time through their association with emotions and body sensations. For the period between our sessions, which would be two weeks, I asked Katie to get to know her parts and to begin negotiating with them for a greater interest in having sex with Aaron.

At our next session, Katie talked about how she tried to reach agreements with Katiebug and Katie Ann about having enjoyable sex with her husband. Katiebug provided the strongest objections, primarily because of

Aaron's attitude toward things involving horses. The couple had gone to a rodeo over the Thanksgiving weekend, and Aaron had flatly refused to make this lifestyle a part of their future. He agreed to participate in a minimal way through not objecting when Katie attended the occasional rodeo, and he agreed to allow Katie and their future children to have horses when their income permitted it. Katie Ann, The Church One, was more flexible. She agreed to permit pleasurable sex for Katie in the interest of "saving the marriage." In the remainder of the session, we explored Katie's internal system of parts with a view toward discovering other possible roadblocks in the way of Katie's movement toward more pleasurable and more frequent sex. There were several parts who wanted to express their feelings, or who had something to say on the topic of sexuality. Ham, a part previously mentioned by Katiebug, turned out to be the internal system's primary manager. She presented herself as age 28, "shapely" in physical appearance, her hair in a bun, and wearing a business suit. Katie described her as "businesslike." She was sad. It was difficult for her to deal with all the pressures of her job at the office while also managing the emotional overload from other parts regarding their relationships with Aaron. Ham said that she had personally never participated in sexual activities, and she was not sure if she ever wanted to. One of her earliest memories was that of being 17 and wanting to look like the professional she was now. Another early memory was that of dating her first husband. "I was working," she said, "and he came up and told me he loved me. I felt a sinking feeling in the pit of my stomach." Ham didn't feel the same way toward him, but "I had to muster up the courage to say it back. I just felt that if someone tells you 'I love you,' you have to say it back."

Among the parts present for this internal gathering was Wife, "who just sat there," said Katie, "like a bump on a log." She added, "That's how other parts see her, too." Another part's appearance was unclear. Her image was "fuzzy." Her name was Just Katie. "She said she was not a manager and that she has had good sex with Aaron in the past but was holding back now, because if she gets hurt so does everybody else." Her goal with Aaron was "to live a long and prosperous life." Currently, Just Katie was sad because Aaron admitted that, while on a retreat for his part-time job, he went to a co-worker's room and "hugged her, but didn't kiss her." She was also sad about his broken promises about having horses in their lives and his back-tracking on being a part of the rodeo lifestyle.

Another part was *Heidi*. Katie described her as age 15, with long, straight brown hair, tanned skin, and wearing glasses. "She doesn't look like me," Katie said. She was "disappointed and angry" with Aaron. Her earliest memory was that of going on a horseback ride with her older sister at age eight. The sister "was always mean. She threw rocks at me and my horse and left us there. We thought we were lost. It wasn't fair. And then mom and dad were mad at me for getting home late." Another early memory was that of her father making her "gas" newborn puppies. "I had to hold the bag of puppies over the [automobile] muffler." Heidi's primary function within the system seemed to be to maintain a sense of fairness about the way things should be. When they were not that way, she became angry.

We had met a range of parts at this impromptu internal gathering, some of them apparently relevant to the problem of low sexual desire and some less so. At the end of the session, I asked Katie if she had a *wild and crazy* sexual part. Katie said that she did when she was drunk. She added that she would talk to her parts about letting out this part while she was sober.

At our next meeting, Katie was feeling depressed and hopeless. Aaron was not responding to her efforts to change. She had been able to bring out the wild and crazy sex part on the weekend, but Aaron seemed not to notice. He did not respond by joining the mood Katie tried to develop. "I expected he would be more affectionate, but he wasn't." She had also tried to engage Aaron in a discussion regarding how each of them could contribute to reha-bilitating their marriage, but he was not receptive. At the end of the session, I explained that if her situation became truly hopeless and her only option was divorce, then she could make that decision easier to live with through unburdening herself of the love some of her parts felt for him. Unburdening love is accomplished in much the same way that anger, sadness, or other painful emotions are unburdened. Love is carried by specific subpersonali-ties and these subpersonalities can choose to let it go. Chapter 7 describes such a case.

Between sessions, Katie had again coaxed out the "wild and crazy sex" part of herself, on both Friday and Saturday nights. Her experience of sex was pleasurable, but Aaron again seemed not to notice anything different in their lovemaking. Once more Katie tried to engage Aaron in conversation, both about their future and about ordinary things. Aaron appeared to her to be a reluctant participant in their conversations.

In the remainder of the session our focus was on changing Katie's difficulty in receiving oral sex, something that she knew Aaron enjoyed providing but which she could rarely accommodate. Katie's earliest memory relating to this topic was that of actually receiving oral sex in a pickup truck when she was a junior in high school. Both Katiebug, the rodeo girl, and Katie Ann, The Church Part, were present, although Katie Ann didn't remember it very well. The experience was "incredibly uncomfortable," disturbing to a level nine on the SUD scale. Because Katie wanted to be able to be open to a variety of sexual experiences with her husband, she convinced Katiebug and Katie Ann to unburden their memories of that first experience with receiving oral sex. This experience appeared to be blocking her openness to lovemaking with Aaron because whenever she thought about receiving oral sex she re-experienced the negative emotions she felt in the pickup truck.

The subpersonalities agreed to unburden themselves of the negative emotions attached to the pickup truck incident through the symbolic action of dissolving them in water. Katie visualized Katiebug and Katie Ann standing in a waterfall as the water flowed over, around, and through them. She asked them to notice where within them they carried the negative emotions and to allow the water to touch and dissolve those emotions and then to allow the discolored water now at their feet to be carried away in the small stream. As the intervention continued, Katie narrated the memories that came to mind. She had finished work that evening at the video rental store and then, with another young coworker, met up with other teenagers for drinking "in the hills." She had become very drunk. An older boy had given her a ride home and parked some distance from her house. The boy, whom she said she didn't like, began kissing her. She said she was too drunk to resist. Her next memory was that of him being "down there," as she was squashed painfully against the door with her face against the window. She noticed that it had begun to snow, and she remembered thinking "how stupid this was," with "no feelings at all." Finally, she remembered walking up the hill to her house, stumbling and tearing her pants, and climbing through her bedroom window. After this narration, Katie's SUD level was down to a two. What remained was her disgust with herself for having this sexual experience with someone for whom she had no feelings, and her embarrassment about an incident that "made me look like a whore." Katie unburdened the remainder of the disgust and embarrassment by visualizing Katiebug and Katie Ann dumping these negative emotions into a bonfire. At the conclusion of the intervention, the SUD value was zero for the oral sex incident.

In our next session, Katie talked of Aaron's continued distancing from her. In spite of her efforts to engage in sex with him more frequently, Aaron largely remained emotionally unresponsive. Christmas would be just three days away, and Aaron had suggested that Katie purchase herself a Christmas card and think of it as a gift from him. Katie did not sense that Aaron was making a weak joke; rather, he seemed to be serious with his suggestion. The couple had had sex twice during the previous week, but on one of those occasions it was Heidi, the angry part, who was in charge of the sexuality. Katie said that she probably wasn't very nice when Heidi was present.

A Solution

Katie remained determined to find a way to engage regularly in enjoyable sex with Aaron. To this end, she convened an internal conference involving six internal parts and negotiated agreements among them for specific behaviors that would improve her sex life with her husband, at least for the near term. Katiebug, at her bubbly best, would handle the sexual interaction with Aaron and provide the verbal stimulation that excited him. Katie Ann, the church part, agreed not to listen to the sexual by-play between the couple so as to minimize the embarrassment that Katie usually felt with sex talk. Katie Ann showed herself in a visualization with her hands over her ears. Heidi, the angry one, agreed to absent herself from the love - making activities altogether. Just Katie, the sad and jealous part, agreed not to speak about her hurt, while Wife also agreed not to speak—she showed Katie an image of herself with her hands over her mouth. Ham, the manager, showed herself with her hands over her eyes. Thus, the entire set of sexual parts agreed upon a plan to help Katie engage her husband in sex in a comfortable and enjoyable way. Parts are not people, although they usually present themselves in that way. There were no actual persons putting their hands over their ears, mouths, or eyes. Rather, different aspects of the whole of Katie were showing in symbolic ways how they would cooperate in achieving a common goal; helping Katie have good sex and doing their parts to rescue her marriage.

Our meeting a week later, between Christmas and New Year's, was our last. Katie said that her internal parts continued to cooperate with her so that she could be comfortable in her sexual experiences. "Sex was good," said Katie. It was more enjoyable and she was not dreading it. She could call upon both Katiebug and the "wild and crazy sex" part as needed. She and Aaron were having sex more frequently; Katie was being sexual "without making an effort." Aaron was being attentive to her now and even occasionally affectionate at times when sex was not imminent.

Katie decided that she had accomplished her goals regarding her sexuality and so she graduated herself from therapy. I saw Katie a total of ten sessions, four of them with her husband and six in individual therapy. I wondered if we had done enough work, and was concerned that there might be other parts not yet known who were also affecting Katie's sex life. Further, I had my doubts about how long the agreement among parts would last. Katie, however, was enthusiastic and confident. "Besides," she said, she could "always come back to therapy if things don't go well." She added that now that she knew how to talk to her parts she was confident she could work with them to solve any further sexual problems that surfaced. About one year later, Katie called to refer a friend for therapy for a similar problem of low sexual desire. She said that her sex life with Aaron continued to be "great!"

Chapter 6
Sexual Swinging and Jealousy

Chapter 2 describes work with jealousy and anger. In this chapter, jealousy is again the focus of therapy, but it is less linked with anger than with a problem of sexuality. What makes it a problem is that the client's particular fixation threatens the marriage and the integrity of the family. It is theoretically possible that another marriage and another family could safely accommodate the client's desired sexual variations. However, that is not the case here.

Carson was a 38-year-old corporate vice president who came to therapy as one of the conditions set by his wife for staving off divorce. He was sleeping on the couch, but back in the family home after three months of separation. Carson had admitted a number of indiscretions to his wife, Nicole, such as frequenting strip clubs without her knowledge and, with one stripper, developing a cell phone texting relationship. These behaviors were the immediate cause of Carson's forced separation from his wife. Nicole now wanted him to address his larger issues in therapy, but did not specify exactly what she wanted him to change. Carson, however, thought her concerns were clear. He should stop checking on her activities; he should stop trying to track her movements away from the home; and he should stop his daily phone calls to her at work, sometimes as many as 12 to 15 a day. Another issue was his powerful desire to involve Nicole and himself in sexual *swinging*. He enjoyed both *wife swapping* with other couples and *threesomes* that included just himself, Nicole, and another man. The threesomes were most powerful for him, although he avoided touching the other man involved. He just wanted to witness Nicole and the other man having sex, or he wanted to have sex with Nicole while the other man watched or touched Nicole. She had indulged him on a few occasions but was now unwilling to continue these activities. Carson's score on the Dissociative Experiences Scale was a low average 4.6 in comparison to the norm of 10.0. Consequently, his world of internal subpersonalities is not likely the result of abnormal dissociation.

Carson agreed to make the changes necessary to correct the problems that stemmed from his jealousy and his sexual interests, but he needed help in doing so. The jealousy that drove him to obsess over Nicole's whereabouts, and his intense need to know if she were seeing someone else, reached a peak during his three months away from home. His sexual interests had no obvious relation to his jealousy, and, in fact, since he encouraged Nicole to have sex with other men in his presence, he might seem an unlikely man to experience extreme jealousy. However, jealousy is not so much about sexuality as it is about fear of loss. With Nicole now refusing any further swinging activities, Carson felt a greater threat of losing her. For Carson, Nicole's rejection of his sexual predilections meant that she was rejecting him. The sexual fantasies that he wanted Nicole to help him experience seemed to derive from an early introduction to childhood sexual activities, especially those of receiving oral sex from an older boy at age seven and multiple sexual adventures with boys and girls in his neighborhood between the ages of seven and 12. This would be the area of focus as we worked on these issues in therapy.

Jealousy

In our second session, we worked directly on the jealousy issue. Carson said that feelings of jealousy were new to him, but they overwhelmed him during the three months when Nicole wouldn't let him stay at home. He found that he no longer trusted her, especially after she and a friend began to visit nightclubs on weekends. He also discovered in her possession a business card from a man unknown to him. This was a particularly provocative discovery.

I had introduced the idea that we all have internal parts in the initial session, and Carson agreed to begin looking for the jealous part of himself in this session. We focused upon an incident that happened during the time of separation. He had searched the city for Nicole until he found her car in a casino parking lot. Desperately, but to no avail, he looked for her in all areas of the casino and the attached shopping mall. During our session, Carson focused upon his remembered feelings of desperation and, following my suggestion, he subvocally asked his sense of desperation to provide a picture of itself. What appeared in his mind was the image of a white room with a black ball, about the size of a softball, lying in the corner of the room. When he addressed the black ball, it very quickly transformed itself into an image of Carson at the age of 19 or 20. His shirt was off and he wore "shredded jeans." Carson thought this younger image of himself appeared to be "almost half-crazed, actually sex-crazed," as he stared back at the current Carson.

The internal image responded quickly to questions. He did not know who Carson was and didn't care. Carson noted that the part "had an attitude." The part reported that its own name was Carson and he was 18 years old, not 19 or 20. Such differences between an observing self's estimate of a part's age and a part's own felt sense of age is not uncommon. The younger Carson gave an estimate of the observer Carson's age as 32, rather than his actual 38. Because *Carson 18* seemed not to understand his relationship to the current Carson, I coached my client to provide a short summary of the nature of parts to the young subpersonality. Carson communicated that he was the self and Carson 18 was a part, one of many parts who make up the whole adult Carson. Such explanations are sometimes necessary to get subpersonalities quickly up to speed so that the therapy can proceed. Carson 18 readily accepted the explanation, although his attitude still contained a bit of *So what!* in the mix. Once the part understood his relation to Carson, we began to collect the set of memories that constituted the primary content of the Carson 18 subpersonality.

His earliest reported memory was a pleasant one of bouncing on his grandfather's feet at age three. The next was of being next door and playing *show and tell* with a neighbor girl at age five. Another memory, at age six, was of "just playing with friends." At this point, Carson pointed out that Carson 18's appearance was "not as crazed" as it had been earlier. We skipped ahead then to find out how much Carson 18 knew about Carson's personal history. He remembered parts of high school but not the graduation. He also remembered parts of college but, again, not the graduation. He knew Nicole, Carson's wife, and remembered meeting her when Carson was 22. Carson 18 also knew the couple's children, but did not consider them his own. He would like it if they were his own, but he currently "loved them more like an uncle." It is common for parts to have a different relationship to a person's children than does the observing self. Carson 18 remembered

Nicole kicking him out of the house for three months and wondered how Carson "could be so stupid" as to let that happen. It is also common for a part, as with Carson 18 here, to be only somewhat aware of current events at the beginning of a conversation and to gain a connection and revived memory of the person's current life as the conversation continues.

At the beginning of our third session, Carson reported continued arguments with Nicole. He said that she had visited relatives out of town on the weekend and was late getting home. When he demanded that she account for all of the activities that resulted in her coming home late, Nicole became angry and the two of them engaged in a "screaming match." With a sense of humor, however, Carson commented that the gifts she brought back from her trip were nice.

Based upon the memories we had collected from Carson 18, we returned to the problem of jealousy with the hypothesis that Carson 18 was not the part who influenced Carson to demand detailed explanations of Nicole's activities. However, Carson 18 seemed to be unaware of any other internal parts. We used an affect bridge to continue our search for other jealous parts. This technique allowed Carson to associate (bridge) to other related memories by focusing upon his feelings of jealousy in the present. He immediately recalled placing a voice-activated tape recorder in Nicole's car before she went out for an evening of entertainment with a visiting relative. When he later checked the tape and listened to the conversations, he thought he heard evidence substantiating his fear that Nicole was seeing another man. We then used the anger produced by this memory to connect to another internal part. Carson simply focused on the anger he was feeling and asked it to provide a picture of itself.

The internal image that appeared was that of a large black ball with which Carson was able to establish communication. We did not investigate the symbolic meaning of the image nor the possibility of connection with the black ball visualized prior to the appearance of Carson 18. These are interesting questions, but they are not as important to the work of Parts Psychology as the development of communication with internal parts and the collection of memories. Carson found that the black ball knew him and understood that it was a part of him—a better orientation than that initially shown by Carson 18, of whom it claimed an awareness. The new part indicated that it was male, about 22 years old, and knew Nicole. It chose the name *Checker* for itself. Checker acknowledged that it was he who timed how long it took Nicole to arrive home following the scheduled touchdown of her plane at the airport. When she did not arrive as quickly as he expected, he became anxious, and later, angry.

Checker's first memory dated to preschool age when Carson walked with his family after church following the death of a church leader. The experience was confusing to him because he did not understand why people were crying. Although the memory was not disturbing to Checker now, it seemed to be significant because of its connection to an early loss, a frequent source of adult jealousy. Checker's next memory was that of a spanking at age six or seven, an event that rated a three or four on the 0-10 SUD (Subjective Units of Disturbance) scale. A more significant memory dated to the age of seven or eight. Their mother had dropped off Carson and his brother for his brother's football practice. His father picked up his brother after practice but left Carson there. Apparently, the father did not know that Carson was also at the practice field. No one in his family missed Carson until dark. Checker rated this experience as a seven on the SUD scale. Another memory related to neighborhood boys who would not allow Carson to play with them. They told him to go home and take a shower because he was dirty. This experience also registered a seven on the SUD scale. At age 12 or 13, Carson and a friend were talking to two pretty girls. Carson had a romantic crush on one of them. For no apparent reason during their interaction, this girl said to Carson, "I can't believe how ugly you are." This experience registered an eight for Checker on the SUD scale.

At this point in the collection of Checker's memory set, Carson reported that with each recollection, Checker's appearance changed to look more like him. He now "looked like a dopier version of me but with elongated features." Changes in the perceived appearance of internal self states are not uncommon; however, such changes most often come during or after unburdening and memory processing.

Checker's later memories, beginning around high school age, were more often positive. The painful memories he recalled were less disturbing than those of childhood. The positive memories included the greater attention he got once he began playing high school football. The college years were also mostly positive for Checker. Exceptions were a breakup with a college girlfriend, and getting in trouble (at a religious college) for possessing a photograph of a woman wearing just lingerie.

Our fourth session was devoted entirely to the unburdening of Checker's heavy load of negative emotions connected to his early experiences. We began with his memory of the spanking at age six or seven and quickly reduced the SUD level to a zero through an imaginary fire intervention. Carson visualized Checker standing next to a bonfire while systematically reaching into himself, lifting out the hurt as if it were a physical substance, and throwing it onto the fire. The next intervention also involved unburdening with fire, but with an interesting variation. The memory was the abandonment until after dark at the football practice field. Carson reported that this time, instead of Checker lifting the burden from himself, he lifted the burden from an image of Carson as he was now at his current age. The SUD level reduced quickly from seven to two as Checker carried out the symbolic action of tossing the burden of emotional pain onto the fire. A repetition of the intervention reduced the SUD level to one. Carson brought the memory to a zero SUD level by asking the present-time image of himself to help Checker remove the final remnants of the emotional burden.

Checker chose a wind intervention to unburden the feelings of rejection by the neighborhood boys. Carson visualized Checker standing in an open field between two posts as the wind blew between the posts and onto Checker. As Checker hung onto the bar that connected the posts, he quickly released most of the emotional burden, down to a level two. Then, perhaps playfully, Checker indicated that the remainder of the burden was stuck between his toes. A repetition of the wind intervention quickly reduced the memory to a SUD value of zero.

For the memory of rejection by a pretty girl at about the age of 13, Checker chose to unburden himself into a waterfall. This level eight experience of being told how ugly he was quickly reduced to a level two as, according to Carson, Checker first felt the water dissolving his burden in his head and shoulders, and then in his midsection, his knees, and finally his ankles. Repeating the intervention produced the level of zero distress we were looking for. At this point, Checker spontaneously shifted to another memory, so far unreported. Carson was about seven years old at his grandmother's house. He was "hyper" and his mother repeatedly asked him to calm down. She warned him that she would shock him with a cattle prod if he didn't behave. Finally, with his grandmother gripping his hand, his mother shocked him with the cattle prod. The memory disturbed Checker at a SUD level nine, but quickly resolved to a level three when Carson visualized the part unburdening in the waterfall. Temporarily, however, Carson could not further reduce the burden. What bothered Checker was that his mother could do something so outrageous to him. Three other interventions were necessary to reduce the disturbance to zero. First, Carson visualized his seven-year-old self, still stuck in the memory scene, speaking up to his mother and saying, "I can't believe you are doing this!" This was helpful but not enough to reduce the SUD value to zero. Next, he imagined his adult self, as he was now in the therapy room, entering the scene and scolding his mother, telling her never to do this again. Finally, he visualized himself removing the boy from the memory scene and taking him to an internal playroom, a safe place for him to be. Following these interventions Checker's SUD level for the cattle prod memory became a zero.

Three other memories required unburdening before the end of the session. The first two were breakups with college girlfriends carrying low-level SUD ratings of four. These losses were quickly unburdened, one after the other, to the symbolic action of dissolving them in the waterfall. The last memory was recent and more of a problem. It was the memory of Carson placing the voice-activated tape recorder in Nicole's car to record conversations between Nicole and her relative. Carson believed the tape provided evidence that Nicole had developed a questionable relationship with another man. This discovery disturbed Checker to a level nine on the SUD scale, and he did not initially agree to unburden the memory. However, because Carson knew how damaging his jealousy-driven surveillance of his wife was to his marriage, he persisted in insisting that Checker do the unburdening. The memory was powerfully disturbing, and Carson developed his own powerful symbolism to unburden it. He first tried to unburden Checker to fire, but quickly found that the part's reluctance was too strong to overcome. He assured Checker that giving up the burden of negative emotions would not cause him to miss danger signs in the future. A repetition of the fire intervention reduced the SUD level to four. Carson then visualized Checker at the top of the mast of a sailboat trapped in a hurricane with the rain and the wind battering him as it dissolved and blew away his burden of anger, fear, and anxiety. Unfortunately, these efforts reduced the burden only to a SUD level of three. Since we were at the end of the session, Carson convinced Checker to unload temporarily the remaining distress into a suitcase that he could keep with him. In this way, Checker could open the suitcase and draw upon his negative emotions if he felt it necessary. At the same time, he could experience life without the burden and perhaps discover that he would still be alert enough to protect Carson from other potential threats. As this temporary solution suggests, we would need to work more with the Checker subpersonality in the future.

Swinging

In the fifth session, two weeks later, we began to collect information about Carson's early sexual experiences, with the goal of discovering those experiences that underlay his desire to bring other men and couples into his marital sexuality. His desire to be present when another man was having sex with his wife was strong, and he could not resist asking his wife to engage again in these activities. She was adamant, however, that she would no longer participate in these threesomes or with other couples. Because he did not want to lose his wife, Carson hoped to reach the point in therapy where he could be satisfied just with sex with his wife alone.

We began by talking about his premarital sexual experiences, with an emphasis upon the earliest in his memory. These experiences included playing sexual *show-and-tell* at age five in a neighbor girl's closet, receiving oral sex several times around age seven from a slightly older male cousin, and, much later, enjoying sexual threesomes (two males, one female) in college. More recently, Carson recalled several experiences of involvement in sexual threesomes with Nicole and another man. A particular focus of sexual energy for Carson was the memory of watching his male friend fondle Nicole during an evening of drinking. I asked Carson to speak to this energy and ask the part that carried it to provide a picture of itself. The resulting internal picture was that of a "sexy looking" woman in her 30s wearing lingerie. She claimed the name *Taylor*. She would be our next focus in therapy.

The memory set we would explore was different from most memory sets because most of the specific memories were positive, not distressing. We would aim to neutralize these positive memories because they were the memories that provided the energy for Carson's urge for sex with multiple partners. Taylor's earliest memory was the age-five show-and-tell memory mentioned above. For her, that memory still contained a SUE (Subjective Units of Energy) rating of three. The SUE scale measures energy invested in a memory that is not negative. In this case, the energy was positive, but in other cases, there can be energy investments that cannot easily be categorized as either negative or positive. Receiving oral sex from the male cousin had a SUE rating of eight or nine. Another early sexual experience for Taylor was finding several *Playboy* magazines that she explored in a childhood fort, a level nine positive experience.

At this point in the process of collecting members of Taylor's memory set, Carson interrupted to say that his internal image of Taylor had changed. The image of a sexy adult female had morphed into that of a little boy who continued to claim Taylor as a name, and who said he was 10 years old. It is important to remember here that the images parts present of themselves are metaphors, symbolic representations that reflect a set of life experiences and a particular view of the world. Parts are not people, although they respond internally as people might respond. From Taylors's memory set, we might conclude that some activities were experienced as masculine in nature while some were experienced as feminine. The part's self-image might change, perhaps, depending upon the kind of experience that is in focus. For example, carrying Playboy magazines to a boy's fort seems to be a kind of masculine experience, while receiving oral sex from another boy might be experienced as a kind of feminine experience. The self-image presented by Taylor would change again by the time we finished unburdening his/her sexual memories.

As a boy now, Taylor continued to list his sexual memories. He remembered playing *doctor* with a new neighborhood girl at age seven, an incident with a SUE level of seven. He saw a magazine depicting sex between two males and one female at age 10, a level eight positive experience. He masturbated in front of another boy around the age of 11, a positive level seven event. Finally, he remembered receiving oral sex from another boy in a treehouse at age 11, with a SUE level of six. From Carson's college years, Taylor remembered three threesomes involving Carson's girlfriend and a male friend, all positive level nine experiences. More recently, there was a foursome with Nicole and another couple with a SUE rating of nine and several threesomes with Nicole and another man that rated as level 10 positive experiences. Taylor reported two other of Carson's memories, both of which were experienced as negative. The first was that of taking his Playboy magazines to school and being caught and punished. The second was a recent incident of jealousy when Nicole came home and told him she had danced with another man. Both of these experiences were unpleasant, registering about a five on the SUD scale. We did not unburden these memories because our focus with Taylor was on reducing positively charged sexuality.

Taylor agreed to unburden the positive sexual energy attached to the early experiences of receiving oral sex from his cousin. He chose fire as the symbolic mechanism for this work. As Carson visualized Taylor standing next to a fire pit, he instructed the part to reach into himself, lift out the targeted energy as if it were a physical substance, and throw it into the fire. Then he and Taylor watched it burst into flame and be incinerated. Taylor's first effort reduced the package of positive energy to a SUE rating of five. Repetition of the intervention reduced the rating to a one, and a final repetition reduced it to the necessary zero. The next intervention also used the symbolism of fire and quickly reduced the excitement attached to the pornographic depiction of a sexual threesome to nearly zero from a level eight. One repetition of the intervention brought the energy level to zero. For the unburdening of the next three memories, Carson chose the symbolism of water. These were the experiences of Taylor finding and taking a *Playboy* magazine to his fort, masturbating in front of another boy, and receiving oral sex from still another boy. These experiences occurred between the ages of 10 and 12. Carson visualized Taylor wading into a moderately flowing river where the water dissolved the positive sexual energy and the current carried it away. In each case, complete unburdening was achieved on the first attempt.

At the end of the session, other important sexual experiences remained to be processed. Consequently, because a part's accessed but unprocessed memories can overwhelm a client between sessions, we asked Taylor to leave behind his strong emotions and sensations. Carson visualized Taylor placing the potentially troublesome energy into a bank vault. We would open the vault and complete the unburdening in the next session.

Our sixth session was devoted entirely to detaching the positive sexual energy from Taylor's memories of engaging in threesomes and foursomes in college and later during Carson's married life. The symbolic discarding of the sexual energy connected to these memories was achieved through visualized fire and water interventions of the sort previously described. Following these interventions, Carson reported that Taylor's image had changed to female again. She appeared to be in her 20s, pretty, and "dressed like a girl on her first date." According to Carson, she was sexy in a "wholesome" way, unlike in her first appearance when she was sexy but in a "slutty" way.

At the end of the session, Carson felt the processing had been successful but was not entirely sure if the zero rating would last. Given his doubts, we made a note to check in with Taylor in the future to assess whether the zero rating had held. At this point, however, it seemed that we had achieved the goal of removing the foundation for Carson's fixation on multi-partner sexual activities. That foundation was the set of exciting sexual experiences in his childhood together with their expansion to threesomes and foursomes through the present. Thus, we now expected that whatever sexual fantasies he might now have, they would not be amplified by the powerful energies connected to previous experiences. He might still be able to enjoy such activities in the future, but he would not be compelled to pursue them. As these remarks show, Parts Psychology makes no value judgment regarding sexual activities. Instead, it addresses the specific problem the client brings to therapy. Carson's problem had to do with marital discord stemming from his fixation on multi-partner sexual relations. I expected that the stress on his marriage would be reduced to the extent that he no longer made frequent requests of his wife to bring others into their bedroom.

For a variety of reasons unrelated to therapy, our next session, the seventh, took place seven weeks later. At this time, Carson reported that he was again sleeping in his wife's bed, and had resumed occasional lovemaking with her. "I'm impressed," he said of the results of his therapy. He no longer thought of threesomes when he masturbated or when he engaged in sex with Nicole. He said simply, "I don't think about it anymore." When I asked him to think purposely about engaging in sexual threesome activities, Carson acknowledged that he still found the idea exciting, but unless so directed he did not spontaneously dwell on such activities.

Jealousy Again

Near the end of the seventh session, we returned to the issue of jealousy, which, although less intense now for Carson, was still an occasional problem. We focused upon a memory from a few days earlier. Carson felt a strong twinge of jealousy and fear when his wife went out "cutely dressed" for morning coffee. When Carson concentrated on his feeling of jealousy and asked the part who carried it to show itself, he found an internal "little boy in a red hat." The boy appeared to be about five years old. His name was *Calvin*. He knew Carson and said, "Carson is me." He was fully coconscious with Carson, knew his wife and children, and thought of the children as his own. This last thought is somewhat unusual in that most of the time child parts do not consider the observing self's children to be their own children, especially when, as in this case, the child part presents itself as about the same age or younger than the person's actual children. We would collect incidents from Calvin's memory set in our next session.

In the next session, our eighth, Calvin reported the mildly painful memory at age nine of falling onto a fence from the rope ladder to his treehouse. The incident bothered Carson mainly because a friend laughed at him. He also shared the age eight experience of having his mother stick a pin in his chest when she tried to attach his newly awarded Cub Scout gold star to his shirt. Calvin's memory was that the pin penetrated his chest to the unlikely depth of one inch. These incidents barely registered on the SUD scale. An earlier incident at his brother's Cub Scout meeting remained disturbing to a SUD level of eight or nine. At this event, a table fell on Carson (as Calvin) and broke his leg. Three visits to the hospital were required before the break was diagnosed. In this and the other injuries, the disturbing element was Calvin's fear that he would be abandoned and no one would take care of him. Particularly disturbing was the separation from his parents at the hospital during his examinations. The disturbing elements in these experiences of body injury were quickly unburdened through the symbolic action of burning them up in fire.

Carson's childhood injuries did not initially appear to be the sorts of memories I had come to expect in the early foundation for adult jealousy. However, when he talked about his fear that he might be abandoned because of his injuries, the familiar theme of threat of loss revealed itself. The next remembered event quite clearly fit the theme. At around the age of four Carson's same-age friend and neighbor suddenly disappeared. When he went to visit her one day, the woman who answered the door told him his friend didn't live there anymore. She had moved. When Carson tried to unburden Calvin of this painful memory by casting the pain into a fire, Calvin was initially unable to release his pain. He was confused, he said, by the disappearance of his friend. Where did she go? What does *moving* mean? Carson explained that moving meant going to live in another place. He also acknowledged the pain Calvin felt over the loss of his friend. After Calvin felt understood, and after he understood that moving was something adults did and that it wasn't his fault, he was able to give up to fire his burden of loss.

In our ninth session, we continued to work on the problem of jealousy by collecting and unburdening other memories of losses. The memory of his young friend moving away had not remained at zero but had risen to a SUD level of two. A memory of having his ailing dog put down at age 11 was disturbing to a level nine. Memories of his brother and cousins preventing Carson from playing with them at the ages of eight and nine bothered Calvin to a level nine also. At age 13, Carson injured himself one night by crashing his bicycle into a parked car. He bruised and lacerated his body badly and fractured his hip. His father reacted in anger to the accident, throwing the bicycle across the yard and making Carson take a shower before taking him to the hospital. Carson was in traction for three days. This incident remained disturbing to Calvin at a level 10. At age 15, Carson's father moved out of the home following a fight with his mother. This event also remained at a SUD level of 10.

We decided to wait before doing more work on the age-four loss of Carson's friend. I hoped that unburdening other losses might eliminate the remaining disturbance without further work. Turning then to other memories, Carson initially tried to unburden Calvin of the loss of his dog through a wind intervention, but succeeded only in lowering the SUD level from nine to six. Calvin remembered that he had gone to school that day but when he returned home, the dog was gone, just as his friend had been gone when he went to visit her some seven years previously. His mother had taken the dog to the pound to be put down. He felt the same sort of sadness as when his friend disappeared. Having expressed these thoughts and feelings, Calvin was able to complete the wind intervention to fully unburden his sadness. For unburdening the memories of his painful treatment at the hands of his brother and cousins, Carson chose a fire intervention, asking Calvin to stand next to a bonfire and unload his bad feelings into the flames. The first effort lowered the SUD rating from nine to four, representing the pain Calvin still felt for being excluded from the company of his slightly older relatives. Repetition of the intervention reduced the disturbance to zero.

The next unburdening involved the bicycle crash and subsequent hospitalization for his broken hip. Carson unburdened Calvin in his first effort with a river intervention, visualizing Calvin wading into the gently flowing water, immersing himself, and allowing the current to carry away his fear and hurt. The final intervention of the session focused upon the incident when Carson's father moved out. For this work, Carson visualized a huge bathroom shower with water powerfully surging out to wash away the burden. The initial immersion in water reduced the level of disturbance from 10 to a six or seven, representing Calvin's fear that the family would be broken up. The next immersion in the shower focused upon this fear and reduced the burden to a level two, representing sadness. Further attempts to unburden the remaining sadness were unsuccessful. We ended the session with Calvin's unburdening incomplete. We now had two incidents that continued to amplify distress at a SUD level of two: that of his father leaving and that of his young friend moving away when Carson was four.

At our tenth session, we did not immediately return to the task of unburdening. Instead, Carson talked about the difficulties he was having in ending his checking on Nicole. He also talked of Nicole's refusal to acknowledge his progress. On one day, he felt significant anxiety when Nicole did not return his phone calls. He felt compelled to leave work and drive by their home to see if she was there. When he saw her car in her usual parking place, he returned to work feeling somewhat calmer. In the evening of a different day, Carson saw that Nicole had washed two pairs of underwear and her bra, leading him to wonder why she would need to launder just these items. For Carson, these items were the sort of intimate female things she would be concerned with if she were having an affair. When he asked Nicole about the matter, she refused to answer his questions, giving him only what he saw as an exasperated look and a headshake in response. Carson acknowledged that his checking on and wondering about Nicole suggested he had more work to do; however, he also felt that if he had a secure relationship with his wife these things would not bother him.

Regarding his progress in therapy, Nicole told Carson she saw no improvement. She reminded him of their recent lovemaking when Carson had once again brought up the matter of sharing their sexuality in a threesome. She added that he had raised the matter on other occasions as well. In spite of Nicole's account, Carson was quite sure that his behavior had changed significantly. He did not remember mentioning threesomes to her, but was willing to do more work on the issue. He was saddened that his wife refused to give him credit for his changes.

In the remainder of the session, we focused on the problem of the distress Calvin still felt for the age-four incident when his friend moved away. Because we had evidently processed Calvin's loss to a zero on a previous occasion, we looked for another part, perhaps a manager, who was not permitting the unburdening for its own reasons. Calvin could not find such a part when he explored the internal space. Consequently, we looked for a younger part, yet unburdened, who might be amplifying its distress onto Calvin. The part turned out to be the four-year-old part who was still stuck in the memory of learning that his friend had moved away. It seemed that the Calvin subpersonality had not fully integrated the younger part into his emancipated state. Thus, there was a four-year-old who functioned as a subpart of the Calvin part. This young subpersonality was aware of the adult Carson but otherwise his only memory was that of discovering that his friend had moved away. For the four-year-old, the loss of his friend was disturbing to a level seven or eight on the SUD scale, considerably above the remaining level two disturbance felt by Calvin. By visualizing the four-year-old standing in the wind as the wind carried away his burden, Carson quickly unburdened the child state of his feelings of loss. Once this was accomplished Calvin's level two SUD rating also disappeared. When we checked on the stability of the SUD ratings in the following session, they remained a zero.

Some interesting Parts Psychology dynamics are evident in the work with Calvin. When we first found Calvin, Carson had visualized him as a little boy in a red hat and appearing to be about five years old. Unlike the four-year-old who remained trapped in the memory scene of his creation, Calvin is emancipated from the particular traumas he has experienced. His memory set includes a number of traumatic memories from age four through adulthood. He is fully aware of Carson and his activities in present time. His self-presentation remains as a five-year-old boy. It appears, however, that he has incompletely integrated his memories because some of these memories are held by parts of varying ages who continue to amplify distress through the system, even when Calvin has evidently completely unburdened himself. Thus, the four-year-old continued to amplify distress because Calvin's symbolic unburdening reached him only tangentially. The memories we will work with below contain scenes with parts also still stuck in the traumas that created them. Like the four-year-old, but unlike Calvin who is emancipated from any given memory scene, their memories do not extend beyond their own individual creation traumas. In completing the unburdening of the emancipated Calvin, we would also work with an eight-year-old and a 15-year-old. Neither of them had any memories beyond the experiences in which they were still trapped. It is unclear what will happen to them as internal subpersonalities in the future. They may be absorbed into existing emancipated subpersonalities, as has happened in the internal worlds of other clients, or they may begin to acquire new memories of their own as newly emancipated parts.

In session 11, we checked the SUD ratings for Calvin regarding other previous work. The maltreatment by his brother and cousins now registered a rating of four, better than the nine we began with, but disappointing because we had previously reduced the rating to zero. Additionally, Calvin once again rated the memory of his father leaving at a level 10 disturbance, although we had previously reduced it to a level two. Finally, Calvin's rating for his bicycle accident and three days in traction at the hospital was back up to a level nine disturbance.

In cases like this, it is generally futile to simply repeat the previous unburdening attempts. In two of the three memories, we chose instead to intervene directly in the painful memory scenes just as we did with the four-year-old. For the memories of maltreatment by his brother and cousins, Carson located the most disturbing incident and then encouraged the eight-year-old part still stuck in the memory to speak to his brother and cousins, telling them how he felt about their unkind words and their exclusion of him from their games. This simple intervention was sufficient to bring to zero the eight-year-old's distress. The boy was happy now and did not want to be taken away from the scene. Instead, he chose to stay and continue to play. The larger result was that emancipated Calvin's SUD level for this incident also reduced to zero.

Additional effort was required of Carson before he could unburden the age-15 memory of his father leaving. Once again, Carson recalled the problem memory scene and spoke with the traumatized part trapped there. He urged the 15-year-old in the scene to tell his father how he felt about him leaving and breaking up the family. This intervention reduced the teen's distress level to a three. Carson then guided the 15-year-old in the unburdening of his remaining distress to water, visualizing the young part flopping in the ocean surf while allowing the water to dissolve the remaining bad feelings. Unfortunately, the SUD level dropped to no lower than a two. Carson then asked the 15-year-old to talk about what continued to disturb him. He said it was disturbing to see his parents like that, hurting and crying. They had called him and his siblings down to the family room, where one parent sat on the couch and the other on a chair. "They said they had something to tell us. They were divorcing." The father said he was sorry and then "he went out and got into his Cadillac and drove away." The 15-year-old followed him out and, as the father drove away, he screamed, "It's not fucking fair!" Eventually, months later, the father returned, but the teenager continued to retain the fear he felt that night when his father drove away. After this talk about the incident, the SUD level was reduced to one. It yielded quickly to zero with another unburdening by water. Once the event had been reduced to zero for both the teenager and for Calvin, Carson moved the 15-year-old to his internal "family room" for continued safety.

The teenager part, previously trapped in the abandonment scene, had no other memories before or after that scene.

For the last member of Calvin's memory set, the one involving his three days in traction in the hospital, Carson thought he could unburden Calvin without intruding into the actual memory. He chose to visualize Calvin wading into a gently flowing river as he allowed the water to dissolve the negative emotions associated with the event, especially his sense of abandonment and his hurt over his father's anger. Calvin released his burden quickly and reported a SUD rating of zero within a minute of beginning the intervention. We would check the stability of this rating in a later session.

At the end of session 11, Carson had complained that Nicole felt he was continuing to monitor her. She would interpret even innocent questions about the events of her day as Carson checking up on her. Although Carson protested his innocence, in session 12 he described certain of his actions that were clearly efforts to monitor Nicole. Following a weekend when he watched the kids when Nicole spent the days away from home, and one evening when Nicole and her sister went out on their own, Carson attempted to check Nicole's cell phone for stored text messages. He found, however, that she had deleted them. When asked why she had deleted her messages Nicole said simply, "Because it was time." Carson tried to gather more information by asking if his wife gave out her telephone number to men for text messaging, but she refused to discuss the matter further. Carson acknowledged that his concern was driven by jealousy, but he insisted that the level of jealousy had reduced greatly from what it had been.

When asked, the Calvin part rated his upset at this interaction between Carson and Nicole at a SUD level of six. Calvin felt that Nicole must have been hiding something or, alternatively, that she was excluding him from something in which he might want to participate. This sounded like what he had previously experienced when his brother and cousins excluded him from their games. Those earlier experiences still rated at a SUD level of two or three, indicating that we still had more work to do. When Carson looked inward to recall the memories, he saw himself as "a little boy who was tagging along with his older brother and cousins." This little boy rated the treatment by the brother and cousins at a SUD level of four or five. He knew who Carson was but had no memory for any events before or after the specific actions by his brother and cousins. He quickly unburdened his distress into a bonfire, with just one temporary stop at a SUD level of one. Before his final visualization, Carson observed that his younger self thought that the other boys were "cool dudes and he just wants to hang out with them, but sometimes he feels like they don't want to hang out with him." Following the unburdening, this little boy chose to go off and play with his toy soldiers. Thus, we learned that there were two subpersonality fragments trapped in the interactions between Carson and his brother and cousins that required unburdening before the SUD level of zero could be sustained.

Carson believed that his attempt to check Nicole's history of text messaging was sparked by his overhearing Nicole telling her sister that having sex with him just once every two or three weeks was okay with her. This comment irritated Carson because it meant to him that he was unimportant to Nicole. When he again looked within to see what other parts were involved in his distress, he found Checker nearby. Checker readily admitted that it was he who checked for Nicole's text messages. Carson described Checker's concern as, "if he's not important enough to have sex with, then maybe somebody else is," meaning that maybe Nicole was having an affair. We were at the end of the session and so we planned more work with Checker in the next (and final) session.

Our 13th session was our last. Our sessions had lasted over a period of almost five months. Carson had been feeling the pressure of work obligations and had previously expressed concern about the difficulty of getting away for therapy sessions. We had earlier agreed that we were close to finishing our work, but there was still a small amount of parts work to do before Carson could feel safe with his personality reorganization. Our final session focused upon Checker, the part who originally presented himself as a black ball in session three and slowly came to resemble an "elongated version" of Carson.

At the beginning of the session Checker was not sure how well he was doing with his jealousy. As the result of his checking of Nicole's text messages to her best friend, he learned that just a few weeks ago she was proud of her sexuality, proud of her responsiveness, her awareness, and her willingness to be open. But the recent text message he intercepted in which she said sex was not very important to her and that she could go without it for weeks at a time disturbed him because it led him to feel that he wasn't very important to her. However, after he and Carson had a discussion of the nature of internal parts, Checker came to accept Nicole's different positions on different occasions as the result of her own parts' influence on her at different times. Thus, he could see that, like Carson, Nicole might feel more or less sexual depending upon which part was influencing her on a given occasion. Checker also agreed that checking her text messages was an invasion of her privacy and he could be strong enough to stop his surveillance of her.

To help Checker in his agreement to stop his checking on Nicole, Carson used an affect bridge to discover the earlier memory that was being triggered and thereby energizing his urgency to know what Nicole was thinking. Carson asked him to focus on his sense of urgency and then to let his mind float back in time to the earliest memory he had which connected to it. The memory that popped into Carson's mind dated to age 15 when he "liked" a girl named Susie, but after Susie met his best friend, she liked his best friend more than him. The same sequence repeated itself at age 17 with Michelle who also came to like his best friend more than Carson. Checker said that he rated these experiences at a level six on the SUD scale but he also thought the experiences were "kinda funny. It's like when someone slips on the stairs and hurts themselves; it's kinda funny but still bothersome." There were no other unresolved memories that Checker could discover at the foundation of his need to check up on Nicole.

With the aid of a wind metaphor, Carson guided Checker in unburdening the memories of losing the affections of Susie and Michelle to his best friend. The initial exposure to visualizing the wind blowing away particles of hurt led to a reduction of the SUD level to a two, which Checker identified as having to do with feelings of inferiority in relation to his best friend. A single repetition of the intervention reduced the SUD level to zero. Carson then asked Checker to accept a different role with respect to questions about what Nicole was doing. Checker agreed to take on the role of reassuring Carson about Nicole's behavior, finding legitimate reasons for her doing the things that formerly disturbed him. When asked to review his entire memory set Checker reported that there were no other disturbing memories. There were memories that once disturbed him, but they were now all unburdened.

Finally, Carson asked Checker about whether he had any knowledge of Carson mentioning sexual threesomes while engaged in lovemaking with Nicole. Checker said no, but suggested that Taylor did. Taylor is the part with whom we had previously worked to diminish Carson's desire for multiple sex partners. This part had presented itself as both a 10-year-old boy and as an adult female, but was now maintaining itself as a female. She admitted that Nicole was correct in saying that Carson (influenced by Taylor) had mentioned a threesome during one evening of lovemaking; however, she said that she did not think about multiple partners very much. She agreed not to mention it again to Nicole for at least six months. Taylor said that she wanted to demonstrate her strength in sexual matters and did not want to fantasize about multiple sex partners even during masturbation.

The work in our final session illustrated two matters of interest. First, there is the fact that Taylor, although agreeing to cease her efforts to involve multiple sex partners in Carson's life, still had an interest in doing so. Time will tell if this remains a problem. The other matter is a general point about internal parts. Carson did not remember mentioning a sexual threesome to Nicole, but Taylor did. The point is that a person can honestly say he has no memory for a specific action or statement, but some part of that person may have the disremembered information. Carson said he would call in six months to report on his progress in reconciling with Nicole.

Chapter 7
Letting Go of Love

Sam was 44 years old and an engineer with a local casino when he first came to see me. His score on the Dissociative Experiences Scale (DES) was a minimal 2.1 in comparison with the norm of 10. Consequently, the internal world with which we would work was not likely to be the result of significant childhood trauma. Sam had been married to Mary, his current wife, for 12 years. However, the couple was separated and in the process of divorce. Sam had two biological children from a previous marriage; Mary had one child, a daughter. They had no children of their own. Sam's final resolution of his loss of Mary involved letting go of the love he continued to feel for her. The original focus of the therapy, however, involved a different kind of loss.

The problem that brought Sam to therapy was the suicide of his twin sister more than two years previously. His was a close family deeply affected by the suicide. Only after considerable urging by his siblings did Sam finally seek out a therapist to help him adjust to the loss of his twin. His dissociation rating was a minimal 2.1 on the DES scale. His sister had committed suicide in a way that traumatized her close family members, especially those who found her remains and later cleaned up the scene of her death. Sam was one of those who helped to clean up the bloody scene. He had to process not only her loss but also his exposure to the circumstances of her death. Fortunately, over the course of five sessions Sam was able to release the pain that had burdened him for so long.

Marital Problems

As Sam struggled with his sister's death, he also struggled in his marriage. With the suicide of his sister successfully processed, he turned his attention to his unresolved marital situation. Almost a year previously, still in the depths of grief over his sister, he had moved out of his home, leaving everything in the control of his wife. He left the city for two months. When he returned, he found that Mary had become bitter and angry. In his absence, she had taken out a six-figure home equity loan on the house and refused to say what she did with the money. She refused Sam visitation with the pets he left behind. She also refused to talk to him directly and cut off her relationship with the two children from his first marriage. These were children she had helped to raise during their 12 years of marriage. Sam filed for divorce. Three months went by as he struggled to come to terms with his sister's death and tried to talk to his wife. Then he stopped the divorce proceedings and tried to reconcile with his wife. He wrote her love letters and pleaded with her to join him in marriage counseling. But it was too late. They communicated with each other minimally through a friend of Mary. His wife was uninterested in reconciling and uninterested in dividing the community property. She wanted Sam to walk away and leave her everything. Through her friend, Mary invited him to the house to visit their pets and then called the police, saying he was harassing her and that he had tried to force his way into the house. Her anger was so great over his abandonment of her that she seemed only to want revenge for the pain he had caused her. Finally, nine months after he had moved out, Sam reactivated the divorce proceedings in order to force an equitable settlement of the community property. He tried to come to terms with the loss of his wife, but it was another five months before he would ask for help in letting go of his love for her.

Letting go of love is sometimes necessary for a person to move forward from the loss of a romantic partner. The extreme cases where this is called for are those where the relationship cannot be repaired; where paralysis grips the partner in pain; and where further pain and loss (including financial loss) are likely to result without intervention. All of these features were present in Sam's case.

There are two important steps to letting go of love of a romantic partner. First, there is the resolution of the pain of rejection. It is quite painful when someone you love wants nothing to do with you, or in Sam's case, where the person actively wants to hurt you. Frequently, resolution of the rejection requires that the person also unburden the pain of previous losses and rejections over the course of his or her life history. For Sam, some of the same historical events that had made it so difficult for him to accept the loss of his sister also contributed to his difficulty in adjusting to the idea of divorce (i.e., the loss of his wife). The second step in letting go of love is the symbolic release of continued loving feelings. Unburdening love works in exactly the same way as unburdening anger, sadness, and other negative emotions. Sam had to unburden both the negative energy of rejection as well as the positive energy of romantic love before he could successfully move on.

During the course of the work that had permitted Sam to reach closure on the death of his sister, he sometimes spoke of the continuing problems he was having in dealing with his divorce. In one of those sessions, I introduced Sam to work with internal parts. The first of Sam's subpersonalities to present himself was a much younger version of Sam, just 20 years old. Sam saw this internal image as "looking insecure," crying, and wearing the same clothing that Sam was wearing that day in my office. The part indicated that he knew Sam and called him *the boss*. According to Sam, the part's function was to drive Sam with energy. His earliest memory was of Sam wandering away from home at age four in search of oil for his cowboy boots. A helpful couple brought him home. In another memory, also from age four, Sam was saying goodbye to a neighborhood friend because Sam's family was moving away. These memories were not very disturbing to the part, registering only a one or two on the SUD scale, but they would come up again in the memory set of another part, described later in this chapter. *The 20-year-old* part at first said that he did not know Mary, Sam's wife. However, when Sam took a moment to visualize Mary, the part indicated that, in fact, he did know her. Sam said that although the part knew Mary he did not love her. In response to Sam's further questions, the 20-year-old answered that he was aware of the part who loved Mary and that he would connect Sam to that part.

There was only a little time left in the session, but there was time enough for Sam to find himself viewing another version of himself, this time at about 30 years old. When I coached Sam in interviewing this part, we found that the part acknowledged loving Mary and was afraid of losing her through what he perceived as her abandonment of him. Like the part who presented as a 20-year-old, this part was not fully aware of current events in Sam's life. His earliest memory dated to Sam's sixth grade and consisted of a simple mental image of his schoolteacher at the time. This memory was not disturbing. The memories that were disturbing were of the ending of two of

Sam's previous love relationships. In each of these cases, he experienced great pain in dealing with his loss.

Following this first attempt to become acquainted with his internal world, Sam did not return to work with internal parts for some time. Sam came to therapy only six times over the next five months. During this time, he wanted a supportive listener, someone he could talk with about what he was going through, and someone he could use as a check on his rational behavior. He chose not to do the deeper work with his internal parts at that time. Finally, however, after his wife accused him of years of physical abuse at one court hearing, failed to show up at two other court dates, and allowed their home to go into foreclosure, Sam decided to do the deeper work that would relieve him of his emotional connection to his wife. It was just too painful to continue as he had been.

Deep Work for Letting Go

To begin this new approach to helping Sam deal with his pain, I asked him to focus upon whatever internal picture he could find that would maximize his negative emotions at that moment. He reported that his picture was one of "losing my wife." With that, I introduced Sam to the Two Fishermen imaging exercise:

> Imagine that there are two fishermen walking past you on either side of you, holding between them a tightly stretched, magical fishing net. The net is magical because it can move through your body without harming you. As the fishermen walk past you on either side of you, the net they hold between them moves through your body but snags up against and around this part of you that causes you so much pain. As they continue walking past you their net moves through you and as it does, it draws out of you the part of you in pain. As the net draws this part out of you, gently place it into a nearby room. Then look into the room and tell me what you see.

Sam saw an image of himself at 12 years old, wearing a white T-shirt and blue-jean cut-offs. As I coached Sam to speak subvocally to this part, we learned that he was well oriented within Sam's internal system. When asked, he said of Sam, "You're me." His name was also *Sam*. He agreed that we could call him *the 12-year-old*.

Before our session ended for the day, we collected three memories from the 12- year-old that seemed to be related to separation and loss. The first two memories had appeared a few months previously when I first introduced Sam to his internal parts. The first of these was the one where, at about age four, Sam's family was preparing to move to a different house. Sam was on his way to his friend's house to say goodbye. The memory was disturbing to the 12-year-old at a level four. The second memory dated to the same period, although it is unclear whether it happened before or after the first memory. In this memory, Sam's family had not moved yet, and Sam was "running away from home" because he did not want to move. "I walked down the street and got pretty far away." Eventually, "an old couple in a blue Cadillac picked me up and took me back home." This memory was not disturbing. The third memory dated to the time after the family had moved and Sam was in kindergarten. The 12-year-old remembered a recurrent dream he had at the time. In the dream, Sam was in the classroom when a scary machine entered the room and "began killing people with sharp knives." This recurrent dream was disturbing at a level nine on the SUD scale. At this point, our session was out of time and so we continued with the memories of the 12-year-old at our next meeting.

In our next session, we returned immediately to work with the 12-year-old. His next memory dated to the time between his seventh and eighth grades. He had been at summer camp for two weeks. When his mother picked him up, she told him that the family had moved again. The house had been sold; everything in it had been moved to the new house; and they were not going back to the old house. The 12-year-old learned he would have no chance to say goodbye to his friends. He was upset with his parents in a "major" way. "How could they do this to me!" he demanded. He felt his distress at a level nine or ten.

The age at which a part presents itself does not necessarily correspond to the limit of its memory set. Consequently, it was not unusual to find that the 12-year-old remembered Sam's high school years. He also remembered quite well Sam's girlfriends, Carla and Candace. He had no knowledge, however, of Sam's wife. Carla was Sam's "first true love." Sam was 16 when Carla broke up with him. Her parents refused to allow her to see him anymore after he involved them in trouble with the police. "I stole my father's truck," said Sam. "Then I got some friends to buy beer. The cops pulled us over for drunk driving and took us both to the jail for juveniles." For the 12-year-old, the memory for the breakup with Carla was not the level 10 it was 25 years ago. It was now only a level three.

The breakup with Candace had a more lasting effect. It was disturbing to the 12-year-old at a level nine or ten. Sam dated Candace for two years between the ages of 16 and 18. "We got into a nasty car accident; my fault. She went half way through the windshield of the car. I'd been drinking. Her parents forbade us to see each other again. I remember driving up to her house. She came out and said we can't see each other anymore. I almost committed suicide after that. We continued talking on the telephone even in college."

All of the memories we collected from the 12-year-old's memory set seemed to be related to a theme of loss, just the sort of experiences one would expect as the foundation of an inability to let go of a relationship and move on. We began immediately to unburden the pain of these losses for the 12-year-old. First, we worked with the low-level distress of saying goodbye to the neighborhood friend at age four. In our initial attempt to unburden the part, Sam visualized the 12-year-old standing between two posts as a powerful wind blew between the posts and over and through him. This reduced his burden to a level two. Sam explained that the remaining distress was "because he lost someone he liked and would never see again." Once the part expressed these thoughts, a repetition of the intervention quickly reduced his distress to a zero. Other wind interventions successfully reduced to zero the other memories in the 12-year-old's memory set. The kindergarten nightmares reduced quickly to a level one and then zero. The loss of his friends at age 12 when the family moved again followed the same pattern. The breakup with girlfriend Carla at age 16 reduced immediately to a zero with a single wind intervention. The pain of losing Candace at 18 was somewhat more difficult to unburden. Our first effort reduced the level of distress to a level three. Here, Sam remarked, "I should have held on to this woman. She was my first [sexual experience] and I was her first. I wish I had gotten her pregnant." Once these thoughts were expressed, the 12-year-old was able to release the remaining pain of loss. We were then at the end of the session. It seemed to have gone quite well. We planned to check the permanence of the unburdenings in our next session and then go on to unburden the loss of Sam's wife.

We began the next session by checking the level of disturbance for the 12-year-old for each of the losses we had unburdened in the previous session. All remained at a zero except for the loss of girlfriend Candace. This memory registered at a level one or two on the SUD scale. Sam described his remaining negative emotions as regret and self-blame. He said, "I really feel like I blew it. It didn't have to be that way. It could have been a lifetime relationship." After he expressed these thoughts, Sam was able to guide the 12-year-old in a final unburdening to wind. Once the memory registered a zero on the SUD scale, Sam was able to say without distress, "We were just dumb kids."

At this time, Sam asked the 12-year-old again if he knew Sam's wife, Mary. Once again, the 12-year-old indicated that he did not. His memory set ended with former girlfriend, Candace. We had to conclude, then, that although the 12-year-old's distress could be triggered by loss of a relationship in Sam's present, he was not the part directly affected by such loss. His triggering appeared to be secondary to that of another, as yet unidentified, internal subpersonality.

In order to find this part I asked Sam to focus on the distress he felt over losing Mary and to ask for the part who felt that distress to show itself to Sam. The result was that Sam visualized himself in his own workshop wearing jeans, a t-shirt and his familiar boots. It was a memory picture from several years earlier; he no longer had that shop. This subpersonality knew he was a part of Sam and acknowledged the pain he felt over losing Mary. He readily agreed to unburden his pain with the help of a wind metaphor. Sam's initial visualization of wind carrying away the part's pain of loss reduced the distress level from a 10 to a four or five. But now the part was stuck on the memory of Mary saying, before Sam walked out, "I have always loved you and I always will." If that were true, then, according to the part, Sam still had a chance to win back his wife. Sam and I discussed then how statements like "I will always love you" may be experienced as true at the time they are expressed, but are often not accurate forecasts of future feeling states. Sam spoke inwardly to this part of himself and asked for his help in "moving on" because Mary had not shown even a single indication that she still loved him over the preceding year as he pleaded for her to return to him. A second wind intervention reduced the remaining distress to a level two, which connected to the part's sadness over "losing a friend, someone I care about." For the final intervention, we asked the 12-year-old to join this adult part in standing between the two posts in the field through which the wind blew, and then both parts together allowed the wind to carry away any remaining distress over losing Mary. Both reported a distress level of zero. We were at the end of the session with time left only to check with Sam on the level of distress *he,* as opposed to the two parts we had just worked with, still felt over losing his wife. Surprisingly, Sam reported a level 10 of distress. Clearly, there was still another part amplifying a great deal of pain.

At the beginning of our next session, Sam was visibly upset. He had learned that his wife was now living with another man. He was so depressed that he intended to tell his attorney to give her anything she wanted, as long as she would sign the divorce papers. He would say to his attorney that he wanted nothing, not his pets, the personal possessions he had left behind, nor any of their community property. He just wanted to walk away and be free of his pain. His pain was greatest when he thought of his wife in the arms of her new lover. Unlike most people whose jealousy leads to anger, Sam's jealousy led him to debilitating depression. I suggested that he work with me for a few more sessions before instructing his attorney to give up on his case. Tentatively, he agreed.

Sam focused on the pain of his jealousy then, and we returned to the therapy. He asked the sensation to give him an internal image of itself. The result was that Sam found himself visualizing "a ball of tangled rope," an image which, although not animated, would serve the purpose of providing an internal focus for Sam to dialog with his internal part. At first, the image was unresponsive. Sam experienced no indication of the part's awareness when I coached him to ask the usual early questions. It had no response to questions of whether it knew who Sam was, how old Sam was, how old *it* was, what its purpose was, or whether it had another image of itself with which we could interact. However, it began to respond with memories when Sam asked questions intended to elicit its memory set. Its earliest memory dated to a few months after Sam met Mary, 12 years previously. They were having an argument. Sam explained, "She was yelling at me. I walked out the door, but I was saying to myself, 'If I leave now, the relationship is over. Or, do I walk back into her apartment and work it out?' I knew it wasn't right even as I walked back in the door." The memory was disturbing at a level six.

The part's next memory dated to a time when Sam and Mary were living together, but not yet married. "Mary [a casino worker] went on a date with a guy when we were living together. She really dolled up for dinner with a big-time player. She said it was just business." The memory produced painful jealousy to a level seven on the 0-10 SUD scale. The next memory also dated to the time when Sam and Mary were living together, but still unmarried. The memory was of "the fight we got into on our way back from Paris. We were going through customs. We weren't married and so I made her fill out her own forms for customs. We had a screaming fight after we got off the plane in L.A." The memory of this event was disturbing to a level six. Of the next memory Sam explained, "After Paris I kicked her out. Five months went by before we got back together. We got married. Three months later, she wanted to start an internet business. So I set her up by giving her the startup money. Mary got into a fight with my friend who was helping her for free, and then she wouldn't come out of the bedroom and talk to him and his wife who helped us for months. She never talked to them again." The event continued as a level three disturbance because of Sam's embarrassment in front of his friends.

There were two more groups of experiences in the part's memory set. The first followed the death of Mary's mother. Sam said, "She locked herself in the bedroom and wouldn't come out for days at a time. She was taking major pills. I remember her screaming, 'Leave me the fuck alone!'" Sam rated these experiences with Mary at a level seven, because he felt "so helpless." The next group of experiences had to do with the illness of Sam's father. "I learn my father has terminal cancer. I'm upset, crying. Mary comes into my office and says, 'Get over your pity party!' How dare she tell me this after she spent a year in the bedroom getting over her mother! She didn't even come to his funeral." Sam's feelings were hurt to a level six because of what he felt was Mary's insensitivity.

Our session was at an end but we briefly talked about unburdening the memory set connected to this subpersonality represented by the image of a ball of rope. During the following week, I had misgivings about doing such an unburdening. On the one hand, Sam continued to carry around considerable negative energy relating to his time with Mary. Unburdening the memory set would contribute to greater centeredness for Sam. If we were doing marital counseling, I wouldn't hesitate to say that it was important for Sam to give up these resentments. On the other hand, the problem with which Sam wanted help was that of giving up his aching need to be with Mary, who had already moved on. It might be better for Sam to hang onto his resentments in the interest of furthering his goal of letting her go. As it turned out, we did not have to make a decision on this unburdening because when we met again we located the part who carried the romantic love for Mary and longed to be with her again.

Letting Go of Love

At our next session, Sam described a dream he had during the week. In the dream, he knocked on Mary's door and found her willing to talk to him. They went for a walk together and eventually held hands. She agreed to begin talking more with him and even to go out on dates with him as they worked to save their marriage. That was the point at which Sam woke up. He realized that his dream was only a fantasy, that Mary continued to hate him, and was living now with another man. Sam's dream images remained clear to him in the therapy office, and so I suggested he experiment with speaking internally with the dream image of himself because it might represent the subpersonality who continued to love and long for Mary. To Sam's surprise, he found he could speak with his remembered dream image. He described the image as himself at about age 30, roughly the time when he first met Mary. He wore boots, jeans, a tan button-up shirt, and was hatless. This *Dream Sam* acknowledged that he still loved and wanted to be with Mary. His earliest memory was of a time when Sam worked as a bartender. He had only recently met Mary. She came into the bar to wait for him to get off work. Another woman, who he had dated a couple of weeks previously, also came into the bar to wait for him to finish work. Sam didn't know what to do. Neither woman knew the other, and each one expected him to join her in about an hour. Sam wasn't even sure which woman he wanted to wait for him. He took his problem to his boss, who told him to choose one of them and then he would make up a story and tell the other one that Sam was unavailable. Sam chose Mary. He never heard from the other woman again. The memory was mostly a positive one for the Dream Sam who chose Mary. He felt pride that two women were waiting for him, but he felt especially good because this was the moment when he knew he wanted to be with Mary.

All memories we collected from Dream Sam were positive experiences. Consequently, we used the SUE (Subjective Units of Energy) scale to measure them rather than the SUD (Subjective Units of Disturbance) scale. The positive memory, above, registered at a level seven on the 0-10 scale. The next memory in the set concerned the celebration of Sam's birthday at the bar where he worked. "My co-workers had hired two strippers to strip for me at the bar. Mary was okay with it at first. Then the girls started dancing, but still had on their bras and panties. That's when Mary got in front of me and told the girls the dance was over. She said if anybody was gonna strip for me it was gonna be her." This memory registered a seven on the SUE scale. Dream Sam's next memories were of what Sam and Mary called their *spa weekends.* These were times when neither of them had custody of their kids and they had entire weekends just to themselves. The experiences registered eight on the positive energy scale. There were two memorable trips for Sam and Mary that registered nine on the SUE scale. The first was a trip to the Caribbean on a sailboat with just the two of them present. The other was a weekend flight to San Francisco soon after Sam got his pilot's license. They had three days together.

Dream Sam had only positive memories of being with Mary, and had only a vague awareness of the bad times between Sam and Mary. This is typical of the romantic parts with whom I have worked. Our strategy was to release the positive energy from the accumulated events of the part's rather narrow memory set. Dream Sam at first refused to agree to the plan. Sam explained to the part that the relationship was over; that Mary lived with another man now; and that she had refused even to speak to him for nearly a year. Finally, Sam reminded Dream Sam that the purpose of his existence was to help Sam and he needed that help now. Reluctantly, Dream Sam agreed, indicating that he would like to help but didn't know how. We explained the process of unburdening the positive energy of his memories by giving them up symbolically in some permanent way.

Dream Sam chose to do all of the unburdenings to a bonfire as Sam visualized him reaching into himself and lifting out the positive elements that made life with Mary so good. Sam gave first attention to the spa weekends, and shortly reported that Dream Sam had only a level two of positive energy remaining. A repetition of the intervention reduced the memories to a zero. The remaining memories yielded their positive contents quickly to the bonfire, beginning with the Caribbean and San Francisco trips and ending with the memory of the birthday strippers. Dream Sam now reported to Sam that there was no remaining positive energy in his memories of Mary. All were neutral. We concluded the session as Sam and Dream Sam negotiated a new role for the part. He would help Sam select a new and appropriate partner for him.

Sam's next session was our last. The previous week, he said, "was a great week, the best in a long, long time." He was not feeling loving toward his wife, Mary. He had thoughts of the other man, the man with whom Mary now lived, but these thoughts were kind, as Sam said that he actually felt sorry for him. This man didn't know what he had gotten into with Mary. Sam had a date during the week with a new woman, his first date in years. He liked her. However, when I talked with him a month later Sam said that the two of them had decided "to just be friends." They enjoyed each other's company but their interests were just too different. Sam looked forward to finding someone with whom he was more compatible. He had reached a divorce agreement with Mary. Only the signing and recording of the agreement remained. He no longer felt pain over his loss.

Chapter 8
Binge Eating, Panic and Rage

This chapter describes a case that began with the problem of overwhelming rage, but quickly turned to two other issues. The first was high anxiety due to a child's health issues; the second was a longstanding eating disorder. Successful resolution of the problem of rage required resolution also of the sources of panic attacks and binge eating.

Brandy was a 26-year-old *special needs* teacher who drove 220 miles from southern California every weekend to attend our Saturday appointments in Las Vegas. Her score on the Dissociative Experiences Scale was an unremarkable 6.4 in comparison to the norm of 10.0 and, consequently, the issues she brought to therapy and the inner world she discovered were unlikely to be the reflection of a problem of pathological dissociation. Brandy also completed the Multidimensional Inventory of Dissociation (MID), a 218-item questionnaire for the assessment of pathological dissociation. Her score was 11.0. The report for this score states, "A MID score of 8-14 suggests that the test-taker has a few, diagnostically insignificant, dissociative experiences. This level of dissociation is common in therapy clients who do not have a dissociative disorder."[20]

Excessive Anxiety

Over the longer term, the major foci of Brandy's work were her rages and her binge eating. However, in the shorter term we worked with her fears about the health of her son. He was born prematurely with a compromised immune system, which led Brandy to be hypervigilant about maintaining a germ-free environment for him. She experienced panic attacks once or twice a month cued by her intense fear of her son getting sick. She used up a box of hand sanitizers every week and hovered over visitors to monitor their contact with her son. To calm herself, she ate large amounts of food, just as she had done during earlier stressful times in her life. Since her son had come home from the hospital a year earlier, she had gained 60 pounds.

Regarding her anger, Brandy said, "It comes out with my students, but mostly with my husband—I get really nasty." Her recollection was that she had been angry all of her life. Her description of her expression of anger fits that of dissociative rage. "I scream and yell and don't think about anyone else. It's like something takes over, and I can't stop myself from saying hateful things." Among the sources for her rage, Brandy cited her mother's verbal and physical abuse of her and her father's failure to protect her from her mother.

Brandy immediately grasped the concept of inner parts and felt comfortable with the idea of working with her subpersonalities. Consequently, near the end of the first session, I introduced her to an image of herself that connected to her fear for her son. When she focused upon this fear and asked it to provide an image of itself, Brandy found herself visualizing a thinner version of herself, but with red hair rather than her own brown, and wearing a starched, white blouse and black pants. This professional image, said Brandy, is what she felt like when she was at home taking care of her son. The part's name was *Nina*. In Brandy's opinion, this part had a problem: she was extreme and inflexible in the care of her son. For example, in her anxiety to keep him safe she required visitors to wear disposable gloves when greeting him and immediately sanitized the area when they left. At the end of the session, Brandy was intrigued by the idea of working with an inner world of subpersonalities, and hopeful about gaining relief from the extreme emotions she had been feeling.

In session two, we returned immediately to work with Nina, and Brandy added a few more details about how she perceived this aspect of herself. Unlike Brandy, Nina wore glasses and her hair was drawn into a bun. She was tall and statuesque. Brandy said that this was the part of herself she knew best. "She is the one who is organized, does paperwork, cleans house." She added that other parts of herself were probably annoyed by this one.

When asked if she knew who Brandy was, Nina indicated that she did not. When asked to guess, Nina had the sense that Brandy was somehow familiar to her, but anything more than that was unclear. I coached Brandy to explain that she was the self and Nina was a part of her, one of many who made up the complete personality. Brandy described Nina's response as confused, disapproving, but ultimately accepting. She, Nina, had imagined her *boss,* Brandy, as being "more professional and better put together." Nina's earliest memory, dating to age 10 or 11, was of her first thorough cleaning of her room. She did it for pleasure, she said. The task took two full days of cleaning and organizing and gave her a warm feeling of satisfaction.

Nina knew Brandy's husband and thought of him as her own husband. She was quite concerned for everything to go well in the marriage, and was pleased to hear from Brandy that all was well. She also thought of the young son as her son. When asked what advice she might have for Brandy, Nina said that she should be more affectionate with her husband around other people so that they could see that everything was going well, proof that Brandy was being a good wife.

Nina said that one reason she had to be so strict in her rules for life in general and care for her son in particular, was that there was another part who could take over and bring chaos into their lives if she wasn't constantly on guard. When asked to do so, Nina connected Brandy to this other aspect of herself. Brandy described the internal image of the new part as "overweight, dumpy looking, rotund and jolly." Her attitude toward household duties was nonchalant; she would rather wait until tomorrow to take care of the household duties that Nina wanted to take care of today. She enjoyed food and alcoholic drinks, and referred to herself as a "lazy homebody." Her name was *Candace.*

Candace knew who Brandy was, and called her *the boss.* When asked how she knew this she indicated that she had been eavesdropping on the conversation between Brandy and Nina. Like Nina, Candace knew the husband, but thought of him more as "a pal, a partner, but not so much as a husband or lover." She sometimes helped to take care of the son when Brandy was relaxing. She thought of him more as a pet than as a son. "It was not," Brandy summarized, "as if she gave birth to him."

The differences between Nina and Candace are a good illustration of how internal parts can have quite different orientations to important aspects of a person's life. Nina related to Brandy's husband and son similarly to the way Brandy did. In fact, she was probably the source of many of Brandy's attitudes and feelings. Candace, however, although she was fond of both the husband and the son, did not consider them as her own. She joyfully participated in their lives but not with the possessiveness of Nina. She was "not present," apparently, at the birth of the son, and consequently, did not have the mother-son bonding experience carried in Nina's own memory set.

Candace appeared to be a relative newcomer in Brandy's life. Her earliest memory dated to Brandy's sophomore year in high school. Brandy said, "I had always been healthy and took care of myself. I was disgusted by my mother's overweight body. But one day I bought some fast food and took it home and ate it really fast." The out-of-control eating "was soothing, even though it was uncomfortable." This novel experience was evidently the creation moment for Candace. "It was Candace," said Brandy, "who felt the rush and the pleasure." This first episode of binge eating was pleasurable to Candace at a level eight on the positive SUE (Subjective Units of Energy) scale. She also indicated that the discomfort she felt was at a level six on the negative SUD (Subjective Units of Disturbance) scale. Later she indicated that the discomfort was not hers in origin, but was coming from a different part.

Because binge eating is a response to anxiety or other stress in a person's life, I asked for more information from Candace regarding the conditions of life when she first achieved conscious awareness. Speaking for Candace, Brandy said that the primary source of stress at the time was her mother. "She was so mean at that time. She cursed me and called me names every day. She said that she and my dad were going to get a divorce and it was all my fault. I had tried smoking, drinking, drugs; and promiscuity was a disaster. But food was the best relief." Candace recognized that she had problems and would prefer to take life more seriously and be less out of control. However, it was easier for her if she simply focused upon her body desires.

In our third session, Brandy learned from Candace that there was a "mean, bullying part" in the system. Candace said that the part encouraged her to binge on food, whispering that it would make things better. But then, after she binged, the part would turn on her and criticize her incessantly. Brandy asked Candace if she could bridge to the offensive part and bring her onto Brandy's internal screen. When Candace did so, Brandy found herself visualizing *Veronica,* who was "very pretty, a bombshell with sluttiness." She had dark hair and wore tight-fitting jeans and a t-shirt. Veronica knew she was a part of Brandy, but wasn't sure about her function. She thought her job might be to keep Brandy in check. She viewed herself as a bully and liked this image of herself. Her earliest memory was of her experiences in the fourth grade when she was "being funny, a joker; it made people want to be around me." Note here that Brandy uses "bully" in an unusual way. It apparently means simply "the center of attention."

Veronica remembered middle school as a time of trying to fit in and "hang out" with the popular kids after football games, drinking and smoking pot. "It was so cool." However, "By the time I was a sophomore in high school," Brandy said, "Veronica was over her wild stage and wanted to study. But she still played a role in making me likeable." When Brandy was a freshman in college, Veronica was active again. "She was partying again to help me make friends, but she protected me from going too far." Regarding Candace's binge eating, Brandy explained that Veronica didn't see herself as manipulative. It was more like, "Go girl if that's what you want," but then she would turn on Candace, asking, "Now that you've done it, was it worth it?" Veronica acknowledged that she was involved in the acquisition of binge food, but indicated that she "stepped away" once the eating began.

Although we were getting good information from Veronica and Candace that would later be useful, the immediate problem was Brandy's extreme anxiety over the health and care of her son. Consequently, we shifted our attention to this concern. Brandy regularly had panic attacks when she thought of her son's health problems; she hoped therapy would provide some relief for her extreme emotions. Nina, the caretaking part, was not the part who experienced the panic attacks and amplified them onto Brandy; we needed to look further to discover their source. Since we had just been working with Veronica, we asked if she could find the part who had the panic attacks. She immediately did so.

The new part, said Brandy, "kinda looks like me, and she's backing away." Brandy asked the image to come closer for a conversation. She found that the part identified herself as *Bonnie*, and claimed the age of 53. She knew who Brandy was and knew that she, Bonnie, was a part of the larger Brandy. She had been watching the other parts come forward and was "keeping an eye on them." She acknowledged that she was the part who had the panic attacks.

Bonnie's earliest memory was the day Brandy's son was born. "It was horrible," she said. "The worst part was when the doctor said the baby had to come out right now." Brandy's blood pressure was at a very dangerous level, and the baby's placenta had already detached. This experience was Bonnie's creation event and registered a level 10 on the 0-10 SUD scale. Other memories with very high SUD ratings punctuated the time the baby was in intensive care. Crises occurred frequently. The baby *coded* and stopped breathing at two weeks after delivery, and then twice more. Brandy had been called to the hospital twice to hold the baby before he died. Each crisis continued to register a 10 on the SUD scale for Bonnie. Because emergencies might happen at any time, Brandy remained in a high state of anxiety during all her waking hours. It was Bonnie who served as the container for this state of high anxiety, and it was Bonnie who had panic attacks when the baby seemed to show any sign of a downturn in health during the months after his release from the hospital.

Beyond her experiences with the baby, Bonnie had only one other disturbing memory. This was Brandy's experience of learning, just a few weeks previously, that her best friend and daily confidant, was going to join the Air Force. This event and the consequent anticipated loss of her daily support, registered an eight for Bonnie on the SUD scale.

We were at the end of the session, but because Bonnie's memory set had been activated, she, and therefore, Brandy, experienced considerable anxiety as we tried to bring temporary closure to our work. In order to ensure that Bonnie would not be overcome with anxiety, and possibly have another panic attack, Brandy visualized Bonnie in the symbolic act of putting her aroused emotions into a storage container until our next session. Bonnie chose a large trash bag for this purpose.

In our fourth session, we returned immediately to work with Bonnie, who continued to amplify her anxiety onto Brandy. Brandy talked about her prolonged fear that her baby boy would get sick. "I'm always afraid of bringing something home that will infect my son. At work, I'm constantly waiting for a phone call saying he's turned blue." It was apparent that our first unburdening work should be directed at the overwhelming anxiety Brandy felt on a daily basis and also at relieving the panic attacks to which she was subject when Bonnie was overwhelmed.

Brandy chose an ocean metaphor for the symbolic act of unburdening the extreme emotions connected to the birth of her son. She visualized

Bonnie standing hip-high among gentle breaking waves as she remembered the crisis surrounding the premature birth of her son. Brandy asked Bonnie, as she dipped beneath the waves, to feel the water dissolve and carry away her remembered fears, her sense of helplessness, and any other extreme emotions she connected to that night. After the initial unburdening, the SUD level reduced from 10 to six. Bonnie attributed the remaining distress to the pain she felt over the suffering her son had since experienced. The repetition of the unburdening visualization reduced the SUD level to four. Bonnie stopped the reduction at this level because she was concerned that further reduction of her fear might lead her to be inattentive and cause her to miss any new problems her son might have. Brandy assured her that this would not happen. She had a job to do, and she could do it better if her mind was clear. The third repetition of the visualization reduced Bonnie's, and also Brandy's, SUD level to zero. Brandy said, "Now I can see it was a good day because it was the day my son was born." She added that Bonnie was surprised because she now felt *more* rather than *less* competent to be alert to her son's health problems.

We next turned our attention to the painful experiences of the first three weeks of the baby's life in the intensive care unit, which included three occasions when the baby coded. "They called us," said Brandy, "and said we had to get there immediately if we wanted to hold him before he died." Using the same ocean metaphor, Brandy attempted to unburden Bonnie's distress for the ICU experience. As she visualized Bonnie among the ocean's waves, Brandy said, "I can see it [the burden] dissolving and then coming back. It won't wash away."

When this sort of pattern of a burden leaving and returning appears, it is inevitably a sign that another internal part is interfering with the process. I asked Brandy to look around for such a part. She quickly found a new part who chose the name *Kendra* for herself. The new subpersonality was afraid that if she let the pain go away she would lose part of herself. "She kinda looks like me," said Brandy. "She's tall, but fit, and she's wearing a workout outfit." Kendra said that she was 22 and knew "vaguely" who Brandy was. Brandy quickly grasped that Kendra had a strong interest in keeping her body in good shape, and so, in an effort at rapport building, she shared her distress over the 50 pounds she had gained since the birth of the baby. She also explained to Kendra that she was a part of her, living with her in the same body. Kendra accepted this explanation and noted, "I thought you looked familiar." Her earliest memories dated to when Brandy was 16 and had first begun to binge on food and gain "a lot of weight." Kendra emerged at this time "to get me in shape," said Brandy. This first bingeing on food, and the subsequent weight gain, registered an eight on the SUD scale for Kendra. Her next memories had to do with two other episodes of bingeing and weight gain. The first was at age 18, before Brandy went off to college; the second was at 22, shortly before Brandy's wedding. Kendra rated these experiences at a level 10 on the SUD scale. It wasn't just the weight gain but also "seeing me fail again, later, after she had helped me get healthy." Kendra's most recent memories were the birth of the son, whom she considered her own son, and the post partum weight gain mentioned previously. The birth experience registered at a level seven, while the weight gain was a nine or ten on the SUD scale. At the end of the session, Kendra agreed to permit Bonnie to continue the unburdening process. She committed to doing her own unburdening as well.

In our fifth session, we continued our work with Bonnie, after first confirming that we had Kendra's permission to do so. The work went quickly. Bonnie returned to the ocean and unburdened her distress over the previous year of difficulties with her son. As Bonnie healed herself and recognized that she was part of a larger system, Brandy helped her negotiate a new role with Nina, the internal manager, and with Kendra, the fitness part. She wanted to continue to be the primary party who watched over the son, and she wanted to continue to be his advocate. Manager Nina agreed to this redefined role for Bonnie provided that she, Nina, got increased responsibility in the future, especially regarding Brandy's work with special needs children. Kendra, all agreed, would take full responsibility for Brandy's physical body and food.

There was a final bit of unburdening to do. Bonnie still carried the painful memory of the four-pound baby's fragility, and, to some degree she continued to see him in that way. Brandy guided her in another ocean unburdening and explained that Bonnie needed to see the baby as he is now, healthy and thriving, rather than as he was. She needed to adjust her view of him as he continued to grow. The unburdening was successful. Bonnie agreed to experiment with the amount of base anxiety she needed in order to be attentive to the boy's future needs.

We would check later on the effects of our work on Brandy's anxiety for the health of her son, and we would monitor any changes in the frequency of her panic attacks. We hoped to have ended them. At the end of the session, we agreed to return to work with Candace, Veronica and Kendra regarding binge eating.

Binge Eating

In session six, we spent the entire session collecting memories from Candace's memory set. We were not concerned as much with the acts of binge eating as we were with the stressful life experiences that led to binge eating as a means of coping with the stress. Candace's first memories relate to the mother's name-calling. Between the ages of 16 and 18, being called derogatory names was a regular feature of Brandy's life, disturbing Candace at a level 10. Over this same period, in addition to the verbal abuse, there was occasional violence as her mother threw things at her or in her direction. Once, her mother threw an ice skate at her. It missed, but its blade stuck in the wall. On another occasion, Brandy fought back physically, slapping her mother in response to her mother's slapping of her. The fight ended when her mother cursed her, spit on her, and manhandled her out of the house. Brandy was greatly ashamed of herself for slapping her mother. Candace rated both this and the ice skate incident as level 10 disturbances.

Brandy's father knew her mother was frequently out of control. Sometimes they fought over the mother's treatment of Brandy. Her mother blamed Brandy for her difficulties with her husband, saying more than once that they would get a divorce because of Brandy. Candace rated the guilt she felt at a level eight. Guilt was a feature of another set of memories as well. When she was 17, hoping her mother could learn to understand her, Brandy wrote an angry letter to her mother detailing her grievances and asking her to stop trying to control everything she did. Her mother responded by not talking to her for three months. Candace rated her guilt at a level seven.

In school, Brandy was "stressed out." She felt like a failure because she wasn't as good at academics as she thought she should be. For Candace, these memories rated a seven on the SUD scale. In her senior year of high school, Brandy experienced extreme loneliness. Her sister, normally her evening companion, worked at night. Her boyfriend was overseas in a student exchange program. She had given up her friendships with classmates because she thought they were out of control with drugs and alcohol. One night, mired in her loneliness, she bought "a huge quantity of food" and consumed it all in a single sitting. This was Candace's first experience with binge eating. She found it pleasurable to a level nine on the SUE scale.

In our seventh session, we began to unburden Candace, who chose a bonfire as the means of letting go of her distress over the years of the mother's name-calling. As Brandy visualized Candace standing next to the bonfire, lifting the burden out of herself and throwing it onto the fire, Brandy exclaimed, "It just dawned on me; my mother was sick! It wasn't me!" This insight was accompanied by a reduction in the SUD level from a 10 to a three or four. Although she now believed the name-calling wasn't her fault, Candace found it still hurt her feelings to be called those names. As she continued to unload more of her burden into the fire, she found herself remembering much earlier experiences and had the sense that another part was also involved in the processing.

Brandy asked Candace to look around and check to see if she could locate the other part. In a moment, Brandy reported the presence of "a little girl, about seven. She looks a lot like me when I was seven." In response to Brandy's questions, the little girl said that her name was also *Brandy* and that "she is me, but little." Evidently, recalling and processing Candace's painful memories of her mother had triggered even earlier memories carried by the younger subpersonality. When this happens, the focus has to shift to the newly appeared part. Otherwise, the unburdening work with the older part cannot be entirely successful. Consequently, we turned to the task of collecting *Little Brandy's* memory set. We wanted to understand its content, and we wanted to do whatever unburdening was necessary in order to continue our work with Candace.

Little Brandy's earliest memory was that of going to preschool with her grandmother at age four. She remembered being excited, "bubbly," running into the school. This excitement registered a nine on the SUE scale. Her earliest painful memory also dated to age four. It was of her mother and grandmother screaming at each other downstairs, and the dog barking at them, as she lay upon her grandmother's bed upstairs. She was distressed because she did not know what to do. Other painful experiences were those of her mother braiding her long hair when she was five. When her mother was upset with her, she would jerk her hair as she braided it into pigtails. Both the hair-braiding and the arguments were disturbing to a level eight.

Little Brandy was a hyperactive child, naturally happy, but "jumping out of my skin". By the second grade, she was having academic difficulties in school. When she was seven years old, with a friend visiting, she was so out of control with joy, loud laughter, and jumping around the room that she was unaware of the effect on her mother. Her mother took her to another room and "shook me so hard I thought she would hurt me. Her eyes were bulging and scary." Little Brandy had never before seen her mother so angry. She was disturbed by this memory to a level 10.

Other memories from age seven related to going with her mother to visit her great grandmother in a nursing home. Brandy remembered being "so scared of old people." She knew the old woman was dying and was relieved when she did so, because after that she didn't have to be around the old people anymore.

By the age of eight, Brandy's life "started getting really, really bad. I felt rejected by my parents and unlovable because of my hyperactivity. I had a constant feeling of a vibrating, a whirling in my mind, a fidgeting in my head. It was constant." For Little Brandy these subjective feelings, in combination with her felt sense of rejection and unlovability, were disturbing at a level eight.

Also at age eight, Brandy was tested and diagnosed with *ADHD* (*attention deficit hyperactivity disorder*). Her mother arranged for her to be prescribed Ritalin, a medication for hyperactivity. "The Ritalin calmed me," said Brandy. Interestingly, after this, Little Brandy's autobiographical memories ended. Brandy drew upon a different memory source to summarize her later school years. "I took Ritalin from eight until I got pregnant with my baby two years ago. Back then, the school district was going to put me in special education because of my hyperactivity. I could talk for hours if people let me. My mother put me in a Montessori school rather than special education. I learned nothing for three years. I went back to public school in the seventh grade. My grades were horrible. But I got serious as a junior in high school. I got a perfect score on the *ACT*." Later, she went on to graduate from a major eastern university and then moved to southern California to take her first teaching job.

We unburdened Little Brandy with a wind intervention, where Brandy visualized the child part standing between two posts planted deep in the ground while hanging onto a bar that connected the posts. Brandy then visualized a powerful wind blowing over Little Brandy. Brandy was successful in helping Little Brandy unburden a number of memories at once. The first intervention took about one minute, during which Little Brandy reduced to a zero rating the fights between her mother and grandmother, mother's pigtail-pulling, and the nursing home visitations. The memory of her mother shaking her with bulging eyes reduced to a level two, but stalled there temporarily because of the fear that the mother might shake her again. Another 30 seconds of the wind intervention reduced that memory to a zero rating. Little Brandy retained her hyperactive way of feeling but was no longer uncomfortable with it. Brandy described her inner vision of the child part: "She's hyper, laughing and running around, jumping over the bar that's between the posts." Brandy added that the child part no longer felt guilty about her hyper feelings. To complete our work with Little Brandy, Brandy visualized a safe room for her and placed her there, where, hands on hips, the child part expressed her surprise to learn that Brandy now had a baby.

As we concluded the session, we returned to Candace and the unburdening of the pain she felt for the teenage years of mother's name-calling. This was the work previously interrupted by the appearance of Little Brandy. Candace completed that unburdening in less than a minute.

Most of our eighth session was supportive therapy as we discussed Brandy's experiences as a special education teacher and her difficulties with her severely disabled students. We would return to this topic in later sessions. Near the end of the session, we continued our unburdening work with Candace, focusing upon the memory of her mother blaming her for bringing about the coming divorce from Brandy's father (which never happened). Brandy first mentioned this issue in our second therapy session, when she talked about her mother's verbal abuse of her. We now knew it was Candace who carried the pain of the memory. For the intervention, Brandy visualized

Candace lifting her guilt out of herself and throwing it into a fire pit. "This is difficult," said Brandy. "It rests in her chest, and she can't pull it out." To help break the impasse, I suggested that Brandy encourage Candace to tell more of her story of the event. "My mother was screaming in a quiet voice how, because of my running around at 13, she was getting a divorce. I remember being in my dad's office and feeling so bad about them getting a divorce because of me. I was gonna tell my friends it was because my dad had an affair, because I was embarrassed it was my fault. I told my boyfriend my dad had an affair. They never did get divorced and so I didn't think about it anymore." Having expressed herself, Candace was now able to complete the unburdening. "It's easier now," said Brandy. Very quickly the SUD level reached a zero for this event. Brandy added, "I felt myself telling Candace it wasn't her fault; it couldn't be; she was just 13 and couldn't be responsible." For our next session, we planned to process the memory of Brandy's letter to her mother at 18 and the three months of her mother's silence that followed.

In session nine, before returning to our work with Candace, Brandy shared the information that our work on her anxiety for her son's health had been successful. Bonnie, the anxious caretaker of Brandy's son, had been calm recently. Brandy had taken her son on a picnic outing and to a friend's house without experiencing significant fear for his health. There had been no panic attacks since therapy began.

Brandy also talked about her anger. She had so far been unsuccessful in visualizing the angry part, although she had searched for it outside of our sessions. The need to work with this part was clear from an incident during the week. She had taken her son for his scheduled MRI and had waited an hour and a half past the appointment time. When called for the MRI, she discovered that the nurse was supposed to have given her son a sedative an hour before his procedure. Consequently, it was yet another hour before the MRI could be performed. "I went off on her! I wanted to go over the counter and strangle her!" Brandy added that she had many fights as a teenager and was still ready for confrontation in the present. "I suffer road rage," she said. "I chase them down." It was clear that we would eventually have to differentiate this angry part and process its memory set. First, however, we had more work to do with Candace.

We began by unburdening Candace of the effects of the accusatory letter she had written to her mother when she was 18. For this, Brandy used a waterfall metaphor, visualizing the water flowing over Candace as she released her hurt feelings over her mother's angry silence. The unburdening was straightforward, with Brandy's only comment being, "I could hear myself saying [to Candace], 'You could have been more tactful, but the things you wrote were true. And Mother was an adult, and she should have been able to handle it.'" A check of the SUD level found that the incident had been fully processed and had reached a zero.

The next unburdening, also using the waterfall metaphor, processed multiple memories over a couple of years and required considerably more effort from Candace. We wanted to unburden Brandy's sense of failure for her college performance. College had been much more demanding than she had expected. The initial attempt at unburdening reduced the level seven disturbance to only a level five. Brandy explained, "Candace did a lot of memories. Just when she thinks she's got them all done, something else comes up. The feelings continued through college. She felt stupid that she disappointed her professors, her family. A few times, I was flat out inadequate. I would go home and stress over what I left out of a test—and then I'd go to a party—it was embarrassing." A second unburdening at this point reduced the SUD level to a one. It was a stubborn remnant of the original level seven. "There's still a low-level feeling of failure. I hear myself telling her, 'Look at how good you are at teaching now.'" After a pause, Brandy shared a related memory: "I was a theatre major and the lighting design manager for a play. Another student was competitive with me and he thought he should be the manager, and he took every opportunity to show me up, embarrass me. I was afraid of heights and he told me to change a light. I refused and he made a big deal of it and put me down in front of other people." Because Candace was unable to easily let go of her embarrassment, we urged her to speak to her internal image of the competitive classmate, and to tell him what she felt about his actions. She did so and immediately felt better. Brandy went on then to talk about other embarrassments. "I skipped a lot of classes because I was hung over. In my small design class, it was noticeable. I made up stories as excuses so I wouldn't get a lowered grade. I believe my professors knew I had a drinking problem but they let me pass. But in my senior year a new professor caught me in a lie and wrote a letter to the Chair and I was afraid I wouldn't graduate." In order to release Candace from her guilt and embarrassment, we coached her to apologize to the remembered images of this and all of her other professors to whom she had lied. After she did so, one additional repetition of the waterfall intervention finally reduced the failure memories to zero distress.

In the preceding narrative, Brandy switches between using the third person for Candace and the first person for herself, as in: "She felt stupid, that she disappointed her professors, her family. A few times I was flat out inadequate." This pattern is common when working with parts. At one moment, Brandy views Candace as separate from her and in the next moment, she views Candace as herself. The narrative also illustrates the difference in difficulty level between processing a single memory, and processing a set of memories that are connected to an attitude or belief. In this case, the belief was that she was a failure, but the belief was founded upon her perception of a number of experiences over several years. Unburdening generalized negative beliefs will usually take more time and effort than unburdening specific beliefs or attitudes that are linked to a single incident.

We thought we had reached closure on the treatment of Candace's major negative experiences. For this reason, it seemed time to begin work on desensitizing the actual pleasurable aspects of bingeing. We turned to Candace's memory of her first episode of binge eating during her senior year of high school. Candace rated this positive experience at a level nine on the SUE scale. She agreed to unburden the energy with the waterfall metaphor; however, she ran into immediate difficulty. Brandy visualized her in the waterfall, but then said, "She's nervous about giving up the energy. It's something that's been so much a part of her life. She's remembering how many times she's said, 'Just one more time and then I'll give it up.'" When Brandy checked the SUE level, she found it unchanged at a level nine. Previous experience with reluctant parts suggested that Candace should still have been able to reduce the SUE level by one or two. Consequently, I coached Brandy to ask Candace about the presence of another part who might be blocking the work. Candace identified an angry part as the one preventing her from unburdening the positive energy of bingeing.

Because we were at the end of the session and did not want the bingeing energy to overcome Brandy during the week, we coached Candace to put it into a container until we had more time to work with it. Brandy visualized herself helping Candace put the energy into a safe in her garage. We planned to process the positive memories of bingeing after we had located the angry part and done whatever work we needed to do to gain its cooperation. We knew from the beginning that we had a lot of work to do with anger. As we closed the session Brandy observed, "I'm scared of the angry part. It's embarrassing to be so crazy. It began when I was 12."

Anger as a Monster

In our next session, the tenth, Brandy had still been unable to access the anger part directly. Consequently, she connected with Candace and asked her to bridge to the angry one and bring it onto Brandy's internal screen. She did so without difficulty. The new part's name was *Phyllis,* a name she claimed she had before Brandy sought her out. Brandy saw her as "an older lady" in her 60s. Her manner of dress was unclear, but Brandy imagined her as having "grey hair pulled into a bun." When Brandy asked, Phyllis responded that she was aware of how she and Brandy were connected. "She said she is a part of me and I'm the head person. 'You're the person who's supposed to tell me what to do but I don't like it very much.'" Phyllis's earliest memory dated to the fifth grade. At that time, Brandy was in a private school and there were two girls, sisters, who were "a big part" of her life. "They were over, and we were making a video about corn flakes and I spelled it *corn flaks.* They made fun of me. I was mortified. It felt like they were ganging up on me." The memory disturbed Phyllis to a level seven or eight. Another memory involving the same friends also registered at a level seven or eight. Brandy said, "I was hyper and couldn't control it, even with my pills. I took them with me when I did overnights. Their mother accused me of spitting out my Ritalin pill. She looked everywhere for it. The sisters egged her on, 'Look here! Look there!' I was so embarrassed."

After these incidents, Phyllis did not have clear disturbing memories, except for being angry with her mother for frequently yelling at her. In middle school, her memories are positive. She had her first physical fight in the summer between her seventh and eighth grades. The fight was with a "random" girl at a county fair; it developed from an exchange of remarks that escalated to a fistfight. Phyllis, as Brandy, knocked the girl down. She ran off with a bloody nose. The fight was pleasurable to Phyllis at a level nine on the SUE scale. After this, Phyllis was involved in many confrontations, usually verbal only, with "a lot of screaming and yelling." In the eighth grade, Phyllis "got in a teacher's face" and screamed at her just as she would a classmate. Brandy observed that following this incident she "got lots of credibility with other kids." This and other encounters during the same period rated a positive eight or nine on the SUE scale.

As Brandy grew older and transitioned from middle school to high school, Phyllis "became more verbally abusive toward her family and friends. She was mean to everybody in high school." In her senior year, Brandy was active in theatre, as she would be in college. One night while working late on a project for a coming play, the school janitor asked her what she was doing at the school at 10 PM. "I was rude, disrespectful, cursing. I had permission to be there but I still got suspended for how I talked to him." Even with the suspension for her actions, Phyllis rated the experience as a positive level five on the SUE scale. She was rating the pleasure of expressing anger and the feeling of power it gave to her.

Brandy pointed out that when Phyllis acted in a mean way to strangers, she did so intentionally; but when she was abusive to her family and friends, "It's like it happens to her. She doesn't realize she's doing it." Thus, Brandy was a victim of dissociative rage, something she experienced as happening to her, rather than something she directed at others. We have seen this in other chapters. What is interesting here is that Brandy made clear that dissociative rage wasn't just *her* experience; Phyllis also experienced dissociative rage. She, too, was driven by the rage as opposed to being its driver. We would come back to this matter later in therapy.

Two more recent incidents fill out Phyllis's memory set. When Brandy was 20, a teenage driver cut her off. Phyllis became enraged and chased the girl for 20 minutes, through parking lots and up and down streets. When she finally caught up to her, she rolled down her window and threw a can of soda at her. "The girl was terrified," said Brandy. For Phyllis, the incident was positive to a level eight. The other incident happened just a few months before Brandy came to therapy, and also rated a level eight score. Phyllis "went off" (i.e., cursed and screamed) on a woman who blocked Brandy's exit from a hospital parking garage as the woman awkwardly tried to maneuver her vehicle into a tight parking space. Brandy explained that these experiences were generally quite positive for Phyllis, although she might experience "a small amount of guilt and embarrassment later for having her loved ones see it." Note here that Brandy is describing Phyllis's feelings, but she is also talking about herself. She went on, "I'm afraid they'll think I'm crazy." We can also note here the likelihood that the "guilt and embarrassment" Brandy feels is probably an amplification from another part, rather than a reflection of something coming directly from Phyllis. Individual parts probably do not experience opposing emotions at the same time unless they combine their own with those of another part.

With a good sense of Phyllis's memory set, Brandy then asked her why she was blocking our work on Candace's bingeing. "She says she likes bingeing, too. She's afraid she'll have nothing left without binging, and she's afraid she'll just be angry all the time. And she'd be angry with the people closest to her." Thus, the bingeing provides Phyllis some temporary escape from her constant anger.

Brandy went on, "She doesn't realize she is being so rude, nasty, and condescending to her husband. She knows what she's saying but doesn't comprehend why someone is offended." This seemed to be at least partially related to the fact that Brandy did not always remember what she said, especially to her husband. She would deny that she said the things her husband insisted she said. Amnesia for things said and done during a rage is characteristic of dissociative rage. Phyllis took over so completely that Brandy didn't remember what she said. We would normally expect that Phyllis would remember the content of her own experience. However, there was a twist here. Sometimes even Phyllis didn't remember what she said in her rages. This finding led us to search for the subpersonality who *did* remember. Thus, I coached Brandy to ask Phyllis to "look within" herself and check to see if there was another part of her who remembered what *she* did not. The answer was, "Yes," and Phyllis herself was afraid of the part. It was, said Brandy, "a monstrous-looking part, a shadowy, demon-looking part." But she could not see the part clearly. Because we were too late in the session to open up disturbing material, Brandy asked Phyllis to "put away" the monstrous looking part until our next session. "That's not hard to do," Brandy said, "because it didn't come out too far." We planned to investigate this internal monster in our next session.

When we returned to the therapy in session 11, the new angry part was our focus. Brandy continued to interview Phyllis, who confirmed again the existence of a "monstrous-looking" part. Phyllis thought of it as she did herself, as having no remorse. She acknowledged that it sometimes took over from her. It had no name, and its image was "shadowy, misty, very dark, very tall—eight feet—and also wide." When Brandy turned her attention directly to this part, she found that she could communicate with it. We began to speak of it as *The Monster*. Brandy described its view of her as "the person who runs the show, although I don't do a very good job." It was also aware that it was a part of Brandy. It did not know its age, but felt "old, like it's been around for a long time." It felt like an adult. It did not have a gender, and it thought of Brandy as a child.

When Brandy asked about its earliest memory, The Monster said it was "having a hard time thinking," and finally said that it did not want to talk about the earliest memory. Brandy asked about any memory at all and was rewarded with a remembered scene in which her mother was "yelling, crying, swearing at a sales person in a store." That was when The Monster realized that "my mother wasn't like other kids' mothers." Brandy observed that The Monster's memories were "quick flashes" and "harder to pin down" than those of other parts. Then, suddenly, it gave her its earliest memory, dating to age four. Brandy said, "A 17 year old boy was in our house. He made me put things in my vagina. He never came back again." From there, Brandy flashed forward to the time when she told her husband she had been molested, but she told him it had been by an uncle. "It felt better to tell this weird story than to tell what really happened." Brandy commented on these memories, saying that she was "just now learning what really happened. It becomes more clear." Evidently, The Monster had kept the details of the memories away from Brandy's awareness. In fact, this is a function of most dissociated parts.

It seemed appropriate to bring The Monster up to date with Brandy's life, so she shared with it that she was an adult, and visualized for it her view of herself as she saw herself in her mirror. She also shared internal pictures of her husband and baby son. She then introduced the idea of changing The Monster's role in her life, from raging to something that would allow Brandy to have better relationships with others. The Monster indicated it was willing to help, but it had heard other parts talk about changing their jobs and he didn't know what other job he could do. "He's just anger and rage," said Brandy, noting that she had begun to perceive the Monster as a male. He agreed to begin unburdening himself of his early memories, but was pessimistic, according to Brandy.

Brandy guided The Monster to the idea of unburdening the molestation at age four, and he quickly took over the visualization metaphor utilizing a bonfire. Very quickly the memory was reduced to the necessary zero level of distress. "It was easy to do," Brandy reported. "He took out different parts of the room where it happened and threw them onto the fire, and lots of other memories, too." The Monster then wanted to unburden other memories, as well. "He lies a lot," Brandy revealed, as she recalled her early years in college. "I lied that I had been pregnant before, about where I grew up, about how much money I made, and that my parents worked in professions they didn't." When asked the purpose of lying, Brandy said of The Monster, "He lies to help people feel that I'm accomplished, or knew or experienced things they had not, so they would like me." He agreed to unburden himself of his urge to lie by throwing it onto the bonfire. In less than a minute Brandy said, "Okay, yes, it's gone."

We asked then if The Monster had other memories to unburden, and his immediate response was, "No." As the interview continued, Brandy learned that he did not consider himself a part of Phyllis, although that was where we found him. Regarding a new job description, he thought that he could learn to be balanced with his anger. With some unburdening accomplished, Brandy noted that The Monster's appearance had changed. He wasn't as large as he once was, and "I can see patches of the real person underneath — a little child — and there's something deformed about him, and he seems to be male." Although The Monster could be seen now as a smaller person, and a "real person," Brandy visualized him as having "holes in his face with pus, missing toes and fingers, and eyeballs hanging out." In his damaged but more human-like form, The Monster acknowledged that there was more healing to do. He still did not want a name of his own.

This initial work with The Monster illustrates some of the familiar phenomena we find in work with parts. First, there are the changes in physical appearance that The Monster experienced as he processed painful memories. As with the unburdening of other parts, these changes are symbolic representations of progress made. Second, there is The Monster's lack of awareness of Brandy's current adult life. Somehow, his rage was triggered by circumstances in Brandy's current life without his awareness of the actual current problem. Finally, he denied that he was a part of Phyllis. Yet, before we began to interact with him directly, Brandy had visualized him as emerging from angry Phyllis. Angry Phyllis experienced him as overwhelming her with rage in the same way that Brandy experienced Phyllis overwhelming her. He denied he was a part of Phyllis just as some other parts initially deny they are parts of the self upon first differentiation. In such cases, it seems prudent to educate the part about the larger system.

We were near the end of the session when we asked Phyllis to join our discussion. Both she and The Monster objected to unburdening Candace, the binge eater. They experienced Candace's food bingeing as somewhat calming to them. Phyllis said that she was no longer afraid of The Monster, and saw him more like "a little, deformed troll." Because we were at the end of the session, and Brandy didn't want The Monster to overwhelm her during the coming week, she transported him to a "safe room" where he could involve himself with the range of toys and entertainment possibilities that she visualized for him. He agreed to work with us again in our next session. Phyllis, apparently still somewhat frightened of The Monster after all, did not want to share a safe room with him, so Brandy gave her an imagined room of her own.

Anger as a Boy

In session twelve, we returned immediately to work with The Monster who Brandy was now calling *Monster Boy*. She had had a difficult time with her special needs students during the week, and she traced some of her emotional difficulties to Monster Boy. "He gets really frustrated and angry with the kids I work with at school," said Brandy. He agreed, however, to unburden his frustration to wind. Brandy visualized him "throwing it up into the wind on a really windy day" and letting the wind carry it away. She soon reported that it was "fairly easy" for Monster Boy to release his anger toward four of her five students, but the fifth child "was more difficult, because he takes seven hours of attention every day and then he goes home and his parents destroy everything I've done." For example, she had succeeded this year in getting her blind and deaf eight-year-old student out of diapers and into using her classroom's built-in restroom facilities. Then she trained him to begin using the regular boys' restroom urinals. Unfortunately, after a weekend spent with his parents, he tried to sit in a urinal rather than stand up and face it when he relieved his bladder. "Monster Boy gets angry with the child and not with the parents, but it's the parents who don't want him to stand [to urinate] because they don't want to clean it up!"

In theory, the unburdening of day-to-day stress, such as that caused by Brandy's difficulties with her students, should be fairly easily accomplished. Unburdening the *current-time* stress in a person's life can be a regular coping strategy for dealing with life events. However, because it focuses only on present-time experience, this sort of unburdening cannot solve a problem exacerbated by *earlier* life experiences. Monster Boy's inability to release his current anger suggested that we needed to look further into Brandy's past for the triggering events that prevented current-time unburdening. Using an affect bridge, Brandy asked Monster Boy to focus on the anger he felt in relation to the handicapped student, and then to let his mind "float back in time to memories that somehow connected to that anger." He bridged to a set of experiences involving Brandy's hyperactivity. "In school, teachers didn't know how to deal with my hyperactivity. I remember being yelled at by teachers and also by my parents. And I felt so much frustration over not being good at school work—my spelling and reading." Brandy then guided Monster Boy in unburdening this childhood frustration through use of the same wind metaphor he had previously used. The intervention was quickly accomplished, and Monster Boy soon reported a SUD level of zero for those experiences. We returned then to unburdening Monster Boy of his current-time frustration of working with handicapped children. As the part's frustration reached a temporary level of zero, Brandy observed, "I see more clearly that it's the parents who I need to work with, but I'm not sure how to do it."

Monster Boy now looked more like a boy than a monster. "Only his hands are monster hands and covered in holes and pus." I asked Brandy to focus on the monster hands and notice how she felt about them as she bridged to her earliest memories that somehow connected to her feelings about the monster hands. The memory that surfaced was connected to the burglary and vandalism of her family home when Brandy was seven years old. "After they broke into the house they trashed the backyard. They threw a lot of stuff into the pool. My parents were cleaning the pool, and my dad was diving into the pool to bring up stuff from the bottom. I wanted to show him a picture I had drawn, but he rejected me. He kept diving into the pool. Then I set out to make him feel bad. I cried and tore up my picture and kept crying until he got out and consoled me." It was Monster Boy who carried this memory, and it disturbed him to a level seven on the SUD scale. However, the memory also registered a nine on the positive energy SUE scale. Brandy first unburdened Monster Boy of the negative energy connected to rejection by her father. She used the metaphor of releasing the burden into a powerfully blowing wind. After processing the negative energy of rejection to zero, Brandy turned her attention to the positive energy Monster Boy felt for being able to control her father. She observed, "This is the pleasure in the power that comes from manipulating people. It's more difficult to let go of." Still, after only about three minutes of Brandy's visualization of Monster Boy giving up this energy to wind, the memory was neutralized. It had reached zero on the positive energy scale. "But I can tell," said Brandy, "that pleasure in manipulating people is a big component of him."

Monster Boy's next memory related to the time when, after age ten, Brandy's hyperactivity got her "into a lot of trouble" in public school. Because of this "trouble," her parents tried to find a better school environment for her. They put her into a private Montessori school that Brandy described as an educational waste of her three years there. The lack of structure meant to her that she did what she wanted and learned virtually nothing. The incident recalled by Monster Boy had to do with his ability to display his power. In Brandy's second year in the school, she got a new teacher. "The teacher was new, young—she seemed okay. But then one day she flipped— she yelled, cried, and generally had a melt down over something in class, I don't remember what. I went to an older teacher and told her that my teacher was crazy and needed help, and I told my parents how scared I was—I wasn't; I was used to that from my mom—and my parents took action and the teacher was fired." The experience rated an eight or nine on the positive SUE scale for Monster Boy. It felt good to be able to affect the adult world so powerfully. Yet he cooperated fully when Brandy asked him to unburden this energy. Once again, the wind intervention reduced the positive energy connected to the memory to a zero. This work brought us to the end of the session. At that time, Brandy noted, "Monster Boy looks more normal now. He looks like a person and not a troll. But he still has more stuff though. I think it's guilt for being like this and for taking pleasure in doing things to people." In our next session, we planned to do additional work with Monster Boy, and, once we had finished processing his memories, we planned to return to Phyllis, the original raging part. We would also check on the previous week's interactions with Brandy's students, expecting that her interactions with them would be from a more centered place.

In session 13, it quickly became clear that we were not yet ready to return to Phyllis. We had more work to do with Monster Boy's rage. Nor was there the stress reduction Brandy expected for working with her special needs children. "Because of our work I thought I wouldn't have so much anger with the kids, but it was actually more intense for the first few days." Brandy did find some improvement in how she dealt with adults. An aide in the school program blew up over things Brandy asked of her and, in the process, said some uncaring things about Brandy's own child. Brandy explained, "Last week I would have told her off; now I don't think it's a big deal. She's a troubled woman; her kids are in trouble and her husband is in jail. It's really not about me."

We examined more closely the "choking anger" Brandy felt during the first two workdays after our last session. She checked with Monster Boy to see if the anger came from him. It did. Monster Boy did not know Brandy was a teacher, but he did know Brandy's most difficult student, the handicapped boy who required almost full-time attention. It was toward this student that Monster Boy felt his "choking anger." Realizing that it was just this one boy who enraged her, Brandy felt a need to follow the anger to its source. She knew her anger was irrational and that it inhibited her teaching. She used an affect bridge to link her (and Monster Boy's) feelings toward the student to memories from her past. Focusing on the feelings, she allowed her mind to drift back in time to the earliest memory she had that seemed to be connected to those feelings. The early memory that surfaced dated to elementary school and was disturbing to a level seven on the SUD scale. The setting was that of doing homework with the help of her father. "I felt my dad was disappointed that I wasn't learning fast enough," and, as Monster Boy's perspective broke through into Brandy's narrative, "that you were stupid." "My father was impatient, always rushing me. 'Hurry up! Hurry up!'" Monster Boy agreed to the unburdening of this memory, and Brandy guided him in releasing his anger into an imagined fire pit, where his negative feelings were consumed in the flames. Only a single instance of the intervention was needed to reduce the disturbance to a zero. When Brandy checked with Monster Boy for further troubling memories involving the father, she found that his thoughts about the father were only "somewhat disturbing" and not significant enough to warrant additional unburdening.

Brandy's affect bridge also connected Monster Boy's "choking anger" with an age 12 incident when Brandy's grandfather told her "You would look a lot better if you lost 20 pounds." The experience continued to disturb Monster Boy to a level seven. Another linking memory was that of Brandy's mother screaming at visiting friends of hers when she was 13. Monster Boy could not remember the reason for the mother's rage, but it disturbed him to a level eight. Finally, Brandy remembered that when she was 14 she was "slim and tall and dressing provocatively and my mother called me a slut a bunch of times." Once, her mother told her, "You take so many showers because you're dirty and a slut!" The mother's name-calling disturbed Monster Boy to a level nine. Evidently, another part of her felt good, however, because she remembered feeling that "If my mother is calling me a slut, I must look good!"

We were at the end of the session and had accessed a lot of Monster Boy's negative energy. In order to protect Brandy from unintentional consequences of this newly accessed energy, we coached Monster Boy to store the energy in appropriate containers until our next session.

At the beginning of session 14, Brandy summarized her experience with anger for the previous week. For the first two workdays after our session, her anger with her problem student remained unchanged. The next three workdays were much better. She indicated that she was able to calm herself before her anger became too great. She looked within herself and talked to Monster Boy during those times. For example, she might ask him, "Why are you so angry?" These conversations were "very helpful" in controlling her anger.

We turned then to the task of unburdening Monster Boy of the negative energy attached to the memories accessed at the end of the previous session. Unlike most unburdening in which I coached Brandy in visualizing the intervention, this time she took charge of the process herself, quickly guiding Monster Boy in dumping into a fire pit his hurt feelings over the grandfather's comments about her need to lose 20 pounds. She next used the fire pit to incinerate her negative feelings connected to her mother's screaming at her friends. "I pictured Monster Boy in the fire, holding pictures [of memories] burning from the center outward." She also unburdened memories of her mother's many remarks "where she assumed I was sleeping around and having sex with multiple partners—but I was still a virgin. She'd say if I got pregnant she wasn't gonna take care of it. And she took me to a gynecologist for birth control. And I also unburdened Mother saying I took lots of showers because I was dirty and a slut."

We had completed the unburdening of all of Monster Boy's significant experiences that he had so far shared with us. We asked then whether he had other memories that should also be unburdened. There were a few more. When Brandy was 11 and 12 her mother required her enrollment in an after-school dance class with other girls her age. "I wasn't as good as the other girls. I didn't practice as much as they did and I wanted to cut back. But she wanted me to do more. On the way home from classes she would compare me to the other girls and talk about how I should be like them and how I sucked." With Brandy's guidance, Monster Boy quickly released his level six or seven distress to the fire pit. Another disturbing set of memories, also level six or seven on the SUD scale, had to do with her mother's criticism of Brandy's friendships with older boys. "When I was 14 and 15 I hung out with older boys—my husband was one of them—my mother tried to keep me away from him. And the boy who introduced us was a good friend of both of us, and he was there, too. I felt that this really good thing with my future husband was being contaminated by all the other stuff." Once again,

Monster Boy successfully consigned to the fire pit the negative emotions connected to these memories.

At the end of our session, Brandy reported, "Monster Boy is exhausted." Consequently, she suggested that we check at the beginning of our next session to see if there were any additional memories that needed to be processed. She also noted that "He looks younger and younger and isn't a monster any more. He's now about three years old and he has normal, little-boy hands." We intended to return to the angry adult, Phyllis, if our work with Monster Boy was finished.

In session 15, Brandy talked first about the week between out meetings. She had had "a big fight" with her sister who lived with her, but she had been better with her problem student at school. She had experienced one episode of binge eating, which she believed had to do with the fight with her sister. However, she pointed out that when she first came to therapy she had been bingeing almost daily, and this was the first instance of it since we unburdened the first set of memories three months previously. Brandy explained that she now understood that she had actually been angry with her sister's boyfriend, and that her sister had been merely a more convenient target for her outburst. "I screamed as loudly as my throat would permit." She had binged on food the day after her fight with her sister, but once they had resolved their differences, she did no further binge eating during the week. Resolving their differences included deciding amicably that having the sister and boyfriend living with Brandy's family was not a good thing for now.

We decided to go inside and check with Candace, who was responsible for binge eating. Brandy summarized her inner conversation with Candace: "She said she had just been feeling low all week and thinking of doing it all week, and so she picked my fight with my sister as an excuse. She says it wasn't a positive feeling like before. The food didn't even taste good." The fact that Candace could taste the food was different, too. "Before, she didn't taste it at all."

Brandy also discovered that *the screamer* in her fight with her sister was Phyllis. "Monster Boy is just concerned with my student. I think Monster Boy is so angry because he hates my student, and that's because he thinks my student caused my premature birthing—with stress—because he [the student] is such an animal." Brandy agreed it would be a good idea to unburden Monster Boy of his hate for her troublesome student. When she began the intervention, which was supposed to use fire to incinerate the hate, she found herself visualizing Monster Boy throwing *her student* into the fire pit rather than his hate. This illustrates again that internal parts are not just passive participants in the process. She went on to help Monster Boy unburden with gentler imagery. In a few minutes she said, "Monster Boy is now exhausted by the fire. He would exude a coating of purple hate and peel off the whole layer and throw it into the fire, and then another layer would appear and he would do it again. Finally, he lay down next to the fire in his natural skin. And then I heard my own voice telling him, 'He didn't know; he didn't know. He didn't mean to. You don't have to love him but I do—I love him a lot—it's okay if you don't like him.' Monster Boy says he doesn't have any more hate." Brandy added, "He doesn't really like the boy; he *is* kind of 'bratty' sometimes."

We were near the end of the session, but we still had time to find Phyllis and ask her about the fight with Brandy's sister. Phyllis pointed out that Brandy's sister and her boyfriend lived with Brandy and her husband at minimal cost. The boyfriend "buys crap from the store and buys stuff from eBay, but the last time he paid rent to us, he was late. He only pays $150 a month. And Phyllis had been thinking, just one more thing and she would go off on him. And then he was gonna take my son to the pool at twelve noon in 100 degree heat. I scolded him. Then the next morning my sister said I didn't have the right to talk to him like that—but I did, and I screamed at her. I screamed as loud as my throat would let me."

Phyllis also acknowledged that it was she who drove Candace's last binge. She said she got some relief from the bingeing, but not nearly as much as she had hoped. This finding is important. It makes clear that working just with the part who is identified as the holder of the problem is sometimes not enough to fix the problem. The identified problem part is enmeshed in a web of relationships such that other parts may have an investment in the actions of the problem part. Resistance should be expected from the other parts who may fear that a change will adversely affect their situations. In the present case, we needed to work with angry Phyllis if we were to successfully help Candace permanently end her binge eating.

Career Developments

In session 16, we did not return to the problems of either anger or binge eating. Instead, we worked with current job issues and Brandy's concerns about making somewhat of a career change. She wanted to enter a second master's degree program at her nearby California university and then move toward work with a different classification of special needs children. This would mean that she had to end work with her current category of children. She had some misgivings about this. The directors of her present work program had been quite supportive of her. Additionally, she was concerned about the students she would leave behind, especially the boy for whom different parts of her felt both love and dislike (formerly hate).

Brandy's career issues provide a good illustration of the value of Parts Psychology in the treatment of current as well as past issues. When Brandy checked with her parts, it was Candace, the binge eater, who felt badly about making a career change. It appeared that she had a broader role in Brandy's life than just providing a physical outlet for accumulated stress. Candace was the part who carried Brandy's desire to feel irreplaceable; she wanted to feel that no one else could do what she did as well as she did. She had that feeling where Brandy presently worked. Additionally, the children she would leave behind might not get a replacement who could help them as much as Brandy could. Thinking about moving on to another program, also led her to feel guilt for "breaking trust" with both the parents of her greatest problem student, and the supervisor who recruited her for her present position. The parents trusted her to give their child what he needed, and the supervisor had supported her in her problems with other parents and with school administrators. In order to bring out Brandy's problematic emotions, I coached her to rehearse goodbye scenes with each of those she had to tell of her decision. Guilt and fear were the most prominent emotions. Following an internal discussion of the difficulties of balancing career opportunities with the problem of weakening or leaving behind important links to others, Brandy asked Candace to unburden her guilt for saying good-bye to old friends and relationships. She visualized Candace standing in an open field as wind blew over her carrying away that guilt. Following this wind intervention Candace reported the guilt was gone, but now she felt fear for how people might react when she told them of her plans for leaving. As Brandy repeated the intervention, she reported that initially Candace couldn't determine the appropriate amount of apprehension to have for the leave-taking. Finally, however, after additional exposure of Candace to the wind, Brandy said, "I think it's okay. It feels better. I'm ready to do it." As this example illustrates, unburdening is not just an intervention for dealing with the past, it also works well in rehearsing for an anticipated event in the near future.

In session 17, Brandy said that the farewell scenes she had rehearsed had all gone well. The supervisor was happy for her and her worries about her existing students were unfounded. She introduced her students to the new class they would join for the following year. They all fit in, especially the one student about whom she was most worried.

Unfortunately, just before leaving home for our session Brandy opened a letter from her new program committee. She was stunned by its contents. The letter stated that she did not qualify for the new program. Phyllis was furious with the committee members; they had previously given her their tentative approval. Now they were saying she did not have the necessary background. Because of them, Brandy had begun the process of letting go that had been the focus of our work in the previous session. Candace now felt "embarrassed and humiliated" that Brandy would now have to "grovel" to get back her previous job.

We spent the remainder of the session doing emotional damage control. First, Brandy chose a fire pit metaphor to incinerate Candace's anticipated humiliation. However, Phyllis interrupted the intervention as soon as it began. She was too angry to cooperate. I coached Brandy then to explain that she needed Phyllis's help over the next few days as she tried to figure out how best to preserve and enhance her career. Once Phyllis was willing to be helpful, Brandy tried the same fire pit metaphor with her. But Phyllis couldn't unload her anger. Instead, she was overcome with panic. Brandy searched for the panicky part and found it in Nina, the part who had experienced panic attacks relating to the health of Brandy's son. Now, said Brandy, Nina was "catastrophizing:" She was afraid of being out of work with no job prospects, of being unable to pay bills, of starving. She would not allow Brandy to soothe her fears. I coached Brandy to utilize a wind metaphor for unburdening current anxiety. She visualized a strong wind blowing over Nina, letting it carry away her fears even as she expressed them to Brandy. Brandy said, "She's afraid of not having a job, of staying at home, or if she gets her old job back, of being thought of as arrogant, of being an idiot, stuff like that." Brandy renewed the wind intervention and said of Nina, "She's disappointed in me. She thinks I blew it. I should never have tried for the new program." Finally, after Brandy once more renewed the wind intervention, Nina gave her permission to unburden Phyllis's anger. Phyllis was unwilling to release her anger, but agreed to permit the unburdening of Candace, who "shouldn't have to pay for my stupidity" in trusting what people say. As the session ended, we were finally able to return to Candace's fire pit intervention. After Brandy visualized Candace burning up her fears and anticipated embarrassment about asking to return to her old job, she was able to say that Candace was better now, but still not at a zero level of disturbance. She added that Phyllis would hold onto her anger "just for those who misled her." We ended the session with the understanding that we would adjust the content of our next meeting according to developments at that time.

Two weeks later, Brandy had good news at our 18th session. She had gone over the heads of those who told her she lacked the necessary certifications for her new program. She found an advocate who negotiated for her directly with representatives of the state of California. Her advocate was able to argue successfully that, although she lacked the specific certification now required of her, her work experience demonstrated that she was more than qualified for the new training program. She would be able to pursue her career in the way she had hoped. She would not have to apologize or "grovel" to anyone to get back her old job.

Resolving Anger and Binge Eating

During the two weeks between our sessions, Brandy had experienced greater control over her anger than she expected. She did not rage during the entire period. Unfortunately, her binging behavior returned. After more than three months with only a single binge, Brandy had binged four times in the last two weeks. She thought the source of the bingeing was entirely Candace. Phyllis and Monster Boy seemed to have tried to help her to stay calm. When she checked with Candace, she found her embarrassed and feeling badly that she binged. The binges were not impulse eating. Each was carefully planned and carried out, just as she used to do. Candace was feeling anxious about leaving behind her severely handicapped problem student. "She loves him so much. Saying goodbye in three weeks [at the end of the term] is really powerful. She's the only part who wants to stay with him."

Candace's anticipation of the loss of her relationship with the student, linked to a previous loss she had experienced during Brandy's final months of college. She and four other students had rented a house together and formed close friendships. As their lease approached its termination, two of the other students moved out and onto their new paths. One of the roommates, however, had stopped coming home at all. All of his possessions were still in the house, but he had become a heavy drug user with another crowd. After two months of trying to get in touch with him and leaving messages that he needed to collect his things because of the ending of the lease, Brandy, who was in charge of preparing the house for its return to the owners, gave her roommate's things to charity and turned over the keys to the landlord. Two days later the roommate called her and demanded his things. He was enraged that she had given away his possessions and told her he would never talk to her again. Candace, experiencing through Brandy, was devastated at the loss of her friend. She registered her distress at a level nine on the SUD scale. We used an ocean metaphor to unburden Candace of her loss. As Brandy visualized Candace swimming in the gentle surf, she coaxed her to feel the water dissolving the pain of the loss she felt. Candace quickly reduced her distress to a level one, which was about sadness—sadness that the incident happened, sadness that her friend was an addict, and sadness that she didn't know what eventually happened to him. A single repetition of the intervention, which included Candace yelling at her friend for "doing dumb things," brought the memory to a zero level of distress.

In session 19, Brandy reported having "a really good week." "It was easy," she said, "to deal with what would have been difficult before. I didn't get angry." Brandy was also pleased that she had found a new role for Candace to replace the old role of soothing through eating. "I want to be a

Vegan [a type of vegetarian], and I think Candace needs a job having to do with food. She agrees with the change." Brandy added that becoming a Vegan wasn't just about her body but was "on ethical grounds, also."

We returned to work with Candace by asking her to scan her memory set and to look for other memories that needed attention. She responded by recalling a memory she had intentionally withheld from us. It was her first memory of associating eating with calming herself. Brandy explained, "I was 13 and a bit chubby. It wasn't a big deal. I had a reputation among my friends as a person who loved food. I remember watching TV and just continuously eating potato chips. I wasn't hungry but I wanted to keep eating. It was the first time I recognized that food didn't have to be used for just nutrition. I realized that the feeling of pleasant/unpleasant stuffing of myself helped me with my stress." The positive energy level for this experience registered at a nine for Candace. Just prior to this incident Brandy had had a fight with her mother, who was angry with her for her poor performance in school. "I was feeling pouty, inadequate, and angry." This incident was important because it was probably the experience that fueled Brandy's use of food as a means of escaping from stress.

Another of Candace's memories also dated to age 13, but a bit later in the seventh grade. Brandy described "sitting at my desk and feeling my legs and stomach, and my stomach roll, and realizing, 'Oh my god! This is how fat people feel.' I had thoughts about how no boy will ever like me." The memory was disturbing to a level eight.

Brandy quickly unburdened these memories through use of a waterfall metaphor, visualizing Candace standing in the water with her hair plastered to her head and her clothes plastered to her body as the water dissolved both the positive and negative energy. She said of Candace, "She's getting better at unburdening. She visualizes the burden as a red-colored liquid in blue water. She gets angry when the last of the burden won't go and she punches it out of her." Brandy added, "Her appearance has also changed. Before, she was a 'schlubby' looking person, dumpy and unkempt. Now she is more slender, like a normal slender body type. She's a more attractive person, pulled together." A final check of her memory set revealed no additional experiences that required unburdening.

We planned to work with angry Phyllis in our next session. In anticipation of that, Brandy said of Phyllis: "She is much more aware of herself now and her role within me. I feel her anger and I talk to her about it. It used to come on suddenly and now it grows more gradually. Being angry at my loved ones has really gone down. She really wants to be able to use her anger for getting things accomplished without losing herself in rage."

Two weeks later, we met for session 20. At the beginning of the session Brandy observed, "The last two weeks have been really good. I think Phyllis is getting close [to finishing her therapy]. She was able to be firm about my sister moving out without raging. I think just two weeks ago I would have gone off on her." We returned then to further work with Phyllis's memory set.

At the age of six or seven, Brandy and her mother were decorating the Christmas tree when her mother's problem knee "popped out of joint." She fell to the floor "crying, screaming, cursing." Brandy's father rushed into the room and demanded of Brandy, "What did you do to her!" "I was so mad that he would accuse me of hurting my mother." Phyllis was disturbed by the memory to a level eight. Brandy unburdened Phyllis of her anger by visualizing her burning it up in a fire pit. Only a single effort was necessary to reduce the burden to zero.

Another of Phyllis's memories related to her anger toward Candace for bingeing, and for Phyllis having to deal with the consequences. The problem arose during the summer between Brandy's 10th and 11 grades, when she was 16. Over the summer, Candace binged so much that Brandy gained 50 pounds by the beginning of classes. After school began again, she lost back about 30 of those pounds. One day during theatre class rehearsal a male friend told Brandy he was glad she had lost the weight because, he said, he had "barely recognized" her at the beginning of the school year. He was unaware of how much his remarks hurt Brandy, but the combination of embarrassment for Brandy and anger toward Candace disturbed Phyllis to a level eight. Candace was disturbed to a level six by the incident.

Another group of memories captured Brandy's bingeing activities over a period beginning about six months after her marriage. Her husband worked nights and Brandy felt isolated from family and friends. To soothe herself, she engaged in a great deal of bingeing. On the way home from work

Candace would influence Brandy to buy large amounts of fast food as well as several extra-large boxes of pizza. Typically, Brandy would visit three fast food outlets and then a grocery store before arriving home. Through the evening, Candace would influence her to consume all of the food. Then, said Brandy, Candace would disappear, leaving Phyllis with the task of cleaning up her mess. In particular, Phyllis felt she had to hide the food wrappers and empty pizza boxes from the husband. It would be too embarrassing for him to know how much food she was eating. The next day Phyllis got rid of the evidence by distributing the trash in dumpsters in several different locations so that no one could get an idea of exactly how much she had eaten. Phyllis was driven both by her anger at Candace and by the embarrassment she wanted to avoid should anyone, especially Brandy's husband, discover the extent of the problem.

Working with Phyllis and Candace together, illustrates that sometimes negative emotions are aroused between parts in the inner world, and unburdening is not just about a part's response to something happening to the person in the outer world. Parts develop and maintain feelings, both positive and negative, toward other parts with whom they share the inner world. In other internal systems, an angry part like Phyllis might direct her anger at the observing self, because she might have no knowledge that another part, such as Candace, was the cause of the problem. However, in this case, because parts were well differentiated, Phyllis was able to identify Candace as the source of the bingeing behavior. It is also revealing here that even as Phyllis focused upon Candace as the source of the problem she also voiced her concern for her. Immediately after observing aloud that it had been six weeks since she had binged, Brandy quoted Phyllis as communicating the thoughts: "I'm very concerned for Candace. She is very fragile. I'm afraid she won't handle it well if something bad happens." Phyllis, said Brandy, saw Candace as "fragile, weak, and feeble."

Near the end of the session, we unburdened both Phyllis and Candace of the age-16 comment by a classmate about her weight. We also unburdened Phyllis of her anger for having to clean up the messes and dispose of the bingeing evidence. Both sets of memories yielded their negative energies quickly to a fire pit visualization.

In session 21, we spent most of the session reviewing Brandy's progress and discussing the events of the previous week. She was bitten on both hands and arms when she and her aide worked to prevent an enraged, low-functioning child from repeatedly banging her head against the floor. During the week, she also said good-bye to students and staff members, and packed and moved most of her things to her new school. She still felt badly that her best friend was joining the military. A big test for Brandy would be on the following night at a farewell party for her best friend. Her best friend's ex-husband would probably be there. She said, "in the past I would have gone crazy on people who hurt my friend." She planned to monitor angry Phyllis throughout the party so as to prevent her from attacking the man.

Yet, she did not binge. Prior to making the four-hour drive to our session she had thought a lot about it, but "I talked myself out of it." She had never before been able to do this once she was deeply into the bingeing mood state. She asked Candace if bingeing would have given her pleasure, and Candace replied that it would not. Candace said her bingeing desires had been about being tired from the moving, and especially because she had been unable to cook for the family, a part of her enjoyable, normal role. "She felt marginalized," said Brandy, "and wanted me to know she should have been cooking."

At the end of the session, we elicited one additional memory from Candace. It related to a significant bingeing episode when Brandy and her husband were still in their large eastern city before moving to take jobs in California. They were moving into an apartment in "a bad neighborhood" of the city, where no fast food was available and there were no food delivery services. At night, it was too dangerous to venture out of the apartment. Because she thought circumstances would prevent her from bingeing at the new location, Candace decided make her last binge a big one. While her husband was at work, she binged off-and-on for 12 consecutive hours, with a positive energy rating at level eight. There were many such *final binges* in Candace's history, and this one was no more final that the others. Brandy related, "Actually, I switched to bingeing in the car on the way home from school. It worked for me, but the greatest pleasure always came from bingeing in the comfort of home." We planned to unburden this and other positive-energy bingeing events for Candace in our next session. Evidently, our work had so far been successful. Brandy's last comment before leaving the office was that she had lost 30 pounds since the beginning of therapy just by reducing the bingeing compulsion.

With little preliminary in session 22, except for noting that Phyllis did not cause a problem at her best friend's farewell party, Brandy turned immediately to unburdening Candace of the energy connected to her intended last binge just prior to moving into a prohibitive inner city environment. For this intervention, Brandy used an ocean metaphor as she visualized Candace swimming in gentle waves and allowing the water to dissolve and wash away the energy connected to the powerful memory. As Candace processed the event Brandy observed, after half a minute of silence, "She remembers the excitement of planning it out, shopping at the stores, bringing the food home and spreading it out." Then, after a short pause as these memories were resolved she observed, "It took a couple of hours of preparation; all of that was pleasurable." Within another half minute, the energy level was reduced to zero for the entire experience. Brandy explained, "She has unburdened this excitement but has managed to transfer some of it to the pleasure she feels now when buying and preparing food for normal meals. I tell her that when she needs the excitement, to use an extravagant recipe that takes a couple of hours of preparation. She agrees. She is cautiously optimistic. She really enjoys cooking and I think this will be a good substitute for her. Driving to Santa Cruz tomorrow will be a good test for her. All my family will be there for the first time in years. Usually she stops frequently to order fast food on a road trip to visit family. She's never been able to do a family road trip without stopping for food."

Brandy also talked briefly about the relationship between Phyllis and Candace. "Phyllis has been really kind to Candace in the last couple of weeks. She's been stepping in to help her. And she's been helping her with saying goodbye to all the people we've been around for the last couple of years, as we move to a new school." Saying good-bye to our therapy relationship was also on the agenda for our next session. Brandy thought she had achieved what she set out to achieve. Our next session would be our last if, as expected, no new problems arose in the assessment we planned for our final meeting.

In session 23, our last, Brandy shared the good news that she had managed to make her road trip to visit family without bingeing. She said that as she approached her city limits Candace felt a strong urge to binge; however, as she headed north on the freeway she quickly released the urge. Then, on the return trip, she felt no urge to binge at all. Brandy was understandably pleased with herself. She was also pleased that "Phyllis stayed home," so that she was not annoyed as she usually was to be together with a large group of her relatives.

Brandy's son was now more than a year old. Her pregnancy with him was the reason she had stopped taking Ritalin, her ADHD medication. She had been considering going back on this medication, but had now changed her mind. She felt less impulsive than before therapy, and was "more aware of what was going on around" her. She had not been doing irresponsible things as she had in the past, such as deciding upon a sudden vacation trip to Mexico with no preparations, or of buying a car she could not afford. "I still make decisions quickly," she said, "but the decisions are wiser, less extreme choices." She went on to say, "I don't feel I need Ritalin. My husband wanted me to go back on it before I started therapy. I was anxious all the time, unfocused, all over the place, and my thoughts switched quickly. Now my husband is impressed with how calm I am. I still get angry, but I'm more in control of it. And it's not a crazy anger that washes over me, leaving me emotionally exhausted. Now I tell people when I'm angry, and I'll say what I have to say, and then it's done."

Finally, Brandy summed up by noting that she hadn't had a panic attack since our work with her anxiety five months previously. She no longer experienced excessive worry over the health of her son. She was able now "to put him in daycare and not think that he's going to get deathly ill." She thought her binge eating needed more work, because Candace was still saying "just one more time," meaning one more of those well-intentioned final binges that never turned out to be the final binge. "But now," Brandy added, "the thought leaves quickly. I used to act immediately on such a thought, but now I'm patient when I tell Candace that it's not worth it. I haven't binged in two months."

Chapter 9
Grief, Depression and Marital Problems

Prolonged grief can be a major component of depression. Often the two cannot be clinically distinguished. The helplessness, hopelessness, and sense of lack of control, characteristic of many who suffer the grief of losing a loved one, are the same emotions that depressed persons feel. When the grief is finally resolved, so too will be the depression. In the case described in this chapter, both dissociated grief and the depressed state which accompanied it were triggered anew a decade after the loss of the client's mother. The triggering circumstance was that of her father-in-law moving in with her family.

Sandra was 45 years old and a seasoned executive recruiter when she first came to therapy. She had three teenage children of whom the eldest, her son, would soon graduate high school and move on to college. Her scores on intake screening tests were all in the moderate range. Her DES (Dissociative Experiences Scale) score was only 3.2, low average in comparison with the norm of 10. The inner world we would later explore was therefore not likely to be the result of trauma and pathological dissociation.

Sandra initially wanted to talk about her strained relationship with her husband, Brian. He had rescued his alcoholic father from a near death coma in his apartment in Chicago, got him through a rehabilitation program there, and brought him to live with the family in Las Vegas until he could find a job and a place to live on his own. Only 16 years older than Brian, his father was still young enough to work. Brian had been raised by his grandparents and related to his father more as a beloved older brother than as a parent. His father had arrived the week prior to Sandra's first therapy appointment. Brian had taken control of his father's remaining assets and assumed responsibility for managing his life. For Sandra, her father-in-law was a major intrusion into her family's life. My initial impression was that a few sessions of supportive psychotherapy would suffice for Sandra to adjust to a temporary situation. The problem, I believed, was just a variation of one faced by a great many mature families: providing temporary support for an aging parent. I did not expect we would be doing the deep work of Parts Psychology. The problem, however, was much deeper than it first appeared. The new family situation triggered a complex of memories whose pain Sandra had managed to dissociate from her everyday experience. Chief among those memories were the death of her mother 12 years previously and Brian's intolerance for the grief she felt at the time.

Depression

Ten days later, when we met for our second session Sandra had spent the previous night in a motel. The precipitating incident was an argument with her son in which he called her a *fucking bitch* while Brian listened passively. Sandra believed that Brian's failure to respond to their son's inappropriate language was further evidence of her marginalization as a decision-making adult within the family. Her father-in-law's constant presence irritated her and magnified everything negative in her life. Brian trivialized Sandra's objections to his father's presence. She wasn't sure if she wanted to go home again. She was thinking about talking to a divorce attorney. Her depression, from which she had been relatively free for about 10 years, had returned.

In our third session, only four days later, Sandra talked more about her depression. She had returned home after three nights in the motel and tried to talk with Brian about the state of their relationship. He was unable to see why the presence of his father was having such a negative impact on Sandra. She had been extremely sad since the addition of Brian's father to their household three weeks previously. She was uninterested in the things that usually gave her pleasure. She had gained 10 pounds, had difficulty concentrating, and felt guilty about being a *horrible mother* and a *bad wife*. She was exhibiting the symptoms of major depression. Although she was not suicidal, she was having many thoughts about death. She remembered the death of her father three years previously and was especially drawn to remember the details of her mother's death 12 years ago.

It had now become clear that Sandra's problems were greater than first indicated. She was now clinically depressed and incapable of viewing the presence of her father-in-law in the way her husband wanted. The memory of her mother's death, and especially the memory of Brian's reaction to her extended grief, would require deep processing. Because of this, I introduced Sandra to Parts Psychology near the end of the session.

Sandra could vividly remember her mother's final hospital scene. Her mother lay in a coma as Sandra paced the floor waiting for the physicians to confirm that there was no hope for her mother's survival. Sandra could see herself in this scene, 12 years younger and wearing a blue denim top with matching pants. I suggested that she concentrate on this image of her younger self and try to get its attention. To Sandra's surprise, the image seemed to look at her when she spoke to it subvocally. I coached Sandra to say "Hi" to this part of herself and to tell her that she would talk to her later. Sandra did so as we ended the session. She observed that it felt "odd" to be talking to herself and to experience the image as if it were hearing what she said.

In session four, Sandra found that her depression had deepened even as her husband showed signs of recognizing they had a problem. They would see a marital therapist in two weeks. In response to Sandra's complaints, Brian had arranged with his father to be absent from the home at noon each workday so that Sandra could come home for her lunch, as had been her custom, without having to interact with his father. However, Sandra described her relationship with her husband as "strained." While he was willing to see a therapist with her, he viewed Sandra as the one with the problem. "He says I get upset when there's a mess, but it's my mess." It was only July but Sandra had already decided that she was "not going to do the holidays this year."

Grief

Suggesting an affect bridge, I asked Sandra to focus upon her upset feelings about her husband and to allow her mind to float back to the earliest experience she could remember that connected to those feelings. The memory that surfaced for her was one in which she saw herself lying on the bathroom floor, sobbing uncontrollably. She wore leotards and a t-shirt, and her hair was pulled into a ponytail. The memory dated to 11 years previously, a year after her mother's death, when she was still in the depths of her grief. Brian found her there in the bathroom. He told her that he had had enough of her "sniveling." He had put up with her "weakness" for more than a year, and it was time for her to give it up. Sandra quoted Brian as saying, "If this is the way our life is going to be, I'll find another wife!" As Sandra described it, she had just lost one of the two most important people in her life, and now the second was threatening to leave her. She was frightened and angry. The scene with her on the bathroom floor, previously dissociated from her consciousness, was now repeatedly triggered as Brian took care of his father. Sandra was only partially aware of this triggering. Unlike his continued patience with his father's present struggles, Brian had shown no tolerance for Sandra's emotional turmoil 11 years previously.

The younger image of herself that Sandra visualized in the bathroom scene responded when Sandra spoke to her. She answered Sandra's question about who she thought Sandra might be by communicating, "You are me." Sandra said the part was 34, so we called her simply *the 34-year-old*. She correctly stated Sandra's age as 45, but she had no knowledge of the events in Sandra's life over the last 11 years. However, she did have memories for events that preceded the bathroom scene. Her earliest memory dated to age 18, when a friend died, a man she looked upon as "a kind of uncle." It disturbed her to a level four on the SUD (Subject Units of Disturbance) scale. At age 19, Sandra found out that her high school boyfriend had cheated on her after they had gone off to separate colleges. The cheating ended the relationship with him. It continued to disturb the 34-year-old part at a level six. In another memory, following Sandra's marriage to Brian, Sandra miscarried her first pregnancy at age 26. This disturbed the part to a level six on the SUD scale. When she was 28, Sandra and her husband moved to another city to pursue better job opportunities. It was painful to move away from the friends and family she had been close to all of her life. The loss of these connections continued to disturb the subpersonality at a level nine. The last memory reported by the part was that of Sandra's devastation at age 33 when her mother died.

Twelve years later Sandra believed that she had successfully dealt with the loss of her mother. But she could not explain why, despite the passage of time, any thought or mention of her mother brought tears to her eyes. Thus, the face she showed to the world denied grief even as the subpersonality who carried the memory blended with her and caused tears to fall. For the 34-year-old part, the pain of the death of her mother continued to register at a SUD level of 10, as did the scene of her husband's threats as she sobbed on the bathroom floor. Sandra had blocked most of her pain over the loss of her mother, limiting it to a level three or four, but the 34-year-old still carried that pain to a level 10, illustrating the value of dissociation to the functioning person. However, the scene in which her husband threatened to find another wife unless she stopped her grieving was no longer dissociated. It disturbed Sandra to a level 10, the same level as for the internal part. What seems to have happened is that this memory became a level 10 disturbance again because of its repeated triggering since her father-in-law moved in. Sandra was now in touch once more with the depression that followed her mother's death. She was also aware of the anger she had felt, then and now, when she felt forced to pretend that she was over her grief.

Sandra had come to realize why her husband's attention to his father's needs disturbed her so much. When she had been lost in the grief and depression following her mother's death, Brian threatened her with divorce. But now, with his father recovering from his own emotional wounds, Brian was understanding and supportive. "It's so unfair," she said. Sandra was reminded of Brian's callousness toward her every time she saw his father in their home and every time she wrote a check, as household financial manager, to cover the man's expenses.

Sandra said that although she took pains to hide her distress from her husband, she had remained depressed for another year following the bathroom incident. She put on "a happy face" around him so that he wouldn't leave her, but she continued to mourn. She was now depressed again, as the dissociated grief from the loss of her mother came flooding back to overwhelm her whenever the 34-year-old part was triggered by the presence of her father-in-law. Additionally, Sandra was angry. "Why," she asked, did this "waste of a man" get to live, while her mother died?

Healing Losses

We began the unburdening process with Sandra by working with her 34-year-old part's earliest painful memories. The loss of her friend at age 18, a level four disturbance, gave way fairly quickly to the imagery of discarding the pain into a bonfire in two steps, first to a level two and then to zero. Next, we used the same metaphor to unburden the loss of Sandra's high school sweetheart at age 19. As the 34-year-old lifted her burden out of herself and tossed it into the fire, Before she released the pain of her loss, Sandra first felt anger toward the boyfriend and then anger at her own "stupidity" for trusting her boyfriend. The part soon reported a SUD level of zero for the loss of her relationship but acknowledged a continuing negative judgment of herself as stupid. An additional visualization of dumping that distress into the fire for incineration brought the negative judgment to zero.

We were at the end of the session and it was time to help Sandra prepare for the coming week. Sandra visualized moving the 34-year-old into a safe room, a family room, metaphorically putting away the memories that we had exposed to her conscious mind. We planned to return to this younger version of Sandra in our next session; we might also seek out the internal part who held such strong antipathy for her husband's father.

At the beginning of the fifth session, we discussed the progress Sandra and her husband had made in reconciling their differences. Sandra looked forward to the marital session they had scheduled for later in the week. She observed that her husband was "trying, but he still doesn't get it! He still puts it on me and says I'm getting back at him for my past." He didn't understand why it was such a problem for her to give temporary aid to his father. Sandra, however, was afraid the aid was not temporary, and that her nuclear family was experiencing the beginning of a permanent addition.

When we checked on the work we had done with the 34-year-old in the previous session, we found that her SUD scores had increased from the zeros we had achieved then to a level two and a level one for the first two memories we had unburdened. As previously discussed, this sort of increase following the achievement of a zero level of distress inevitably means that there is another part involved. Sandra focused upon the distress she now felt for the two experiences of the death of a friend and the loss of her boyfriend. She followed that distress to another, younger part. She found a child version of herself, about nine years old. The part called herself *Sandi*. She wore pink shorts with a plaid top. Her hair was braided into pigtails. "She's a little heavy," said Sandra, "and she is self conscious about her weight." We quickly found that Sandi knew who Sandra was—an adult version of herself—and she understood that she was a part of Sandra. Her earliest memory came from the time when she was six years old and filling up water balloons in the bathroom. One of the balloons exploded prematurely, causing a mess in the room. Her father spanked her for her mischief. The memory disturbed her to a level seven or eight. At this point, it was unclear how Sandi's distress related to that of the 34-year-old; we only knew that there seemed to be a connection. In our next session we planned to explore more of Sandi's memory set and then to unburden her.

In our sixth session, we returned to work with Sandi with little preliminary. We found that she continued to rate the water balloon incident at a seven or eight on the SUD scale. She had few other memories in her memory set. At around age seven, her dog appeared on her school playground and she was required to take her pet to the school office and then take him home. The incident was not disturbing. At age nine Sandi had her tonsils removed. The overnight stay in the hospital away from her parents, was disturbing to a level six. Also, at age nine her fourth grade teacher revealed to her class that Sandi had received a very high score on a national achievement test. She was proud of her score and was not disturbed by the teacher's announcement. The last memory Sandi could recall was also from the fourth grade. Her classmate, Maria, had a birthday party but did not invite Sandi. On the following Monday she criticized Sandi for not being there. Although Sandi had been hurt by the lack of an invitation, their talk on Monday revealed that it was just a mistake in sending out the invitations. Both girls were okay once they realized that neither had been snubbed by the other. The incident was no longer disturbing.

Sandi evidently had no other significant memories. She had no memory of Sandra going on to junior high or high school and no knowledge of Sandra's current life. After Sandra quickly brought Sandi up to date on her life since the fourth grade she unburdened her of her two disturbing memories, the water balloon and hospital incidents, guiding her in releasing her burden as a powerful wind carried her hurt away. Nine-year-old Sandi decided not to accept Sandra's invitation to move to an internal playroom, but chose instead to stay on her memory playground and play with her classmates.

Just before the end of the session, Sandra mentioned that when she had asked Sandi about memories from high school, she had glimpsed another part in the background. When she returned to this momentary event, she found an image of herself at age 19, wearing jeans and "a white fake fur coat." The part chose to be called *Janet*. We would return to her in our next session after checking on whether our work with young Sandi had had an effect on the level of distress carried by the 34-year-old.

At our seventh session, Sandra reported that she thought the couples session she had attended with her husband had gone well. Her husband seemed to be listening to her concerns. We returned then to check on our progress with the 34-year-old. The SUD level for her earliest memory, the death of an older friend, was once more a zero. It appeared that our brief detour to work with the child part, Sandi, was justified. The second memory, however, the loss of her first boyfriend, continued to rate at a level one on the SUD scale. Sandra thought that this might have been a reflection of the feelings of Janet, the teenage part we had met at our last session. We would work with her soon, expecting that, as with Sandi, once we unburdened the younger part, the 34-year-old would no longer be disturbed by the incident.

Before turning to that work, however, we worked again with the 34-year-old on other painful memories. She was able to release quickly to a waterfall metaphor the burden of the miscarriage of her first child, although Sandra noted that she could sense the presence of another amplifying part. Unexpectedly, when we tried to unburden the 34-year-old of the loss of her friend and family relationships consequent to Sandra's career move from one city to another, we found that the part was unwilling to release the pain. Sandra said that the 34-year-old was afraid the unburdening would lead to her "not knowing who she is." Sandra noted that right after her mother died, "I wanted to move back to [the home city] to be among my lifelong friends and family." Rather than pressure the 34-year-old further at this point and risk alienating her, we chose instead to return to the teenage part we had discovered at the end of our last session. Before doing so, we checked the 34-year-old's SUD levels for the move away from home and for the loss of her mother. She reported a distress level of three for the move, down from nine, and a distress level of seven, down from 10, for the loss of her mother. Clearly, we seemed to be on the right track. The distress levels for these events had spontaneously reduced without our working directly with either of them.

We returned then to becoming acquainted with Janet, the 19-year-old part who wore a "fake fur coat." We found that she was current with the events in Sandra's life but felt herself to be an observer rather than a participant. She did not consider Sandra's children to be her children. Her earliest memory dated to age 18, the first time she had sex. Another early memory was of her high school boyfriend visiting her when she was in college. When asked for her earliest painful memory Janet recalled that after three years of dating her boyfriend, she thought she would marry him. At one point, she thought she was pregnant and visited the clinic for a pregnancy test. The test was negative. Although she had previously indicated that this was her earliest painful memory, she now rated it as a zero on the SUD scale. Perhaps just talking about it released any remaining negative emotions. She rated as a four on the SUD scale her discovery that her boyfriend had cheated on her while away at his college. The issue of cheating and the issue of ending the relationship were not separable, so the SUD score reflected both the betrayal and the loss of the relationship. Another of Janet's memories was of her first date with a different man. It was notable as a step in moving forward from her loss, but it was not otherwise significant.

When asked, Janet indicated that she was aware of the death of the mother, but she did not consider this event to be a part of her own experience. She did not respond to the question of whether she knew of any other internal parts who had personally experienced the death of Sandra's mother. However, when Sandra requested that Janet connect her with a part who did experience the death of her mother, Sandra found herself visualizing an image of herself at the age of 24 or 25, wearing a business suit, tennis shoes over her hose, and with her hair "a little *poofier*." We would interview this part in our next session.

In our eighth session, following a lengthy discussion of the difficulties of having her father-in-law living in her home, we returned to the part we had discovered at the end of the previous session. The part claimed the age of 25 and, although she said that she, too, was named *Sandra,* she chose to be called *Vanessa.* She felt the loss of the mother at a level four on the SUD scale. Her earliest experience was that of having a miscarriage early in her marriage. She also rated that loss at a level four disturbance. She rated the discovery that her husband's career required moving away from her hometown at a level three. Another painful experience was that of living alone for six weeks in the new city while her husband trained elsewhere for his new career. She rated this time of being alone at a SUD level of three.

We had planned to unburden Vanessa in our next session and we hoped to continue the unburdening work with the 34-year-old. However, the strain of having her father-in-law living in her home as well as the diminished attention she felt she was getting from her husband, meant that our next session, number nine, was devoted entirely to a discussion of how to cope with the stress of her family situation. Sandra felt that the marital therapy she and her husband were getting had provided little help. Her father-in-law was still in her home and her husband was doing little or nothing to move him into his own place.

In session 10, as with the beginning of most sessions, Sandra felt a need to express her frustration with her father-in-law and her husband's tolerance of his problems. She had just received the cable bill for their television. She discovered that her father-in-law had downloaded porn movies on two separate occasions while the family was out for the evening. "He said he didn't mean to," Sandra reported. Another concern of hers was that her husband would be in Chicago all of the next week for a business trip. She felt uncomfortable being in the home with her father-in-law without her husband also present.

We returned then to work with 25-year-old Vanessa, who carried the loss of Sandra's first pregnancy through miscarriage. We guided Vanessa in unburdening her sadness with a wind intervention, and as Sandra visualized the wind blowing over and through Vanessa and carrying away her sadness, Sandra discovered that Vanessa was angry. She was angry that she had lost her baby, which she wanted so badly, and yet there were people who didn't want their babies and intentionally aborted them. She felt both anger and sadness. It was confusing to her. She didn't understand why her baby died. "Bad things weren't supposed to happen to good people. Losing the baby switched my life. I probably would not have stayed home all those years if I hadn't lost the baby." Although these words came from Sandra, the thoughts originated with Vanessa. Expressing them helped with the unburdening. "She's feeling better now," Sandra said of Vanessa. "She just needed to explain." A short visualization of the wind blowing away her remaining negative emotions from the memory of the miscarriage completed the intervention. Vanessa's remaining troubling memories, the death of her mother, living alone for six weeks as her husband underwent training, and the discovery that her husband's career meant that they would have to leave their home town all yielded quickly to one additional visualization of the wind intervention. The distress levels for all of these memories reached zero for Vanessa.

At the end of the session, we checked the distress levels for the 34-year-old regarding Sandra's losses. The death of the mother was now down to a SUD level of two or three. The move away from the hometown held a level four. And the miscarriage memory was now at a zero. We planned to check these levels again, both for both the 34-year old and for Vanessa, at our next session.

Anger

Unfortunately, we could not return to the unburdening in session 11 because of Sandra's upset with her husband. While in Chicago he had taken the time to call and check-in with his father, but he did not call Sandra. The result was that Sandra was again overwhelmed with the hurt and anger that had been a part of her life since her father-in-law moved in. She was uninterested in working with her inner world while her anger was so great. The anger seemed to be originating with 25-year-old Vanessa, while the hurt came from the child part, Sandy. We used the session to help Sandra become calmer and more centered by focusing on each negative emotion and asking it to step back from her in turn. In this intervention it was not necessary to identify all of the self states involved. Just by speaking to each negative emotion as she identified it—for example, sadness, rejection, resentment, fear, etc.—and asking it to step back without going far away from her, she was able to achieve a degree of calm by the time she left the office. We repeated the exercise several times before that state arrived.

When we met again in session 12, little had changed in Sandra's home situation. She had decided, however, to return alone to her hometown to visit her family over the Thanksgiving holiday. She wanted a break from the household stress she had been experiencing, and she wanted to consider how much more she was willing to tolerate. Sandra thought that her plan to spend the holiday away from her husband and children had finally gotten through to Brian how important it was to make changes. Brian had indicated that he would work at finding a place for his father to live while she was gone. It had now been four months since he brought his father home. Sandra had doubts that Brian would actually follow through on his plans, but she was hopeful.

We met for session 13 following Sandra's return from visiting her family. During the week of her absence, Brian had helped his father find a job as well as a place to live. Sandra thought Brian "got scared" when she chose to visit her family without him. He had also purchased a used car for his father's transportation. His father would move out in four days.

In this session, we explored Sandra's distress more deeply by connecting to the 34-year-old part and the memory of her sobbing on the bathroom floor as she grieved over her mother's death. The focus for the processing was Brian's devastating comment when he found Sandras lying there 11 years previously. Brian's words were "I'm only 35. If this is the way it's going to be I'll get a divorce and start over!" This remembered scene was triggered each time Sandra was faced with another accommodation to having her father-in-law living in her home. Here are Sandra's words as she tells the 34-year-old's story of her trauma.

> He left me floundering. But he bails out [his father] who blew 30 thousand dollars partying. My resentment is deserved. My mother died suddenly. It put me into depression for a couple of years. I didn't want to get out of bed. I wasn't able to work; I was taking care of the kids. It was a year after she died. I was on the floor in the downstairs bathroom, and he came to the door and that's what he said. He left and I sat there and I never said anything more about it to anyone until now. I had to put on a happy face for Brian. That was a horrible thing to do—it rocked my world. I was depressed another year after that. I just ate. I had lost 75 pounds before my mother died, but I gained it all back. I don't feel special with him anymore. Sometimes I get angry that he's so clueless about how fragile our relationship is. He didn't call me from Chicago but he called his father. I think I don't want to

leave him. I think I love him. Am I willing to take second place indefinitely? Maybe not.

At this point, I asked Sandra to check with the 34-year-old on her level of distress. She reported a SUD level of five for the painful event. We continued then with the exercise, but Sandra switched from a first person to a mostly third person account.

She was trapped. And then she was yelled at for something she couldn't help. It made the sadness worse. Maybe she wants to keep the burden to justify the hurt and resentment she has for being depressed so long. Why was I threatened with discarding, while he totally enabled his father?

We were near the end of the session and I hoped that Sandra would not continue to feel her extreme distress during the coming week. Consequently, I asked her to help the 34-year-old visualize putting her activated distress into a container for storage until we could return to it. The part chose a purse for this purpose. We planned to continue working with the 34-year-old in our next session.

Life Stresses Trigger Adolescent Memories

In session 14, however, new issues arose to postpone our plan. Although her father-in–law was now out of her house and into his own apartment, Sandra found herself in a "meltdown" over the demands of her work and her children. On the day prior to our session she had worked extra hours at her job, had spent more than two hours arranging for repairs for her son's car, and finally had to deal with her hysterical 14-year-old daughter who demanded help for her homework. Sandra was shaking, she said, as she tried to move her daughter out of her room so that she could have some relaxation time. She finally went out and drove around for a couple of hours to calm herself down. In our session, Sandra identified her greatest concern as her current dislike for her daughter.

We decided to look for the internal source of the strong reaction she was experiencing to her daughter. I asked Sandra to connect to her current dislike for her daughter and to ask that feeling to provide a picture of itself. The initial image that came to Sandra's mind was that of her high school rival, a girl towards whom Sandra still felt significant animosity almost 30 years later. What Sandra seemed to have done was to bridge to the memories in her past that were most like the feelings she was having in the present. Thus, she was feeling toward her daughter as she felt toward her high school rival, but she hadn't yet located a visual image for her internal self state. I suggested she focus on the image of her rival and speak to the part who was doing the focusing while subvocalizing, "I see who you are upset with, now let me see you, please, the part who feels the emotion." When Sandra tried this technique, she found herself with an image of herself as she remembered herself in high school, with her hair down, and wearing a striped sweater, a match with that of her boyfriend. The new internal image responded when Sandra spoke to her, indicating that she knew who Sandra was. She was aware, she said, of current events in Sandra's life. She surprised Sandra by volunteering that her name was *Lana*. She acknowledged that she was the part who didn't like Sandra's daughter, at least at the present time. Lana thought that the daughter was acting like a peer and a competitor rather than like a daughter. She was crying to get help with her homework just as Sandra's high school rival cried to get better grades. In fact, said Sandra, her high school rival became the school valedictorian ahead of Sandra only because she cried over her grades in a math class. As a consequence, Sandra ended as number two in her class while her rival held the number one spot.

Lana's earliest memory dated to a bus ride with other members of the school speech team to a competition at another school. She remembered that her rival was also on the bus. This memory did not disturb her. Her most painful memory was the night she graduated high school when the class rankings were announced. She was number two behind her rival. Lana believed that she was unfairly demoted from the number one position because of her rival's propensity to cry to her teachers when she was in danger of getting a lower grade, and also because Lana's math teacher made an error in computing Sandra's grade for his course. By the time she could convince the teacher of his error, the graduation was over and Lana was forever relegated to the number two position. The announcement of Sandra's position as number two in her class disturbed Lana to a level 10.

Lana's other disturbing memories were also related to problems with her high school rival. When we unburdened the class rank announcement we would also be unburdening Lana's other problem experiences. Lana had no autobiographical memories for the years after high school. As Sandra put it, "She's pretty much stuck in high school." She had no memories of going to college, although she was aware that Sandra had gone. She was aware of Sandra's husband but did not consider him her own husband. Nor did she consider Sandra's daughter to be her daughter.

We unburdened Lana with a wind metaphor. Sandra visualized her standing between two posts in an open field as Sandra brought a powerful wind to blow through the posts and over Lana. The first effort reduced Lana's burden to a level two, effectively unburdening the announcement of class rank but not yet neutralizing all of the smaller incidents of fierce competition between Lana and her rival. A final visualization brought the SUD level to zero. We expected that Sandra would now be less angry with her daughter. We hoped also that some of her anger toward her father-in-law might be reduced. With the temporary problem with Sandra's daughter now alleviated, we planned to return to work with the 34-year-old in our next session.

At our next session, the 15th, Sandra was not yet ready to process the 34-year-old's memories of the death of her mother and the abandonment threat by her husband. Instead, she wanted to talk about Christmas, just two weeks way. She had decided not to decorate the house or a tree for the holidays because of her depression She had gained 20 pounds since her father-in-law had arrived; she still felt angry with her daughter; and at work, tempers were high. She had failed to fill an important executive position and her company was distressed over the loss of anticipated revenue. Finally, she was feeling guilty about her decision not to decorate for Christmas. She was feeling "like a bad person" for not guiding her family into the holiday mood.

When Sandra focused upon her guilt and asked that feeling to provide an internal picture of itself, she saw herself as she was in her 20s, wearing winter boots, a red dress, and a white, wool coat. The part knew Sandra and said she was "Me." Her name was *Rose*. Her earliest memory dated to about age 14 when she remembered her father trying to sing "Silent Night" with the family. Other memories were about past Christmases, and they blended together in her mind. She acknowledged that she was the part who was sad that Sandra would not do Christmas decorations this year. "It doesn't feel right," Sandra quoted her as saying. The sadness did not seem to be out of proportion to the issue, so we decided not to do any additional work with Rose. Once again, we planned to return to work with the grieving part, the 34-year-old in our next session.

In session 16, Sandra checked with the 34-year-old part regarding her distress over her husband's ultimatum to stop grieving 11 years previously. Her SUD level for the event was now down to two on the 0-10 scale. She was unwilling to do any further processing of the memory until she knew how her husband would continue to deal with his father. One of her concerns was whether any of the substantial money spent on rescuing her father-in-law would be repaid.

Sandra noted that she felt a "nasty" feeling in her chest as she interacted with the internal 34-year-old. With the use of a sensory bridge, she focused on the sensation and allowed her mind to float back in time to the memory source. The event that came to mind was her mother's funeral. That was not surprising since that was the source of grief for the 34-year-old. However, Sandra had the sense that the "nasty" feeling did not originate with the 34-year-old, but with another part. We planned to seek out the mystery part in the next session.

We met for session 17 in the New Year two weeks later. Sandra wanted to talk about her job situation rather than her family situation. At home, things were "better" but Brian was now somewhat depressed over his father's failure to keep his spending under control. He was "blowing money on slot machines." At work, Sandra had discovered that her holiday bonus was half of what many coworkers had received. We spent the session discussing what steps she might take with management in order to bring her pay to parity with her coworkers.

In session 18, Sandra reported that she had pointed out to her boss the pay disparity between her coworkers and herself. She was optimistic that her boss would increase her pay. With some aspects of her life thus normalized, Sandra was ready to return to Parts Psychology. She agreed that it was time to stop mourning her mother's death and she was ready to seek out the new part who seemed to be involved with that event.

Mourning and Letting Go

We began this work with Sandra focusing upon the sadness she felt as she remembered her mother's casket during her church's funeral service. When she directed her concentration to her sadness and asked for an image of the sad part of herself, she found herself viewing an image of herself sitting in the cemetery where her mother was buried. The part wore a black coat and sat next to her brother on a bench on the snow-covered grounds of the cemetery. Although she initially thought she was visualizing the time following her mother's burial, she slowly realized that the memory actually dated to the more recent burial of her father, 10 years after her mother's death. Both of her parents were buried in the same cemetery. When Sandra spoke internally to what she called her *Mourning Self,* the part indicated that she knew who Sandra was. "You are me," Sandra quoted her. The Mourning Self had a quite limited memory set, containing only three memories. The first memory was that of viewing her mother's casket during the funeral service. The second memory was that of waiting during the visitation period at the funeral parlor where her father's service was held. The last memory was the one where the Mourning Self was now stuck, in the cemetery a few days after her father had been buried. The part's SUD level for the death of her mother was only a three. Her father's death was at a level five. Probably, these events did not register a 10 because of the earlier unburdening work we had done with other parts. We planned to unburden the Mourning Self and to move her out of the cemetery to a more pleasant place in our next session.

In session 19, we unburdened the Mourning Self as planned. We checked again to be sure that there weren't other memories in her memory set that we had overlooked. There were none. Not only did the part have no other autobiographical memories of her own, she also had no awareness of events in Sandra's life between or after the two deaths. Further, the Mourning Self felt no connection to either Sandra's children or her husband. For the unburdening of the part's three memories Sandra chose a novel symbolic intervention. She helped the Mourning Self to bundle up her sadness in snowballs and throw them away. The first effort brought the SUD level for the death of Sandra's mother to a two. When she repeated the intervention,

Sandra thought the part's distress level was down to a zero, although she wasn't entirely sure. Turning then to unburdening the sadness connected to her father's death, a single visualization of the snowball intervention reduced the distress level to zero. Even with the distress level reduced to zero for the Mourning Self, Sandra felt uncomfortable with leaving her stuck in the cemetery scene. Consequently, she installed the part in a window seat in her home, so that she could sit in the sunshine and watch the events of her neighborhood. The part found the idea a pleasant one. Before closing the session, we wanted to see if the work on the Mourning Self had had an effect on the 34-year-old, the active part with the greatest expressed grief over the loss of the mother. This part's level of distress was now down to a one. Sandra thought that was appropriate. Her tears no longer welled up when she spoke or thought of her mother, but she believed that she should continue to feel at least a small amount of sadness for someone who had been as important to her as her mother had been. At the end of the session, Sandra decided to take a month away from therapy so that she could assess how well she was doing.

When Sandra returned for session 20, she had decided to graduate herself for our work. She could talk about her mother's death without distress. Things were going well with her husband. He was making an effort to check in with her more frequently and helping her feel that she was important to him. Her father-in-law was less an issue now, but was still somewhat of a sore spot for her. Sandra believed that her life was good enough. She was comfortable with leaving some conflicts in her life incompletely resolved.

Chapter 10
Body and Beauty

This is the second of three chapters that describe the therapy of a single client, Georgia. The first was Chapter 4, and the third is Chapter 14. The presence of these three chapters illustrates that Parts Psychology is suitable for longer-term therapy. Even with this longer-term view, however, the focus of the book remains on resolving specific issues within a shorter frame.

After therapy on her original problems, Georgia felt she had more work to do. There were certain mini-mysteries that we might have tried to solve, such as the meaning of The Thinker and The Monster subpersonalities, but Georgia chose to continue the problem-focused approach with which we had begun. She had acquired such confidence in Parts Psychology that she was ready to see if she could get help with a very personal issue. She wanted to change the way she felt about her body and her appearance. She said, "I would like to improve my body image as perceived by others, and desensitize myself to what others think." While this way of stating the problem was problematic because of its emphasis upon others' views rather than her own, I did not want to influence unduly Georgia at this early stage of problem formulation. I felt confident that she would eventually locate both the problem and the solution within herself. In all, we spent 16 sessions on the problem of body image. Unfortunately, the first six of those sessions accomplished little in the way of alleviating Georgia's concerns with her physical appearance. It was not until she restated her problem with a necessary focus upon her own perceptions that we were able to make rapid progress. The description that follows is the story of the final 10 of the 16 sessions we gave to the problem.

In the first of this block of sessions, we decided to redefine the problem on which we worked. There were several reasons for this. First, Georgia had no-showed for our previous session because she "just forgot." Certainly, people can "just forget" their appointments, but that usually happens at the beginning of therapy before the weekly pattern of visits is established. It is unlikely, however, for someone as responsible and committed to her agreements as was Georgia, that she would "just forget." Something wasn't working right in our sessions. In addition, Georgia reported that she had fallen back into old, unwanted patterns at work during the previous week. She had worked through lunch and stayed one or two hours after work in order to increase her paralegal billing. In the centered state that resulted from therapy, Georgia held back from doing this extra work. This had been one of her primary reasons for coming to therapy in the first place. Finally, it seemed that our therapy sessions had begun to meander somewhat as we lost focus on the problem of body image. For example, we had spent time again in trying to figure out the significance of The Monster subpersonality in Georgia's inner world. While this question was a legitimate one, it was not a priority in Georgia's life at that time.

Self Acceptance

Georgia wanted to continue with psychotherapy but with a differently stated goal. Her goal would now be self-acceptance of her body, whereas previously she had stated her problem in terms of the perception others had of her. We began with her startled response to seeing a reflection of herself in the bathroom mirror. "Yuck!" had been her reaction. She was surprised that she "looked that bad. My head seemed too small for my body, and I looked like a big round ball." When asked to focus on the feeling that accompanied the startled reaction of "Yuck!" and to search for the responsible part, Georgia found herself visualizing a clenched fist.

There was some initial difficulty in establishing communication with the fist image. There was no response to ordinary greetings such as "Hello" and "How are you?' There was an affirmative response, though, (the fist moved up and down) to the question of whether it could hear Georgia. When asked if it knew Georgia its response was a slammed fist. There was a lack of response to the question of whether it knew it was a part of Georgia, an affirmative response to whether it had a name, but a lack of response to a request to share its name. The fist also provided no response to separate questions as it whether it was female, male, or lacking a gender. When Georgia found that the image was fading, she looked for White Dragon, the helper part we had met during the work described in Chapter 4. After about 30 seconds of concentration, Georgia said that White Dragon was present. The helper part indicated that the fist was indeed a part and that it was female. She didn't know why there was difficulty communicating between the fist and Georgia. She said that she could see the rest of the body attached to the fist, and was able to help Georgia see the rest of the arm to which the fist was attached. White Dragon interpreted the meaning of the earlier image of the slammed fist to be that Georgia was the boss, the one in charge. She also affirmed that the fist was the part with the "Yuck!" response to Georgia catching sight of herself in the mirror. Additionally, said Georgia, White Dragon was now referring to the fist as a he rather than a she. In the next session, we would learn that the part presents itself as a male. It is not unusual for inside parts to be mistaken about their first conclusions. They are as fallible as outside persons are. At the end of the session, Georgia asked White Dragon if she could teach the new part how to speak. She said she would try. Speaking directly to the part presenting with a fist, Georgia gently said that she did not want to hurt it, but to work with it. She thought that the part understood. As we closed the session, Georgia suggested that maybe the part could work on its speaking ability during the coming week.

As we began our second session in the series, Georgia recalled that during the week the office manager had assigned her full-time secretarial work. Because of her secretarial load, she had to explain to one of her attorney bosses that she had no time to do the paralegal work he wanted. She pointed out to him that she was caught between conflicting directives. For as long as she had to do all the secretarial work for a just-fired secretary, she couldn't also do paralegal work. She was proud of herself for not silently working extra hours without pay to do both paralegal work and secretarial work. This new, more functional set of responses reflected the earlier successful work we had done with her work stress, as described in Chapter 4.

We began the internal work in this session with Georgia seeking out White Dragon to help her reconnect to the part presenting itself as an image of a clenched fist. Shortly, Georgia said, "The fist is here and I can see more of the arm—a bulging bicep—a body builder, and I can see some of the shoulder." After a few moments more, Georgia added that she could see the full image. It was a cartoon bodybuilder, with large, exaggerated broad shoulders at the top, tapering down like a V at his legs, a caricature of what a bodybuilder looks like. He had "big, white teeth, a bright smile and a square jaw." His name was *Smiley*.

The Problem of Normal

We began to collect Smiley's memory set immediately. His earliest memory was from Georgia's fourth or fifth grade, when she played at her best friend's house. "Her mother always wanted to fix us food. She always said I was skin and bones and needed to eat more." For Smiley, these experiences were negative because the implication for him was that there was something wrong with Georgia. He estimated his distress at a mid-level five on the SUD (Subjective Units of Disturbance) scale.

Smiley's next significant memory dated to the seventh grade of junior high school. "It was when I started to wear my first bra. Around the same time, I got my first pair of jeans. Over the summer, I went from *Girls* [in children's clothing] to *Misses* [in adult clothing]. I skipped *Juniors* altogether." It was disturbing at a level eight to Smiley because, said Georgia, "I wasn't normal."

In the eighth grade, Georgia had her first period and used a tampon because she was a swimmer. Other girls on the swim team had to take off practice for a day, or even up to a week, Georgia she had no problems with her periods and did not need to skip swimming practice. Her mother was surprised, Georgia said, that having periods didn't slow her down in any way. Georgia's experience with adjusting to having periods was disturbing to Smiley at a level five because she was different from the other girls. "I wasn't girly enough," said Georgia. It is interesting to note how representative Georgia is here in her response to the natural developmental process of growing up. She represents the very normal human tendency to find problems where others find success. She was negatively affected by her success in adjusting to her monthly cycle because she wasn't girly enough; she was different from the other girls who struggled somewhat with the same adjustments. Yet, it is likely that at least some of the girls who had to take time off from their practice schedule also found fault with themselves for an assumed weakness in being female. Some might even have compared themselves to Georgia and found themselves lacking in whatever qualities Georgia had that allowed her to breeze through the process. This example makes the point again that trauma is relative to the individual. In doing psycho-therapy, we have to understand pain relative to the individual's own framework, rather than to a presumed objective observer's idea of what should or should not be painful.

In the summer between her eighth and ninth grades, the local newspaper did a feature article on Georgia's family, with its five student swimmers, as part of publicity work for an upcoming championship meet. For the publicity photograph, Georgia's mother borrowed a skirt and blouse from Georgia. The Smiley part of Georgia was disturbed by this to a level six "because my clothes fit my mother and she was so old [age 42 or 43]."

Then, in the summer between her ninth and tenth grades, Georgia noticed spots on her hips. Because she spent so much time in the sun wearing just the bathing suit in which she practiced and competed for her swim team, there was a significant contrast between her overall tan and the white skin underneath the suit. Yet she had dark spots on her hips where her suit covered her skin. She feared some sort of bruising or, at worst, skin cancer. The spots were definitely not normal. For Smiley, the concern reached a level six on the SUD scale. Eventually, Georgia discovered that the spots represented tanning from the sun that corresponded to the portions of her brown and white bathing suit that were a part of its design of alternating brown and white coloring. Evidently, she had spent so much time in the sun that tanning marks appeared where sunlight broke through the white portions of the design.

We were at the end of the session again but planned to do further work with Smiley in our next session. Before closing the session, Georgia noted that another part must also have been present during the session when, at a couple of points, tears came to her eyes. She said that when that happened she asked White Dragon for a blast of wind from her powerful breath to blow away the tears. She could then again focus on the work with Smiley.

A Forced Break in the Work

At the beginning of our next session (third in the series), Smiley was difficult to locate when Georgia turned her attention to her inner world. However, White Dragon was present, and Georgia asked her to help locate Smiley. Unfortunately, Georgia continued to have trouble in maintaining her focus on the search for Smiley. After some two minutes of intense internal focus, Georgia reported, "I'm seeing random images of a Ferris Wheel, a circus acrobat, and other carnival features." Shortly after that she said, "I'm not sure what's going on. Whenever I get close to Smiley, I see something spinning, an acrobat, a light bulb on the end of a pole, or other things that don't register enough for me to remember them." We suspected that another internal part was interfering with our plans for doing internal work. Consequently, Georgia asked White Dragon to locate the interfering part. White Dragon wasn't sure who this part might be but, said Georgia, "It's someone who really wants my attention." Georgia continued, "I said hello; it said, hello, and it's jumping, like on a pogo stick. It's kinda like a caricature of a cat, green in color, all over." When Georgia asked the new part to describe its function in her life, the part responded with, "I'm here to have fun." It acknowledged that it knew Smiley and that it was "sort of" intentionally blocking work with Smiley because, "I wanted to talk to you." It went on to say, "We need to have more fun." Georgia told the part that two college friends would be "coming to town tomorrow and that will be a lot of fun." The new part agreed with her. When asked if it had a name the part said it was *Funky Monkey*. In response to Georgia's questions, it also said it was a monkey and not a cat; it knew the difference between boys and girls but would not indicate its own gender; and its age was 10 years old.

When Georgia asked Funky Monkey for its earliest memory, it provided her with an internal memory picture of a small firemen's carnival in the small town where she lived as a child. Another memory was that of getting ice cream cones at an ice cream stand in the same small town. Georgia said that her school bus driver would take the kids on the bus to this ice cream stand on the last day of school and buy everyone an ice cream cone. With this description, it is clear that Funky Monkey represents an exception to the usual rule that parts are created at painful or difficult moments. As with the case of Funky Monkey, parts are also created at high energy, positive moments.

When asked, Funky Monkey also produced a painful memory. Georgia was in the fourth grade and participating in a games carnival at her elementary school. A friend of hers fell and broke a wrist at the end of a race. "It was really out of alignment and scary looking," said Georgia. The memory was disturbing to a level six on the SUD scale because of the fear Georgia experienced. "They put her on a stretcher and put her on an ambulance, so we didn't know what was gonna happen to her. I also felt guilt, because I was playing in another part of the playground and I was having fun and continued to have fun because I couldn't see who it was who got hurt." Another painful memory Funky Monkey recalled was from Georgia's sixth grade. She was playing *dodge ball* when she fell and broke her own wrist. The memory was disturbing to a level eight because it was physically painful and also because Georgia had to stop having fun and go to the nurse's office. There appeared to be no other disturbing memories in Funky Monkey's memory set.

We were at the end of the session when Funky Monkey finally revealed its gender: he was a boy. Georgia asked if he spent a lot of time around Smiley, and Funky Monkey said that he did. "Yes, we have to stick together because we're both boys." When asked if he wanted anything else from Georgia, Funky Monkey said he wanted her to "get a life." "He wants me to leave work on time and use the extra time to have fun." He agreed to permit us to return to work with Smiley in our next session.

Georgia began the next session, the fourth in the series, by talking about the good times she had on the weekend with her visiting friends. They saw a show, played keno, slot machines and more. Funky Monkey was pleased. At the office, the company hired a new secretary and planned to hire a second. Georgia got her own office, that of the paralegal who had previously been dismissed along with the secretary. She was no longer working in a closet-like workspace.

Body Image Again

We began the session's parts work with Georgia going inside to find Smiley and White Dragon. After helping a somewhat unfocused Smiley to settle down, Georgia was rewarded with another of Smiley's significant memories. It dated to her 11th grade in high school. She had been playing soccer when she found that her left knee was swollen, although she hadn't fallen. A trip to her doctor provided her with an immobilizing brace on her knee that left her walking awkwardly. Smiley didn't like the way the brace affected her appearance and rated its effect as a four in embarrassment on the SUD scale.

We seemed to be at the end of Smiley's memory set, at least of those memories that he judged to be significant. Georgia revealed that she had been having difficulty maintaining Smiley's interest and had to call upon White Dragon a couple of times to bring Smiley back into focus. We asked him a series of questions to find out how well he was oriented to Georgia's current life. He said that he remembered Georgia going to college, but he didn't really know what she was doing for a living now. He had no memories of her going to law school. He thought the year now was 1989, rather than the end of 2007. He believed that Georgia was 25 years old and not her actual 41.

In cases like this where there is a significant discrepancy between the age of the client and the age perceived by an internal part, I have found that there is generally another, unseen part somehow blocking this internal part's observation of the self. In such cases, I prefer to differentiate the suspected part from the observing self so that we can continue the process of discovery. It is important to do this because otherwise the first part remains stuck in its own pocket of time and hinders the solution of the client's problem in real time. Since it is the part (in this case, Smiley) who has the problem perception of the self, the procedure is to ask the problem part to speak to the part he perceives and to ask that part to step aside so he has a view of the observing self. At first, Smiley resisted doing this. "He doesn't seem to want to see me any other way," said Georgia. Georgia asked Smiley to listen as I spoke directly to him, telling him that we thought there might be a 25-year-old part standing between Smiley and Georgia and that we wanted this part to join our conversation, too. Georgia reported, "I asked him if he understood what you said and he nodded. But when I requested him to ask the 25-year-old to step aside he shook his head, no. I asked if White Dragon could help by giving the 25-year-old a ride, but he shook his head again. I asked him if he needed the 25-year-old to be present [and not flown away by White Dragon], and he nodded his head, yes, again. I asked Smiley and White Dragon to form a circle with me so that we could all be together with the 25-year-old." After a pause, Georgia said, "I think Smiley is trying to move her. His muscles are bulging-but it doesn't seem to be working." Then

Georgia spoke directly to herself as if she could perceive the new part and asked the part to step aside. Georgia said, "I think I was talking to her a little bit. I saw a profile of a female face. She thought I was rude for talking to Smiley about her but not talking directly to her. I apologized and asked if she would join the circle. She seems to have softened, but she doesn't move. She seems to have turned away so I see the back of her head." This beginning proved to be sufficient for Georgia to interview the new part with some of our standard questions.

Princess Reveals Herself

Yes, the new part was 25 years old. And yes, she knew Georgia. "She thinks of me," said Georgia, "as a pest." Asked if she knew Georgia's age, "She says I'm too old, and over the hill." The part's name was *Princess*. When asked what she wanted Georgia to know, Princess said, "You suck!" We were out of time for our session, and Georgia had to return from her inward concentration to the therapy room. She said that as her conversation with Princess continued she was able to get a clearer view of her. She seemed to be posing, almost as if she were on stage, moving her arms dramatically around and over her head." Princess was definitely a cartoon-like image of a woman, and not a realistic image of a person.

Before Georgia returned to the inner work with Princess in the fifth session, she shared that she had had flashes during the week of more distinct images of the new part, confirming her impressions from the end of the previous session. Princess wore an evening gown. Her hair was up and there was something theatrical about her. She seemed to be on a stage, and she struck various poses as she moved about. When Georgia returned to her inner world in our session, she found Princess willing to talk, with Smiley and White Dragon standing by in the vicinity. Remembering that Princess had showed some hostility ("You suck!") in the previous session, Georgia took pains to speak to her in a civil tone. She greeted Princess courteously and engaged her in conversation. "She said she's very busy, but will talk to me for a while." She seemed to Georgia to be brushing her hair and getting ready for a performance. "She says she can do it all—she can sing and she can dance."

Princess dodged Georgia's request to explain the nature of their relationship with each other. Instead, she asked whom Georgia was talking to (in
the outside world). Evidently, she had not been sufficiently aware of
Georgia's life to register that Georgia had been in therapy for most of the
previous nine months. Georgia explained that she was talking with her
therapist, who helped her to talk to Princess and other internal parts. When
Princess came back to the original question, she identified Georgia as the one
who dragged her down and held her back. She was surprised when Georgia
asked her how her life would be different if Georgia gave her her freedom,
but then she said that she "couldn't really say because she had never had
that freedom." As Georgia continued to ask questions and report Princess's
answers, we discovered that Princess was sometimes aware of Georgia's
current life, but sometimes she didn't pay much attention. She knew that
Georgia was an attorney working as a paralegal. She acknowledged that she
did pay attention whenever Georgia was getting dressed. When asked if she
had any comments on Georgia's dressing habits, Princess responded that
she "could write a book about it." She said that Georgia's dressing style was
"too boring," and that Georgia should spend more time on her appearance.
Then she wouldn't look "so dumpy." Georgia asked Princess to expand on
her "You suck!" comment from the previous session. Princess acknowledged
that she "may have been a little harsh," but then she justified that judgment
by asserting that Georgia was simply "not good enough." She didn't "measure up." When Georgia explained our therapy project to help her accept her
own body, Princess was not sympathetic. "She doesn't like that idea. She
thinks I should improve my body. She says I should drop 30 pounds, do
something new with my hair, and wear more makeup. At first, she said I
should drop 50 pounds, but I told her I wasn't going to accept that. She says
I should get some exercise, but not too much. She doesn't want me to look
like a man, with muscle. She wants me to be lady-like."

Princess agreed to share her memory set with us. Her earliest memory
was hazy, but came from the fifth or sixth grade. "I noticed a scar on my
right knee that I hadn't noticed before. It was really ugly. At first I was
shocked by it, but then I realized I skinned my knees all the time, like when I
played in the woods or crashed my bike." The memory of discovering the
scar was disturbing to Princess to a level four on the SUD scale.

When asked to explain her relationship to Smiley, Princess said that she thought of him as "a buffoon." "He follows her around and does whatever she tells him to do." She also acknowledged that their memories overlapped to some extent, but she had more memories than he did.

Princess's next significant memory dated to "the day I fell and broke my left wrist. While I was waiting in the nurse's office for my mother to pick me up and take me to the hospital, my wrist got really swollen, with a big lump. [Princess] doesn't remember the pain, just how it looked. They cut off my favorite shirt to put ice on the break." It was disturbing to Princess at a level six on the SUD scale. What was disturbing to her was "watching the swelling get worse and not being able to do anything about it. She was horrified by the deformed look of my arm." By the end of the session, Princess had softened her attitude toward Georgia. She agreed to talk more to us during our next session. "She likes the way we listen," Georgia added.

In session six, of the series Princess continued to share her significant memories. However, before beginning this work, Princess emphasized that she wanted Georgia "to behave differently," especially regarding how she dressed and ate. She wanted Georgia to make more of an effort in how she dressed and presented herself publicly. She also emphasized again that she wanted Georgia to agree to a weight-loss plan.

The next significant memory came from Georgia's seventh grade. "This was maybe a year after I broke my wrist. I was playing with my brothers and sisters in the basement. I struck my foot against the base of a table. I think I broke my toe. It had a big V-shaped gap between the little toe and the second toe. It just didn't look right, and it looked deformed." The SUD level for Princess for this seeming deformity was eight.

"In the ninth grade I had to change into a uniform for P.E. —shorts and a knit top that zipped up. With an elastic waist. It looked terrible—because I had no waist and no butt, according to Princess. I wore it higher or lower to make it look better, but nothing worked. None of the girls liked the uniforms. I don't know if others thought they looked as awful as I did." The SUD level was five for Princess.

"In the summer between my eighth and ninth grades everyone 12 and over shaved down [i.e., shaved all exposed body hair] for the championship swimming meet. We all did it together. The guys shaved down, too. The memory that Princess showed me was the hair as it grew back in—it was really dark and kinda spiky." It was disturbing to a level three—"because of the way it looked, with the hair kind of sticking up out of the skin and really dark brown, and before I shaved it, it was bleached blond—because of the chlorine and the sun."

The next memory was "one we've talked about before, but from a different perspective. The sun made spots on my hip, coming through my bathing suit. She noticed the skin wasn't all one color the way it should be. She remembers the pattern very vividly." The memory was disturbing to Princess to a level four "because it looked like there was something wrong with the skin." The slightly differing perspectives of Princess and Smiley are apparent as Georgia explained, "Smiley thought it was a bruise, but she thought it was more external, like a stain or spot on a shirt. I remember now I tried to scrub it off, like it was dirt or something."

In another memory provided by Princess, Georgia recalled her eighth grade. "I started having seriously bad acne on my face. When I was inducted into the honor society, my parents took a picture of me with the school principal. It was shocking how bad my skin looked [in the picture]. I went to see a dermatologist." The memory was disturbing to Princess at a level seven, "because instead of seeing me [in the picture] all I saw were pimples."

The next memory Georgia recalled had to do with the surgery she had on her upper jaw during the summer between high school graduation and the beginning of her first semester of college. "When I went to college the pictures of me from the first semester showed my cheeks were bigger than before. My face looked like it had been squeezed between my forehead and my chin, and the excess ended up in the round part of my cheeks." The SUD level was a five for Princess, "because my face looked like the face of a fat person."

During her second year of college, Georgia suffered a severe ankle sprain. What Princess remembered was "how unattractive my leg appeared, wrapped in a bandage, and how big it looked." The SUD level was eight "because my leg looked bloated and fat." Later, after finishing college and while working full time before changing careers to go to law school, Georgia "had a really bad perm—my hair. Princess said I looked like a poodle." The

SUD level was a three. Later again, when Georgia was in law school, she exercised on a treadmill. On one occasion, she fell and scraped her knee, leading her to wear a bandage for a few days. Princess said this was "completely unacceptable. A woman in her 30s shouldn't have skinned knees."

In response to the question, "What about aging?" Georgia said, "Princess doesn't like the lines under my lower eyelids." She was disturbed to a level nine. "Part of it is because they seemed to come out of nowhere. It was a shock to see them. They're only gonna get worse."

We were at the end of the session again but, before closing, we asked Princess about her willingness to unburden the disturbing memories she carried, memories that led her to judge Georgia so harshly in the present. "She agrees to try it," said Georgia, "but she's a very strong-minded person." Georgia also added that at one point during the collection of the memory set, Princess asked her if she was feeling okay and if she needed a break because "we were dealing with pretty painful stuff." It was clear that Princess had changed her initial attitude of disgust and irritation with Georgia to one of sympathy. This was a good sign for cooperation in the unburdening process. We intended to help Princess become less judgmental and more accepting of Georgia's 41-year-old body. The result should be that Georgia would become less judgmental of herself. Actually, Princess was the one distressed by the "pretty painful stuff." Georgia was not bothered much by the memories. They were just a part of her history. She remembered the pain and inconvenience of her injuries more than their negative appearance.

Healing Georgia's Body Image

In our seventh session, we thought it was time to begin the unburdening. However, new information came to light that led us to postpone that work. Once Georgia located Princess for the evening's work, she asked her if she would be willing to give up some of her demand for body perfection in Georgia. Princess said that "she would try." At this point, it became clear that Princess's model for body perfection was developed almost entirely from Georgia's extensive experience with watching the black and white movies of a different generation. As Georgia pointed out, blemishes are hardly visible in such films. In answer to the question of whether movie scenes were the one foundation for Princess's views on beauty, Georgia answered, "Yes. She showed me a couple of them: *Mildred Pierce,* starring Joan Crawford; *Notorious,* starring Ingrid Bergman; Katherine Hepburn in *Philadelphia Story;* Rosalind Russell in *His Girl Friday.* She shows me the characters in black and white, except *Notorious* in color. She just showed me a scene from the animated movie, *Sleeping Beauty.* I think she most wants me to look like Katherine Hepburn." Because she had yet to see Princess clearly, Georgia asked her to provide a picture of herself. Then she said, "I'm getting images from a black and white cartoon. There's like a crooner, a singer—a caricature of Frank Sinatra. I caught a flash of a picture of a woman in carica- ture, a stylized drawing of a Hollywood starlet." Asked if Smiley was there Georgia said, "No, he's a newer model. He comes from a different style." Georgia went on to describe Princess, "She has shoulder-length wavy hair. Her skin is smooth. It's a cartoon version of a variety show. I was young, maybe third or fourth grade when I saw the cartoon. I think it had *Melody* in the title, maybe something like *Melody on Broadway.* It was probably made in the late 40s."

The source of Princess's view of female beauty thus became clear: ani- mated drawings of stereotypically beautiful women, and female stars from the era of black and white movies. In these films, women never showed blemishes or unattractive bulges. They were never overweight. Before be- ginning the process of unburdening Princess's memories of Georgia's blem- ishes and bulges, we tried to broaden Princess's ideas concerning female beauty in the real world. We talked about Katherine Hepburn still acting in movies in her 70s. Princess acknowledged that "Hepburn made it work." Georgia also tried to give Princess a more balanced view of Joan Crawford, "Yes, she gained weight, but she was still Joan Crawford." She went on to say, "I reminded Princess that Joan Crawford was a dancer and had to work out hard and got swollen feet, and she says 'I hadn't thought of that.'" Georgia pointed out that normal aging and body changes happened to models and to Georgia, too. Princess accepted this truth.

Our effort to broaden Princess's framework for judging female beauty was partly successful, as shown when we turned to doing unburdening work. Princess's judgment of the seventh grade memory of how distorted Georgia's foot looked after she broke her little toe had spontaneously re- duced from a SUD level of eight to a level three. We went on to ask Princess to unburden the remainder of her distress of the foot's distorted look. She chose fire as a means of unburdening but was unable to release her distress. Georgia discovered that the problem was that Princess thought she was supposed to burn up the memory in the fire so that she wouldn't have to look at it anymore. Georgia explained that that was not the intent of unburdening. Princess would keep the memory but release her negative emotional reaction to it. Once Princess understood the process she accepted Georgia's visualization of a rain shower which easily washed away all of the negative energy attached to Princess's memory of the distorted toe.

At the end of the session, Georgia asked Princess if she had any response to this evening's session. Georgia chuckled at the response and said, "She wants me to wear some fabulous jewelry one day, something with pizzazz! I told her I'll do my best." Then Georgia added, "When we talked about Joan Crawford and Hepburn [regarding aging] she was saying Sleeping Beauty never got old, but I think she was just arguing for the fun of it." Georgia also pointed out that "in *Whatever Happened to Baby Jane*, Joan Crawford was older and the camera gave her a more realistic look."

In our eighth session, we approached the continuing unburdening of Princess somewhat differently. Rather than focus on particular memories we asked Princess to package all of her negative memories of Georgia and try to unburden them all at once—the injuries, apparent deformities, and body imperfections. She chose to use the symbolism of a rain shower washing away her negative feelings as the means of unburdening. The initial effort reduced Princess's burden to a level three on the SUD scale. After this, further progress required considerable discussion and negotiation. The remaining level three disturbance was "because we're asking her to ignore the evidence that she can see." Georgia told her that her view was not quite accurate. We were asking her to accept rather than ignore what she sees; we were asking her to embrace self-acceptance. "She doesn't like that," said Georgia, "because that would just be an excuse to really let myself go." Georgia then told Princess that "she doesn't really need to carry around her burden of dissatisfaction, because she still has her primary job and she knows what to do to help me stay in shape, to take care of myself, and to dress well. And I told her it might even help her to be better at her job because I would listen more." Finally, Princess agreed to go back to the rain shower and let the water wash away more of her negative energy. The intervention went something like this:

> Okay, visualize Princess standing in a pleasant rain shower, gentle but with a lot of rain. Notice how every part of her is soaked, as the water flows over her, around her, and right through her. And ask Princess to focus within herself where she stores the memories of all the problems she remembers about your body. And then ask her to allow the water to dissolve the negative energy attached to these memories and wash it away.

It is similar to hypnotic suggestion, but formal hypnosis is not involved, just Georgia focusing inward on her own imagery.

Soon Georgia said, "Okay, we're down to a one—just a kernel of negativity, the idea of accepting imperfection." Georgia added additional explanations regarding the pretend-world of film and the actual outside world in which she lived. "Okay, she understands the difference between the actual world that I live in and the fantasy world of film. Okay, she's ready to try the rain shower again." This time Georgia said she could handle the imagery by herself. She visualized Princess standing next to her by a lake as the rainstorm approached. When it arrived, she asked Princess to let the rain wash away the remaining negativity. Then she said, "It looks like it's gone down to a zero." In order to be sure that Princess had indeed given up all of her burden of negative feelings, we checked several memories to verify that all registered zero on the SUD scale. Finally, Georgia asked Princess a few more questions and was satisfied with the answers. "Yes, she still feels committed to her job. Yes, she will be my coach as long as I listen."

Commenting on her own different perceptions following the unburdening, Georgia said, "Interesting; Princess started to look a little differently after the last rain shower. She had been in black and white, but at the end there, I thought I could see her arms in color. I had been concentrating on washing away the darkness or graininess from the pit of her stomach, but then it seemed like it was more on the outside—I don't know if her arms got colored or just got shinier." Looking back at her processed memories, Georgia said, "Amazing! I can see that picture with my acne and it doesn't bother me at all." As we ended the session, I gave Georgia the homework assignment for the coming week of looking at herself in the mirror, nude, and recording her responses.

In session nine, Georgia talked briefly about her progress at work, which was going well. Then she reported back on her homework assignment.

It was amazing! The difference [from her previous 'Yuck!'] was unbelievable! When I looked at myself in the mirror, it was like looking at a normal person instead of a blob. Also, I felt like I had lost 20 pounds. Actually, I haven't lost any, or at most five pounds. On the Monday before our session, I looked in the mirror and still saw a big fat blob. But on Thursday and Friday [after our Wednesday session], it looked like I'd lost a ton of weight. Now I've gotten used to realizing that this is how I really look. So it's not so much of a shock. But I actually felt lighter on my feet on Thursday and Friday and on into the weekend.

Georgia also described a change in her view of her clothing:

While considering what to wear yesterday I remember thinking about a necklace, 'Oh, Princess will like that.' Over the weekend while going through the closet to discard too big and too small clothes, I found myself finding lots of nice clothing that I hadn't been wearing. I was able to think more about how the clothes and jewelry could look on me because thinking about my body wasn't such a negative experience. It was like a weight lifted off my shoulders that I didn't realize was there. I realize that I had been dressing to hide myself rather than to draw attention to myself. I had been wearing four pairs of pants and three shirts and rotating them. There were so many clothes in my closet I wouldn't think of wearing. I don't know why I bought them. Maybe Princess influenced me to buy them but couldn't get me to wear them.

Following my comment that Georgia seemed to be dressing differently, she said, "I know that I had promised Princess to try to look better, and so I am not surprised that you have noticed a difference in what I'm wearing. There were a couple of times on the weekend I was so happy to look in the mirror and like what I see. A couple of times I even started to cry I was so happy. It was amazing! When I look in the mirror now, I feel like it is the core of me who is looking there."

When we returned to deep work, Georgia had some initial difficulty locating Princess, but when asked to help, White Dragon quickly brought her onto Georgia's mental screen. Princess said she had heard most of our conversation at the beginning of the session. Georgia commented, "Princess was glad that you [the therapist] had noticed that I was dressing a little better. And she appreciates the effort I've been making. And she was definitely helping when I was looking at the clothes in the closet this weekend." Regarding the question of a change in Princess's skin color, Georgia said, "It's just more shiny and gives a clearer image of her, but she is still in black and white." When Georgia asked Princess about the role of Smiley, she found:

> She says he can be childish, and you have to watch out for that with him. She really sees him as a kind of pest, like a younger brother who wants to tag along. I asked her if she knew if he worked with any other parts, and she said she doesn't pay that much attention, but seemed to think he would follow anybody around who let him, and he would do things for that part if asked. Yes, she asked him to do things for her, but she is hesitant to say what she asked him to do. She definitely had him try to get my attention sometimes when she thought I wasn't listening to her. She had him run errands for her, but it's the kind of stuff like get beauty cream for her, stuff like that. She never paid attention to what he was doing. She would tell him what she wanted and then didn't worry about it because she knew he would do what she asked. She didn't care about his methods.

In answer to the question as to why she was more difficult to locate for this session, Princess indicated that "She's not stepping back from me, but she reminded me that when I first started communicating with her I used the knot in my stomach about how I looked to locate her, and that knot isn't there anymore." Georgia thanked Princess for working with her and got the response, "Anytime!" Once Georgia was fully oriented to the external world at the end of the session, she said, "Princess was right about that knot in my stomach. But when White Dragon helped she was right there as usual. But she did have that bit of attitude about being interrupted from being busy with important things."

In our tenth and last session in this series, we turned our attention to Smiley to see if there was more work we needed to do with him. Georgia had some initial difficulty in locating him, but White Dragon soon brought him to Georgia's internal attention. He acknowledged that he had been listening when we talked with Princess about him. "He said when he hears Princess talking about him he likes to check it out." When asked about his function in the internal system Smiley said he didn't know the answer to that. When asked if Smiley had a job, Georgia answered, "Yes. He listens to other people, both in the inside and the outside world. He says he listens to everything. He listens so he can figure out what people think about me. And yes, he will try to influence my behavior depending upon what people say about me, but only when Princess tells him to."

"He thinks Princess is fantastic. It's like he's a fan of hers. He helps out because he wants her to like him. And no, he doesn't do things for other parts like he does for Princess. He says also that his burden is not a problem. He can handle it." Georgia negotiated a new, more constructive, role for him. He would help coach her toward physical fitness. "He definitely likes this idea. 'No problem,' he says. And he is willing to give up his burden now—so he can be a coach and not be bothered by his burden." Smiley chose to do his unburdening with fire. Georgia visualized a pit of flames for him, and he walked through it, allowing all his negative feelings to be burnt up in the fire. When we checked the SUD level for the individual incidents in his memory set, each one scored at a zero level. As a fitness coach, Smiley will get together with Georgia and Princess to work out a plan for Georgia to get in shape.

The end of the session approached, and we would take a two-week break from therapy as Georgia devoted herself to the coming Christmas and New Year's holidays. Before she left the office, Georgia paused to say, "The work on how I look was huge! I'll spend the next two weeks thinking about what to work on next."

Postscript

Six months after concluding our work on body image I interviewed Georgia again on the same topic. At my request, she produced two written descriptions of herself, the first for how she viewed herself at the time of our first meeting, and the second for how she viewed herself after the work on body image. The first description follows:

> Tall (5'8") with fair complexion, brown eyes and dark brown hair cut short and worn spiked up on top. From my shoulders to my knees, my body looked like an apple-shaped blob. I saw the same shape whether I looked at myself straight on or in profile.

After our work with Princess and Smiley, Georgia described herself as:

> Tall (5'8") with long arms and legs. Fair complexion, brown eyes and dark brown hair cut short and worn spiked up on top. My body has a curvy, hourglass shape and all the parts are in proportion to each other. When I look at myself in profile, I now see the contours of my body.

Georgia said she now put more thought into how she dressed, and she mixed things up more. She changed her jewelry every day now, and she more often wore "fitted clothing." She also said that she thinks differently about clothes and jewelry. Previously, "I looked at clothes as camouflage, a way to cover up and hide my unsightly appearance. Now, although I still see clothes as primarily functional, I also see clothes as decoration or adornment."

Chapter 11
Gay Porn Addiction and Low Sex Drive

Henry was 37 years old when he came to see me for help with his addiction to pornography. He was successful and prominent in his profession as an emergency room physician. His compulsion to view porn had become a serious issue with his male spouse and threatened their 13-year committed relationship. Their relationship therapist had referred Henry to me for more specialized work. Henry's score on the Dissociative Experiences Scale was only 4.1, and consequently, the inner world with which we would work was not likely to be the product of a dissociative disorder. The kind of pornography to which Henry was addicted was that involving late adolescent males. His fantasies were actually more strongly drawn to early adolescent boys, but he worked hard at avoiding porn involving the younger boys because it was illegal. One problem was that it was often difficult to tell the actual ages of the young participants depicted in the videos. Henry was fearful that he might destroy his career if he was somehow found in possession of videos that turned out to be child porn; that is, where the participants were actually under the age of 18. The second problem was that Henry's spouse was strongly opposed to his fantasies of adolescent males, even older adolescents found on the internet. It was an issue that threatened to end their relationship.

Until recently, intermittent, overwhelming rage was also a problem for Henry, but he appeared to have resolved this issue through his work with his previous therapist. The work with rage had significantly improved his relationship with his partner. Now he wanted to remove what he believed was the one major remaining source of conflict: his addiction to gay porn. Henry estimated that he typically spent two hours a day on his computer looking at pornography. During a two week period when his partner left him, just prior to his committing to our therapy sessions, he took a leave from his work. For those two weeks, he spent virtually all of his waking moments, 16 hours a day, on porn websites.

Parts Psychology treats behavioral addictions such as pornography, gambling, binge eating, etc. through two sets of interventions. Both involve unburdening memories of their attached emotional energies. In one set of interventions, we locate and then neutralize the positive memories associated with the addiction. In the other set, we locate and neutralize the painful memories from which the addiction is an escape. These negative experiences are always a feature of behavioral addictions. Without them, ending the problem behaviors would be a simple matter. In Henry's case, we began with the positive emotional energy of viewing porn, but the negative emotional energy of other life experiences were soon a target of our work as well.

Beginning Parts Work

Henry's previous therapist had introduced him to Parts Psychology. As a consequence, he needed little additional information about working with parts. It was the sort of work he had come to expect. We began our work with subpersonalities in the first psychotherapy session. I asked Henry to recall and think about some of the pornography that he found particularly powerful. He was able to locate within himself a "slight response" to remembered pictures. When he focused upon that internal response and asked it for an image of itself, the first image that came to mind was an erect penis. We might have been able to use this image as a representative of the addicted part, but when there was no response from the image to our first question, I suggested that it might be more helpful if Henry worked with an image of an internal person. With my coaching, Henry directed his thoughts toward the penis image, saying, "I understand this is your response to sexual pictures, but now let me have a picture of you, the part of me who responds sexually in this way." The result was a different internal image that Henry described as "the shadow of a person looking at a computer screen." Such an image is consistent with the internet as the primary source of Henry's pornography. As we worked with this image, Henry would eventually come to visualize this shadowy figure as if it were looking back over his shoulder at him as they carried on their conversation. The image responded readily when Henry directed our orienting questions at it. Yes, it knew who Henry was. Henry was "Me." "Of course," said the part, he was the one addicted to pornography. His name was *Yogi*. Later, Henry would describe the image as a version of *Yogi the Bear*, the animated cartoon figure popular in children's television in the 1960s. Yogi said that he knew of Henry's partner and of Henry's desire to improve their relationship, but that was not his concern. Henry had the sense that Yogi was irritated about being interrupted and wanted to return to his computer.

Working successfully with an internal part requires rapport and a sense of cooperation. The observing self and the internal part need to work as a team with a common purpose. With the early hint that Yogi had an agenda different from Henry's, and with the intent to help the two of them develop a positive working relationship, I urged Henry to thank Yogi for being a part of his life and for helping him to enjoy it. Unfortunately, Henry found himself unable to direct these thoughts toward Yogi. The problem was that Henry had another part, as yet unidentified, who felt threatened by Yogi and considered him an enemy. I asked Henry to do two things. The first was to speak inwardly with the part of himself who disliked Yogi and request that it step back; the second was to permit me to thank Yogi on his behalf. Initially Henry argued that it was he and not a part who refused to thank Yogi. Eventually, after I explained that the self had no extreme feelings, he accepted that it might be a different subpersonality who refused to work with Yogi. Still, he could not say the things I urged him to say to bring about a cooperative relationship. He gave me permission, however, to speak through him, directly to Yogi. I thanked Yogi on Henry's behalf for being a part of his life, and for providing him many sexual pleasures over the years. I also thanked him for providing an escape and release for Henry when life's stresses were great. I pointed out that only Yogi could give Henry the help he needed now. He was too powerful for us to make changes with respect to porn unless he cooperated with us. I thanked him again for his many efforts to help Henry in the past, and then asked him to help him now in a new way. Henry wanted to give up his porn addiction and only Yogi could help him do that. A therapist can never lavish too much praise on a recalcitrant part. After I spoke, Henry reported that Yogi said that he had been happy to help over the years, but he wanted to know what was "in it for him" to work with us now. I suggested that his cooperation would improve Henry's relationship with his partner and that Yogi would gain significant respect among other parts in Henry's inner world. He agreed to cooperate, Henry said, but pointed out that he was less concerned with Henry's personal happiness than with his *own* standing among other self states.

The preceding interactions illustrate that the preferred way of doing Parts Psychology, by working through the observing self, sometimes has to be temporarily set aside. Henry had brought a sense of urgency to our work. Consequently, rather than take a more circuitous route to getting Yogi's cooperation, I spoke directly to him. The part who didn't like Yogi wanted to solve the problem of the porn addiction by simply getting rid of Yogi. Parts, however, rarely disappear, and never do so through direct interventions for as long as they continue to be empowered by the energies locked in their memories. It is futile to try to dispense with a part. The most that can be accomplished is to send the part into temporary hiding. A part is a collection of memories with a linking theme or two, consciousness, a sense of self, and a desire to continue its existence. Memories, the primary content of internal self states, cannot simply disappear. The most frequent reason initially given by parts for their refusal to cooperate with parts therapy is their fear of dying or disappearing. They need to know that the therapist and observing self value them. And they often need assurances that unburdening will not threaten their continued existence. We ended the session with a plan to locate the part who disliked Yogi, so that we could facilitate cooperation between them. The strongest feelings that Henry could identify in the unknown part were embarrassment and fear.

Unburdening Positive Energy

In session two, we tried to connect with the part who disliked Yogi. Henry explained that the fear the part carried was the fear of being arrested and sent to prison if he acted out on his fantasies. Our attempts to bring the hidden part into our conversation failed, so we returned directly to our work with Yogi.

Because Henry was so worried that he might act out on his fantasies, I wanted to be sure that when he left my office at the end of a session he was not sexually aroused. With this in mind, I suggested that we unburden each memory as we elicited it, rather than collect the entire memory set before starting the unburdening. Yogi's earliest memory of porn dated to when he was six years old. Henry's male cousin had porn magazines that he kept in a coffee can in the woods. Yogi's recollection of the heterosexual porn produced an energy response of only one or two. In this case, we used a SUE (Subjective Units of Energy) scale rather than a SUD (Subjective Units of Disturbance) scale because the energy connected to porn memories was positive rather than negative. Henry chose a frequently used wind metaphor to unburden this first memory. He visualized Yogi standing between two posts in an open field as a powerful wind blew between the posts and over and through Yogi. The SUE level for the porn memories quickly reduced to zero. The pornography itself was less important than the sex play his 13-year-old cousin introduced to six-year-old Henry. For Yogi these memories of "fooling around" retained a SUE rating of five. Our first attempt at unburdening this energy was unsuccessful. Yogi simply didn't want to let it go. However, Henry explained that this memory was his earliest memory of sexual experience as a boy and with a boy, and it was triggered when he watched gay porn in the present. As such, it was a foundation memory for later sexual responses to gay porn. Finally, Henry reminded Yogi that he didn't want even the slightest chance that he would act out on fantasies of young boys because of the possibility that he could go to jail. After Henry stated his position, Yogi allowed the wind that blew through the posts to carry away the sexual energy connected to the memory. The result was a reduction of the SUE level to one. Because this final amount of sexual energy was resistant to unburdening, we used a technique also drawn upon in other chapters. We worked directly with the six-year-old still stuck in the memory of fooling around with his cousin. After Henry introduced himself to the six-year-old in the memory scene and guided him in releasing his sexual energy to the wind, the boy was no longer interested in sex play and "ran off to play with his trucks." The intervention with the six-year-old also brought Yogi's SUE level for the early memory to a zero without further intervention.

Yogi's next memory was similar to the first. It involved sex play with the same male cousin when Henry was eight and the cousin was 15. The level of sexual energy was a three on the SUE scale. Henry guided Yogi in releasing the energy to the wind-and-posts intervention, and quickly brought the SUE level to zero. The next memory was of watching heterosexual porn at age 12 with a male friend. Yogi reported that the memory was almost boring to recall. There was no unburdening necessary.

Yogi then reminded Henry of a two-week period of sex play when he was 13. He and a male neighbor watched *straight* porn while masturbating. It was not the porn that was exciting; rather, it was the masturbation in the presence of another boy that remained exciting to Yogi. The SUE level was six. Over this exciting period of time, Henry and the neighbor boy watched porn and masturbated on four different occasions. There was no overt homosexual contact, but the memories remained very stimulating to Yogi 25 years later. After Henry prepared the intervention scene by visualizing the wind blowing between the posts and onto Yogi, he soon reported that Yogi was not cooperating. "He wants to know why he has to give up the excitement of the memories," Henry said.

Henry and I took a brief time-out then from trying to persuade Yogi to unburden the adolescent memories. We talked further about the reason for the present unburdening. My thinking was that the memories of adolescent sexuality were important to unburden for two reasons. Some of the memories were associated with stimulation with porn, even if it was straight porn rather than gay porn. The other reason was that the memories of adolescent sexuality were often triggered during Henry's current use of porn. We also discussed the possibility that Henry might be able to heal his compulsion to view adolescent gay porn without working with his porn-free adolescent sexuality. We could avoid work with those memories if he chose to do so. Then, if this approach proved unsuccessful, we could go back later and include the memories that didn't involve porn. It was his choice, but logic suggested that since the adolescent memories were triggered by porn use, those memories should also be unburdened of their sexual energy. Henry asked, "So I lose this whole window of my life?" In responding to this question, it was important for me to remind Henry that unburdening does not involve the loss of memories; rather, it involves detaching the problem energies from the memories. His memories would remain intact, and he would also retain whatever knowledge he had acquired from the experiences. The aim of the intervention would be for Henry to become emotionally neutral when recalling his adolescent sexual activities. Ultimately, Henry chose to go ahead with the full unburdening because he thought the seriousness of the problem required him to be as thorough as possible. Yogi, who had followed our conversation, accepted Henry's decision. Within two minutes of visualization, Henry reported that Yogi had fully unburdened the four earliest memories of adolescent sex play.

We were near the end of the session when Henry announced, "There are dozens more of these adolescent sexual experiences. The first four were just the beginning." He also talked about his first boyfriend, Tommy, and their four-year relationship when he was aged 15 to 19. His boyfriend was two years younger than he was. He felt that his experiences with this boy were not related to later porn use or to the current problems with his partner. Yogi said that if he didn't have to give up Tommy he would give up the rest. Henry and I thought that was a reasonable trade-off.

In session three, just two days later, Henry reported that he had felt no compulsion to look at porn on his computer since our last session. Yogi, according to Henry, was saying, "See! See! We're all done, right?" We reminded him that he had agreed to give up the sexual energy connected to dozens of other adolescent memories, provided we left alone the memories of Tommy. Yogi agreed to stick to the bargain. Since our last session, there had been a change in the way Henry visualized Yogi. Instead of seeing him at the computer looking back over his shoulder, Henry said, "I'm picturing him sitting in a brown chair looking directly at me. He acts like he's in a hurry." But he was ready to unburden the other adolescent memories.

Henry had by now accepted the process of unburdening and chose to do the work without my guiding the imagery. He used the same metaphor of bringing a powerful wind to blow over and through Yogi as he stood between two posts. With his eyes closed, Henry was silent for about five minutes. He opened his eyes then and said, "He's pretty much finished." Before fully accepting such judgments, it is always important for the therapist to check the results. I did this simply by asking Henry to check with Yogi and ask him to scan his memory set for additional problem memories. Henry said, "There's a few more he forgot about." I suggested that he take Yogi back again to the wind-blowing-through-the-posts metaphor. Before doing that work, Henry checked again with Yogi and reported that there were other sexual images, but they were not triggered by porn, including some with girls. Then he added, "Okay. He says there are other memories but only about ten are triggered by porn." Henry guided Yogi in unburdening the sexual energies from these 10 memories. After another minute with his eyes closed, Henry said, "Done." I asked him to check to see if any of the targeted memories had even a level one of sexual energy. He did, and said, "They are at zero."

We moved on then to Henry's college memories involving pornography. He recalled that the only porn available to him at the time was legal adult porn. He did not have access to porn involving underage boys. When I asked if he wanted to unburden the memories of adult porn, Henry responded, "I should probably give up all gay porn since the links [on the computer] take you to younger and younger boys. It's like climbing down a ladder." The experiences of adult porn while Henry was in college were all related to "adult book stores" or "gay arcades." The unburdening of these experiences took only a few seconds.

The next set of memories Yogi carried were formed during the years when Henry was in medical school. Those years, said Henry, were his first experiences with illegal porn. He chose to continue unburdening through use of the wind metaphor. Within about one minute of concentration with his eyes closed, he said, "Okay." The medical school memories were done. Then, when I asked Henry to check for any unresolved porn memories from this period, he began unburdening later memories without further prompting. After about three minutes, he opened his eyes and said, "There are millions of images and Yogi's going through them one by one. This is gonna take a long time. Maybe we can group them somehow." I agreed and suggested grouping them by year of viewing them. "My mind can't deal with that," Henry responded. We had momentarily forgotten that it was Yogi who carried the memories, and it was he who probably had a better sense of how to group the porn images for efficient unburdening. Henry decided to leave the grouping up to Yogi and again closed his eyes. After four minutes of silence Henry nodded, opened his eyes and said, "Yogi let his collection go." He had sorted the porn images into four groups: men with boys, women with boys, boys with boys and boys by themselves. "He just burnt right through them, right up to the last, about two weeks ago." The sexual energy, previously bound to the pornographic pictures from more than a decade of compulsive viewing, had been released. Those years of memories were no longer connected to Henry's sexuality.

As we approached the end of the session, I asked if there were additional experiences with porn that needed unburdening. After a few moments of inward searching, Henry said there were. He was unsure, however, whether they came from Yogi or another source. We would search for the source at our next session.

A week later when we met for our fourth session, Henry reviewed his progress in therapy. The rage on which he had worked with his previous therapist remained a nonissue. Internet pornography was not a problem throughout the week. The night before coming to our session, Henry was home alone and didn't even turn on his computer. During episodes of love-making in the previous week, there were no pornographic fantasies. "My mind was a *whiteout*." There were no images either of previous partners or of the pornographic pictures that had been a part of his sexuality for almost all of his adult life. Although the absence of these fantasies reduced some-what the sexual energy in his lovemaking, Henry said that the trade-off was worth it. He felt no guilt about having sex. He did not want back the energy of the porn images. Before seeking out further work with other possible internal sources for his porn addiction, we discussed other thoughts and fantasies that he might use to replace the whiteout he now experienced when having sex. Among those ideas was that of asking Yogi to focus on the earliest and most powerful images from his early history with his partner.

Manager Tiberius

The only disturbing experience for Henry during the week occurred dur-ing sex with his partner. "Yogi tried to bring in a recurring fantasy—no, it wasn't Yogi, but a more power-hungry part. I can feel it. Yogi is more sub-missive. No, Yogi wasn't involved at all." We searched then for this more dominant part. I asked Henry to think of the fantasy and allow it to evoke a response in him, and then ask that feeling to show itself. Henry described the image that came to mind as that of "a man, 55 years old, thin and bald on the top of his head, but with the baldness framed by white hair around the sides and back of its head." It was, Henry said, a Roman bust of Emperor Tiberius, and the fantasy scene involved young boys from the movie,

Caligula. The fantasy was less important as pornography than it was as domination. The part was not very cooperative. Henry said the part had a name but would not share it. We decided to call him *Tiberius.* He was neither shy nor angry; he simply "refused to be told what to do." He knew Henry, and accurately insisted that he and Henry were the same person. "He's kinda pissed to be bothered over a handful of images." Tiberius was evidently fully coconscious with Henry, aware of everything happening in his life. He was the part in charge when Henry dealt with matters in the hospital's emergency room. He liked being dominant. And he was the one worried about legal issues related to Henry's porn use. He agreed to give up the fantasy from the movie scene, but not his dominance.

Henry visualized a powerful wind blowing over and through Tiberius in order to unburden the energy attached to the movie fantasies. Less than a minute after closing his eyes, Henry opened them again and said, "Let's try something else. I can't get a wind strong enough [to do the unburdening]." After a brief discussion, Henry decided to use fire. He would guide Tiberius in unloading the sexual energy attached to the images into the coals of a fireplace. Within a few seconds, the unburdening was finished. As Henry reflected on his past, he observed that Tiberius was "the one who was there when I got in trouble in school. He's the one who said to himself, 'Well, fuck you then! I just won't say anything if you don't want the right answers!'" Henry went on to say that Tiberius "thinks of Yogi as a masochist, that he enjoys having the guilt over the porn. And he's the one giving Yogi the guilt. He's verbally abusive to Yogi."

Henry suggested that Tiberius was not a problem in his life. His energy and his drive to be in control helped to make Henry a successful man. Tiberius did have a problem before beginning therapy, a problem with moments of rage. But his previous therapist, who also practiced Parts Psychology, had healed him of that issue. Tiberius believed, according to Henry, that he now had control over the porn. "It's not an addiction anymore." We tentatively accepted that judgment, but planned to check on the matter after Henry returned from a Caribbean vacation.

As we concluded the session, Henry noticed that his internal image of Yogi was now clearer. He was "a big stuffed bear, a Teddy bear version of *Yogi the Bear.* He was like a big beanbag bear. He has holes in him, and his stuffing is leaking out." Because I had previously worked with parts with damaged self-images, I suggested that when we met again we should probably look for the cause of the holes Henry saw in Yogi. Henry agreed and said that he had a part with whom he wanted to do some work —a part who could rarely turn down his friends when they asked for money or other assistance.

An Embarrassed Part

Following Henry's return from vacation for our fifth session, the first of the New Year, he said that pornography had not been a problem at all for the entire 10 days he was gone. We did not do further work on the porn issue during this session because of the disturbing presence of another part, a part who felt great embarrassment about Henry's porn use, as well as embarrassment over Henry's actions as a gay man. The part was not concerned with Henry being a gay man, but about the ways he acted in the pursuit of his sexual interests. The porn use was one example; another was Henry's visitation during medical school of *gay parks,* places where men went to connect with other gay men in a sort of random way. The part felt such actions were undignified and beneath Henry. Henry should meet men in more normal environments—work, social events, friends of friends, etc. "The embarrassed part," Henry said, "is exactly half of me." The other half consisted of Yogi and Tiberius. When I asked Henry to focus on the embarrassment he felt and to ask that emotion to provide a picture of itself, Henry found himself looking into a cave, too dark to see inside. He couldn't find anyone in the cave. In the absence of an image upon which to focus his questions, I suggested that Henry simply speak to the dark cave and see what happened. It would be a simple experiment with nothing lost if there were no response. To Henry's surprise, his questions were answered. An 18-year-old part appeared who looked like Henry when he was nearing the end of his senior year of high school. He knew that Henry was 37. His earliest memory was of riding in a car with his mother at the age of four or five and listening to the music of James Taylor on an "old-style tape player." When asked for significant memories, the part responded with memories of Henry involved in "lots of boy scout and other hiking and camping experiences. Henry had been an Eagle Scout. The recollections involved a significant amount of charity work: "soup kitchens and clothing drives." The part reminded Henry that he had been good at sports. As Henry spoke of these memories, he noted a strong sense of connection to his grandmother, with whom he had lived for several years during his youth.

Other memories carried by the 18-year-old part were of "sitting in the restroom, stoned" in Henry's first year of college, an event that was embarrassing at a SUD level of seven; playing volleyball at his fraternity house; and a fraternity house photograph of him with "wild hair and a full beard." Later, when Henry was in medical school, he occasionally met other gay men in "a pick-up-park." The 18-year-old part disapproved of this activity and rated those visits at SUD levels from four to six. Henry observed that it was also the 18-year-old who had previously judged that those meetings "were beneath me." The connection to his grandmother's view of propriety was evident to Henry as he experienced his disappointment in himself.

In session seven, Henry noted the absence of any urges to view pornography. However, unwilling to give himself too much credit, he also indicated that he had "mostly stayed away from the computer," using it only for specific tasks such as booking a hotel room and *Map Questing* directions. He had also not experienced any urges to pull up porn on his Blackberry, which, in any case, "is slow and the images are not as clear."

We returned then to the themes of disappointment and embarrassment that had surfaced in our previous session. The 18-year-old part, said Henry, was embarrassed by "gay behavior." He did not mean Henry's sexuality. He considered himself bisexual. "Sex is just sex. Boys are just sex. Oral sex is not gay sex, just sex." He did not disapprove of sex with males. Henry might even have a girlfriend, and that would be fine with the 18-year-old. What he disapproved of was "acting like a *femme on a float,*" or "going to a *pick-up-park,*" or otherwise displaying mannerisms that were stereotypically gay. He found fault with Henry because Henry was "faggier" than he was. This was embarrassing to him. He was most concerned with Henry's "perversion," by which he meant his interest in boys, an attitude he attributed to Tiberius.

Tiberius Again

Henry described Tiberius as "a boy lover." "I want him to give it up, but I'm in for a real fight. Tiberius is indignant," Henry explained, "at being singled out as a problem. "Tiberius says it's *another sexuality*. Under the right circumstances, there is nothing wrong with it. He generally does not find women or men attractive." Henry described Tiberius as "a dominant sexual part."

In contrast to Tiberius, the 18-year-old "liked it all—women, girls his age, men and boys, and hunky muscle-builders. He is afraid to talk to Tiberius, and Tiberius won't listen to him." I suggested that Henry speak to Tiberius on behalf of the 18-year-old. Tiberius responded quickly to this attempt to communicate with him. Henry explained,

> He talks over me. He says he gave me Bobby [Henry's boyish 32-year-old spouse] as a compromise. That's why there is a sexual problem [of libido]. It's the 18-year-old who has sex with Bobby, and that's just not as strong a sex drive as Tiberius has. His sexual excitement is about power, archetype, and beauty. It's just what he is sexually attracted to. He has no interest in men and women. It's like the way a *screaming queen* would look at a woman.

We were near the end of the session, and Tiberius was not responsive to Henry's desire to move him away from boy love. Instead, Henry experienced Tiberius as angry and overbearing. He was the most powerful of parts in Henry's inner world, and we could do little without his cooperation. Consequently, I guided Henry in thanking Tiberius and showing appreciation for his work as a protector and manager throughout Henry's life. We hoped that Tiberius would work more cooperatively with us in our next session. Experience with other systems shows us that flexibility and cooperation often follow when the therapy focuses on the importance of a part's role rather than on convincing the part of the necessity for change.

In our eighth session, just a day later, Henry reported that he had fought "all day and all night" with his spouse. "Bobby thinks my anger is out—it was; it spilled over from yesterday's session. We fought like a parent and child or older brother and younger brother. I hope we can get past this." I assured Henry that he and his partner could indeed get past their fighting, as least to the extent that it related to the sorts of problems we were working on in therapy. In the remainder of the session, we focused all of our attention on getting to know more about Tiberius, our purpose being to do the work that Henry believed was necessary to heal his relationship with Bobby.

We began by thanking Tiberius for being a part of Henry's life and for providing so much help over so many years in aiding Henry's growth into adulthood. Henry acknowledged that his success in his profession was due in good part to the guidance of Tiberius. He acknowledged as well that Tiberius's management of Henry's inner world had been excellent and wise. Now Henry wanted Tiberius to help him even more, to help him in a new direction in life. All of this praise—and one can never praise an inner part too much—was aimed at gaining Tiberius's cooperation in a way he had not yet shown. Once Henry had finished lavishing praise upon Tiberius, he said that Tiberius seemed to have "less attitude" and to be ready to share his memory set with us.

The earliest memory Tiberius could recall was that of watching the impeachment proceedings of President Nixon on television. Henry estimated that he had been about 10 years old at the time. While the memory was not disturbing, it was consistent with the sorts of things—the maintenance and loss of power—in which Tiberius had great interest. Another memory, earlier than this one, was of riding upon his father's shoulders at a carnival. This memory contained positive energy at a SUE level of nine. In fact, all of Tiberius's memories were connected to positive energy and required the use of the positive-energy SUE scale. The earliest memory he could identify in this session dated to Henry's pre-school experiences. "Another girl stole my toy," said Henry, "and Tiberius beat the living shit out of her!" This event measured a level six on the SUE scale. Another event involving childhood violence rated at a level nine or ten, and happened in the first grade. Henry was in a military school and, like all of the school's students, had been drilled in the importance of the honor code. On one occasion, said Henry, "A boy stole my paper while the teacher was out of the room, and he wouldn't give it back. When the teacher came back, the boy was bloody and on the floor in the back of the room." Tiberius had evidently severely beaten the boy, but Henry didn't remember the details. When coached to ask Tiberius for details, Henry reported that *he* didn't remember the details either. Tiberius remembered a "swirling" in his mind following his demand that the boy give back the paper, but he had no memory for the actual fight. This amnesia for such a high-energy event sounded similar to the amnesia that adults experience following rage-induced battering or destructiveness. Because such events seem always to involve a subpersonality in executive control of the body, I asked if Tiberius was aware of another part who was also involved in the incident. He acknowledged that there was another part. It was the anger part who we believed had been successfully treated by Henry's previous therapist.

Other significant memories Tiberius held, included playing chess with the headmaster (level six positive energy), being attracted to his best friend (level 10), and wrestling in gym class with other boys (erotic at a level seven or eight). These memories all dated roughly to Henry's age eight or a little later. While they were important for understanding the role of Tiberius in Henry's life, they did not appear to be the sort of memories that underlay Tiberius's problematic relationship with Henry.

One of my early hypotheses was that Tiberius had projected himself into the molester role in the incident at age six when Henry's 13-year-old cousin had molested him. However, Henry reported that Tiberius was not present at that event. Such an absence is often the case in exploring a person's inner world. Not all parts are present at the significant events of a person's life, and this leads to each part having its own unique memory set. Tiberius was the part involved whenever Henry exhibited dominant behavior with respect to other persons. One such incident involved "using a younger, weaker boy sexually in the third grade." The memory rated at a level six on the SUE scale for Tiberius. This was the first memory so far reported by Tiberius which seemed to be connected to the theme of "boy love" that Henry objected to and wanted to change. When asked, Tiberius agreed to unburden the positive energy connected to this memory. We used a wind metaphor to help Tiberius release the energy connected to the memory, with Henry visualizing Tiberius standing in an open field as a powerful wind flowed over him and carried away the problem energy. Tiberius said that this was not the age of boys to whom he was attracted. He was not troubled at allowing the memory to be unburdened. However, when we checked the SUE level for what remained after the intervention, it still registered at a level four. We were at the end of the session and did not have the time to explore the source of blocking, although Henry did report the internal image of his grandmother expressing anger because Tiberius couldn't let the energy go. I asked Henry and Tiberius to find a suitable symbolic container in which to store the unresolved energy that had come up during the session. Henry chose to visualize putting it into my office refrigerator until our next session.

In the following week at our ninth session, Tiberius indicated that he was still willing to unburden the energy connected to the incident in Henry's third grade. For the intervention, Henry chose a metaphor of Tiberius discarding the problem emotions into a fireplace for its incineration. Surprisingly, given the block to our work that had appeared in our previous session, the intervention went quickly. Within a few seconds, Henry reported that the memory was neutral. It is not uncommon for resistance to disappear between sessions, and it is always a pleasant surprise.

We continued then in collecting other memories from Tiberius's memory set. One subset of pleasant memories involved Henry's participation at age eight or nine, "down the street," in mutual masturbation with four brothers, aged 10 to 14. The experiences registered at a level two on the SUE scale for Tiberius. Other of Tiberius's memories involved feelings of attraction for a couple of different male friends. "No sex," said Henry, "just an attraction." Henry went on to say that the memories of attraction and sexuality with boys his age and older represented "the gay part of me; they are not a part of the *boy love.*"

I then asked Henry to request from Tiberius only those memories that connected to the problematic boy love. In response, Henry described two incidents involving boys younger than him. The first involved sexual contact with a sixth grade boy in the billiards room of a motel when Henry was in the eighth grade. The second was paired closely in time and occurred on a cruise ship. The boys touched each other through their clothing but went no farther than that. The experiences rated a level four on the SUE scale. I continued to follow the practice of encouraging Henry to unburden problem memories as they surfaced rather than to elicit a full memory set. Henry immediately made use of his fireplace metaphor to rid himself of the unwanted sexual energy connected to these experiences with younger boys. In just a few moments he said, "That was easy."

The next set of relevant memories was linked to Henry's participation in the Boy Scouts for two years between the ages of 14 and 16. He estimated that there were more than 50 incidents of sexual contact between him and younger boys during this time. There were additional contacts with neighborhood boys during this period as well. Tiberius agreed to unburden the positive sexual energy from these experiences. Henry said that the overall rating was a positive eight on the SUE scale for these many experiences. He added that giving up that energy represented a significant sacrifice by Tiberius. We began the intervention with Henry and Tiberius using the fireplace metaphor, attempting to incinerate the associated positive sexual sensations. However, after less than a minute Henry opened his eyes and said, "There's just too many; I'll have to break them down first." I suggested that Henry allow Tiberius to sort the memories for unburdening since we were working with his memory set and he was most familiar with them. Following an internal discussion with Tiberius, Henry said, "I'll do the easier ones first," then he closed his eyes and worked with Tiberius in stripping the memories of their sexual energy. When he opened his eyes again four minutes later he said, "I got the big bulk of them out. Then there is a big jump from 16 to when I was in [medical] school." Between his teenage years and medical school, there were no memories of the sort that bolstered Tiberius's boy love fixation.

When Henry attended medical school, he met a younger boy in a gay park and developed a relationship with him that lasted for two years. Henry was 24 and the boy was 19, but "he acted younger. Emotionally he was younger." Tiberius agreed to unburden these memories, once again using the fireplace metaphor. Within a minute, the memories were unburdened to a zero level of sexual energy. Henry commented, "He was tied to more than I remembered. There were incidents with other boys during this same time period."

Next, Henry turned to two other similar experiences. Tiberius rated one of them at a level one on the SUE scale, but the second received a rating of ten. Henry said, "I'll do the easy one first." Almost as quickly as he closed his eyes, Henry opened them again to say, "That's done. Now the other one." After two minutes of effort, Henry opened his eyes and said, "Tiberius doesn't want to let this one go. Because this one was close to perfection. It's like collecting the most beautiful statues you can collect, and you want to keep them for yourself." At my suggestion, Henry expressed to Tiberius that he knew what a powerful sacrifice he was asking him to make. Yet he believed it necessary in order for Henry to have the best chance of continuing his relationship with his partner. Henry did so and returned to the unburdening effort. Shortly, he reported, "It's still a 10 [on the SUE scale]. It may even have been a nine at the beginning, but now it is a 10. It's also the last time I've done anything with anybody under 19."

In cases such as this when a subpersonality takes a stand in direct opposition to what the observing self and the therapist wish to accomplish, it is never helpful to try to force the intervention on the part. Consequently, I asked Henry to pass on my appreciation to Tiberius for the work he had already done and for considering the request we were currently making. In return, Henry reported that Tiberius also thanked me for working to help Henry. I went on to question Henry about the inner changes we had made to date. I wondered if Henry still felt there was a danger of him actually acting out on his fantasies. He said that he believed he was safe now and that neither he nor his career was in danger. He didn't know, however, if the changes would be enough for Tommy, his partner. Then, without further prompting from me, Henry tried to explain Tiberius's position. He said, "It would be like asking a straight guy to give up his memory of a sexual experience with the most beautiful of *Playboy* center pages." Then, without any request from me, Henry said, "Let me try this again." One minute passed with Henry keeping his eyes closed. When he opened them he said, "It's done. He gave up the sexual energy but kept the artistic appreciation. It's like keeping an appreciation for Michelangelo's *David*." When I asked Henry how he came to decide to try again, he said that the idea just came to him, a way to do the unburdening with which Tiberius might agree. As we ended the session Henry added, "I still think there is more boy love, but Tiberius says there is not. It's more that they are just pretty. He doesn't have to own them. He doesn't have to have sex with them."

The Angry One

At the beginning of our tenth session, Henry noted the absence of any urges to view pornography. He added that he still found boys attractive, but felt no danger of acting on this admiration. He was bothered, though, with what he felt was a diminution of his sex drive in general. He had always had a lower sex drive than his partner, but the work we had done seemed to have driven his libido to new lows. He wanted to see if there was anything we could do about this problem. Shifting our focus to this new problem led us to check with the sexual parts we knew about and to look for others we hadn't yet met. We knew that Yogi and the 18-year-old were sexual parts. Tiberius, as we were surprised to discover, claimed that he had never been involved in a sexual experience with Henry's partner. We wondered if the angry part who had been the focus of work with the previous therapist might be a sexual part also. When Henry inquired within his internal world, he quickly discovered that this part, which he called *The Angry One*, was indeed a sexual part. It was apparent that we would have to include this part in our work. Unfortunately, the intervention used by the previous therapist to subdue the rage led to The Angry One becoming psychologically constricted rather than unburdened. He had been placed in a symbolic prison, guarded by Tiberius. It appeared that we would have to do the incomplete unburdening of rage in order to draw upon The Angry One's sexual energy. However, releasing The Angry One from his internal prison might endanger Henry with his untreated rage. We decided, therefore, to work with The Angry One while he remained in confinement. We planned to unburden him of each of his painful memories as they surfaced and then to return him to Tiberius's control at the end of each session.

When Henry first dialoged with The Angry One, he confirmed that the part carried sexual energy and wanted to help Henry in therapy. He had had sex with Henry's partner and would like to do so again. He was frustrated with being "tied down." It made him angrier. He understood, however, why it had been done. He believed that it was Tiberius who had "locked him up" and who "held the key." When asked about his earliest memories, he presented Henry with a flash of recall of great frustration as a pre-school child when he could not open a bag of cheerios. The frustration rated a level six on the SUD scale. Another early memory was that of Tiberius drawing him out to "beat up" a little girl in preschool. The memory rated a level three on the SUE scale—it was neither negative nor positive, he said, just "something I was told to do." Another level three rating on the SUE scale, dating to about the same time period, was the memory of playing "show and tell" with a little girl in an uninstalled, above ground, sewer pipe. And from the first or second grade, The Angry One recalled a recurring fantasy he had of throwing knives to hit the board close to his first girlfriend as she spun around on a carnival wheel. The excitement of throwing knives at her and the danger inherent in the possibility of actually hitting rather than missing her rated a level eight on the SUE scale. Another experience came at age seven when he was mean to a girl he had become attached to at a Christmas camp. Tiberius didn't know how to say goodbye to her at the end of camp, so he caused The Angry One to be "vicious" toward her when the camp was over. The Angry One also had many memories of getting into fights with other boys as a child.

We moved through the last few memories quickly, without collecting a rating on an energy scale, because we were approaching the end of the session and we wanted to introduce the unburdening process to The Angry One before we ended the day. Before we could begin any unburdening, however, The Angry One spontaneously reported to Henry that "Tiberius was dishonest when he said he doesn't remember beating up the kid in the first grade. Tiberius was watching and even telling him how to beat him up. He remembers the other kids in class taking off to the other side of the classroom and the girls screaming. 'The little bitches were running and screaming while I beat the shit out of this little motherfucker.' Tiberius told him to kick the kid in the head, and I did as he lay on the floor."

The preceding powerful observations by Henry are interesting for several reasons. First, there is the switching between first and third person in Henry's narrative, which we have seen in other chapters. Second, it is clear that Henry's angry and violent part developed early in his childhood. Third, we begin to see that the angry part did not act as a free agent, but was under the direction of a manager part at an early age. It may have been that The Angry One was even a part of Tiberius, similar to how Monster Boy was a part of Phyllis in Chapter 8. Finally, if The Angry One is correct in his contradiction of Tiberius's previous reports, we have an illustration of how internal subpersonalities are capable of lying, at least by misdirection or underreporting. In any case, both parts cannot be correct.

Henry and I turned then to the unburdening process with The Angry One. Henry, like Georgia in Chapters 4 and 10, preferred to provide his own imagery rather than have me narrate the intervention. We began with The

Angry One's earliest reported memory, that of his level six frustration with opening a bag of cheerios. Henry said, "Let's try the fire; he likes that." Then, "Nope, that made it worse. I'll try the wind." Within a few moments, Henry reported, "Okay. The baby [i.e., preschool child] is just bored now; he's not angry." The SUD level had been successfully processed from six to zero. Henry added, "Tiberius is teasing The Angry One about making a big deal about opening a bag of cheerios when he was the part who kicked a kid to unconsciousness." Continuing the unburdening, Henry said that a puff of wind was all he needed for the memory of beating up the little girl in preschool. However, when Henry chose wind to process the fantasy knife-throwing at the first girlfriend, he quickly said, "It's getting worse; the wind is blowing the fire over the girl now, and she's screaming." Evidently, Henry had begun to visualize a powerful wind blowing over the scene, but the fireplace imagery he preferred had intruded into the process. Whenever there is this sort of interference with unburdening, it is important to look for another part who is interfering with the work. When asked, Tiberius said that he was not interfering, but we were out of time to investigate further. We quickly helped The Angry One to visualize putting his aroused emotions into a container until we could return to him in our next session. As a final note, Henry observed that based on the memories we had so far collected, The Angry One seemed to be "more straight than gay."

Enhancing Sexual Energy

At our eleventh session, Henry noted that he had had an urge to go onto the internet to view porn only once during the five days since our last meeting. He thought the urge might have come from the awakening Angry One, a part he had tentatively identified in our last session as more straight than gay. He added, "My fantasies have predominantly been *hetero*." This posed a problem for Henry because he was in a committed gay relationship, and he wanted that relationship to continue. He and Bobby, his spouse, had had no sexual contact over the previous week, and this was worrisome to Henry. He knew that Bobby's sex drive was greater than his was, and he was concerned that Bobby might stray if he did not keep him satisfied.

Consequently, we decided to take a break from our work with The Angry One to see what we could do to heighten Henry's current sex drive, especially his gay sexuality. Logically, it seemed that if we could reduce sexual energy through guided imagery, we ought also to be able to increase sexual energy through guided imagery. We began by returning to Henry's memory, accessed through the Yogi part, of his first meeting with Bobby in the gay park and returning to Bobby's house for their first sexual encounter. The memory registered a level seven on the positive energy SUE scale when we accessed it, but by focusing on it and exploring all of the pleasant details of the meeting—the sounds, sights, smells, activities—Henry was able to elevate the SUE scale from seven to 10. Before proceeding further, Henry talked about how, before meeting Bobby, "I was 80 percent straight. I even had a girlfriend for three years. I don't find most men attractive, except those who are younger and slim. But that leads to the slippery slope to underage boys we're trying to avoid."

We returned to additional work with Yogi by asking him to think about lower-level sexual experiences with Bobby, as measured by the SUE scale, as Henry visualized Yogi standing openly in the sun and drawing upon the sun's energy to amplify the SUE level for pleasure in those early memories. As Henry continued this visualization, he recalled that he had met Bobby when Bobby was 19 and that "he is my best friend in the whole world." Shortly thereafter, Henry reported that he had been able to amplify Yogi's earlier low-level sexual memories with Bobby to "close to 10." We continued this work with more recent memories of sexual activities with Bobby; however, we were interrupted by the intrusion of memories of *mercy sex*, occasions when Henry did not want sex but consented anyway for the sake of pleasing Bobby. Because these were unpleasant memories, we took the time to unburden the negative energy attached to them. With that work accomplished, we returned to the intervention in which Henry used the power of the sun to enhance Yogi and *his* sexual response to his spouse. Henry concluded this work saying, "I think we're done." Finally, in order to maintain the gains we had made, Henry asked Yogi to work at being more a part of Henry's daily life with Bobby. Henry also asked Tiberius to permit this greater influence. Tiberius, Henry said, had no problem with that.

Before ending the session, we talked again with the 18-year-old and asked him to be more involved with Bobby as well. "He hasn't had much influence lately," Henry pointed out. "He wants more fun in sex and he'll bring more ideas, like different places, more teasing, maybe use a feather, add some light kinky stuff." Henry was pleased with our session and said he was looking forward to being with Bobby that night. Assuming that all went well, we would return to work with The Angry One in our next session.

Two days later at our twelfth session, Henry said that Yogi's sexual response with Bobby after our last session rated a seven on the SUE scale. He was quite pleased with this because in the absence of porn, his usual response rated a level two or three. We wondered if the level seven response could be increased for Yogi. Consequently, Henry tried again to use the drawing-energy-from-the-sun intervention to heighten Yogi's most recent sexual memories. Henry was unsuccessful in doing so. He said that Yogi wanted to borrow energy from The Angry One, but Tiberius vetoed that idea with the observation that "Yogi wouldn't be able to handle it."

The Angry One Becomes Banger

We tried then to work directly with The Angry One with the goal of accessing his sexual energy in order to enhance Henry's sexual response. We found him "locked in a cage" and watched over by Tiberius. We asked him if he could explain the difficulties we had two sessions previously when Henry tried to unburden the memory of his fantasy of throwing knives near his childhood girlfriend. In that intervention, when Henry tried to use wind to blow away the positive energy connected to the fantasy, Henry's efforts were interrupted by the intrusion of the fire from a previous intervention. The Angry One's response to the question was, according to Henry, "You started the fire; I just let it get out of control." Then, rather than respond to Henry's request that he permit the unburdening, The Angry One ignored the conversation. According to Henry, The Angry One refused to engage further with him and distracted himself with internal noise and extraneous commentary. In order to develop a cooperative relationship with The Angry One, I guided Henry in praising him for his talents and in thanking him for being a part of Henry's life. We also thanked him for all of the help he had given over the years to help Henry survive and be successful. Those efforts mollified The Angry One somewhat. Additionally, according to Henry, Tiberius also lent a hand in "calming him down."

When The Angry One was prepared to work with us, Henry asked him about his earliest memory. This time we learned that just minutes before the incident of frustration with opening the cheerios package, Henry's parents had been engaged in a loud and scary argument. The Angry One had been trying to protect Henry from his fear through banging together the pots and pans he had pulled out of a low-level cabinet. The conflict was disturbing to The Angry One at a level seven on the SUD scale. In recalling this incident, Henry said that his ears were actually hurting and ringing with tinnitus as he sat in the therapy room and remembered the racket he had made so many years before. Henry quickly unburdened The Angry One's emotional distress for this incident through the wind-blowing-through-the-posts meta-phor. An additional unburdening with the same metaphor was necessary to clear the ringing in the ears experienced by both The Angry One and Henry.

Following the pots-and-pans intervention, The Angry One cooperated fully with the project of unburdening painful memories, but he wanted a name of his own. When he couldn't decide on a name for himself, Tiberius suggested — with a chuckle, Henry said — that he take the name *Killer*. Henry, however, found this suggestion unhelpful. Then, spontaneously, the part chose the name *Banger* for himself, evidently connecting to his early expe-rience of banging together pots and pans. We agreed to address him with this name in the future. Henry noted that he now visualized Banger as hav-ing less fire around him. Evidently, the fire had been leftover imagery from our first attempted unburdening with him.

As the session concluded, Henry turned his attention to Tiberius and quickly unburdened him of his level one guilt for the manner in which he broke up with his girlfriend at age seven. For our next session, we planned to process the beating up of the boy in the first grade. We wanted to keep in mind as we worked with Banger that we were looking for sexual energy to boost Henry's interest in his partner. We also wanted to be careful not to release the restraints on this angry part until we had unburdened enough memories such that he would not do further damage to his relationship with Bobby through explosions of rage. Consequently, we did not aim to collect his entire memory set before unburdening. We aimed to unburden each memory soon after eliciting it.

A week later at our 13th session, Henry talked briefly about his growing awareness of the actions of his internal parts. At a staff meeting he had directed at the hospital, Henry "could almost feel Tiberius saying, 'Hey, what about me?'" during the introduction of new staff members. Henry added that after a full day of high-energy responses to emergency room crises, he could feel Tiberius still experiencing an emotional high. "I tried to put him away on my way home, but it was difficult. He's definitely on the manic side. He was ready to go look at porn when it was done. I knew I was at risk, so I took the battery out of my Blackberry and went to visit my mother." Henry added, "I could definitely sense him talking some of the time, and dealing with all of the emergencies was such a rush that he wanted to do something to come down from the high."

When we returned to our work with angry Banger, Henry reported that he was still in jail, where Tiberius kept him so that he would not rage. Regarding Tiberius's manic mood on the previous day, Banger, according to Henry, "was aware that Tiberius was pumped. Everybody was. But he didn't experience it." When we checked on the level of energy for the first-grade beating of the boy who violated the honor code, Banger indicated that it was only a one or two. Henry quickly unburdened this remaining energy through his favorite metaphor, burning it up in a fireplace. The next memory Banger recalled was that of driving "really fast" at age 16 following a break-up with Henry's girlfriend. They had not had sex. "She offered, but I couldn't perform. She screwed my best friend." Banger was angered over his girlfriend's behavior only at a SUD level of one, but was upset at a level six because of the betrayal by his (male) best friend. Driving fast actually came at the direction of the 18-year-old part who was more active then than in recent years. In fact, said Henry, it seemed to him that the 18-year-old had been largely "shut down" since college. The 18-year-old's reaction to the breakup was the inverse of the reaction by Banger. He was disturbed to a level six with the girlfriend, but only to a level one with the best friend.

While the breakup with the girlfriend was a memory we planned to neutralize, it seemed to me that there had to be other painful experiences between the first grade and age 16. As a means of exploring this question, I asked Henry to check with Banger and ask what he was most angry about now. His answer was that the noise of the fan in my office was disturbing him to a level nine. He wanted to get up and "smash it." It was easy enough to turn off the fan and look for underlying anger issues. Banger acknowledged that he was angry with Bobby, Henry's spouse, but only to a level five. We would later learn that it was Tiberius who was most disturbed by Bobby's behavior, at a SUD level of 10. Working with Banger, however, permitted the use of an affect bridge to earlier memories. Henry asked Banger to stay connected to his anger with Bobby as he allowed his mind to float back in time to his earliest memory "that somehow connected" to the anger he was feeling now. The memory he accessed through this technique was an incident in the fourth grade. "My friend Roger pissed on me. I had an attraction for him." The memory was disturbing to a SUD level seven. We were at the end of the session, so we asked Banger to put into a container the negative affect we had activated in this session.

In our 14th session, Henry observed that Banger had been "out of his cage" since our last session, but was under the control of Tiberius. He believed that this was the reason the sexual parts, Yogi and the 18-year-old, hadn't been around; that is, because his consciousness had been dominated by Banger and Tiberius. "Banger likes being out," Henry added. "And I notice the way I'm speaking is different when he is out. And Bobby asked me what I was mad about, but I wasn't."

We had not previously talked about how Henry was different before the work with his previous therapist had brought his anger under control. We took some time to explore that remembered state, because we wanted to ensure that he didn't return to his older, angry ways. He said that previously he had often raged at Bobby. "I would scream at him and be emotionally cruel. I would take out my frustrations on those I loved—Bobby and my mother." Even as a teen, Henry raged frequently. When he lived with his grandmother and a cousin, he would turn his anger on them. Only once, however, had he actually struck anyone. That was when Bobby was wrapping Henry's injured knee after a fall and a shooting pain had triggered his reflex to punch his partner. Two other ways that Banger had previously affected Henry was through his tendency for binge drinking and his claims of being suicidal.

Unburdening Banger

At our last session, we had ended with Banger's memory of being "pissed on" by Henry's friend, Roger during a holiday outing. Henry returned to this memory in our 15th session and, without my coaching, proceeded to unburden Banger of the distress of this memory. He used a wind-and-posts metaphor, where he visualized Banger standing between two posts while Henry brought up a powerful wind to blow through the posts and over and through Banger. Within 10 seconds, he reported that the SUD level for Banger was zero and that Banger was feeling "a tiny bit better."

Banger next recalled that, in the seventh grade, his teacher embarrassed him by revealing to the entire class her plans to have Henry tested because she thought he was "mentally challenged." The tests revealed that far from being mentally challenged, Henry was quite bright, with an IQ of 154. As a result, said Henry, "I was removed from her class and put in with the gifted kids." The damage, however, had already been done; the embarrassment registered at a level seven on the SUD scale. Henry unburdened Banger of his distress through the fireplace metaphor, visualizing Banger removing his negative emotions and throwing them into the fire. During this process, he decided to unburden all of the negative events of the entire seventh grade, a year of considerable awkwardness and unhappiness. Afterwards, Henry noted that Banger had also thrown the teacher into the fire and watched her transform into the *Wicked Witch of the West* (from the movie, *The Wizard of Oz*) before she burst into flame. Within a couple of minutes, Banger had achieved a zero distress level for all events of Henry's seventh grade.

The next significant event for Banger occurred when Henry was 17. At this time, Henry lived with his grandmother and a male cousin just a year younger than himself. The cousin was a meek and overweight boy who had been prescribed Ritalin for his attention deficit disorder. One day a classmate had bullied him into giving up the pills for his own use. The bully overdosed on the pills, ended up hospitalized, and blamed the cousin for his situation. Banger blamed his cousin for forcing Henry to deal with the fallout. He was angry that he had had to pick up his cousin from school following his expulsion. (His grandmother was out of town). He was embarrassed in front of the vice principal, a teacher who Henry liked and respected. He was concerned with the possible effect on his grandmother's health—she wore a pacemaker. Finally, he was upset that his cousin "had almost killed another kid." The incident disturbed Banger at a level five on the SUD scale, but yielded quickly to Henry's visualization of the wind-blowing-through-the posts intervention.

The next memory involved Henry's experience as a varsity wrestler in high school. It was normal practice for the second-string boys to *challenge* the first-string boys to wrestling matches. The winners would represent the school in their respective weight classes at the next match. Henry had been challenged for his position by another boy and was angry about it. During the challenge match, Henry had the boy *pinned* with a wrestling maneuver called the *guillotine*. Still angry, however, Banger gave the challenger "an extra pop" at the end of the match and "tore his *lats* [i.e., lateral back muscles]." Deciding upon the unburdening work required some discussion because it registered on both the negative SUD and positive SUE scales at a level five. For Henry, wrestling was sometimes a sexual *turn-on*. Once, another boy had noticed that Henry had an erection and made a rude comment about it. Although Banger unmercifully attacked the boy verbally, the incident remained a sore spot in his memory. The challenger paid for the other boy's comment when Henry injured him. The 18-year-old part accepted responsibility for the erection on the previous occasion, and Tiberius acknowledged that he was involved in the pleasure of hurting the boy who had challenged Henry. Henry asked for and received permission from both Tiberius and the 18-year-old to unburden the wrestling incident. The unburdening involved all three parts, Banger, Tiberius, and the 18-year-old, discarding both their positive and negative emotions into a visualized fireplace. The intervention was accomplished in less than one minute. The 18-year-old also unburdened his remaining distress for having been noticed with an erection on a previous occasion.

At the end of the session, Henry took time to thank Banger for his cooperation in doing the unburdening work. In return, Banger asked permission to "stay out of the cage" in which Tiberius had kept him. Henry then led a short discussion involving himself, Banger, and Tiberius on the question. Tiberius pointed out that if Banger stayed out it could make life difficult for Henry's relationship with Bobby because of all the anger Banger had for

Bobby's suspected relationships with other men. Banger countered with the suggestion that he could just "step back" from day to day interaction with Bobby without having to return to his cage. Finally, Tiberius relented, saying Henry could give it a try, as long his blood pressure—which correlated with anger outbursts—stayed down. Henry asked Banger to step back from him, and then asked for a further step into dissociative space, until Tiberius felt Banger had achieved enough distance from Henry to make him safe from rage.

The following four days between sessions went well with the absence of rage, and so, in the 16th session, Henry asked whether we might work directly on his rage toward his Bobby. Until now, the strategy had been to elicit painful biographical memories in the order in which they occurred so as to benefit from the generalization effect on later memories that follows from working first on earlier memories. It was the rage Banger generated toward Bobby that Henry viewed as the greatest block to their continued life together. Because Banger had done well during the previous four days, we temporarily abandoned the plan to work from his earlier to later memories and skipped to the memories that directly impacted Henry's relationship with Bobby in a negative way. The decision was not a good one, but it was instructive and emphasized the value of staying with the protocol of working with earlier memories before tackling the more recent ones.

Henry described his history with Bobby since they moved to Las Vegas four years previously. They had "an okay relationship" when they first arrived, but Bobby soon "shut down." He was depressed; he stopped working; he stopped going to school. He took a job at a high-end department store where he developed an extended network of social relationships. Henry estimated that after Bobby took the job at the department store "he cheated hundreds of times." In contrast with this period, Henry thought that over their previous years together each of them had cheated only "a handful of times." One year earlier, Henry had discovered "thousands of emails" between Bobby and other men. He found also that Bobby had had a boyfriend for six months, and "he was connecting with about 12 guys a week." Two months prior to beginning therapy with me, Henry discovered again that Bobby was cheating. After a huge fight, Bobby left to live with his boyfriend in another state for a time. During the year after Henry discovered the emails, he and Bobby entered couples counseling. "I think he cheated less then or stopped cheating altogether for a while. He probably cheated 12 to 15 times. I cheated maybe two or three times that year."

Bobby stayed with his boyfriend only a couple of weeks before returning to Henry. But shortly after their reconciliation, Henry found Bobby being affectionate with another man at their hotel during a weekend getaway trip. This event led Henry and Bobby to stop their couples therapy while each of them sought out individual therapists for their own work. As Henry finished his historical summary, he noted that it was Tiberius who claimed the anger over the betrayals. It was also Tiberius who investigated and uncovered the many ways Bobby had strayed.

Near the end of the session, we began to work with the rage Banger carried. Banger thought that his greatest disturbing memory was the one where he found himself looking at the thousands of emails Bobby had made to other men more than a year previously. We quickly discovered that Henry was not yet ready to process this memory. It was disturbing to him at a level 10 and was physically painful. "I don't think I can hold this [rage] even a single day," Henry said. His left arm and the left side of his body were in pain and his entire body felt tremendous pressure. He was sure that his blood pressure was skyrocketing. In order to help Henry better tolerate his stress for the remainder of the day, we worked with container metaphors to put away Banger's rage for later work. Henry visualized Banger putting his distress into a cell phone and placing the cell phone into a freezer. That helped significantly but left "a little patch of pressure in the left of [Henry's] chest." Henry then visualized putting the remainder of the rage in the glove compartment of Bobby's car.

As we ended the session, Henry and I agreed to return to the original protocol of working through each incident or set of experiences in the historical order in which they occurred. The experiment in moving ahead quickly was not successful. On the following day, Henry said that while the containers helped him in controlling his anger he experienced considerable distress after leaving the session. "I was an asshole all day!" he said. He added that it was a good thing that there was only one day between our sessions.

In our 17th session, we returned to systematic work through Banger's memory set, including some initial work with low-level events that we had earlier skipped. In Henry's sixth grade, while sitting around with friends after school, a female friend took a keen interest in the contents of Henry's book bag, and began pulling out and examining the items in it. Henry told her to stop, but she wouldn't. Banger took executive control at that point and kicked her in the head, fortunately not causing serious damage to her. The incident was embarrassing to Henry and disturbed Banger to a level four. Henry quickly unburdened Banger of the energy still connected to the memory, using the wind-through-the-posts metaphor. Also in the sixth grade there was a level five incident involving a school bully. "He tortured me all year," said Henry. "He was forty pounds heavier and six inches taller. One day I was drinking from a water fountain. He pushed my head into the metal of the fountain. I turned and beat him up. I remember hitting him so hard my hand ached. He collapsed and I kept kicking him in the gut over and over again. Nobody tried to stop me until a teacher grabbed me. I think I got suspended for a couple of days." This incident was a pleasurable one for Banger and also, therefore, for Henry. However, because it was a part of the base of memories that underlay Banger's rage, Henry agreed that it too should be unburdened. With the use again of the wind-and-posts metaphor, Henry quickly neutralized Banger's energy investment in the memory.

A final pre-college memory for Banger involved fear at a SUD level of three while attending the high school prom. Henry had confronted and broken up with his high school girlfriend because he discovered "she was sleeping with my best friend." Her angry response was to tell the vice-principal that Henry was using cocaine. He was afraid the vice-principal would believe her and accuse him during the prom. Consequently, he did not enjoy the event, anticipating instead that at any moment he might be accused and expelled. Henry once more unburdened Banger through directing the wind to strip the memory of its attached fear. After about a minute of internal concentration with his eyes closed, Henry opened his eyes and reported that he had unburdened more than just this single incident. "I was actually able to unburden all the stuff with her. She tried to trick me into believing I was the father of the child she was pregnant with. I tried to have sex with her but I couldn't. She wanted to have sex so she could say I was the father. I never had sex with her. Later, she told me about stripping for some marines and having sex with them. I was a sophomore in high school, and she was a senior. She aborted the fetus."

Before continuing the unburdening, we asked Banger to review his memory set to check for any additional high energy experiences preceding college. He indicated that there were none with a rating greater than level one. For a long time after the girlfriend incident, he added, he was happy.

His next disturbing memory dated to Henry's first year of college. The experience rated a level eight on the SUD scale, with some anger but a predominant mood of sadness. During that first year, Henry and a male friend had gotten drunk together and become sexual with each other. Unlike Henry, his friend had previously claimed to have no sexual interest in males. "Two weeks later, he became furious with me and made death threats against me. He tried to turn our other friends against me. I went into a giant depression. It freaked out my girlfriend—the first girl I ever had sex with. She was concerned with whether I was gay. At that time, it was dangerous to be gay. You could get beat up for it." Henry explained that what angered him was that the boy "was just as drunk as I was, and he knew what he was doing." For the unburdening of this memory, Banger chose a new metaphor: dissolving the negative energy in a swimming pool and having it disappear down the drain. Henry visualized this scene for him, and within 30 seconds, reported the disturbance level was now zero.

The final memory we accessed during the session was the breakup with Henry's girlfriend at the end of his sophomore year. By then she was by his fiancé. Banger rated the SUD level at an eight or nine. "I chose to break up with her," Henry said. "Yogi wanted freedom and so did the 18-year-old." [Note that at that time Henry was unaware of his subpersonalities]. "Banger did not want to break up. It's kinda like a sweet loss, a tender moment, like in the movie, *Casablanca*. Banger was angry with the other parts for choosing to break up." Henry went on to explain that at that time he was also involved with a boyfriend who was still in high school. Henry was 19 and the boy was 16. "Both relationships were sweet," he said. At the end of our session, Henry chose not to unburden the memory of breaking up. It was not a memory that fueled Banger's rage. Instead, "it was a good sad, a sweetness."

At our 18th session six days later, Henry reported that he had had no impulses to view porn between sessions. He did admit to "innocuous" emailing with men he would never meet—they lived 2,000 miles away. Henry described it as "flirtations at a distance." He identified the subpersonality Yogi as the driver in this activity and Tiberius as the manager who put a stop to the activity. Henry attributed his actions to his nervousness about the upcoming *Valentine's Day*, and to his and Bobby's wedding anniversary a few weeks later. After being together for more than a decade, Henry and Bobby had married two years previously.

When we returned to our work with Banger, Henry recalled a college relationship when he was 20 and his boyfriend was 18. The relationship lasted about six months and was a passionate one, fueled by the novelty that his younger partner was "just coming out." For Banger, the experience rated only a level one on the positive energy SUE scale. There was nothing about it that required unburdening. Henry indicated that he had only brought it up because it was a memory that he had not recalled until Banger brought it up. We filed it away as a potential source for later work aimed at increasing Henry's libido.

Another memory that surfaced for Banger was the experience of visiting gay porn booths in adult bookstores. Henry recalled that he thought this was the only way to be gay at the time because he was too young to enter the two gay bars in his city. What he remembered was the stench of the booths that still disgusted Banger to a SUD level of five. He rated the positive memories of watching the pornography in the booths at a level six or seven. In this case, we wanted to unburden the positive memories of watching gay porn in order to extinguish the addiction. We also wanted to unburden the disgust for his surroundings in order to continue to decrease Banger's foundation for rage. The unburdening intervention was almost instantaneous as Henry visualized Banger cleansing the memories of both sorts of energy in a bucket of bleach. Henry noted the sense of reality of the intervention when he said, "I can smell the bleach."

The next memories Banger brought out for Henry involved the pick-up-park Henry visited while in medical school. The energy attached to these memories was relatively low, but involved "the excitement of meeting men," "the disgust of meeting men," and "the danger of being found out."

The negative emotions of guilt or embarrassment rated only a level one on the SUD scale, while the positive energy rated a three on the SUE scale. These memories seemed to have little impact on either the problem of porn or the issue of rage, and so we did not unburden them.

One memory that continued to enrage Banger linked to Henry's short residence in a dorm during his first year of college. Banger continued to feel anger at a level eight for the memory. He and other students had been "busted" and expelled by school authorities for smoking marijuana in their dorm room. "A stupid girl left the door open when she left, and the smell wafted out." By this time, Henry was doing his own visualization for the unburdening interventions, requiring no verbal guidance from me. He chose to utilize the familiar metaphor of causing the wind to blow over Banger as he stood between deeply planted posts in an open field. After a minute of silence, Henry opened his eyes to say, "There was a lot of anger, and not just for the girl. A lot of stuff was going on at that time. There was a computer I had to bring back for repair again and again—I wanted to hit the snide salesman in the mouth. It was the first time I realized I had rage. It was the first time I realized I was poor in comparison to the rich kids at the school. I felt isolated there. Back home my boyfriend attempted suicide while I was there. Two other guys I knew also tried suicide and one succeeded. One friend was a *cutter*. He wasn't gay, but I knew his father had molested him."

It is a common pattern for clients to begin with the unburdening of a single event and then to find themselves working quickly through other, associated memories. In this case, Henry had unburdened most of his anger for the newly recalled events as they appeared during his initial unburdening. At my suggestion, he took a few moments to complete the unburdening of any of the memories that still required work. He quickly reported that the SUD level was zero for everything except for his anger over his friend's cutting and the molestation that caused it. Henry thought of his friend as a lot like Bobby except that he was straight. Henry helped Banger put his remaining distress into a container for further work at our next session.

In our 19th session, we returned immediately to work with Banger and the leftover problem of distress for his friend's self-harming behavior. Henry closed his eyes for about one minute as he did his own unburdening work. To my surprise when he opened them again, he had spontaneously used a means of unburdening that most clients use only at my suggestion. He had spoken to the memory image of his friend and explained to him that he could not help him through his anger because the issues belonged to him and not to Henry. It was *the friend* who had to deal with his history with his father, not Henry. Thus, metaphorically, Henry returned the negative energy to his friend, rather than keep it himself. With this intervention, Henry realized that a portion of Banger's rage had been misdirected anger that resulted from his compassion for others.

Henry turned next to his first year of medical school. It was a bad year for him. His beloved grandmother had died; he didn't like the people he met in medical school; he felt isolated and angry with the world; and when he read fiction, it was dark and depressive. It was the year as well when he began to view internet porn. When Henry tried to unburden Banger of the distress associated with this year, he found that he could not do so. Banger's internal experience was that a film or plastic membrane seemed to separate him from the memories of that year. When Henry searched his internal world for the part who might be blocking our work, he found that our first suspect, Tiberius, was innocent. However, Tiberius shared his belief that the interference originated with Yogi, the part we had earlier unburdened of his unacceptable sexual experiences. The first two years of medical school were years of frustration and depression for Yogi. "He just really felt sick during that time," said Henry. Both Banger and Tiberius felt sad for Yogi. Henry used the wind-through-the-posts unburdening metaphor for Yogi, and then observed, "That's better, but it's not zero." Henry continued, "It's the depression about the porn—he's sad because he had fallen so low. He was living in a ghetto; smoking cocaine; looking at child porn; sleeping with teenagers; barely trying in school." Henry added, "It's definitely encapsulated, with a definite beginning and end; two years of hell." Henry visualized each of the three involved parts, Yogi, Banger, and Tiberius, giving up their negative emotions to the fire in a blazing fireplace and then said, "That helps, the SUD level is down to a two for all of them." A repeat of the fire intervention for the embarrassment that Banger and Tiberius felt for Yogi reduced their distress to zero. Spontaneously, Yogi's distress reduced to zero as well. Henry finished the session by saying, "I'm glad those years are over."

Couples Issues

In session 20, we thought we were ready to focus on the issues that had developed over the 13 years that Henry and Bobby had been together. These were the issues that enraged Banger and had led to his temporary imprisonment through the work with the previous therapist. Unfortunately, that work had to be postponed because Henry and Bobby had fought almost every day during the previous week. Bobby had spent one night out by himself while Henry waited at home, unsleeping, and thinking of the flight test he would take the following day—he was trying to acquire a pilot's license. He flunked the test "miserably." This period of intense relationship stress meant that Henry's internal parts were not willing to cooperate in the therapy. *Henry 18* (as we had begun to speak of the 18-year-old) "was not around." Tiberius "didn't want to talk, because he was angry with the world—Bobby, work, the world." Yogi had "wanted to view porn. When he's hurt, he's like that. He was hurt by Bobby and by the noise inside me that includes both work and Bobby."

Yogi presented a set of memories from the time when Henry was in medical school. Some of those memories had to do with the turmoil he felt as he struggled with his sexual orientation. He had finally accepted that he was "not bisexual, but really gay." But most of his memories from this period were about school—"the frustration of doing school." He did not like medical school—"the raw competition between students, the condescension of professors, the unrelenting demands to study, study, study." We developed a therapy plan that involved redirecting Yogi away from a professional role and toward an internal advocate for leisure time activities. To that end, Henry focused upon unburdening Yogi again. He easily accomplished it. "There wasn't much there," said Henry. "It's mostly current stuff." Henry and Yogi then began to flesh out the plan for Yogi's new role. Yogi, they decided, would begin by learning all of the hiking trails in the nearby *Red Rock Recreation Area*. As the session ended, we hoped to return in the following session to unburdening Banger of his anger for the painful memories, especially of infidelity, that Henry had accumulated during his years with Bobby.

At the beginning of our next session, our 21st, Henry talked about two days of argument with Bobby about "opening up" their relationship to seeing others. Bobby opposed it, insisting that he wasn't cheating. Henry argued for it, thinking that if there was an "open marriage" agreement he wouldn't be so distressed over Bobby's relationship with other men. He also said that he really didn't think Bobby had been cheating recently, "from the waist down," but his development of close, intimate ties with other men was just as disturbing, perhaps more so, than actual physical infidelity. Henry had also been considering a career change.

Finally, we began unburdening Banger of those memories that seemed to underlie his rage. The first memory rated only a two or three on the SUD scale. It involved Henry's first separation from Bobby, when he went to California ahead of Bobby to find a house for them and to begin settling in with his new hospital job. During that separation, Bobby called Henry at 5:00 AM from a party celebrating his 21st birthday. What irritated Henry was that Bobby went to a party without him. The memory yielded quickly to an unburdening with a wind metaphor.

The next memories that continued to disturb Banger related to the times when, after Bobby joined him in San Francisco, Henry had to leave the city to attend conferences and additional training. Banger was irritated with those of Bobby's telephone calls that displayed his helplessness when it came to doing simple tasks such as "changing the light bulb," or "unstopping the toilet." Henry believed that unburdening this anger, a level five on the SUD scale, would be difficult because it was "still happening today." However, by focusing just on previous memories of Bobby's helplessness, and ignoring the present, Henry easily guided Banger through another unburdening to wind.

Henry's rage with Bobby had as its greatest source the memories Banger retained of Bobby's infidelity. It was while they lived in San Francisco, during a drive across the Golden Gate Bridge, when Bobby confessed for the first time to cheating on Henry. For Banger, the memory of this confession was indelible in his mind. He even remembered the color of the girders of the bridge as they crossed the bay. Eight years had passed, but for Banger the event was as clear as if it had happened yesterday. It continued to bother him to a level nine on the SUD scale. As we talked about the necessity of unburdening this memory if Henry were to rejuvenate his relationship with Bobby, Henry said, "It's difficult to unburden because it's still going on." By this, Henry meant Bobby's emotional intimacy with other men rather than actual sexual relations. He said, "I can't just arbitrarily cut into pieces a cylinder across time where the same kind of stuff is in it." I assured Henry that he could indeed do just that. If he could imagine it, he could probably do it, because the inner world of imagery has different rules than the physical world outside the self. And so Henry visualized cutting through his cylinder metaphor, setting free this first confession from later events so that he could unburden it. Then he used the symbolic imagery of rainfall washing the memory clean of Banger's pain and anger. Henry was surprised at how quickly he was able to release Banger's anger. In about half a minute, he said that Banger no longer felt distress over the incident. Then, with the same "cutting" imagery, he separated the memory of Bobby's close friendship with his boss from later memories and unburdened that distress as well. It was only a level three disturbance to Banger and the negative energy was immediately washed away when Henry brought the rainfall intervention to the memory.

After completing this last unburdening, Henry observed that the next group of problem memories all followed the couple's move to Las Vegas five years previously. We would continue with their history in our next session. However, even the anticipation of these next memories stirred a considerable amount of distress for Banger. Consequently, I coached Henry to help Banger store that distress in a suitable metaphorical container before we ended the session.

At the beginning of session 22, Henry spoke briefly of how he and Bobby were getting along better than usual, with fewer fights. They had discussed and agreed upon ways to cut their expenses as they moved forward. Both of them were in therapy and feeling optimistic about the future of their relationship. Returning to the work with Parts Psychology, we picked up the narrative of events following the move to Las Vegas. Our continuing aim was to unburden the painful memories that underlay the rage Banger felt toward Bobby. We wanted to bring Banger into the larger community of internal parts, into a situation where Tiberius would not have to keep him caged in order to prevent Henry from being overwhelmed with rage. The first six months in their new location was difficult. Henry felt taken advantage of by Bobby and by another relative who lived with them. Henry was the only one producing income. Bobby wasn't trying to get a job, and both he and Henry were depressed. They hadn't been intimate during the entire first six months of living in the new city. Henry was furious at being taken advantage of. He said that his fury came from both Banger and Tiberius. Henry could now do all of his own unburdening without my coaching once we agreed upon where the work was needed. He chose to unburden Banger and Tiberius through visualizing the wind blowing over them as they stood between two posts. After a minute of silence, Henry opened his eyes to explain that he was wrong in thinking Banger was angry; all of the anger had come from Tiberius. He went ahead then and helped Tiberius to release his burden. Unfortunately, more serious problems began for the couple after the six months mark. Bobby found employment and, according to Henry, developed a wide circle of relationships with other gay men with whom he had sexual contact. The next year was extremely painful for Henry. Both of the Banger and Tiberius subpersonalities felt betrayed repeatedly, and both felt anger to the point of rage. Henry found himself asking almost daily if Bobby were cheating. Recriminations, accusations, and Henry's demands for explanations dominated their lives. Then, after about a year, Bobby confessed to sleeping around with other men. He also admitted to having a boyfriend in another city. He had previously stayed with that boyfriend when he left Henry for three weeks. When Bobby returned to Henry, they tried to reconcile and began to attend couples therapy. It was this period of pain and high drama of which Henry wanted to unburden himself.

Henry first worked with Tiberius, again using the wind metaphor. Henry closed his eyes and worked with his internal world for about four minutes. When he opened them again he explained, "First I tried to get rid of the pain for each instance [of fighting or suspected cheating], and then I started making excuses for Bobby but I realized that wouldn't work. Then I decided I needed to forgive Bobby, and Tiberius did that. He's okay now." It was near the end of the session, and we had yet to work with Banger. Henry closed his eyes again to unburden Banger of the jealousy and rage he carried for Bobby's cheating, using the same wind-and-posts metaphor that he had used with Tiberius. After about two minutes, he opened his eyes again to say that "Everything is a [SUD level of] zero, except for his boyfriend. That's gonna take more work." Because we needed to end the session, I coached Henry to help Banger put his rage over the boyfriend into a container until we could work with it again. Henry chose a visualized steel safe for this temporary storage. Putting away the rage took a full minute. After doing so, Henry commented, "It was like pulling out a deep rooted weed, and I had to pull more and more out until I got it all." As we shook hands at the end of the session Henry observed, "I feel a lot better."

Goal Achievement

In session 23, Henry chose not to continue with the deep therapy of parts work. Instead, he needed to talk about the problems he was having with Bobby and the conversations they were having. There was a kind of progress in that Henry's use of pornography was no longer an issue. Instead, they talked mostly about money issues, about whether Bobby would get a job and whether he could adjust to the simpler lifestyle Henry now wanted. Tiberius, Henry's controller part, was the driver in wanting to reduce Henry's workload. "He's tired," Henry said. "He feels like he's the only one doing any work." Henry and Bobby were considering divorce. We planned to return to deep work with Banger in our next session if Henry's relationship issues had sufficiently improved.

Unfortunately, five days later in Session 24, Henry shared the news that he and Bobby had decided to separate. Bobby had remained in contact with Robert, the man with whom he had briefly lived when the couple was separated nine months previously. Bobby was going to return to Robert. A moving company had already been dispatched to prepare the transportation of Bobby's possessions to Robert's home in another state. There was still some discussion, however, of the possibility of Bobby staying with Henry.

In fact, Bobby did leave Henry, although not right away. The moving was postponed for a few weeks, but the couple's problems were never resolved. Henry continued in therapy for many more months after Bobby left, with conventional talk therapy often replacing the intense parts work that had characterized our first 24 sessions. Henry was proud of what he had accomplished in letting go of his need for pornography and in overcoming the rage that originated in his early childhood. Banger, the raging part, no longer needed to be kept as an internal prisoner. Henry had achieved what he had hoped to achieve through releasing Banger from his imprisonment. His sex drive was now normal again. "My sex drive is now as high as it was in my 20s. It seems like the absence of porn as a trigger has opened up ordinary sex interests." We had accomplished the major goals Henry had established early in therapy. When Bobby left, Henry adjusted quickly to life without him. He felt more relief than sadness. The relationship had been more a burden than a source of support for many years.

Chapter 12
Bulimia and Child Abuse

Maria grew up in Argentina, the 9th of 10 children, and came to the United States when she was 22 years old. After perfecting her English language skills, she became a successful real estate agent. She was 46 years old when she brought her 12-year-old son to treatment for his social withdrawal and uncontrolled rages. When, after four months of treatment, her son graduated from therapy, Maria revealed that she had issues of her own that she wanted to resolve. Chief among them was her lifetime eating disorder. She was slim and attractive and looked 10 years younger than her actual age, but she had maintained her thin body only through regular purging with self-induced vomiting. She had purged on most days of her life over the last 30 years, often as many as four or five times a day. She thought that it was now time to finally heal her *bulimia*. She had worked with many other therapists over the years without any lasting effect on her binge-purge cycle. Now, having seen her son respond so quickly to Parts Psychology, she hoped to find similar success for herself.

Our first sessions were in support of her son's therapy because Maria's own unresolved anger affected that of her son. With Maria entering therapy in this way rather than through the normal intake process, I initially neglected to ask her to complete the *Dissociative Experiences Scale (DES)*. This is the scale I used to ensure that other clients in this book had average or below-average dissociation scores. When I decided to include a case description of the treatment of bulimia, I called Maria to get her permission to use her story. I also asked her to fill out the DES, although it had been 18 months since she completed her therapy. Maria's score on the DES was 15.8, a high-average score for dissociation in comparison to the norm of 10. I chose not to exclude Maria's story from this book in spite of her high-average score. I thought it was important to show that bulimia does not have to involve years of therapy. Additionally, the description would illustrate that there are few significant differences between low-average and high-average dissociators in the way their internal worlds are organized. Then, because I wanted to assure readers that the presence of Maria's subpersonalities did not indicate undiagnosed *dissociative identity disorder* (previously named *multiple personality disorder*), I asked her to complete an additional questionnaire. This was the *Multidimensional Inventory of Dissociation (MID)*, a 218 item written test used to diagnose dissociative disorders. Her score was 8.3, a relatively low score that suggested that Maria did not experience significant abnormal dissociation.[21]

Our first sessions began before she shared her concern with bulimia. These sessions were aimed at supporting my work with her son. Our first individual meeting focused upon how Maria's expression of extreme anger toward her son worked against his healing. She talked about a recent argument in which both she and her son raged at each other. She had screamed at her son and "kicked him in the butt," but justified her actions, saying, "He disrespected me. He broke the rule. He broke his promise." The issue concerned her son calling her a *bitch* when she scolded him for coming home late. In this first session, Maria hadn't fully accepted the importance of looking to her own childhood experiences as a source of her anger rather than blaming it entirely on her son. However, she knew she had to work on herself and change the ways she interacted with him. She couldn't continue to scream and be violent with him if she expected him to master his own emotions. She soon agreed to focus inward and begin the work with her subpersonalities.

A Mother Introject

When I asked her to think about whatever it was that angered her most at the present time, she thought of her fiancé's ex-wife. When I asked her to focus upon the anger generated by thoughts of this person, and then to ask that anger to give her an internal picture of itself, she was surprised to find herself visualizing her mother as she probably looked about 30 years ago. This sort of subpersonality is a *mother introject*. It is a part that forms in a client's life in the image of a parent and represents the continuing influence of that parent even when the parent is not physically present. We are all influenced to various degrees by our perception of our parents or caretakers. The introject is different in that it is a representation of the parent in the form of a subpersonality which, when questioned, will usually claim to be the parent and not a part of the self. The characteristics of the introject will be those of the parent as perceived by the child at the time the part was created. Its memories are those of the child, but reconstructed so as to present them from the point of view of the parent at the time of the experiences. Most often, introjects appear to express an angry, critical, or hostile attitude toward the self or other parts. Only occasionally will a parent introject be experienced by a person as nurturing.

Maria spoke inwardly to the mother introject and summarized for me her interactions with her. The part claimed to know her. In an angry voice, she demanded of Maria, "What do you want!" When Maria asked for the other's name, the response was brutal: "Don't you fucking know my name! What fucking name you want to call me? Ana, you asshole!" *Ana* was, in fact, the name of Maria's mother. In cases like this where an internal part is a hostile introject, it is important to do two things in order for the therapy go well. The first is to make an ally of the part; the second is to convince the introject that it is a part of the client and not the parent of the client. Nothing can be gained by confrontation and argument with the problem part. Instead, the introject must be approached with respect. Consequently, I asked Maria to thank Ana for all the help she had given her over very many years. I guided her in acknowledging the help Ana had given her in being cautious in the face of her mother's anger and violent threats. The result was that Maria had survived to adulthood. She explained that Ana's sacrifice in taking on such a harsh inner role in her life permitted Maria to find joy and happiness while Ana could only continue to suffer with her negative emotions. Maria also acknowledged that Ana was extremely powerful and we could not proceed in our work without her cooperation. Finally, I asked Maria to explain that Ana was not Maria's mother, but a part of Maria who had acted in the role of Ana's mother for the benefit of all of Maria's parts. Eventually, the mother introject provisionally acknowledged that she was not Maria's mother.

We asked Ana for her earliest painful memory. What came to Maria's mind was an incident when she was 13. Her mother had told her to stop her nervous habit of pulling out hair from her eyebrows. When Maria did not stop, her mother pulled her into another room and, cursing her, cut a large swath of hair from the top of her head as punishment. Ana viewed the incident from the point of view of the mother while Maria remembered it from the viewpoint of the child she was. The event still registered with Maria at a level ten on the SUD (Subjective Units of Disturbance) scale more than 30 years later. Maria could still feel her mother's rage.

An Adolescent Part

I suggested to Maria that she give her attention to the trauma scene she held in her memory. In this scene, she could easily visualize herself at age 13. Maria asked the 13-year-old internal image to step outside of the scene so that the two of them, Maria and the 13-year-old part, could talk. The part identified herself as a younger version of Maria and accepted the name *Maria 13* as an aid to communication. When asked, she rated her anger for the violent incident with her mother at a 10 on the SUD scale. Maria said that Maria 13 was so angry that she wanted to kill her mother. Then, because we were at the end of the session, we asked Maria 13 to leave her anger in my office in a filing cabinet; we planned to return to her in our next session. We had done a lot in our first session, perhaps because of Maria's familiarity with the last two months of Parts Psychology work with her son.

At the beginning of our second session, Maria talked about some of the problems her son was having. He had been talking about dying and he was often crying and depressed in his room. He believed that the other kids at school didn't like him. At this point, because Maria had come to therapy as an adjunct to her son's therapy, she was providing the background information that would continue to be helpful with my work with her son. She was there to work on her own rage because she recognized that she had been acting in exactly the ways she wanted her son to avoid in his own actions.

Returning to her internal world, Maria easily located the mother introject. Now, while continuing to express herself in a hostile way, the part acknowledged that she was not actually Maria's mother. Maria 13 was also easily located. Initially, I had hoped that less intrusive techniques might be sufficient to soften the effect of the introject. For that reason, I suggested that Maria guide the two parts, Maria 13 and Ana, the mother introject, in an internal dialog. The exercise accomplished little but it went like this:

Why did you hit me so much?
Because you deserved it!

All I wanted was love and affection. I disobeyed to get your attention.
That's the wrong way to get it!

After this exchange, Maria 13 expressed her anger toward Ana the introject,
and this devolved into mutual name calling, ending with "I hate you!" and
"I hate you, too!" The exchange ended, and Maria said of Maria 13's feelings
for the introject, "She loves her but doesn't like what she does," and "her
mother doesn't believe her and laughs at her." The dialog was not as successful as I had hoped, but we seemed to have made some inroad toward
softening the relationship between the two parts. Unfortunately, while the
mother introject acknowledged that she was not the mother, both she and
Maria 13 continued to interact as if they *were* mother and daughter. It
seemed clear that internal dialog between the parts would not be sufficient
to bring about a change in their relationship. Consequently, we moved
forward to do unburdening work with both of them.

First Unburdening

Maria 13's earliest memory dated to the age of two. She was playing
with her brother at her adult sister's house. Her mother slapped Maria's
brother and, when the sister told her mother to stop, her mother hit both her
brother and her sister. Her sister did not hit her mother back; covering her
face instead. More than 40 years later the memory was still sharp in Maria
mind, measuring 10 on the SUD scale. We immediately turned to unburdening Maria 13 of this early memory, utilizing a waterfall metaphor. As Maria
visualized Maria 13 in the waterfall, she asked her to locate where within her
she stored this age two memory and to allow the water to dissolve her fear
and other bad feelings and wash them away. Fairly quickly, Maria said that
the unburdening was almost finished, with the SUD scale down to a level
one. Maria said that the level one was because of "the sadness in her [i.e.,
Maria 13's] heart." We repeated the intervention, and within half a minute,
the SUD rating had reached zero.

Transforming the Introject

We turned then to work with the mother introject, beginning with con-
gratulating her on having done her job well and adding other positive comments about her as we did in our first session. She had succeeded in helping

Maria to grow up. She had done well in keeping Maria alert to possible threats from her mother, and she had succeeded in helping Maria establish the behaviors she would need to avoid her mother's wrath. Then, having thanked and congratulated the mother introject, we pointed out that Maria was now 46 years old and her mother was no longer a threat to her. She could now be the little girl underneath the mother costume. Finally, we used the waterfall metaphor to wash away the mother introject's burden of playing the role of internal mother in Maria's life. As Maria visualized the introject in the waterfall, and imagined her washing away the negative energy from the memories, she described what she was witnessing: "She says she's letting bad emotions go. Yes, she is remembering all the hitting and verbal abuse of herself by her mother and some of her sisters—they were jealous of me." As she completed the intervention Maria continued, "She glows now. She has beautiful dark hair. Her skin is beautiful. She's very pretty. She looks like she is 16. She looks like me at that age. As we ended the session, Maria brought together the 13-year-old and the 16-year-old and suggested that the older teen could now nurture the younger rather than treat her with anger.

In our third session three weeks later, Maria began by confessing that she let her anger overwhelm her in the preceding week. In a moment of rage, she had kicked her son "in the butt" again. Her ongoing relationship with her son was the topic for most of the session. When she looked inside to find the part who had influenced her to kick her son, she discovered the responsible part was not the 13-year-old as she expected. Instead, it was the newly differentiated 16-year-old who had originally presented as a mother introject. The 16-year-old reminded Maria that her older sisters were angry with their parents because they left the care of the younger children in their hands. "The sisters took out their anger on us," the teenager said. She went on to recall how her sisters had "put me down; they were always putting me down." When she kicked her son, she didn't really want to hurt him. She "just wanted to show him that she was strong, the boss, and no one can put her down [now]."

Maria asked the teenager part about her earliest memory. Maria found herself remembering her attempt to visit her niece and nephew when she was seven or eight years old. She had gone to her married sister's house to see them, but when her sister answered the door, she demanded "What do you want!" When told of the reason for the visit, her sister refused and told young Maria to go home. Maria found this memory quite disturbing, but when she asked the teenager part for a SUD rating of the event, the part said that it didn't bother her. Because we were not aware of another part bothered by the memory, I suggested that Maria directly address the child (whom she could clearly visualize) still stuck in the memory scene. The memory image responded quickly and indicated that she was seven years old. She knew Maria and said of her, "That's me." We were at the end of the session with no time to collect more information and so Maria asked the child part if she wanted to leave this scene of rejection at her sister's door. She did, and so Maria visualized taking the child to the family room she had created for Maria 13 and *Maria 16*. Maria 7 joined them.

In our fourth session we returned to work with Maria 7. Maria said of her, "She is skinny with short hair, alert. She wanted to play but her sisters made her do what they wanted." Her earliest memory of negative interactions with her sisters had to do with food her sisters prepared. "She didn't want to eat it because her mother prepared it differently. They said something mean to her." In another memory, the family was eating when one sister's young daughter burped. Everybody laughed "because it was cute. But when *I* burped they called me a pig." Maria 7's negative experiences with her grown sisters yielded quickly to an intervention utilizing a waterfall metaphor. The experience of being sent home and not being permitted to play with her nieces was the first to yield its negative emotions as the water flowed over the memory and cleansed it of pain. The early experience of having the sisters say something mean to her when she didn't want to eat what they prepared was no longer disturbing. The first cleansing by the water reduced the SUD level only to a three for being called a pig, but a repeat of the intervention reduced it to zero.

Near the end of the session, we returned to examine what it was about her interaction with her son two weeks previously that caused her so much anger. Maria 16 was able to identify her problem emotion as a feeling of rejection. Then, Maria guided Maria 16 with an affect bridge to the earlier memory that had been triggered by her son. With this technique, Maria asked the teenager part to stay connected to the feeling of being rejected by her son as she searched her memories for the triggering experiences. The result was that Maria recalled how her sisters would regularly disparage her in front of their customers in the small store they operated. She felt a similar rejection in her sisters' treatment of her then to what she had felt in her argument with her son. Maria visualized a waterfall to help Maria 16 cleanse these memories of "rejection and put downs" but was not immediately able to release the negative emotions. Repeating the intervention, Maria said, "It's a little hard to do it this time." However, after several minutes she reported that the memories of being criticized to the store customers had reduced to a level one, caused, said Maria, by a sadness still clinging to the memories. Repeated efforts to unburden this sadness failed. There were "so many memories" of rejection that needed to be neutralized. "And my mother was worse." Maria visualized helping Maria 16 place the remaining sadness into my file cabinet for storage until our next session.

Child Abuse

In the following session, our fifth, we explored the abuse Maria experienced growing up, especially at the hands of her mother. "My mother would physically abuse us. She would hit me with anything; she pulled my hair; she called me names. She said no to anything I asked, so I went out without permission. She beat me so badly I had marks on my legs." Maria talked about how she often ignored the demands of her mother and sisters that she live the home-bound life they did. She went through an early puberty and looked much older than her biological age. When she was 11, she had her first boyfriend, a young man 20 years old. "I went out to night clubs with my friends at night. [My mother and sisters] called me *puta* [whore]. My mother locked me out sometimes. When I was 12 and came home at midnight one night, she slammed the door in my face. I went to the roof of our apartment building and then to the garage to keep warm with the cars. After a few hours, my sisters came for me. My mother waited with a belt." Maria continued to describe her history. "I became a liar. That is the worst memory I have of my family. My mother said I had the devil inside me. But I wasn't doing anything bad; no sex, no booze, no drugs. My friends gave me attention, and at home I just got criticism from my family. Guys gave me lots of attention. They said my body was pretty." Near the end of her turbulent teen years, Maria tried to find the nerve to go out on her own. "At 18 I rented a room, but I didn't have the guts to leave. I was 22 when I finally left. I went to L.A. I flew from Rio all by myself. At this time my niece said I was a puta and having sex with all the athletes who were going to go to the Olympics."

This sketch of Maria's history came from her 16-year-old part. For this reason, we began to work directly with her as *Maria 16* in order to neutralize her painful memories. Maria visualized the teenaged part standing in a waterfall so that the water could cleanse her memories of her mother's abuse. Maria observed that "I see the clean water pouring into the top of my head and pouring out dirty." After a few moments, Maria said of the teen-ager, "She was very scared and sad and now she's happy." But the intervention wasn't finished. "She has a pain in her heart," Maria explained. She focused upon that pain and repeated the waterfall intervention. As Maria processed additional memories, she continued, "My mother was always abusive. She called me names, *asshole, sonofabitch;* she always made fun of me. One time a friend invited me to go to a coffee shop. I was 15 or 16. I asked my mother for permission to go. She told me she would make my legs as black as coffee with the bruises she would give me." The unburdening appeared to be stalled when Maria said that her 16-year old-subpersonality didn't want to let go of the hurt. "She is scared," Maria said. "She's afraid to lose even the negative attention from her mother. She knows her mother went through this with *her* mother and so she never learned how to love, to give love."

Because Maria seemed to think that unburdening involved letting go of memories, I suggested that she explain to Maria 16 that the intervention had to do only with letting go of the hurt and that she would keep all of her memories intact. Maria reported back that as soon as she gave the part this explanation, "She jumped into the water," and very quickly released all of the negative energy still connected to the memories. Maria concluded, "She feels relieved, free of that pain she was feeling." She also released the sad-ness she had retained for how her sisters treated her.

The Problem of Bulimia

The end of this session marked a change in the way we would do therapy. Her son had completed his anger work on the previous day and Maria now wanted to work on an issue she had been dealing with for forty years: her relationship with food and her body image. She was pleased with what we had accomplished in work with her son and this gave her hope, she said, that she could get relief for her bulimia. She had not previously mentioned a problem with food but now revealed that when she was younger she purged through vomiting three or more times a day. Even now, she purged at least three to five times a week. She began seeing a psychiatrist in Rio de Janeiro when she was 20, but after a year of treatment her eating disorder was unchanged. Her mother was involved from an early age in Maria's problem with food. She said that her mother beat her from the age of six to 12 in order to force her to eat. She felt sad when she recalled these memories but, with no time left in our session, Maria visualized placing her negative emotions in a filing cabinet until we could meet again.

One week later, we met for the sixth time. Previously, I had viewed our work as adjunct to work with Maria's son. However, Maria now made it explicit that with her son's work completed, our work together would be about her own issues. We would begin with the bulimia she revealed in our previous session.

Maria's problems with food began by the age of six. She recalled that, "I wasn't hungry and I didn't want to eat. I didn't like the food." She craved sweets but did not remember ever being given any. She remembered that an ice cream truck would drive around the neighborhood, and other parents would give their children money for the treat. Her father, however, refused to spend the money. Later, at age 17 when she had her own money she would buy loaves of sweet bread and eat them all at once. Then she would vomit up the contents of her stomach.

The first time Maria purged she was 16. She lived with one of her sisters and sometimes helped her out in her store. She stole a package of glazed cinnamon rolls before going home. She described the experience:

> I really craved a roll. My mouth watered as I thought about them. I
> took the package home and opened it. After the first roll I wanted

another, and then another. I didn't even remember eating them all but suddenly they were all gone. Then I felt guilty. I thought, 'I'm gonna get fat and the boys won't like me.' I threw up in the sink and didn't clean it up. My sister came home and got angry about the mess, but she was also angry because she thought I had a problem. She said I was a problem, a trouble-maker for the family.

In our seventh session, we returned immediately to talking about food. Maria proudly reported that she had purchased a large box of doughnuts for her family of five—she and her son plus her fiancé and his two children— but resisted eating any of them. Unfortunately, she binged on the following day. She began the afternoon with a bowl of healthy soup and then had a tortilla. Then she had another and another until she was overfull and in need of relief, both from the feeling of being overfull and from the guilt she felt for bingeing. She vomited quietly in the bathroom before rejoining the family. No one else knew she was bulimic.

The Cecelia 11 Part

I asked Maria to focus upon the remembered feeling of wanting to eat more and more and to ask that feeling to show itself. Immediately, Maria visualized a younger version of herself. "I see myself pretending to others I have no problems. Like to [fiancé] Victor who thinks I am perfect." She saw herself as if she were looking down upon herself from above. She wore her hair in a ponytail, and appeared to be 11 or 12 years old. When Maria spoke directly to the subpersonality, she learned that the part viewed herself as 11 years old and called herself *Cecelia*. I will call her *Cecelia 11* to distinguish her from other Cecelias we met in later sessions. This name is Maria's middle name and the name she used when she lived in Argentina. She knew Maria and said, "I'm you." She had no awareness, however, of Maria's present life. She was pleased when Maria explained that she now had a 12-year-old son. Her earliest memory dated to the age of two or three when she was "naked, running around the house." At about the same age she remembered being at her sister's wedding when her mother was pregnant again. Maria, drawing upon Cecilia 11's memory, remembered the two-year-old being at the wedding reception. "She sat on a chair with [her] legs stuck out." She was angry because "her mother was mean." She had wanted to hold her mother's purse for the wedding pictures, but her mother refused, and "was rough with her in making her turn around for the pictures. She was mad in the pictures."

Cecelia 11 also recalled that as a young child she would sometimes stand outside, near the door of her house, and harass other children. "I would stand by the door and hit or do something bad to kids passing by in the neighborhood. My mother hit me hard several times." A memory from the age of four related to an occasion when her mother was fixing her hair. "I was crying while my mother combed and brushed my hair. I stuck out my tongue at my mother in the mirror. She hit me hard a lot." From the age of six, Cecelia 11 remembered having surgery for a tumor on her leg. After the hospital released her to go home, she learned that her mother had made a promise in her prayers to a Catholic saint that if Maria survived the operation she would dress her to resemble the saint. "We had fights over me wearing the costume," Maria said. "Kids made fun of me." Maria remembered one big argument about dressing like the saint, which ended with her mother "packing my things and then telling me to get the hell out." This experience at the age of six was traumatic for Cecelia 11. It still disturbed her at a level eight on the SUD scale.

From the ages of five, six, and seven Cecelia 11 remembered "a lot of jerking and pulling of hair" by her mother. Also during this period of her life, the earliest painful experiences regarding Maria's weight and body size appeared. She was a skinny child who created a lot of anxiety in her mother and older sisters. "My mother and sisters would force food into my mouth. They would make me sit at the dinner table for hours. I would dump food wherever I could, like in the toilet, whenever they took their eyes off of me."

At our eighth session, Maria talked about how frequently she had been bingeing and purging. She had no problems from Friday (the day of our session) through Sunday, but on Monday "things got crazy." She binged on each of the next four days, sometimes more than once. Maria also acknowledged that her binge-purge episodes occurred more frequently than the three times a week she had previously estimated.

Before beginning the unburdening work with 11-year-old Cecelia from our previous session, we elicited two additional painful memories. Because Maria was so skinny in mid-childhood, her family continued their efforts to increase her body weight. "They wanted me to eat beef liver," she said. "It was disgusting, horrible. It made me sick to my stomach." The memory disturbed Cecelia 11 at the maximum level 10 on the SUD scale. Later, in another incident involving food at age 11 or 12, she was embarrassed in front of her sisters and their friends when she was scolded for taking food for herself at a picnic. "They had so many goodies in the car. She wanted to take some [food] items too, as everybody else was taking items. She waited until she thought her sister wasn't looking and took an item, but her sister grabbed her hand and told her to put it down. She was embarrassed." Cecelia 11's SUD level for the incident was a six.

During the remainder of the session, we focused upon helping Maria unburden the memories we had previously collected from the Cecelia 11 subpersonality over the last two sessions. Maria visualized the part among the gentle waves near an ocean beach as she focused upon the early memory of being upset at her sister's wedding. In this case, Maria did not limit her unburdening work to that incident; instead, she associated to many other memories, some previously elicited and some new. The following passage summarizes that work, as Maria moved from topic to topic and I asked questions to help her maintain her focus. The insert [Pause] indicates short periods of silence as Maria continued to process her memories or as she considered my questions. The starting point was the memory from age two of being angry with her mother because she wouldn't let her hold her purse in the wedding pictures.

> She remembers being an unhappy baby. She was mad or she was sad. She would pull her own hair until she was exhausted. She has a memory of being sick with diarrhea. She always had dirty diapers. Poop ran down her legs to her shoes, and they didn't clean her. [Pause] She's playing in the [ocean] water and thinking about it. [Pause] It feels like they didn't want her around. Her sisters were tired of raising kids for their parents. There were 10 of us.

When we checked on the unburdening process to this point, Maria reported that the SUD level was zero for Cecelia 11 regarding being soiled from diarrhea and also for the sense that her sisters didn't want Maria around them. However, the SUD level for Cecelia 11's pulling of her own hair in frustration was still "a little bit" disturbing. Other memories were at zero, including her upset at not being permitted to hold her mother's purse for pictures at her sister's wedding, for being slapped for hitting other children when they passed by her house, and for being slapped for sticking out her tongue at her mother. Maria said that this last memory caused her to feel sadness, but the sadness wasn't Cecelia's, it was her own. Because the self does not experience strong emotion in the absence of blending parts, this meant that a different part with her own unresolved issues was blending with Maria. I coached Maria to ask the part with sadness to step back. When we checked again on the remaining memories that Cecelia 11 had been processing, all were at a zero level of disturbance. These were the memories of being dressed like a saint, mother's threat of abandonment, being forced to eat food and sitting for hours at the table until all food was consumed, and the incident where Cecelia was embarrassed during the outing with Maria's sisters and friends. We were at the end of the session, and we closed with Maria visualizing Cecelia 11 in an internal safe room, a family room for parts. We planned to check on her and on Maria's frequency of bingeing and purging at our next session.

Two weeks later at our ninth session, Maria talked about her internal experiences since our last meeting. She had been "confused" and she felt a lot of "push-pull" regarding bingeing and purging. She had also been reflective during the break and recalled many sad memories. She remembered how cruel her mother was to her and to her younger brother. Once, when she was eight, her angry mother took her brother's feces-stained underwear and rubbed them under his nose and on his teeth. She had a few positive moments as well. On her own, Maria guided the Cecelia 11 part in the unburdening of some of her sadness. She also reported her reduction by half in the frequency of her binge-purge episodes for the previous two weeks. "There were lots of times I had the power to not do it," she said, although she added that "I did do it this morning."

The Cecelia 2 Part

We returned to the deep work of parts therapy by again locating the Cecelia 11 subpersonality. She remained free of distress for the unburdened memories. Interestingly, however, Maria, but not Cecelia 11, was still bothered by the wedding pictures incident. We had seen this phenomenon in the previous session. It was time now to seek out the additional blending part. By focusing internally upon her sensation of distress, Maria was able to visualize this other part. It was a child part presenting herself at roughly the age of two. Her name was also Cecelia and so Maria called her Cecelia 2 in order to minimize confusion with other parts with the same name. Cecelia 2's earliest memory was of raising her hands to her mother to be picked up, and feeling rejected when her mother refused her. In another early memory, she remembered going out to play in the neighborhood with lots of other children. Someone was carrying a baby and young Cecelia remembered wanting to bite the baby. In another memory involving anger with other young children, Cecelia 2 wanted to hurt a little girl with curly hair. She ran to where the girl was sitting, pulled her hair, and then ran home. Some other children told her mother of her behavior, and she was punished. She also remembered eating food she picked up from the ground. She associated this with having a lot of diarrhea. She also got into trouble when she withdrew from the trash and ate the pulp from oranges her sister used to make orange juice. Finally, she remembered staying at her sister's house following surgery on her leg (That surgery occurred when Maria was six, illustrating that the presenting age of a part does not reliably predict the age content of its memories).

Near the end of the session, we began the unburdening work with Cecelia 2, beginning with the memory of her mother refusing to pick her up. I had failed to collect the SUD levels for these memories, but the first memory yielded quickly to a metaphor of washing the child's feeling of rejection down the bathtub drain during a bubble bath. Following this intervention, Maria said that the SUD level for the child part had reduced to zero, although Maria herself still felt a slight discomfort with her mother's rejection. We planned to find the part who continued to feel some distress about the rejection at a later time. The part was not, however, Cecelia 11 whom we had earlier met.

Before we ended the session, we unburdened Cecelia 2 of the memory of wanting to bite the baby being carried by its mother. The memory did not immediately give up its energy to a bubble bath intervention. Maria observed that there was a lot of energy in the memory picture of the baby getting what she herself wanted from her mother. Her sense of rejection was quite disturbing. She was envious of the baby and envious as well of the other children who were playing joyfully with each other. They seemed to be feeling the comfort of acceptance that she so badly wanted to feel. However, after she had expressed her hurt, a second unburdening reduced the SUD level to zero.

We had helped the two-year-old to put into temporary storage any remaining distress and were about to end the session when Maria said she wanted to add two additional memories that had just come to her. She did not attribute them to any particular part-self. She remembered that both her sisters and her mother sometimes called her "God's punishment" for their sins. And her mother frequently said that she had a devil inside her. These memories were potentially important for understanding Maria's inner world because when young children are called devils or demons they often respond by creating internal parts in the images of what they understand to be devils or demons. I have met many such parts while doing Parts Psychology with other clients. Doing therapy with them is no different from working with other parts. If such a part presents itself as if it actually believes it is a demon, then I treat it as a kind of introject. After thanking it profusely for its help in protecting the client, I ask it to take off its demon costume and just be the child underneath. This intervention has never failed to work. Fortunately, Maria did not develop an internal demon part.

Mother

A week later at our tenth session Maria said that she had been "keeping food down for a few days at a time, although she had purged on Friday, Monday, and Tuesday. It had now been three days since her last purge. She also reported a change in the experience of purging: "Lately, when I purge I feel weird and tired. I used to not even notice it."

In this session, we did not return to the work with the two-year-old part. Instead, Maria wanted to talk about the mother she experienced when she was older. "My mother was psycho, really sick. When she got angry she would pretend to pass out." Maria recalled that when she was 13 she was the queen for her small town's annual celebration. "People came to the party to celebrate. I was attracted to a boy there. He asked me to dance again and again." Unfortunately, she and the boy belonged to families who were in a permanent state of feud. Maria recalled that during the dancing her mother made frequent threatening gestures at her, and went home early. Maria spent the night at her grandmother's house, but when she went home, "My mother beat the crap out of me and told me all kinds of nasty crap. Then she fainted. I was terrified. I called the doctor because she was unconscious. He came over but didn't do anything. There was nothing wrong with her. It hurts my stomach that my mother was a fake." The entire experience surrounding Maria's time as a queen rated a 10 on the SUD scale. Maria went on to say:

> My mother was unreal, evil. One time we were mad at each other, and she made a big thing of it. She cried all morning and screamed a lot. Then she left to go to her mother in another town. My grandmother came over then and told me my mother was devastated and how could I do such a thing to my mother? She took me back to her house to apologize to my mother. I thought she would be upset and in bed, and I was gonna say I was sorry. But she wasn't there. I found her at my grandmother's store and she couldn't see me. She was laughing and joking with customers. I went home and when she got there she started crying again and screaming at a picture of a saint. I was so embarrassed at people hearing how loud and hysterical she was. This is when I discovered she was a fake.

Maria said that it made her sick to her stomach when she thought of these memories. When she spoke inwardly to that sick feeling and asked it to give her a picture of itself, Maria found herself visualizing an adolescent Maria in the act of vomiting. This young subpersonality knew who Maria was and knew that she was a part of Maria. She said she was 12-years-old and claimed as her own the memories of the mother as a fake. Like many other internal parts, her name was *Cecelia* and so we called her *Cecelia 12*. Although we were near the end of our session, we went ahead and tried to begin the unburdening of this subpersonality through a rainfall metaphor. Maria visualized Cecelia 12 standing in the open in a pleasant, warm rain and asked her to feel the rain dissolving the despair she felt for her mother's treatment of her when she was the queen of the town. Unfortunately, Cecelia 12 was not able to release her pain. "She's having a hard time," Maria reported. "She feels that all these problems are her fault. She knows she's not a bad person, but she feels like it." We tried to continue the unburdening by asking the young part to focus on the feeling of being a bad person and to let the rain wash that feeling away. However, we made no additional progress with this shift of focus.

It appeared that we had been premature in trying to unburden Cecelia 12 without collecting more information about her larger memory set, and especially her earliest memories. My working hypothesis was that Cecelia 12 would be able to release her anger at her mother once we elicited and unburdened the memories of events that appeared earlier in her life. We planned to do this in our next session. In closing the session, so that she would not be unduly influenced by Cecelia 12's traumatic materials, Maria visualized putting the child part to sleep for a week until our next session.

At the beginning of our eleventh session, Maria summarized her progress with her eating disorder. She observed that "the problem is there, but changing. The frequency is less. Some days I don't purge. Previously, I purged every day. I feel like a little girl when purging. I feel food protects me. When something is wrong in the house, I wake up unhappy and I have to eat."

Witchcraft

We were unable to return in this session to work with Cecelia 12 because of a new development in Maria's life. She had heard rumors that her fiancé's ex-wife was doing witchcraft against her. "I feel sick," Maria said, as she talked of these rumors. I asked Maria to connect to her sense of feeling sick and to ask the part who experienced those feelings to give her an internal image of itself. This exercise brought to Maria's mind an image of herself, enraged, wearing a white shirt and with her hair down. The part's name was *Maria,* and she said that she was 18 years old. We decided to call her *Maria 18.* She did not know she was a part of Maria and believed that she and Maria were separate people. We took some time then to demonstrate to the new part that she was indeed a part of Maria and that they were not separate people. Maria asked Maria 18 to look through her eyes to see me waving my right hand. Then, Maria closed her eyes and asked Maria 18 what I was doing with my right hand now. Maria 18 could see nothing. A few repetitions of this exercise convinced Maria 18 that if she could only see when Maria had her eyes open, then she must be a part of Maria.

Maria 18 acknowledged that she believed in witchcraft. She talked about her experience at age 18. Her mother had complained to a friend about how badly Maria was acting. "She was doing all kinds of things, rebelling against her mother and her sisters." On the advice of the friend, her mother took Maria to a witch. The witch said that someone from Maria's boyfriend's family had cursed her with a spell. They were doing black magic on her and had placed "things" outside her house. The witch said that she knew how they had done their magic on Maria, and she would heal her. For 14 days, Maria's mother brought her to the witch for cleansing with herbs of various kinds. When the treatment was finished, Maria 18 "felt much better inside her body."

The boyfriend was Maria's first. They had met when Maria was 11 and the boy was 20. Maria lied about her age and told the boy she was 12. They became lovers when Maria was 13. Maria recalled that his family "did everything they could to separate us, and they did. After they did their [black magic], I didn't love him anymore." As Maria continued her conversation with Maria 18, she reported that Maria 18 was enraged that she had responded to black magic. In preparation for the unburdening we would do, Maria visualized removing Maria 18 from the scene in which she was trapped and taking her to a safe place, a "family room," in Maria's present life. Then she began to unburden Maria 18 of her anger by visualizing a powerful wind blowing over her. The unconscious connection between the experience at 18 and Maria's current life became clear when, as the unburdening proceeded, Maria said, "The wind blew the anger away, but while that was happening I saw myself like I am now beating up [my fiancé's] ex-wife. Then I left her alone because whatever she was doing, it wouldn't harm her." That is, the beating Maria was giving to the ex-wife was not harming her. The unburdening of Maria 18 continued, with Maria observing that "the wind is still blowing pieces of black magic out of her." A few moments later she said, "She is calm now, settling down."

Maria had apparently succeeded in unburdening Maria 18 of her anger and the negative effects of what she believed was black magic from roughly 30 years previously. I wanted to be sure, however, that Maria's strong belief in witchcraft and magic that was established at age 18 would not continue to affect her in the present. For this reason, I asked Maria to focus again on all of the memories Maria 18 associated with witchcraft, and then to unburden her of all energy of any kind still attached to those memories. At the conclusion of a final unburdening wind, Maria said that the SUD level for those experiences were all at zero. Maria 18, she added, would stay with her. "She feels loved and protected. She laughs with me at [the ex-wife's] witchcraft."

The Cecelia 12 Part

In our twelfth session, Maria said that she had been purging less often, only two times in the last seven days. She had gone five days without purging at all. Doing this, she said, "felt weird, like something was missing." She could not remember another time when she went five days without purging. The purging in which she did indulge was related to her feeling states. She said that she "wasn't feeling good," and that she "felt anger and then purged." She added, "I got overwhelmed this week."

We returned then to the work we had begun with Cecelia 12 two weeks previously. This was the part we had previously tried and failed to unburden of her pain for the events surrounding her party as queen of her town. Rather than repeat the attempts we had already tried, we collected additional memories from the part and prepared to work systematically through them before working on the queen experience. The first memories that came up for Cecelia 12 were memories of inappropriate sexuality. "When I was 11 or 12 my mother put me in bed with two of my brothers because there wasn't enough room. "Both of them kissed and rubbed against me. One brother tried to penetrate me." In another incident, when Maria was 12, her mother worried that she might be pregnant because she hadn't had a period in a while. "My mother questioned me, and I said I hadn't done anything wrong, but she didn't believe me. She had a doctor friend. I think she loved him, but I think he was more interested in me. She called him to the house. He had me go into the bedroom and lie on the bed. He pulled down my panties and put two fingers into my vagina. I could see pleasure in his eyes. I knew that was wrong."

The earliest memory that Cecelia 12 could recall dated to when Maria was three years old. Her mother was about to give birth to her younger brother and was leaving for the hospital in a taxi. Family members told the little girl she couldn't go because she had no clothes on. When she ran into the house to dress, the taxi left. She was afraid that her mother wasn't coming back. Her recollection was that no one comforted her or told her why her mother was leaving or when she would return. The memory disturbed Cecelia 12 to a SUD level of eight. Another set of experiences had to do with babysitting by an older sister. Maria was in a group of the three youngest of her mother's 10 children. One of her sisters was in charge of these three. This sister was "mean" to all three of the younger children but especially so to Maria. "She was always mad. She pulled my hair, said I was ugly, no good, and other things." Cecelia 12 rated her experiences with this sister at a level five disturbance.

Maria continued to speak for Cecelia 12 as she recalled a memory from the time when she was four or five. "Her mother had friends who were old people. One of the ladies had a son who was filthy. One time the boy sat on a bench with a blanket over him. He gave her 20 cents to go buy candy. Then he asked her to sit on his lap, and he wrapped the blanket around her and he put his hand in her panties and stroked her down there. A woman sent me home and told my mother what happened." Cecelia 12 rated the SUD level as an eight. This and other memories Maria elicited from Cecelia 12 show the familiar pattern of switching between first and third person pronouns as Maria tells the story. Additionally, although Cecelia 12 presents herself as 12 years old, the memories date to Maria's early childhood. In another system, there might have been a separate part who handled the molestation memory, but in this case, Cecelia 12 had fully integrated the memory into her own memory set. There was no need to work with a separate four- or five-year-old part.

Maria's relationship with her father, although not as abusive as that with her mother, was also disappointing. Cecelia 12 reminded Maria of how she was ashamed of her father and didn't want other people to know that he was her father. "He wasn't like other dads. He was irresponsible, no affection, no love." She remembered that he did once buy her a new pair of shoes, but "he made her put on old shoes for a dance." Once, when she was living with her sisters but visiting her mother and father in another state and it was time for her to return to school, her father "put her on a 12-hour bus ride with no food, no drink, and no money. She was starving. It was so hard to watch other people eating." This experience remained disturbing to Cecelia 12 at a level eight or nine. We planned to unburden this and other memories from Cecelia 12's memory set at our next session.

A Three-Year-Old Part

It was two weeks before we met again for our 13th session because Maria had taken a vacation to visit her family in Argentina. She proudly reported that she had purged only three times during this period. It appeared that healing her childhood wounds was the route to healing Maria of her bulimia. The visit with family was a good one. Her sisters were "nice" now and so was her mother, who was in the early stages of Alzheimer's. Currently, Maria noted that she binged and purged most often when she was unhappy, especially when she was frustrated by the demands of blending her new family of son, fiancé, and his two children. Through a dream in which Maria found herself floating on a mattress in the ocean with a little girl, Maria realized how strongly she felt the responsibility to properly raise the three children in her household. In her dream, Maria felt great anxiety for the future, and she was fearful of her ability to meet her responsibilities for the children.

We turned our attention then to unburdening Cecelia 12 of the age-three memory of not being allowed to go to the hospital with her mother for the birth of her younger brother. She had chosen a waterfall metaphor for the unburdening. To her surprise, though, when Maria visualized the intervention she found a three-year-old self and not her 12-year-old self in the waterfall. Evidently, the three-year-old was not fully integrated into Cecelia 12, and so she needed to process the memory on her own. Maria described the beginning of the work: "The three-year-old is there in the water. She's in a lot of pain. She has difficulty in letting it go. I think Cecelia 12 is preventing her." The memory of a later event had intruded into Cecelia 12's consciousness and had temporarily overcome her. When Maria's grandfather died — murdered, according to Maria—Maria's mother had become hysterical. "She was screaming and running down the street, calling out the doctor's name and acting crazy." Cecelia 12's anger was directed at what she thought of as her mother's habit of bringing attention to herself when others were the proper focus. Somehow, the distress experienced by the three-year-old at not getting the attention she needed was linked to other memories where the focus of attention was on her mother rather than on herself. In this case, Cecelia 12 was triggered by the work with the three-year-old as her resentments of the mother's failures overwhelmed her. We took the time then to unburden Cecelia 12 of the blocking memory. Maria visualized Cecelia 12 in the waterfall and asked her to feel the water wash away all of her bad feelings about her grandfather's death and of her anger at her mother for being hysterical. Guided by Maria, Cecelia 12's first effort in the waterfall reduced the SUD level to a three. Maria described this remaining level as the result of Cecelia 12's "anger toward her mother for calling attention to herself—for acting stupid—she wanted to slap her face!" Once again, Maria guided Cecelia 12 through the waterfall intervention. The result this time was a SUD level of zero. "The water took away all of her pain," Maria said, "and she's not angry anymore."

With the blocking memories resolved, we could return to the interrupted work with the three-year-old. I suggested that Maria get the permission of Cecelia 12 to continue the unburdening of the three-year-old part. Cecelia 12 readily assented to this request and, in an action Maria did not request, she took the three-year-old into the waterfall with her and helped her with the unburdening. Maria described the scene: "She is helping her, standing in the water and helping her, encouraging the three-year-old, who is crying hysterically. It is so painful. At that time, no one paid attention to her and she would cry herself to sleep." Within a minute, Maria reported the intervention was successful. The SUD level for the memory of rejection had reached zero for both the three-year-old and for Cecelia 12.

In our fourteenth session, we returned, as planned, to processing the memories of Cecelia 12. Maria had time, however, to report briefly on her progress with managing her eating. She said that her bingeing was less and that it was now "torture" for her. Feeling tortured was not an intended consequence of the work, although the reduction in bingeing was. If the tortured feeling continued, we would direct our attention to neutralizing that emotion. Fortunately, Maria never again referred to her bingeing as torture; she just gradually did less of it.

As a child, Maria was overly thin, at least in the eyes of her mother and sisters. They often forced her to eat regardless of her appetite and protests. Being forced to eat was, for Maria, as abusive as the physical and verbal abuse she sometimes endured. It was Cecelia 12 who carried most of the painful memories of neglect and abuse by her sisters. "Her sisters were mean to her. She is so angry." Together, Maria and Cecelia 12 chose the waterfall metaphor as the intervention for processing these memories. I failed to collect a SUD level before the beginning of the intervention, but based upon other memories and the context, the level was probably a seven or eight. Shortly after beginning her visualization of Cecelia 12 in the waterfall, Maria said, "She's feeling the emotional turmoil in her stomach." She added, "Yes, this is where she carries her anger and hurt." I coached Maria to ask Cecelia 12 to focus on the sensations in her stomach and to allow the water to wash them away. Maria began the visualization again, and then said, "She's very destructive. She's not concentrating on getting unburdened. She is thinking of her brother and her family. Her brother is so messed up [i.e., psychologically damaged by abuse]. She feels very sad for that." At my prompting, Maria again renewed the visualization. She then observed, "Her feelings are kinda numb. She numbed herself to what they did. It was an everyday thing—constantly, every day. She doesn't want to talk about them anymore."

We had reached an impasse in unburdening Cecelia 12. It is important in such situations to look for the source of the resistance rather than to attempt to force the part to continue the non-productive interventions. As I have noted in other chapters, resistance to unburdening seems always to come from one of two sources. The first is a manager part who may fear that healing a younger part will decrease its own power. The other is the presence of a younger part who is amplifying its distress in such a way that the targeted part is overwhelmed. Whatever the targeted part is able to unburden is immediately replaced by the child's amplified distress. We had already worked with a young amplifying part who was closely linked to Cecelia 12. This was the three-year-old who had been left behind when her mother went to the hospital. Maria located this very young part and brought her to the current scene of unburdening.

Maria found the three-year-old part and visualized her joining Cecelia 12 in the waterfall. Both parts could then release the negative energy attached to the abuse. Shortly after beginning the intervention again, Maria, with tears falling from her eyes, said, "It's very powerful. [Pause] Yes, she is ready to let it go—the pain, the sadness. [Pause] Cecelia 12 is exhausted now. She feels a little sad." Maria then repeated the intervention, asking Cecelia 12 to focus on the remaining sadness. She said of the part, "She's in the water, walking through the waterfall, having a hard time. [Pause] It's washing away. It's crystal clear water now. It doesn't bother her anymore. [Pause] The three-year-old is still in the water. She was scared of being left in the water. Cecelia 12 helps her out." We ended the intervention—and the session—with Maria visualizing both parts in a safe room where they could simply rest, or, if they chose, enjoy the many amusements that Maria imagined as available in the safe room. In our next session, we planned to check with Cecelia 12 to be sure that the SUD levels for her sister's and her mother's abuse had remained at a level zero. Then, if no other issues intruded, we planned to process the disturbing sexual experiences she had with her brothers and the visiting doctor.

In session 15, we continued to work with Cecelia 12, but we did not process the sexual memories. Instead, Maria wanted to work with the frustrations she remembered from her mother's controlling behavior as she grew up. As a child, she wanted to be involved in community activities and develop friendships, both male and female, outside her family. Her mother, however, "kept her down and wouldn't let her do these things." She was still upset about the restrictions her mother placed on her and about her sisters' treatment of her as well. "Her sisters made fun of her, talked about her in front of other people, made fun of her legs—she got lots of compliments from other people but not from her family." As Maria continued to talk about this time in her life by summarizing Cecelia 12's view of it, she switched easily into the first person pronoun to conclude her observations: "I think it was a problem for them that I acted mature for my age. I wanted to see the top of the world and they didn't."

For the unburdening of Cecelia 12, Maria chose a campfire metaphor. She visualized Cecelia 12 lifting the negative emotions out of herself and throwing them onto the campfire where they burst into flame. After the initial effort, Maria observed, "It still bothers her. Her mother was always forcing her to eat certain foods, to drink milk, or eat a meal. It was so unpleasant having her mother force her to eat. She never had any positive comments about her. Her mother was constantly putting her down, calling her names, telling her she was stupid, [that] she didn't know anything."

Two More Mother Introjects

When unburdening doesn't immediately release the negative emotions, it is generally useful to encourage the part to express itself more fully. Then, a return to the unburdening metaphor will usually bring additional progress. We followed this procedure in eliciting the previous quote. Maria then asked Cecelia 12 to focus upon the unhappiness she felt when she thought of how her mother treated her and to discard once more her negative emotions into the campfire. Maria soon said of Cecelia 12, "She's having a hard time doing that." Cecelia 12's repeated failure to release her negative emotions suggested that another part was somehow involved. I asked Maria to look around the scene of her focus in the internal world and to ask Cecelia 12 to look around also so that they might become aware of the likely interfering part. The response was immediate. "It's the mother," Maria said. It was, in fact, another mother introject, a subpersonality that took on the physical appearance of the abusive mother and acted out the role of the mother within Maria's internal world. Maria's other parts would view the mother introject as the mother, and they would respond to her internally as Maria did in the external world. Following Maria's discovery of the introject, she said of her, "She looks mad, unhappy. She's giving [Cecelia 12] looks, making threatening gestures—that she'll get her later." Maria judged the image of her mother as 46 or 47 years old. In current time, Maria's mother was actually in her 80s. The introject was initially uncooperative, indicating that she did not know who Maria was and didn't want to know. When Maria informed the part that she was the grown-up Cecelia 12 [Recall that Cecelia is Maria's middle name], the mother introject was "shocked and surprised." Maria went ahead then, following my coaching, to praise the mother part for having done well in ensuring that Maria would grow up strong like the mother was. She thanked her profusely for being there to remind her how to behave appropriately. Then Maria informed the mother introject that she wasn't really Maria's mother but a part of Maria who was acting as the mother to help Maria to grow up well. Because she had been successful in her work, she did not have to carry the burden anymore of acting mean and uncaring and so it was time to take off the mother costume. Beneath the costume, Maria found another image of herself. "She looks like a 12-year-old girl now. She's jumping around, smiling, and wants to run off to the park to play." At the end of the session, Maria named this part *Sweetie*.

Before Sweetie ran off to play in the park, Maria suggested that she could stay awhile and observe us unburdening Cecelia 12. She also offered to relieve Sweetie of her own burden. The former mother introject then began to share with Maria the pain of her own experiences with her mother. "She says [the burden] has been on her for so many years. She feels afraid and sad. She feels turmoil in her stomach, agitation." Maria and Sweetie decided to unburden the part's emotional distress with the campfire metaphor. Maria visualized Sweetheart standing before a crisply burning fire and releasing her pain to the flames through vomiting. "She's throwing it up into the fire." In a few moments Maria added, "She's still vomiting." Then, she explained, "She stopped to tell me what she's throwing up. It's all the bad things [her mother] told her, and she never said anything back." Maria redirected Sweetie back to the visualization: "She's very glad she's vomiting up all the negative memories." A check of Sweetie's SUD score revealed that she had almost finished her unburdening, but there was still a level one of distress remaining. A repetition of the intervention produced no change. "She doesn't want to do it," Maria said. "She said there's something she doesn't want to give up, but she doesn't know what. [Pause] She says it was the wrong love and attention she got from [her mother and sisters]." Once the problem was identified, one more repetition of the campfire intervention brought the SUD level to zero. The completion of Sweetie's unburdening brought us to the end of the session. We planned to check on Sweetie in our next session, as well as Cecelia 12 and Cecelia 3.

As we began Session 16, Maria reported that she had binged and purged on six of the seven previous days. "I didn't feel good about myself this week," she said. It was difficult for her to avoid eating large amounts of food because she "felt so calm after eating." Unfortunately, her calm would short-ly give way to guilt and anxiety about gaining weight, and so she would cause herself to vomit her food into the toilet. It was a difficult week, made worse by a sense of dread about returning to therapy. "A part of me is saying no to the work," Maria confided. In cases like this, my choice is to try to find the resistant part and bring it into the therapy process. Consequently, I asked Maria to connect to the feeling of not wanting to do the therapy and to ask that feeling (i.e., part) to give her an internal picture of itself. Immediately, Maria visualized her mother. She saw her as she was in her 40s, "wearing a gown with short sleeves and flowers on her blouse. She has wavy dark hair and a mad face." We had evidently found another mother introject. As I coached her, Maria carried out a conversation with the part. "She says she had too many kids and my father didn't treat her good. He was stingy with food and money. She said her own mother abused her." Surprisingly, Maria went on to summarize, "She says she's a different mother. She's very sorry for what she did to me. She wishes she could change that, but she was ignorant and didn't know other ways. She wants me to forgive her." Finally, responding to Maria's question, the mother introject indicated that she was not the part responsible for the week's bingeing and purging.

Although this part is another mother introject, a part of the self presented in the image of the mother, it is a different sort of introject from that usually seen in the inner world. Rather than being a critical part or a persecutor part, it is a part that is closer to being a nurturing part than most introjects. What appears to have happened in its creation is that Maria's unconscious mind collected all the information she had learned about her mother that would soften the effects of the persecutor mother, and in so doing allowed Maria to maintain a positive attachment to her mother. Pulling together information that explained her mother's behavior helped Maria to hold the negative impact of the persecutor introject at somewhat of a distance and thereby allow Maria to feel okay about herself. Normally, I would follow the procedure of making an ally of the part and then requesting a costume change, but in this case that seemed unnecessary. This time, because the introjected part held Maria in a positive light, I decided to see if we could unburden the part of the painful memories she claimed as her own and then keep it as an inside source of nurturing for Maria.

Maria chose to unburden the mother introject through use of the wind-blowing-through-the-posts metaphor. She visualized the part standing between the posts as the wind blew through her. In less than a minute, Maria said,

> Yes, she is letting go of some of her pain. [Pause] She says she had a lot of trauma in her family. [Pause] She was the only child. Her father killed a lot of people and some people killed his brothers. [Pause] She cried a lot when I was a child. I used to go and hide behind the stove and cry because she was crying. [Pause] She says she had some kind of mental problem. She wants to let that go.

Maria asked the introject to focus on what she feels is her mental problem and to permit the wind to blow that away too. In a few moments, Maria reported that the introject said, "Daughter, I'm fine now." Maria added, "She looks pretty good and fresh." Maria and I discussed the meaning of introjects for about 10 minutes before Maria said, "The mother is feeling empty and sad now." We focused again on the wind-and-posts intervention for the mother introject, this time for the sadness and emptiness. Soon, Maria said "It's blowing away. [Pause] She said it's very painful, but she's doing it. She wants to take a break because she is tired." With this information, and because we were again at the end of the session hour, I asked Maria whether the mother introject might like to go to sleep until we could come back to her in the following week. The part agreed to do that.

A Two-Year-Old Part

When we met for our 17th session, Maria talked about how she had been sad and sentimental all week. She attributed these feelings to her awareness of the apologetic mother introject she had discovered in the previous week. We had only one more interaction with this subpersonality. Maria asked the mother introject whether there were other disturbing memories that needed unburdening. The response was Maria's recall of her mother's brother's funeral when she was just a little girl. She remembered it from her own perspective rather than that of the introject. "I see my mother crying. I cried because my mother was so sad. I covered my face with a shawl as I cried. [Pause] A man said if I don't stop crying he would put me in the hole with my uncle." From this memory, Maria generalized to other times of her early childhood. "When I was little I felt helpless and sad when I saw my mother cry. When she cried, I felt scared, like something bad would happen. So I went to hide in back of the stove and cried."

Maria could visualize herself behind the stove and so I coached her to speak with this very young part. The little girl did not know who Maria was when she spoke to her, and so Maria explained that she was the same as the little girl but grown up. The child part didn't know her age, but Maria thought she was roughly two years old. The little girl was also unaware of her name, and so Maria decided to call her by her own name because *Cecelia 2* was already taken. Thus, she would be *Maria 2*. Our next step was to begin unburdening Maria 2 of her sadness and her fear. Maria visualized the child part in a calm sea near the shore where she could dissolve her negative emotions and allow them to be dispersed in the water. Shortly after beginning the intervention, Maria said, "She's still scared — of the unknown, of something bad, but doesn't know what it is. She's scared now the water will take her away." It was a simple matter for Maria to change the imagery from that of an apparently frightening ocean to that of a little girl's wading pool. Maria went on, "She likes the little pool. She not scared. She's smiling. She feels safe with me. [Pause] She feels loved and protected. She throwing water at me and squealing. She wants me to get wet." A memory intruded then of Maria 2 left unattended in a lake near her mother's home. She remembered screaming and not knowing what to do. Maria quickly guided Maria 2 in unburdening the fear and confusion of that memory in the water of the wading pool. In a few moments, it was done. "She feels safe," Maria said as we concluded the session.

In the next session, our 18th, Maria said that she had been happy since our last session. She had binge-purged only once. She added that the little girl felt safe now. The remainder of the session served as a break from the intensity of the deep work of Parts Psychology. Maria explored her differences with her fiancé and hoped that he, too, would do parts therapy for his anger.

Lorena, a Six-Year-Old

In our 19th session, Maria again reported only a single instance of bingeing and purging. Her difficulties with her fiancé continued, and she was upset with him when she arrived for her session. Just moments before arriving he had hung up on her, abruptly ending their phone conversation. When asked who among her internal parts was most upset about her fiancé hanging up on her, Maria looked within herself and found another little girl, scared and angry, wearing a flowered dress. Her hair was "cut short like a little boy." The child part knew Maria and Maria's name but did not immediately state her own name. Soon, however, she said that her name was *Lorena* and she was six years old. Her earliest memories were of her mother hitting her because she didn't do what her mother wanted. Her mother wanted her "to be a good kid, quiet, sew, do something feminine," but "I always wanted to play and run and jump, and she called me names and that kind of stuff." Lorena remembered being spanked frequently by her mother at the age of three and four. She also remembered her sisters' critical comments about her. She readily accepted Maria's invitation to release her painful feelings through wind. Maria visualized Lorena standing in an open field as she brought up a powerful wind to blow over, around and through her. She had asked Lorena to locate within herself where she stored her painful emotions. As Maria carried out the intervention, she said of Lorena,

> She's scared—she doesn't know of what. She's not scared of her mother—oh! She's scared of her sisters. [Pause] The wind blows away her sisters. [Pause] She feels light.

At this point, I suggested that Maria check the SUD levels for the memories that previously disturbed the child part. "She's not afraid of something in particular, but afraid of something that could happen." Following gentle probing, Maria said of Lorena, "Yes, she's afraid of Victor [Maria's fiancé], especially the sound of his voice."

Sandra, an Adult Part

It appeared that the anger in Victor's voice triggered memories from Maria's childhood, either the voices of her sisters or that of her mother. Maria then refocused Lorena's attention on the angry sound of Victor's voice. But it wasn't Lorena who was having the difficulty; Lorena appeared to be calm. There was a new part intruding into the intervention. Her name was *Sandra* and she was sad. She was 23 or 24 years old and she vividly remembered the time when Maria moved to Las Vegas. It was a time of great loneliness and homesickness. She had "left her family, her country, had just run away from her problems." "Yes," she answered to Maria's question, "she wanted to run away now." Sandra agreed to allow Maria to unburden her of her sadness and of the distress she felt for the problems she had tried to leave behind in Argentina. Maria visualized Sandra standing in the open as she brought up a powerful wind to carry away her negative emotions. As Maria maintained her internal picture of the wind blowing away Sandra's burden, she talked about what Sandra was sharing with her: "She says running away makes her feel safe, peaceful for a while, but she doesn't want to do that now because she would just have to start over again." Sandra was referring to the problems of being with Victor and blending their two families into one. Maria added Sandra's additional thoughts: "But it makes her feel powerful to be able to do that, to turn her back on her problems and run away." As we ended the session, Maria asked Sandra to focus on that place within her where she held the desire to run away, and then to let the wind blow away that desire. Within another minute, Maria said, "Okay," and both the intervention and the session ended. We planned to do additional work with Sandra, and possibly Lorena, in our next session.

We met again five days later for our 20th session. The days between our meetings had been difficult for Maria. It was now a Wednesday. We last met on a Friday. As the result of an argument with Victor on Friday night, Maria had carried a high load of anger from Friday through Sunday. On Monday, she was still angry but much less so. She continued to carry this lesser anger through our Wednesday session. Not surprisingly, she had binge-purged on three of the previous five days: Friday, Saturday, and Monday. We spent the entire session exploring her relationship with Victor. The three-day rage she felt for Victor was, she said, "the first time I have been mad at him for so long. I hated him. I couldn't stand him. I stayed in my room and pretended to have headaches. Victor got really upset because he knew I got really bad headaches. He wanted to marry me and put me on his insurance to take care of my head. He didn't know I was mad. Every night and morning he asked how is my head. He brought a lady to do massage on me."

During the course of her silent rage, Maria turned her ire on Victor's children and then on his parents. She was not aware of the powerful, raging subpersonality who was directing her moods. Yet the presence of such an internal part would be obvious to any therapist doing Parts Psychology. When we talked about the lesser anger she felt by Wednesday, that subpersonality was less blended with her, and Maria could see more clearly that Victor was not as bad as she had been thinking. Still, she said, "I don't look at him the same. It's a combination of love and hate. I don't like him. I look at him and feel I don't want to be with him. I wanted to leave him this weekend." Clearly, we had more work to do with the Sandra part.

We became briefly acquainted with Sandra in our previous session. It seemed that this was the part who carried the negative feelings toward Victor. Consequently, I introduced Maria to the step-back technique for momentary coping with strong emotion. I asked Maria to find Sandra in her inner world and to ask her to take a step back. Immediately after asking Sandra to step back, Maria felt a calm she hadn't felt for days. "I feel compassion for Victor," she said. "We have differences but I am managing to change him a little bit at a time." As we closed the session, Maria noted that she could now see Sandra's influence in her two previous two marriages.

Two weeks later when we met for session 21, Maria reported that she had binge-purged three times. She was again upset with Victor. "Lately I hate him, and I know he's trying. I am getting irritated at all of the money I'm spending [on Victor's children]. I have frequent thoughts of running away." The theme of wanting to run away was the feature that again revealed the influence of Sandra in her feelings toward Victor, and so we returned to do additional work with this subpersonality. The earliest memory this part could recall dated to the time when Maria was 18 and had just purchased new clothes and brought them home to display for her mother. Her mother's response was critical; she said that the clothes were ugly, in both color and style. According to Maria, Sandra knew that her mother was intentionally "putting her down." This sort of response from her mother happened frequently. From Sandra's memory of her mother's critical view of her tastes, Maria quickly connected to the present where Victor also viewed her manner of dressing with a critical eye. "Victor does this all the time," Maria shared. "He doesn't like me to wear [sexy] underwear. He doesn't like me to wear short skirts or dresses that are revealing. He asks me to change my clothes a lot."

The Sandra subpersonality was at first unwilling to unburden the negative emotions attached to her mother's criticisms. She felt she needed to be irritated by those memories in order to be alert to new criticisms, so that she could protect Maria from them. I have found that a temporary unburdening will often allow continuation of the therapy process when a part fears that unburdening will weaken her ability to play her protective role. Thus, I asked Sandra, through Maria, if she would be willing to remove the negative emotions from herself and place them into a container that she could keep in her possession. Then, if she felt any weakening of her strength or alertness, she could open the container again and retrieve the negative energy for her use. She agreed to do so, and chose to place the negative energy connected to the memories of her mother's criticisms into a "treasure trunk." First, however, she had some things she wanted to say. "She says Victor reminds her of her mother constantly. He brings up her feelings for her mother again. They had been dormant. She remembers one time she wore a bright yellow sweater, and her mother stared at her. Then she said the sweater looked horrible." At this point, evidently because she had been able to express herself, Sandra did the temporary unburdening. "She's doing it," Maria said. She's putting the feelings in the trunk." With this intervention, we had reached the end of the therapy hour. We planned to check with Sandra and the contents of her trunk in our next session.

Maria 2 and a Mother Introject

The next session, our 22nd, revealed the complexity that is sometimes associated with parts work. Maria had binge-purged on four of the previous seven days. It had been a difficult week for her. It began with Maria's preparation of a dinner for Victor's parents at his request, but the parents failed to show up for the meal. Then, she and Victor took a weekend trip to Mexico and Maria "had an attitude the whole time." "Yes," she said, "I think Sandra was around." That is, Sandra had been affecting her mood. She added, "I think it was more the little girl part. We've talked to her before." This was the part we called *Maria 2*. Maria located the little girl and asked about her earliest memory. Maria said of her that "She cried a lot at that age. She was neglected a lot. She was abused a lot. No affection or love." When asked about the child's level of distress, Maria answered simply, "A lot." Maria then returned to her feelings about the dinner she had prepared for Victor's parents. "I felt used, disrespected," she said. He can do whatever he wants. He reminds me of my mother. She didn't care about what I was feeling. I was so furious. I hated him." Maria acknowledged that the welling up of these feelings was due to the Sandra part. Additionally, when Maria checked with Sandra, she found that the part admitted reviving the distress of Maria 2, causing the little girl part to blend strongly with Maria over the previous weekend. "What happened to me on the weekend was not like me. I was like a little kid. I think the mother part was there, too." As we ended the session, Maria indicated that she felt some remorse for her behavior by saying, "Victor loves me a lot, but I have a temper that is coming out." We hoped to work on unburdening Maria's anger in the next session through further work with Sandra, Maria 2, and, if necessary, the mother introject.

In session 23, Maria reported purging on only one of the previous six days, although on that day, the day before our session, she had binged and purged throughout the day. She talked then about her adult anger by recalling how she had treated her son during his early school years. "I became enraged when he couldn't do his math homework. I think I traumatized him for years. I feel guilty for what I did to him in preschool and elementary school."

Returning again to the childhood sources for her anger, Maria quickly located Maria 2. She soon said of this young child part, "She telling me what bothers her a lot is being neglected by her mother, and her sisters' cruelty of her." Maria asked Maria 2 if she was aware of any other part who might be blocking her unburdening. In a moment, Maria reported, "It's the mother who is not letting her give up all her pain." Evidently, we had found another mother introject. Maria described her as "young, pretty, dark hair, chunky, in her thirties." Maria added, "She denies that she was neglectful. She didn't do anything wrong. That's what she said every time I confronted her [i.e., when Maria confronted her mother as an adult], she didn't do anything wrong, I was a difficult child, blah, blah." Following our usual procedure of allying with introjects, I guided Maria in working with the part by suggesting that Maria thank the part for helping her so much over the years and for being a very good actor, etc. Then I suggested that Maria gently explain to the introject that she was not her mother, but a part of Maria. She could now take off her mother costume and just be the Maria part underneath. Following this procedure, Maria soon said that the part had pulled the costume over her head and revealed herself to be another little girl of about age two. Maria introduced the two children to each other and invited both into the waterfall that she had visualized for the final unburdening of Maria 2. Within a few moments, Maria said that Maria 2 had let the water wash away the last of her pain and that the other two-year-old had helped in the unburdening. The two little girls had decided to play together. "They are holding hands and walking through the park."

Ending Therapy

The work with Maria 2 and the mother introject had cleared the way for us to return to do further work with Sandra. Maria shared that she had broken up and got back together with Victor on the weekend. She said that he had a Sandra part inside of him, too. She meant that Victor had an angry part created by childhood abuse. She went on to say that her Sandra was "really angry at her mother and sisters." When asked for a painful memory that still bothered her, Sandra brought to Maria's mind how her sisters had treated her during her teenage years. "Her sisters called her puta [whore] because I went out with my friends and to clubs and other places. One time my sister told me, 'Don't be so puta!' and I cried and cried." The memories of being called puta by her sisters disturbed Sandra at a level 10 on the SUD scale. She readily agreed to unburden the pain she carried from these memories. Maria guided Sandra in beginning her unburdening through the visualization of a waterfall that washed over Sandra to carry away her pain and anger. Unfortunately, soon after she began the intervention, Maria said of Sandra, "She doesn't understand why they did that. They had no proof, nothing! [Pause] She can't calm down. There is so much anger." We were at the end of the session, and so I asked Maria to guide Sandra in storing her remaining anger in a container so that Maria wouldn't be upset easily during the week. I did this because, often, when we have opened up a painful memory but failed to resolve it, the emotion connected to that memory will negatively affect the client during the week. We planned to work more with Sandra in the following session.

In session 24, Maria said that she had had a "good week." "I binged [and purged] only one time—on Mexican candy." She added, "Sandra kept coming when I argued with Victor, but I kept telling her to calm down, to stop it. It worked!"

In an excellent example of how body sensations from the past can affect sensations in the present, Maria observed,

> I have been feeling a weird feeling in my feet, between my toes. Kind of like a tickle, an energy. I had a drink of tequila and two cigarettes to stop it. It feels like an anxious feeling. Sometimes I feel it with Victor on his way to visit his [rental] properties, and when I am waiting in the truck for him.

When she checked with Sandra, she found that this part did not experience the sensations with her; however, "Sandra says it has something to do with her because of her bad behavior. She feels guilty. She says it's the mother— who used to take a brush and brush her feet when she was bad." We looked then for another mother introject. Maria found her without difficulty and described her as "young, in her late 40s, maybe 50. She looks heavy. She's wearing a white shirt or gown. Her hair is dark and wavy and she has wide, fat feet. She is looking at me sadly. She says I'm Cecelia. She's sorry about all the abuse by her. She's kinda distant to me, but feeling sorry for me." I coached Maria to question the mother introject about whether she might somehow be causing Maria's tingling feet.

> She says, yes, she has energy in her feet. She's a very nervous person and has always been that way. And she knows Victor. She likes him a lot, but some things she doesn't like. But it isn't her who gets nervous feet going to Victor's properties in his truck. [Pause] Now she says maybe it's her. Last night I slept with Victor. I was feeling dislike for him. I didn't want sex. But she had sex after Victor got her in the mood. Afterwards, I felt energy in my feet. It was the mother part.

Note here the familiar switching of first and third person pronouns as Maria talks about her experiences. In this case, she described her experience of having sex with Victor while the mother part was blended with her.

Maria went on to explain what the uncomfortable feelings in her feet meant to her. The sensations:

> meant that she was frustrated. She didn't want to be submissive. I felt blocked from expressing myself. I have to keep my mouth shut, or there will be problems. My mother had the propensity to say whatever, whenever and I did too. But now I can't do that with Victor.

As we ended the session, we planned to return to the mother introject as well as Sandra, the part who seemed to be most unhappy with Victor. However, our next session would be our last. It was more than three weeks before we met again because Maria had taken an extended vacation to visit family and friends in Argentina. When she returned, she expressed her concerns with the mounting financial pressures that had been building for her blended family with Victor. She planned to concentrate on getting a new job to help with expenses. The national recession and the problems in the local real estate market now made it difficult for her to earn enough selling homes to pay all her bills. She had decided to graduate herself from therapy.

During more than three weeks of vacation, she had binge-purged only once. She believed that her bulimia was cured. Except for the one occasion when she ate too much food one evening, she had no desire to binge and purge. Everything was going well in her life. After visiting her family, Maria said, "With my mother, I don't feel hate anymore. She was nice, happy to see me. My sisters have changed, too. When I go there, they are nice to me." She believed that her relationship with Victor was going well and that her anger was under control.

Postscript

As her therapist, I believed that Maria had done well in working through her issues. I thought she was approaching the time when she could safely move on without therapy. However, I also thought she could benefit from a few more sessions of work with her parts. There were issues that we had examined but had not yet resolved. Still, I thought she had a good chance of doing well. When I contacted her 18 months later, she and Victor had married and managed to stay together in spite of significant financial problems.

They wanted to stay together but, according to Maria, they had occasional angry outbursts that made her want to get a divorce. She occasionally binged and purged, perhaps once in three or four weeks, when life with Victor threatened to become unbearable. She proudly reported that she once went three months without purging. In comparison with her former rate of binging and purging four or five times a week, Maria thought that she was doing well with her eating disorder. Her greatest problem was her occasional experience of great anger with victor. She acknowledged that the Sandra part was prominent at those times. She and Victor planned to do marital counseling to help them gain control of their tempers.

Six months later, after eight sessions of couples counseling with Victor, Maria chose to do another 12 sessions on her remaining problems with bulimia. Her binge/purge activity had increased to two or three times a week as her anger issues with her husband escalated. In effect, Maria finished what she had not finished two years before. She completed the processing of her years of oppression by her mother and sisters. Most importantly for her marriage, she also processed the memories that triggered her anger with Victor. (Victor worked on *his* anger with his own therapist). When, just before this book went to press, Maria completed her work, she had binged and purged just once in six months.

Chapter 13
Lifetime Depression with Anxiety

Richard was a 38-year-old schoolteacher, and feeling that he could barely function when he first came to therapy. He was not significantly dissociative, with a DES (Dissociative Experiences Scale) score of only 7.5 compared to the norm of 10. He had panic attacks "out of the blue" that felt like he was having heart attacks. His everyday anxiety left him wide awake at bedtime, unable to sleep for an hour or more after going to bed. He was depressed and cried for no reason, sometimes four or five days in a row, although he described his longer term pattern as crying only about 10 days in any given month. He had been on antidepressant medications for 10 years. He was currently taking nefazodone (formerly marketed as Serzone) and bupropion (Wellbutrin) for depression. For his panic attacks and generalized anxiety, his psychiatrist had prescribed lorazepam (Ativan) and risperidone (Risperdal), a medication generally used for schizophrenia and bipolar disorder. He was seriously overmedicated and still not receiving significant relief. One of our first session's stated goals was to wean him off his medications. With proper psychotherapy, most people do not need such a soup of psychoactive substances circulating in their blood.

Richard talked about having "a lifetime issue with happiness." He didn't remember ever having an extended period of happiness, although he enjoyed brief respites for a week or so, as when on vacation. His last month had seen more crying than usual. He cried most often about his sense that he was not a good enough father and husband. Looking back over his personal history, he now believed that his depression began in childhood and became particularly problematic in high school and college. He had finally been diagnosed with major depression when he was in his late 20s. His score on the *Center for Epidemiologic Studies Depression Scale (CES-D)* was 28. Scores over 21 suggest the possibility of major depression.[22] We would use the CES-D to check his depression symptoms several times over the course of therapy.

In addition to depression, Richard acknowledged a problem with his anger. His pattern on a given occasion was to become more and more upset until he "lost control." He might come home from work, for example, and begin to talk about work and the people and conditions that caused him stress. As he talked, he would become more and more angry until he found himself yelling as his wife looked on with bewilderment. He had "yelled a couple of times" at his wife, but "never at the kids." He noted that his two elementary-school children had witnessed his yelling. After an episode of yelling, Richard would typically turn to self-criticism and then back to his continuing depression. He had experienced angry episodes all of his life, but they had increased in frequency through time.

"As a child," said Richard, "I got picked on a lot. I was always the tall kid, the one who didn't fit in easily with others." By the fourth grade, Richard hated school. As a means of connecting to his earliest memories of distress, I introduced Richard to an affect bridge. I asked him to notice how he felt about the demands of work, with insufficient time to accomplish what he was supposed to do in the course of a day or a week, and then let his mind drift back in time to what was happening in his life when he first felt like this. When he did this, he remembered nursery school and being picked on at that time. "It made me angry," he said of his nursery school treatment. Evidently, Richard's experience of his bosses' work demands was triggering long ago memories of how he had been treated in preschool. This is exactly the sort of experience that Parts Psychology helps to explain. After a brief discussion of the universality of internal parts, we planned to explore Richard's work stress in our next session, paying particular attention to how an understanding of his internal parts would aid in the therapy.

An Angry Part

In our second session, Richard easily differentiated his angry self. I asked him to notice how he felt about work and about being at work. He felt "overwhelmed all the time, and overworked." When he focused on his anger and waited to see if an internal image appeared to represent this feeling, he soon visualized a man, "red-faced and tall, with brown hair and clean-shaven." His clothes were "grayish." "He doesn't look like me," Richard said. "His hair is combed up and is sticking out from his head." When I coached Richard to begin a conversation with the part, he reported that the part did not know who Richard was. When asked to guess who

Richard might be, the angry one said, according to Richard, "You're an asshole!" Richard then explained to the image that he was a part of Richard, but the part refused to accept this explanation. He also indicated to Richard that he had a name of his own but could not, for some reason, share that name. As a means of demonstrating to the angry part that he was indeed a part of Richard, I used a simple but usually effective technique. I coached Richard to ask the part to look at me through Richard's eyes and to notice what I was doing with my left hand. I waved my hand at Richard, and the part correctly noted what I was doing. Then I asked Richard to close his eyes and ask the part what I was doing with my hand then. The part didn't know. I moved my hand to place it upon my shoulder and asked Richard to open his eyes and ask the part what I was doing with my hand. When Richard did so, the part was again able to state correctly where my hand was, but could not do so with Richard's eyes closed. Another repetition of the eyes-open, eyes-closed cycle convinced the part that it was indeed a part of Richard. In using this exercise, a part will sometimes guess that the hand is still waving, and so it is important that the therapist move his hand to a different position before asking the client to open his eyes again. As a general rule, the parts of dissociatively normal people can be readily convinced that they are a part of the person. However, with people diagnosed with a dissociative disorder, such as those with dissociative identity disorder, a part will typically resist the idea that it is a part of the person, even when this technique is used.

Once the part was convinced that he was a part, Richard shared his name with him. The part acknowledged "a vague memory" of Richard and was now amenable to further discussion. He answered "Yes" to the question of whether he was the one who was overwhelmed and overworked, and "Yes" again to the question of whether he was angry. Regarding why he thought Richard was an asshole, Richard summarized, "He doesn't like the kind of person I am, someone who doesn't stand up for himself." In response to another question, Richard answered for the part, "No, he doesn't stand up for me. More that he thinks I make poor decisions. So he is angry with me, not other people."

The part's earliest memory was of Richard being picked on. Richard did not know what to do; he was confused. He would "shut down," and the part was critical of that. The earliest memories of being picked on dated to nursery school, when Richard (and the part) felt confused. It wasn't until "maybe the next day, thinking about it," that the part became angry. When asked for his next significant memory, the part provided Richard with a memory from when he was "fairly young," somewhere between five and seven. He remembered that "two friends thought they were being funny, and paddled me on the butt. Then they pulled down my pants and continued to paddle me." Richard was humiliated. The part was disturbed to a level 10 on the 0-10 SUD (Subjective Units of Disturbance) scale. Another memory dated to "a snowy day" in the fourth grade when Richard wore snow boots to school. Some of the children teased him for wearing the boots. The teasing led to Richard's first fight. The teasing disturbed the angry part to a level eight on the SUD scale.

As we concluded the session Richard said of the part, "He wants to be in control, able to be mad without blowing up." In response to a couple of closing questions, the part also indicated that he was not aware of Richard's wife or children, even when Richard visualized his family for him.

In spite of the rather poor initial awareness the part showed of Richard and his current life, Richard experienced a successful introduction to working with his inner world. His earlier, unstated worries about how parts therapy would work were assuaged by his ability to interact with the angry part. He observed that prior to differentiating his first internal part, "I couldn't imagine how this worked. The picture of him helped. It gave me something to grab onto."

In our third session, we returned immediately to work with the angry part. "He definitely knows me now," Richard said. "And he's more friendly." He was still unable or unwilling to provide a name for himself, but midway through the session he chose the name *Eric* for himself. Evidently, he did not previously have a name for himself after all. He experienced himself as being in his "mid 20s." We began to collect memories from Eric's memory set, asking for his earliest significant memories. He responded by recalling a series of events in Richard's life, although they often did not follow chronological order. Eric remembered that "in high school my father was upset at something I did. He hit me for the first and last time. He remembered my father's anger and how [my father] lost it. A friend observed it and that made it worse, but it also made it more okay for me to [get angry]." The memory was disturbing to a level seven on the SUD scale. There were also memories Eric hinted at between the ages of 10 and 16, but he could not recall the specifics of the events. The next significant memory dated to his later high school years. It was after school and Richard was waiting for a ride home. Some older students who Richard did not know approached him and began hitting him in the head. Eric "was angry because I didn't respond. I didn't say or do anything." The incident was disturbing to Eric at a level seven. When asked about other significant memories, Eric communicated to Richard, "I hate feeling like I've been wronged. There were many of those times." When asked about feeling angry toward Richard's wife, who he now recognized, the part indicated that he had "felt anger toward her, but not because of anything she did. She was just there. She was just the one who got the bad end of it when I was under stress. He says he likes her. He likes how she listens."

When we turned to recent memories, the part's focus was on "work overwhelm," disturbing to a level 9.5. The part was angry "because I've been set up for failure. There's more work than anyone can possibly do. Doing a good job makes him happy, so if it's impossible to do a good job how can he not be angry?"

When asked, Eric was willing to try to decrease his anger, but "he doesn't know if he can." Given this willingness, I suggested to Richard that he use the wind-and-posts metaphor to unburden the powerful experience of being paddled by his friends at the age of five or six. Following this suggestion, Richard visualized Eric standing between two posts as Richard brought up a powerful wind to blow away his burden of anger. In a short time Richard said, "I have trouble letting it go—he can't see how to do it." Because clients vary in the amount of help they need or want from me during the intervention phase, I had given Richard minimal help in animating the metaphor. Given this difficulty, however, I went ahead to give a full description of what we were asking Eric to do. In a calm and steady voice, I said to Richard:

> Imagine an open field where there are two posts stuck deep in the ground, with the posts connected to each other by a bar, about chest high. Visualize Eric holding onto the bar as you bring up a powerful

wind to blow between the posts, and over, around, and through him. Ask Eric to find within himself where it is that he stores the memory of the paddling by his two friends, and ask him to feel the wind touching this memory, cleansing it of the anger and other bad feelings attached to it.

This guidance was apparently all that Richard needed to carry out the unburdening. Within a minute, he rated the SUD level as "a zero or a one." When asked about what made the remaining burden register at a possible one rating, Richard said, "The memory of it is so ingrained that it's hard to let it go." I suggested that Richard ask Eric to focus on the remaining resistance to letting the burden go, and to visualize the wind blowing again. Within a few moments, the SUD level had reached zero.

We turned next to the unburdening of Richard's nursery school experience, when Eric was angry with him for freezing rather than responding to being picked on by other kids. Before beginning the intervention, Richard noted that Eric said the unburdening "will be easy. He accepts the fact that I was inexperienced, and probably a lot of people went through the same thing." Indeed, the SUD level for the experience reached zero shortly after the wind-and-posts intervention began.

For the last intervention of the session, Richard brought up a new incident that he had just remembered. "I went to a private school for kindergarten and first grade, and then to public school for the second grade. I was shocked by how different it was. During recess, I was sitting by myself inside a concrete tunnel on the playground because I didn't know anyone, and a girl picked on me. "What's wrong with you?" she said. "You're weird!" The incident bothered Eric to a level eight on the SUD scale. We began the wind-and-posts visualization, but soon Richard said, "I can see the green dust [representing the negative emotions] blowing away, but the wind keeps blowing and not finishing because there needs to be a stronger wind for some of it." The SUD level had reduced to a two but hadn't gone further "because it's hard to forget." I coached Richard then to explain to Eric that unburdening isn't about forgetting and that he would retain the memories and the knowledge that came from the memories. It was the negative emotions attached to the memories that we were unburdening.

Richard soon observed, "He's letting it go and focusing on the learning experience." The SUD level reached zero. As we concluded the session, Richard said of Eric, "I'm feeling no resistance from him."

Child Parts Amplify Distress

At the beginning of the fourth session, Richard talked about his continuing irritability at work due to his heavy workload. Additionally, the week at home had found Richard blowing up at his wife when she asked him to assemble a small piece of boxed furniture. Checking with angry Eric after the incident, Richard found that Eric was disturbed by his lack of control. Because we had accomplished a significant amount of unburdening in our previous session, it was somewhat surprising to find that Richard had experienced so much anger during the week. Consequently, we checked with Eric to see if the unburdening had held. In fact, it had not. His level of distress for the paddling incident was back up to a SUD level of eight, and the experience of being picked on in nursery school registered a seven. As noted elsewhere in this book, when negative energy returns to unburdened memories between sessions, the source is either a powerful manager who wants to use the energy to carry out its own agenda, or there is a young part, sometimes more than one, who has not been unburdened and who continues to amplify its distress through the system. In such cases, we do not have to repeat the unburdening previously completed.

Richard easily differentiated the part who had experienced the problems in nursery school. He was a five-year-old version of Richard whom we called *Richard 5* in anticipation that we might find other young Richards as well. He was immediately agreeable to giving up his distress, so Richard visualized him standing in a waterfall as the water washed away his hurt for being picked on. With just one run-through of the intervention, Richard 5's SUD level had reduced to a two or three. It had not reduced to zero, Richard explained, because "the memory is so intense." A second visualization of the waterfall washing away Richard 5's remaining distress reduced the SUD level to zero.

When questioned further, Richard 5 indicated that his memories also extended into kindergarten and first grade. At that time, he went to a private, Catholic school, and continued to be distressed over "getting in trouble" there. Once, he was caught by a nun when he was running around the church and the altar. He remained disappointed in himself. His distress measured an eight on the SUD scale. Richard attempted to use the waterfall visualization again, but shortly reported that Richard 5 couldn't unburden because of interference from another, as yet unknown, part. The new part reminded Richard that he had been a disappointment all of his life. I coached Richard to ask the part to *step back* and permit the unburdening because we weren't working on all of Richard's life, just the incident of getting in trouble for running around the church. Then Richard repeated the waterfall intervention, and in a few seconds was able to report a SUD level of zero for Richard 5. We would return later to the interfering part.

We moved on then to Richard's second grade when he changed from a Catholic to a public school. In an incident previously mentioned, Richard felt he was picked on in the first grade by a little girl. The memory was distressing to Richard 5 at a level 10. Richard decided to utilize the same waterfall metaphor that had previously worked for Richard 5. Unfortunately, he was less successful here: "I picture him in the water, and some of the pain is trickling away," but further movement seemed to be blocked. The SUD level was down to seven but did not reduce further because, a voice said, "You didn't do anything back." We decided to look for this interfering part. Richard turned his attention to searching for a representation of the second grader who directly experienced the first day of public school; he easily found the new part.

The part's internal image seemed to Richard to be just as he remembered himself in the second grade. His name was also *Richard,* and he said that he was seven years old. He agreed that we could call him *Richard 7.* He was well oriented and knew that Richard was himself, but grown up. He understood that he was a part of Richard. He was not, however, familiar with his five-year-old predecessor. Richard introduced them before we continued our work. This sort of transition between parts who carry a person's painful memories is not unusual. Evidently, Richard 7 replaced Richard 5 following the incident at the beginning of the second grade, although they overlapped each other in their memories of the incident. Richard 7, however, was the primary participant in that experience. After that incident, Richard 5's memories fade away.

With Richard 7's agreement to continue unburdening childhood memories, Richard visualized him in the waterfall, washing away the SUD level 10
experience of being treated poorly by the little girl on the first day of the
second grade. In an interesting addition to the intervention, Richard visualized Richard 5 joining Richard 7 in the waterfall, because "they have different experiences of the incident." In less than a minute of visualization,
Richard reported that both parts had reached a zero level of distress for the
memory.

When we checked with Richard 7 regarding the memories we had previously unburdened for Richard 5, we found that Richard 7 remembered the
paddling incident and was still disturbed by it at a SUD level of four. The
distress yielded quickly to the waterfall intervention and soon registered a
zero on the scale. Following up with angry Eric, the part with whom we had
originally worked, but whose SUD scores rose again even after we had
unburdened the painful childhood experiences, we found that Eric once
again rated those experiences at a SUD level of zero. This is a confirmation
of the principle that once we have successfully unburdened a part of its
painful memories, we need do no further work with the part for those memories. We need to find the parts who are amplifying their distress onto the
part we were working with. In this case, and as is so often the case, we
needed to find the young parts who directly experienced the incidents in
question. Once they were unburdened, they no longer amplified distress
onto angry Eric.

Martin, a Teenaged Part

We returned then to seek out the part who had briefly interrupted our
work with Richard 5 when we were trying to help the young part unburden
his distress about getting in trouble with the nun. The intrusive part had
expressed the opinion that Richard had been a disappointment all of his life.
At that time, we asked the intrusive part to step back so that we could work
just on the single incident involving the church. Richard had no difficulty in
finding the part when he focused upon the idea of his long-term disappointment with himself. He visualized the new part as of high school age
and resembling Richard, but not as an exact representation. He wore glasses
where Richard did not, and he had pimples and wore his hair in a "bowl

cut" where Richard remembered that his *own* hair was "more styled." In the initial interview, Richard found that the part knew who he was: "You're the person I'm a part of." According to Richard, the part knew this before we began our work with the other parts. The teenager said that he was 15 years old and did not have a name, although he wanted one. He wanted Richard to give him one. Richard chose to call him *Martin*. When asked about his earliest memory, Martin initially had no response. However, when asked about his earliest *painful* memory, he said that he "had been there all along" but didn't become aware of himself until the fourth, fifth, and sixth grades. In one incident, he remembered being in gym class and playing kickball. When the ball was rolled slowly to him, he kicked too soon and missed the ball entirely, ending up with his kicking foot on top of the ball before he fell to the ground. The other kids laughed at him. Martin said the incident bothered him at a SUD level of 10. We planned to return to Martin in our next session.

In our fifth session, Richard spoke of his improved mood. "A pretty good week," he said. He pointed out that he had remained calm in spite of a "snippy" comment from his wife, the sort of comment that would previously have bothered him. He had asked her for something from her purse, and her response was sharp. "I could tell that her response was because she was thinking I wanted it right then. So I knew she misunderstood me, and let it go."

We returned to 15-year-old Martin and began to collect disturbing incidents from his memory set. His first response dated to his freshman year of high school when, because he knew the coach of the football team, he was accepted as the team's statistician. During one game Richard, on the sidelines, "was hit on an out-of-bounds play." Martin was embarrassed by being knocked down when he didn't get out of the way. "I was making notes and didn't see it coming." The memory was disturbing to Martin at a SUD level of seven. Another memory from the same period also involved deep embarrassment. When, during the introduction of the players, Richard was introduced as the team's statistician, the crowd booed him. He was not a popular boy. The booing disturbed Martin at a level 10. Richard had experienced this sort of treatment by others since the fourth grade. He had been picked on frequently, and called *nerd* and other unflattering names for years. Martin's SUD level for this pattern of experiences was 10.

When Richard prompted Martin for additional distressing memories, Martin was silent, but eventually turned Richard's thoughts to his college years. "He says college was starting over with a fresh slate. He was present there but was more of an observer. I enjoyed socializing in college and Martin did too." In response to Richard's question, Martin indicated that he was not the part who guided Richard in socializing.

Before we turned to the task of unburdening Martin's painful memories, Richard asked a few other questions about Martin's relationship to family members. He found that Martin knew and liked Richard's wife. In fact, he considered her to be his wife as well. He acknowledged that he was often present during lovemaking with her. However, although he also knew and liked Richard's children, Martin did not consider them *his* children. They were Richard's children. Martin acknowledged that he was disappointed with the way both he and Richard had conducted their life, and he was eager to engage in the unburdening work he had observed us doing with the younger parts.

To begin the unburdening, Richard and Martin chose the visualization of bringing a powerful wind to blow over Martin as he stood between football field goal posts. The focus of the intervention was the many years of Richard feeling picked on, from the fourth grade onward. Richard closed his eyes to better visualize, and within a minute opened them again to say that he had completed the task. The important SUD check, however, revealed that Martin was still disturbed to a level three on the scale. The problem, Richard said, was "low self-esteem." "Martin can let go of the fact that those things happened, but the result of the incidents was me not liking myself and of dwelling on those incidents—for a week, months, or years." I then coached Richard to repeat the unburdening, as Martin focused on not liking himself and on his low self-esteem. The SUD level reached zero in less than half a minute.

Next, we returned to the kickball incident, which had spontaneously reduced from a level 10 to a level five following the unburdening of the experiences of being picked on. Richard decided to continue with the wind visualization to relieve Martin of his distress for this incident. In 15 seconds, the SUD level reached zero. The next incident was that of being run over on the sidelines during an out-of-bounds football play. Between these two experiences, there seem to have been no major incidents that required unburdening. Richard said of Martin's memories for the intervening years, "He doesn't notice any particular incidents." Martin quickly released his burden for the out-of-bounds hit and followed that by unburdening, within 30 seconds, the experience of being booed when introduced as the football team's statistician. We asked Martin to scan his memory then for any other significantly disturbing incidents that we had so far overlooked. There seemed to be none. "The big things are about being picked on. The kickball incident was about being embarrassed for being uncoordinated. He hated gym classes. There was a long line of embarrassing incidents in gym." Without checking the SUD level, we guided Martin in unburdening the gym class embarrassments. Using the same wind-through-the-goal posts metaphor, Richard focused on helping Martin unburden these incidents. Unlike previous experiences, these took a bit more effort to neutralize, but after about one minute of visualization, the SUD level had reached one. Two additional, short repetitions of the intervention finally produced the desired zero level of disturbance.

We were at the end of our session with just enough time left to try to redefine Martin's role in Richard's life. "He would like the chance to be more positive," Richard said. "He will take the job of trying to help with potentially embarrassing incidents." With our detour to work with Richard's younger parts seemingly at an end, we planned to return to work with Eric, the angry one, in our next session.

Work Stress

We did not return immediately to work with Eric in our sixth session. Richard had experienced a particularly bad day at work. He said that his job was having a negative impact on his family and his health. "They've taken away my talent and creativity in teaching! Now everything is scripted from a textbook. And I have my worst class, ever. They don't stop talking. I feel helpless. I can't sleep. I have pain in my stomach." His students, always difficult to control, had been especially troublesome for Richard on the day of his session. His frustration over his inability to get their attention, and to engage them in teaching and learning, led him to express a sense of failure. The sheer amount of work it took to do all of the paperwork the school administration demanded was always overwhelming. "I stay late and I come in on weekends just to keep my head above water. I'm burnt out. There is non-stop work. There is not enough time to do what they want you to do. I wish I could get in the car and just go away."

Richard was too distressed to do the deeper work with parts that we had planned. Consequently, the session was devoted to providing Richard with a safe place to explore all of his frustrations and, hopefully, for Richard to feel that he was being heard. I hoped that we could return to deeper work in our next session.

By our seventh session, Richard had reached a temporary peace with his work obligations. "I've accepted that it's out of my control. I'll do the best I can and be okay with that." This was precisely the attitude we aimed for in doing the inner work with parts. We returned then to the work with angry Eric.

As we had hoped, the work with the younger parts had reduced Eric's SUD levels significantly. They were at zero for both the experiences of being picked on in nursery school and for the humiliation of being paddled by Richard's friends somewhat later. The memory of being hit by his father was now at a SUD level of one or two. It was quickly reduced to zero through the wind-and-goal-posts metaphor. The memory of being beat up by older boys was now at a SUD level of four. It, too, yielded quickly through a single use of the wind-and-goal-posts intervention.

We next turned our attention to the current problem of work over-whelm, and tried to reduce the SUD level of six through the wind metaphor that had worked so well with previous experiences. Unfortunately, the matter was more complex than a single intervention could resolve. Use of the wind-and-goal-posts metaphor actually led to an increase in Eric's dis-tress, to a level of nine or even ten. Richard said it was because of Eric's "feeling of loss of control; even though at times he can be cool about it, there will be times of instant anger." We asked Eric to focus on his feeling of loss of control and to bridge back in time to his earliest experiences of this feel-ing. Richard remembered his first job after college, for a company that ser-viced ad agencies and helped them get satellite space. "Lots of clients, and everybody has an emergency, and everybody needs it now!" Eric dealt with it with anger. I would go to the restroom and isolate myself in a stall and just steam over. Sometimes I'd break a pencil in half. I had a need to damage something." Richard guided Eric in releasing his anger and other negative emotions for these memories to the wind-through-the-goal-posts metaphor, and quickly helped him to achieve a zero level of distress for that time in his life.

When we checked Eric's SUD level for his current job frustration, it had dropped from a nine or 10 to a seven, but that score indicated we had more work to do. We asked Eric once again to bridge to the past from his feelings of not being in control. This time he found memories from grade school. They were memories of frustration about doing and finishing his schoolwork. The SUD level was three. Richard visualized Eric releasing his frustration to the wind, and then said, "I always struggled because of ADD [*attention deficit disorder,* later included in the category *attention deficit/hyperactivity disorder*], so I was labeled *learning disabled.* Concentrating was so difficult." Turning his focus again to visualizing the wind unburdening Eric, Richard said, "I'm remembering situations and struggling through stuff." Unfortunately, even after these early memories reached zero on the SUD scale, Eric's distress for current job overwhelm remained at a seven. We were at the end of the session with only enough time left to help Eric store the day's unresolved negative energy in a container. Richard chose to leave this energy in a small lockbox. Before leaving, Richard briefly summarized his academic experience. He said, "I was a poor student in elementary school and in college, until my senior year, when I took a course in the history of broadcasting. I found I could focus. I got an easy *A.* In graduate school I was almost perfect. I got a 3.9 grade point average."

Prior to returning to our work with internal self states in our eighth session, Richard surprised me with the information that he had been entirely off Risperdal for eight days. In our initial session just eight weeks previously, we had agreed on the goal of Richard weaning himself from his psychoactive medications. Evidently, he was sufficiently concerned with the potential side effects of Risperdal (e.g., tardive dyskinesia, diabetes) that he immediately reduced this medication by one-half after the first session. Then, as his work in therapy gave him more confidence, he continued to reduce his Risperdal intake. A week ago, he had stopped taking it entirely. He was experiencing no noticeable withdrawal symptoms. I told him that I was proud of him, but exacted his promise that he would work closely with his psychiatrist as he discarded his remaining medications.

Alex, an Anxious Young Adult

As we prepared to continue our deep work, Richard noted that, during the previous week, he had been better able to handle his work stress. His home life had also been "pretty good." He could see that the experiences he had been calling *work overwhelm* had a large component of anxiety mixed with them. With his recent weaning of himself from the antipsychotic drug (which had been prescribed for his high anxiety), he felt he would like to focus more directly on anxiety in therapy. This meant that we would postpone our return to work with Eric, the angry one.

Richard had described his problems with anxiety as including *panic attacks*. These were periods of acute anxiety when he was unable to think clearly and take appropriate action. Only once, about two years previously, had his anxiety been so great that he could not function. On that occasion, his extreme anxiety had lasted from a Friday evening through Sunday morning, ending only when he took the anti-anxiety drug, Ativan (lorazepam). "I felt like I was losing my mind. My body felt weird. I paced back and forth for hours. I was scared of being alone, and sweated all day." He believed that this drug had prevented additional acute periods of anxiety over the last two years. However, he did experience short periods of high anxiety "when there were too many stresses at once. When there are too many, I panic and can't deal with any of them. I start sweating and my heart pounds." Richard recalled experiencing this sort of anxiety at the beginning of the current school year. "I felt anxious and inadequate," Richard recalled. I asked him to focus on that remembered feeling of anxiety and to speak to it inwardly, asking it to give him a picture of itself. There was, however, no response to the request. Then, making use of his knowledge of his system from previous work, Richard asked the angry one, Eric, if he knew the part we were looking for. When Eric replied affirmatively to the question, Richard asked Eric to connect him to the anxious part. The image Richard visualized was that of "an overweight male, very curly hair, a fat face, as well as torso, arms, and legs; light brown hair. In his 20s. Not as old as I. He's wearing jeans and a t-shirt." In response to questioning, the part indicated that he knew Richard and added, "I'm a part of who you are." His name was *Alex*. Before ending the session, we had time only to ask about Alex's earliest memories, which dated to middle school in the sixth or seventh grade. The memories related to anxious moments preceding oral presentations. They continued to disturb Alex at a SUD level of six. Richard helped Alex symbolically store his anxiety in a coffee can so that we could return to this work in our next session.

In our ninth session, Richard again said that things were better at work. He was "not trying to be *Superman*;" he was just trying to comfortable with doing the best he could do. There was one day, however, that had been especially difficult for him. It was a "staff development day," which Richard described as a "meeting where they tell us everything I have to get done." During and after that meeting he felt panicky, with "heart pounding, perspiring, a pit in my stomach—I couldn't eat lunch." Richard could still call up and experience a degree of that panic in our session, and so I asked him to focus on it and to allow himself to connect to the self state from whom the panic was coming. He connected to Alex. Alex was well oriented to the present in the sense that he knew who Richard's wife and children were, although he did not consider them his own. He was aware that he worked with Richard in teaching and that he was a part of Richard who carried the feelings of being overwhelmed by his job.

When Richard asked about Alex's significant memories, Alex responded by referring to every oral presentation he had ever made from grade school through graduate school. Thinking of those presentations continued to disturb Alex at a SUD level of eight. He had been fearful of "making a fool of myself," and of "being picked on." He did not remember specific events, only that he did not want to make a fool of himself. Being in gym classes and joining in group games were also disturbing, because Richard was poorly coordinated and always fared badly in competitive sports. His memories of gym classes still disturbed Alex to a SUD level of nine. Richard also talked about how he had never gotten good grades in school until he had graduated college and entered graduate school. He experienced his low grades as a form of criticism. In the early years, his first grade of *D* did not bother him but over time, "when it kept happening year after year," he came to understand the importance of grades and to believe that he wasn't very smart. However, after success in graduate school, and after becoming a teacher and being accepted by his peers and bosses, he overcame much of his concern for his earlier poor grades. Those memories bothered Alex now only at a SUD level of two.

In the remainder of the session, we unburdened Alex through four discrete interventions, all of them through use of the wind-through-the-goalposts metaphor. All of them were successful in reducing Alex's distress level to zero for the targeted experiences. The first was his earliest remembered oral presentation in school, followed by the unburdening of all other oral presentations through the completion of college. The third unburdening targeted Richard's fear of making a fool of himself in gym classes. Finally, we unburdened the memories Alex carried of Richard's fear and dread of criticism throughout his school experiences, including his years of poor grades. With this work apparently successful, we planned to check how well the gains had maintained themselves during week, and then, if no new problems arose, to work on Richard's continuing depression.

At the beginning of our tenth session, Richard reported that his wife had noticed a difference in him, saying that he was "much easier to get along with," and that he seemed to be happy. Additionally, it had been three weeks since he had fully weaned himself from the antipsychotic drug Risperdal. He was now ready to begin taking himself off his antidepressants. He had been taking 600 mg daily of Serzone (nefazodone) and would reduce that to 300 mg daily. He said that he had checked with his psychiatrist and received an okay to proceed in that way.

Returning to the deep work of Parts Psychology, we checked first with Alex regarding his anxiety about public speaking. Richard said that Alex was fine, and that "public speaking was no longer much of a concern." He was, however, still feeling somewhat overwhelmed with work. Using an affect bridge, Richard asked Alex to stay connected to the feeling of being overwhelmed and to let his mind float back in time to his earliest memory of having that sort of experience. The memory that surfaced had to do with schoolwork as a student rather than work as a teacher. In the ninth grade, Richard found his schoolwork particularly demanding. "I had so much trouble focusing that I would be overwhelmed with ordinary things like studying for a test. Alex rated the SUD level of the ninth grade experiences at a seven. Once more, through use of the wind-and-goal-posts metaphor, Richard guided Alex in unburdening the distress still bound to the ninth grade memories. In less than a minute, the SUD level had reached zero. Checking with Alex for overwhelming schoolwork memories either before or after the ninth grade, Richard found no other problems. Whatever other schoolwork-overwhelm memories there might have been, they were evidently unburdened in the previous intervention.

We returned then to Alex's memory for the panic attack discussed in the previous session. It was after this experience that Richard's psychiatrist prescribed Risperdal. Thinking about this experience still caused a level six anxiety response on the SUD scale. However, this anxiety was quickly unburdened to a zero level through the same wind metaphor we had been using so successfully.

Although we had unburdened Alex's experiences of overwhelm as a student, we had not checked on other memories of overwhelm for the years of Richard's work as a teacher. When Richard checked with Alex about this period of his life, he found several other occasions when his professional demands were temporarily too great for him. Without specifying times or settings, Richard left it up to Alex to locate these memories, and quickly unburdened them to wind. This seemed to have completed our work with Alex, but we planned to check for additional anxiety in our next session. Assuming, however, that our work was indeed finished, Richard negotiated a new role for Alex: this part would now be responsible for *appropriate anxiety*, the sort of minimal level of anxiety that enables a person to meet commitments and finish work at a reasonable pace.

Exhaustion

In session 11, Richard described himself as "exhausted all the time." He had also experienced increased restlessness in sleep and a greater difficulty in going to sleep. Additionally, he noticed some difficulty concentrating and some hand-shakiness but no increase in irritability. These symptoms might have been withdrawal effects due to cutting in half his Serzone dosage. Since Richard found them tolerable in the interest of getting off of the prescription drug, he decided not to change anything about his withdrawal program. The increase in symptoms was consistent with the lack of a significant reduction in his score on the CES-D, the depression screen introduced at the beginning of this chapter. His score was now 24, still in the range of possible major depression.

When Richard examined his experience of exhaustion more closely, he found that both Eric and Martin felt it, but not Alex, Richard 7, or Richard 5. When Richard interviewed Eric and Martin, he learned that they believed that feelings of exhaustion usually had an explanation, such as not enough sleep, or too much physical exertion. Coffee helped them to overcome this sort of lack of energy. However, the exhaustion of the last week was different, in that drinking coffee had no effect, and they couldn't point to any particular cause of the condition.

With continued discussion with his parts, Richard learned that their exhaustion was linked to hopelessness, especially as to whether things would get better in the future. The experience of hopelessness is a prime symptom of depression, but it could have been a part of the withdrawal response to cutting his dosage of antidepressant medication. It is also possible that the medication had been masking some of the worst feelings of depression. Whatever its source, however, the appearance of the hopelessness gave us something to work with. Richard asked Martin to connect to the feeling of hopelessness and bridge to his earliest experiences of having this sort of feeling. Martin reminded Richard of his move to Las Vegas 10 years previously at a time when he felt stifled in his previous career in sales. There seemed to be no way out of the stagnation he felt at that time. Those memories were disturbing to a SUD level of eight. When asked about other memories since that time that also connected to his feeling of hopelessness, Martin came up empty, according to Richard. There was just his unhappiness over his current teaching career and his inability to see anything changing significantly in the future. Before examining his dissatisfaction with teaching, Richard guided Martin through an unburdening of the negative feeling states he brought with him to Las Vegas, especially his dissatisfaction with his sales career and his sense of being blocked in moving toward a successful future. He accomplished the unburdening quickly through visualizing Martin burning up the negative emotions in a bonfire.

We were near the end of our session, but there was still time to identify some of the sources of Richard's frustration with work. Richard spoke first of the difference between what he had hoped to do in teaching and what he was actually required to do: "I thought I'd have the opportunity to be creative, but everything is scripted out a textbook." By that he meant that every class in the same grade was expected to have virtually the same lessons on the same topics presented in exactly the same way. Richard felt that there was little opportunity for him to fit his lessons to the individual needs of his students, or to bring in ideas of his own that might capture their imagination. Richard's other major complaint was of "multiple directives from many sources—they don't communicate with each other." The result, for example, was that Richard was overloaded with paperwork required by the district, but also expected to prepare his students for national testing, while daily recording online his students' grades and attendance so they would be accessible to their parents. There simply was not enough time to do all of the things that different administrators demanded of him. We planned to return to these issues at our next session. We would also look for any significant withdrawal symptoms linked to reducing his intake of Serzone.

In session 12, Richard reported feeling less tired than he had in the previous week. It appeared that if the tiredness was due to withdrawing from the antidepressant medication, those symptoms were abating. It was impossible to know, however, whether the reduction in fatigue might also have been due to the unburdening work in the previous session. In any case, Richard did not notice any other likely symptoms connected to reducing his medication.

We spent most of the session discussing other details of Richard's frustration with his teaching environment. We then unburdened Martin's negative affect, noted at a SUD level of seven, connected to the *scripted teaching* and the *multiple directives* identified in the previous session. Richard used a wind-blowing-through-the-goal-posts intervention for Martin, visualizing him as the wind blew "over, around, and through" him, carrying away particles of negative emotion. The first run-through of the intervention reduced the SUD level to one—which Martin indicated was due to his "lack of faith that he could stay free of the frustration." A single repetition of the intervention reduced the SUD level to zero. For our next session, we planned to check again for medication withdrawal symptoms and then to assess Richard's degree of depression and frustration.

In session 13, Richard reported that his most significant emotional experience during the preceding week was that of intermittently feeling anxious or nervous. He was unable to locate the source of this emotion. When I asked him to connect to that feeling now and to request that it provide a picture or image of itself in Richard's mind, there was no response. Consequently, we tried other means of finding the part what was amplifying its distress. In turn, Richard located the parts, Martin, Alex, and Eric, and asked each of them if the anxiety emanated from them. Each subpersonality denied being the source. Each one also indicated that he had no knowledge of who the part might be.

Jim in a Straitjacket

Alex, when asked directly, communicated that the source of the anxiety was Richard, himself, and not a part. What this sort of internal perception generally means is that the part carrying the emotion is so strongly blended with the self that other parts are unable to distinguish the self from the blended part. However, it is axiomatic that the self does not experience anxiety or other strong emotions directly. The emotion must come from a part. When all other efforts to find a blended part fail, I ask a known part to speak to the problem emotion and ask it to *step away* from the self so that both the known part and the observing self are able to perceive the part carrying the emotion. In this case, I coached Richard to speak to Alex and request that Alex follow this procedure. The result was that Richard was able to visualize a new part. He said, "I see someone in a straitjacket. He vaguely looks like me, too—his skin and hair color, the same length hair. He's tall, too, but maybe not as tall as me." When asked, the part said that he did not know Richard. When asked to guess who Richard might be, he responded, "I can't guess because I have no idea." Additional questions revealed that the part thought he was 38 years old, the same as Richard, and that his name was *Jim,* a name he possessed prior to being differentiated a few minutes earlier. Richard explained to Jim that he was a part of Richard. Jim accepted this explanation, but still did not know Richard's name. Richard shared his name with Jim.

Richard asked Jim about his earliest memory and was confused by the response. "He's acting very strange," Richard said, "like someone who should be in a mental institution. He's coherent one minute and then off on something completely different in the next minute—like the details of what I had for lunch. It makes no sense in the context of the conversation." Richard persisted in his questions and soon added, "He says he wasn't part of my life until post college." Richard asked Jim to share a significant memory with him. "He's telling me that I somehow damaged myself, my brain. In college I experimented with drugs, and he's bringing that up—like maybe I did something that damaged my brain." I asked Richard if Jim participated in his experimentation with drugs. He replied, "Yes, almost as if he was a part of me all along, but whatever that part was, it changed. So he's not who he was before he went to college. Damaging my brain with drugs is what he thinks caused it. Marijuana and LSD. He liked both of them, but he's not interested in doing them again because of possible long-term damage, particularly from LSD."

Jim acknowledged that he was the part of Richard who was experiencing anxiety. "It just happens to him. He doesn't understand why." Regarding why Jim wore a straitjacket, Richard said, "He says he's dangerous and needs to be in the straitjacket for my safety. He doesn't mind it. It's like a security blanket. There are times when he cannot control himself. Sometimes the anxiety will just overcome him, and he just has to ride it out." An early disturbing memory for Jim dated to Richard's age 25: "The time I got so depressed I called a psychiatrist." This period in Richard's life rated a SUD level of eight for Jim. Another memory was "when we moved to Las Vegas and I stopped taking the *Prozac*, cold turkey. It was a really dark time." It rated a nine on the SUD scale. Other of Jim's memories also rated a SUD score of nine: "feeling on edge, agitated, thoughts racing. It happens regularly." As we concluded our session, Richard observed of Jim, "He is definitely the one with the mental health issues—depression and anxiety."

In session 14, Richard described his work stress as high, but unlike previous high stress periods, in this one he described things as going well. During this and the next week, he was doing parent-teacher conferences, but they were going well. At home, life was going well with his wife, also. They were moving into a better time in their lives, Richard said.

During this session, we collected the difficult memories that constituted most of straitjacketed Jim's memory set. In the following session, our 15th, we would unburden Jim of the negative energies connected to these memories. Jim's earliest memory did not date to adult life, after all. Instead, it was the occasion when his parents took him for psychological testing. Richard said of Jim, "He can still remember the ink blot test." The event was not disturbing for Jim, but it appeared to be the event that brought about his first appearance in Richard's life. As a result of the test, Richard's parents were told that he had a *learning disability;* later, he would discover the problem was *ADHD (attention deficit hyperactivity disorder).*

When asked specifically about Jim's earliest painful memory, Richard replied, "He relates it to depression, in that in general we weren't happy. We were down most of the time; there wasn't a specific event. Also, being shy. Also, having trouble with my peers. I felt uncomfortable not knowing what to say in social situations. Not fitting in because I was unable to verbally interact." Not fitting in was a problem throughout Richard's life, but the most difficult time was during middle school. One way Richard found of easing his anxiety was through the friendships he made. "There wasn't so much pressure if there was someone else who also didn't fit in. A good friend in grade school was a dwarf. In high school, a friend was extremely smart. I have a friend now who is 'really weird.' I'm comfortable with these people." Asked about other difficult aspects of growing up Richard said, "The problem became worse as social groups became more important. I was troubled that I was in the nerd group." All of these troubling memories rated a seven or eight on the SUD scale.

When asked about the disturbing aspects of college life, Richard said it was his drug use, especially LSD. He quoted Jim as saying, "the problem is not being able to control himself." "That's why he wears a straitjacket. Without that he would lose even more control."

Before beginning our 15th session, Richard once again filled out the CES-D, the depression screen we had previously used. Unlike the results of the previous screen just four weeks previously, Richard now scored below the cutoff for depression. Richard scored 13, while the cutoff score for mild depression is 15. Scores above 21 suggest the possibility of major depression. At intake, Richard scored 28, and four weeks previously, probably suffering some medication withdrawal, Richard scored 24. We appeared to be on the right track in treating Richard's issues.

After brief observations on the unusual experience of having watched snow fall in Las Vegas earlier in the day, we returned to the work of unburdening straitjacketed Jim of his painful memories from childhood and early adulthood. In every case but one, Richard guided the unburdening with a waterfall cleansing metaphor. Spending just a few minutes on each memory or group of related memories, Jim readily gave up the associated negative energies to the flow of water and reached a SUD level of zero without incident. Richard began with the early depression and shyness, moved on to not fitting in in middle school, and quickly dispatched the pain of being classified in the nerd group. He shifted then and moved to unburden the depression of his mid-20s, dealt with the losses and challenges following his move from the east coast to Las Vegas, and ended with neutralizing his current experience of feeling on edge, being agitated, and having racing thoughts. Only this last intervention required a repetition of the waterfall intervention. The first run-through of the visualization reduced the level seven current-time experiences to a level two, and a second visualization reduced the negative emotions to zero. When we asked Jim to examine his full set of memories in search of additional problem experiences he found none

As we concluded the session, Richard disclosed that Jim wished that he had never used LSD. He continued to believe that Richard might have suffered some brain damage as the result of that drug use. He also acknowledged, according to Richard, that the therapy was now helping Richard. He was concerned, however, with the continued plan to wean Richard of antidepressants. He intended to keep wearing his straitjacket until he was sure it was safe to take it off. We ended with Richard saying he intended to cut immediately his intake of Wellbutrin from 450 mg to 300 mg per day, taking two equal doses of 150 mg daily. He would maintain his reduced level of Serzone. Before walking out the door, Richard noted he was not feeling any anxiety and that he was enjoying the parent-teacher conferences. As an indication that the bulk of our work was finished, we did not have a specific plan for our next session. We would work with whatever issue Richard brought to the session.

We met for our 16ᵗʰ session after a two-week break for the Christmas holidays. Richard had followed his plan to reduce his Wellbutrin dosage to 300 mg a day without any noticeable withdrawal effects. He planned to reduce the dosage to 150 mg, once a day, if no problems arose during the coming week.

Angry Eric

During the previous week, Richard said that he had been short with his wife "a couple of times." He had snapped at her. He did not believe his behavior was related to the withdrawal effects of his antidepressant, but he accepted my suggestion that he keep an open mind about it. Regardless, however, of whether possible withdrawal effects might have influenced his shortness with his wife, the behavior was influenced by a part—because strong behavior is always directed or influenced by a part. I suggested that we could work on the behavior problem without trying to manipulate the medication dosage. Because Richard's actions seemed to be linked to a kind of anger, I suggested that he locate the part originally found to be associated with anger. He found Eric quickly. Eric readily acknowledged that it was he who snapped at Richard's wife. "He was just in a bad mood, but not about anything in particular." We tried an affect bridge with Eric, asking him to connect to his feelings at the time he snapped at his wife and to allow himself to search his early memories for a similar set of feelings. "Nothing comes up," Richard said of Eric's efforts to find early underlying memories. When I asked Richard to talk about an incident from the previous week, he described how he felt about giving the kids a bath. "It felt like my wife was *telling* me what to do rather than *asking* me to bathe them." With this more specific emotional response to his wife, we asked Eric to try another affect bridge. This time he reported "a general memory of just growing up and not liking being told what to do, like mowing the lawn. As a cub scout, I was told to go into the snow and do something, and I felt cold and miserable.

Eric readily agreed to unburden the negative energy attached to these memories. In less than a minute of visualization of the wind-and-posts intervention, his SUD level reached zero. Richard observed that there were three memories in particular that influenced his reaction to being told what to do: mowing the lawn, going into the snow, and, when he was on a soccer team with his father as temporary coach, he remembered his father telling him where he should go on the field. He felt that he did not need to be told where to go; he knew how to play the game. As the session ended, we checked Eric's SUD level for being told by Richard's wife to bathe the kids. It was zero. It is impossible to know whether Richard (and Eric's) irritation with his wife was related to cutting back on his medications, but my guess is that it was related. Increased irritability is a common withdrawal symptom for many drugs, including common ones such as the caffeine in coffee. In any case, the same procedures for unburdening negative affect are effective even when the problem is triggered by medication withdrawal.

In our 17th session, Richard noted that he had halved again his dosage for Wellbutrin. Instead of taking 150 mg twice a day, he had begun to take 150 mg only once a day. He was looking forward to being entirely free of psychoactive medications, but he wanted to continue to take a cautious approach to ending his dependency upon them.

A Moody Teenager

At the end of our last session Richard had stated his desire to explore his moodiness—his tendency to develop a bad mood for no reason. For example, he sometimes withdrew at a social gathering and avoided the cheerful conversations. We returned to that issue in our new session. Eric, the angry one, was aware of the problem but said that this moodiness was not his doing. He only became involved if anger was going to be a part of Richard's behavior. Richard recalled that he hadn't wanted to go to the Christmas party a few weeks previously. He felt he wouldn't know what to say and didn't feel like interacting with anyone. Richard asked Eric to connect him to the moody part who hadn't wanted to go to the Christmas party. Within a few moments, Richard found himself visualizing an image of himself. "It's me," Richard said, "as I am now. He's wearing *Dockers* and a black shirt." However, although the part presented himself as Richard in the present, he *felt* himself to be a teenager, 14 or 15 years in age. The part was well oriented to Richard's present and to the internal world. He knew who Richard was and he knew Eric as well. Eric said that he *knew of* the moody part, but didn't *know* him. *The Teenager* acknowledged that he was the one who carried the problem of moodiness.

As the interview with The Teenager illustrates, it is important to query a part regarding its felt age even when the apparent age seems clear. This part experienced himself as a teenager, but Richard visualized him at his own adult age. Sometimes the disparity can be even greater. In an unrelated case, a part presented an image of itself as an adult but, when asked, said that it felt itself to be six years old. The opposite can be true as well. A part may present itself as a child, but interaction with it may reveal an adult perspective.

Richard described The Teenager's response to the question about his earliest memory: "He keeps talking about my father, who was and still is moody. He says he was a part of my life by the age of six or seven. At this time, he was aware that moody was what one ought to be. Later, about 10, he learned that moody wasn't required, but was an option that coincided with me being awkward and not fitting in at school." The Teenager rated the experience of not fitting in at a level six on the SUD scale. When asked about other painful memories, The Teenager brought to Richard's mind an experience from high school. "I was taking American history. I liked the teacher. I had attention issues. One day she called on me, and I was in a bad mood. I didn't know the answer because I wasn't paying attention. She said something about how I would know the answer if I paid attention. I snapped back that I could pay attention if she wasn't so boring. Later I apologized." The memory was disturbing to The Teenager at a level eight on the SUD scale. A level nine disturbance related to an experience during college. There was a social gathering in Richard's dorm room, and his roommate was talking about other guests she had invited. "I was in a bad mood and snapped at her in front of others. I demanded to know why she invited all those people. I embarrassed her and hurt her feelings. The event chilled our friendship." As we ended the session, The Teenager made Richard aware of how his moodiness led to snapping at his wife. There was "a group of instances with my wife over the years where I snapped at her." The teenager felt badly to a level seven on the disturbance scale. In the next session, we planned to unburden the teenager's moodiness, and perhaps we would unburden angry Eric as well.

At the beginning of session 18, Richard reported on his progress in weaning himself from his psychoactive medications. It had been a week now since he reduced his Wellbutrin to 150 mg a day. The only side effect he had noticed was that he needed to go to bed earlier for the first three nights after cutting the dosage. Because he was so pleased with his progress in reducing his medications, he had decided to reduce his Serzone dosage from 300 to 200 mg beginning that night.

We then returned to our plan to unburden the moody teenager. We began with the waterfall metaphor to dissolve The Teenager's distress for Richard's awkwardness in school. Shortly after Richard began his visualization of the teenager in the waterfall, he opened his eyes to say that The Teenager's distress level had been quickly reduced to a level three, but these were powerful memories and he would try again. He decided to increase the amount and impact of the water on the teenager. Within a minute, the distress level had reached zero. After checking for other significant memories from grade school and middle school and finding none, we went on to problems from high school and later. We dealt quickly with his rudeness to his history teacher and his college roommate, and then processed his snappishness with his wife. Each memory or set of memories reduced to zero with only a single run-through of the visualization.

It was time for The Teenager to choose a new role, since the role of maintaining moodiness was no longer helpful to Richard. Richard and The Teenager decided that a good job for The Teenager would be to provide support to Richard through encouraging him to remember the things that brought happiness. In conjunction with this role change, we guided The Teenager in an intervention aimed at removing the modeling influence for moodiness provided by Richard's father. Richard emphasized to his teenager part that the moodiness he had acquired at about the age of six or seven belonged to his *father*, not to *him*. Consequently, Richard guided the boy in symbolically returning the moodiness to his father. He did this by working with The Teenager to visualize himself as a six- or seven-year-old giving it back (as if it were a physical substance) to his father.

As we neared the end of the session, Richard checked with angry Eric to see if he had anything he needed to unburden with respect to The Teenager's life experiences. Eric reported that he had no problems with those experiences; they belonged to the youngster. Previously, he had only been reacting to The Teenager's distress. The burden belonged to the boy.

Richard and I also discussed how close he might be to graduating himself from therapy. We agreed that our work was approaching conclusion. Richard was especially pleased that he was becoming "unlinked" to his medications. He felt a new sense of freedom.

Continued Medication Reduction

In our 19th session, Richard talked about the anxiety he had felt over the previous four days. We wondered if it might be connected to his further reduction in medication, or if there was a new issue that we had so far failed to notice. The anxious body sensation Richard felt was localized in his stomach, providing an easy connection to the part who carried the anxiety. Our first efforts, however, to connect to the anxious part failed. I had asked Richard to focus on his stomach sensation and to ask the sensation to give him an image of itself. Richard saw only blankness. We then used the fishermen metaphor, a visualization in which Richard imagined two fishermen walking past him on either side of him, holding between them a tightly stretched, magical fishing net. As the fishermen walked past him, the net moved through his body, captured the sensation, and pulled it from his body. As the net pulled through his body, Richard visualized himself gently placing the net's contents into a nearby room. After doing so, Richard observed that the room appeared to be "a shack, with tools and shovels." He added, "Now I see the owner of the shed inside." The owner was a part of "average height, thin, with brown hair, and a beard and mustache." He wore overalls and a flannel shirt. In answer to the initial orienting question, the part indicated that he didn't know Richard. When asked to guess, he suggested that Richard was a tourist. "You must be lost," Richard quoted the part as saying. His name was *Jack.* I coached Richard to explain to the part that although the conversation was taking place in Jack's shack, Jack and his shack existed only in Richard's mind, and Richard wanted to become acquainted with Jack. Richard relayed from Jack that he was "slightly confused but willing to accept" that he was a part of Richard. In order to further solidify the orienting framework, and to convince Jack that he was indeed a part of Richard, I coached Richard again in interacting with Jack. I suggested that Richard ask Jack to look through Richard's eyes and to notice me waving my hand. Once Jack acknowledged that he could see my waving hand, I asked Richard to close his eyes to demonstrate to Jack that he could only see the external world through Richard's eyes. Another repetition of this exercise, but with me snapping my fingers instead of waving my hand, was sufficient to convince Jack that he was a part of Richard. The process seemed to have oriented Jack sufficiently that he could now look back at his [i.e., Richard's] memories relating to anxiety.

When Richard asked about Jack's earliest memories, he found that the part claimed to have "been there all the time," but he didn't begin to have problems until after Richard finished college. When Richard tried to elicit recall of particular anxious moments, Jack could not isolate any specific memories, because, he said to Richard, there had been "no specific reasons for him to be anxious. [Even] when things were going well, we would go through periods of being anxious for no particular reason." Although Jack was now well oriented to being a part of Richard, there was much that he didn't know. He didn't know Richard's wife or children, or even Richard's age of 38. He considered himself to be in his late 40s and had *always* consi-dered this his age. He remembered going to college, but claimed no specific memories for that time in Richard's life. He did remember that public speak-ing produced high anxiety. For example, said Richard, "I won an essay contest in high school sponsored by the YMCA. I had to give a speech in the YMCA building on MLK [Martin Luther King, Jr.] day." The incident both-ered him now only at a level two on the SUD scale, but before therapy it bothered him more. "What would have been debilitating was making eye contact, so I just looked down at my essay. Some other part got me to the podium in spite of my anxiety, and then I just read my essay without look-ing up."

We continued to interview Jack in an effort to understand more of his role in Richard's life. Jack explained that even before Richard made contact with him in therapy, he could remember his own life history. Now he un-derstood that what he remembered was just a part of Richard's life history. He remembered Richard's girlfriend, Sandy, from college, and he remem-bered another girlfriend, Carrie. However, he did not remember that Richard and Carrie lived together in Pennsylvania or that they married in Indiana. He only discovered that they were married during the course of the conversation. Jack did not remember the births of Richard's children, but he knew about his anxiety for the responsibilities of parenthood. He did not consider Carrie to be his wife nor the children to be his children. They were Richard's relationships.

As this interview with Jack reveals, parts do not have to be fully aware of their connection to the self in order to have a significant effect on the self. His primary purpose appeared to be to contain a portion of Richard's anxiety, but even that was somewhat vague. We ended our session with an effort to unburden Jack of his current anxiety through a waterfall metaphor. Shortly after beginning the visualization Richard reported, "I don't think I'm getting anywhere." We decided to return to Jack's anxiety in our next session. Richard guided Jack in storing his current anxiety in a safe until that time.

In our 20th session, I asked Richard about his current anxiety and found that he experienced "none at all." "It was a great week," Richard said. When he went inside and located Jack again, he found that this part was similarly without anxiety. On the chance that Jack felt no anxiety because he had successfully maintained it in the metaphorical safe he had utilized at the end of the previous session, we asked him to check this container as well. He could find no anxiety. These findings about the free-floating anxiety that we had discussed in our previous session suggested that we were correct in our suspicion that the anxiety in question was related to the withdrawal effects from reducing Richard's medications. Unlike the anxiety we had found to be related to life experiences, and which could be reduced through the unburdening technique, the anxiety we worked with in our previous session appeared to have a physiological origin, and was not responsive to unburdening. This interpretation was also consistent with the vagueness of Jack's responses when we asked him to bridge from his felt anxiety to previous life experiences. He could not do so. His life experiences did not produce his anxiety; instead, his anxiety was apparently due to reducing the addictive anti-anxiety medications. Jack might be a representation of Richard's withdrawal anxiety, and not a pre-existing, dynamic part of Richard's life, since recalling significant instances from Richard's history produced no emotional responses from him. Richard planned to reduce his Serzone even further that night, from 200 mg to 100 mg. If there were no further withdrawal symptoms connected to this reduction, Richard planned also to cut his Wellbutrin dosage again.

Our session was on a Wednesday and Richard reduced his Serzone as planned. By Sunday, he felt significant anxiety. Although the anxiety faded during the course of the day, Richard awakened each morning feeling anxious. At our 21st meeting on another Wednesday afternoon, he was unable to connect his anxiety to any particular internal subpersonality. "It's not Jack," Richard said. "He's confused by it. It doesn't make sense. He says it's not a part, and it's not me. I can feel it in my stomach, an unsettled feeling, like I'm worried about something but I don't know what about. A feeling of anxiety without a reason." We assumed the anxiety had to do with withdrawal from Serzone and that it was not due to any particular life experience or current situation. Consequently, we worked on reducing the anxiety through a set of breathing and relaxation techniques. By the end of the session, Richard was no longer feeling anxious.

By the time of our 22nd session, Richard had reduced his dosage of Wellbutrin to 150 mg and continued the reduced dose of Serzone at 100 mg. During the week, he continued to awaken most mornings at 4:00 AM, but "it was less than last week." Jack acknowledged that he was experiencing the anxiety at the 4:00 A.M. awakenings, but insisted it was good for Richard. "He says it's good for me because I'm going over the things I need to do or forgot to do." Richard convinced Jack "to try to wait until 6:00 AM for going over things." Richard also noted that he and his wife were doing well, and she was pleased with the results of his therapy. He was "not going off on her in front of the kids," a sensitive issue prior to therapy. In fact, he wasn't *going off* at all. At work, he was "accepting that I can only do my best, and that is pretty good." We appeared to be on track for Richard to reduce his medications even further.

At our 23rd session, Richard said that he had not experienced any significant anxiety during the previous week. Consequently, he planned to stop the Serzone completely. Then, in the week before our next session, following the complete cessation of Serzone, he experienced some mild anxiety on each of the last four days before our 24th session. He was unsure whether the anxiety was due to withdrawal from Serzone or from his anticipation of the end-of-the-term testing he would be doing of his students in the following week. He found that the subpersonality, Jack, acknowledged some anxiety over the demands this testing would make upon him, but that anxiety was quickly unburdened with the waterfall metaphor. Richard then guided Jack in an additional unburdening of his anticipation of future anxiety by focusing on the thought of how he would feel on the following Monday when testing began. We ended the session with Richard feeling calm and without anxiety.

Concluding Therapy

Our next three meetings could be described as *supportive psychotherapy*. We reviewed Richard's significant activities and interactions and talked about his satisfaction with his current life. There were no significant problems and consequently no need for the deep work of Parts Psychology. We continued to monitor withdrawal effects from his medications but found no significant problems. After the first of these three meetings, Richard cut his Wellbutrin dose to 75 mg, and after the second he stopped this medication altogether. By the last of these three sessions, it had been four weeks since he had weaned himself completely from Serzone and two weeks since he stopped the Wellbutrin. He was now free of all psychoactive medications. The problems at work of too much paperwork, inconsistent or contradictory leadership from different elements of the administration, and the over-structuring of teaching duties continued. What had changed was Richard's attitude. He just did the best he could and let himself be satisfied with that. At home, he and his wife had only mild arguments; the powerful arguments of the past were now history. The *triggers* were missing, he said. Because he was doing so well, Richard decided that he was almost ready to graduate himself from his therapy; however, just to be on the safe side he scheduled a final session for four weeks later.

At the beginning of our 28th and final session of the eight months of therapy, Richard once more filled out the depression screen (CES-D) we had previously used. His score was now five. At the beginning of therapy, Richard scored 28. At our 11th session, he scored 24 at a time when he may have been experiencing withdrawal effects from his antidepressant medications. In the 15th session, his score was down to 13. Fifteen is the cutoff score for a suggestion of possible depression.

Richard felt secure with the changes he had made in therapy. His home and work experiences continued to improve. He said that he neither wanted nor needed medications. He added, "There was a time when I felt I couldn't live without them. But now I feel better than I ever felt while taking medications." Four weeks prior to this last session, Richard was concerned that part of the reason he was feeling good may have been that the effects of the medications had not worn off entirely. He was afraid that when the medication effects finally wore off he would "come crashing back." But that never happened. After an additional month free of the drugs, he still had "more energy," and a "clearer mind." He had neither cried nor blown up in anger in half a year, and had experienced no panic attacks since beginning therapy. His concluding comment before we closed his graduation session was that he felt good about being a husband and a father.

Chapter 14
Scaredy Cat and The Monster

This chapter is the last in a series of three that describes Parts Psychology work with Georgia, the attorney who stepped down to work first as a paralegal, and then as a legal secretary, and then once more as a paralegal. Georgia's long-term therapy continued as this chapter was written, and there appeared to be a good chance that she would reactivate her license and return to full-time work as an attorney. She was currently classified as a paralegal but was doing high-level attorney work, writing briefs and responding to motions, defending her company's clients with her research and writing skills. Her company, who paid her significantly less than they would pay an associate attorney, appreciated her. In turn, she appreciated that her company allowed her to leave work promptly at 5:00 PM with other hourly staff.

In the current chapter, we revisit some issues from earlier sessions and discover answers to some questions for which we had no answers at the time. This chapter also addresses the symbolic aspects of Parts Psychology. In one way or another everything that transpires in the internal world is a symbolic communication; it is not an action in the world outside the mind of the person. Internal parts are not physical actors in the external world of the client except in the extreme cases where a client can be diagnosed with dissociative identity disorder. Nevertheless, internal actions are quite significant for understanding the external world.

After a two-week vacation for the Christmas and New Year's holidays, we returned to therapy with a new agenda. Georgia had two concerns. With her intellectual curiosity piqued, Georgia wanted to find out more about a mini mystery that had appeared much earlier in our work. This was the wound suffered by *Fluffy*, the *Scaredy Cat*, at the hands of *The Monster*. We did not pursue this question at the time because it seemed peripheral to Georgia's primary goals. Her second concern involved how to "give up the regrets for the way I lived my life." This chapter addresses the first concern.

The second concern was more complex and required many more months of therapy.

Scaredy Cat's Wound

Scaredy Cat was a stuffed-toy Easter Bunny who lived in a wicker basket. Very timid, she held a set of memories related to Georgia's sense of separation from or distance from significant people in her life. Scaredy Cat was a name given to the part by others in the system. She called herself *Fluffy*. Georgia remembered that Fluffy would not talk about her wound. "She just showed it. It was a pretty ugly open wound." We decided to find the helper part, White Dragon, so that she could help us connect again to The Monster who wounded Fluffy. The Monster, we had previously learned, had been locked behind a door inside a cave, because "it was mean and hurt people." We hoped to get the cooperation of The Monster by unburdening it of its terrifying memory of the huge snake it had seen crawling behind the family's woodpile. Our reasoning was that The Monster might be more flexible and cooperative after he had released the negative energy still connected to his traumatic memory. That memory had been disturbing to The Monster at a level eight on the 0-10 SUD scale.

As Georgia sat in her chair in the therapy office and turned her attention inward, it took about three minutes before she indicated that she had located her internal helper, *White Dragon,* who had in turn located The Monster for her. Then she said, "Okay, I think The Monster is here. I got a lot of close-up images of an eye and a mouth, but it took a while to get an image of the whole." When asked if he remembered us, The Monster merely growled. But he responded with a "Yes," when asked if he knew who Georgia was, and another "Yes" to the question of whether he recognized that he was a part of Georgia. Finally, he also stated that he would like to unburden the memory of the terrifying snake behind the woodpile. The unburdening went quickly. Georgia visualized The Monster standing in the wind as his fear blew away like particles of sand. In less than a minute, the memory was stripped of its negative energy.

As we had hoped, The Monster was more cooperative after the unburdening. He said he gave Fluffy her wound when he "sliced" her with his arm when he hit her. Georgia asked when and why did he hurt Fluffy. "He said it was a long time ago. He did it because he felt like it. I get the feeling he was angry about something, because Fluffy wasn't taking him seriously. So he hurt her to make her afraid of him. He was in charge—at least he wanted to be in charge—and she wouldn't do what he told her to do. They were playing a game. It was something outdoors. They were playing, running around. He wanted the outside me to lead people somewhere, and Fluffy wanted me to follow someone else's lead." In answer to my questions, Georgia continued, "Just my brothers and sisters were there. It was about a combination of things. We were talking about playing in the woods behind the house, and The Monster wanted me to take the lead in doing that." Georgia remembered that when the kids went into the woods she was always the leader. "Fluffy wanted to do what someone else suggested, staying in the yard and playing *tag* or *hide-and-seek*. It wasn't that she was afraid of the woods. It was more an element of we were not supposed to go into the woods that day. She was more afraid of getting in trouble [for disobeying Mother]."

As we ended the session, we agreed to ask two questions of The Monster at our next meeting. The first was whether he was a monster at the time of the wounding. The second was whether the wounding had a lasting effect on The Monster and Fluffy, and more importantly, whether Georgia was significantly affected by the incident. We did not expect The Monster to provide a definitive answer to this question, but it was a question we would be considering as we continued our work.

In our second session of the New Year, before further work with The Monster, I asked Georgia whether Fluffy's wound might mean that since Fluffy was a follower, and she was wounded, could that mean that Georgia did not do well in following the lead of others? That is, was Fluffy's wound a symbolic communication that the follower aspect of Georgia's personality was somehow stunted? She responded by observing that for most of her life she had not been a follower, but rather an *anti-follower*. There was a time in her life when she refused to listen to popular music, avoided trendy clothes, and ignored popular hairstyles. She also added, "I was the oldest child and I was quite bossy with my brothers and sisters."

Transforming The Monster

When we returned to work with The Monster, Georgia asked him if he was a monster at the time he "sliced open" Fluffy. "No way!" he said. "I was just a regular boy." Georgia described his response to the question of what caused him to be a monster: "At first he said he didn't know, and then he said he felt bad about hurting Fluffy. And the others wouldn't play with him anymore after he hurt Fluffy. The other parts were afraid of him, and so they just left him alone. And that made him angry. So he decided to show them how scary he really could be. That's when he became a monster and terrorized the others. I asked him if he was alone after that, and he said 'Yeah, pretty much.'" Then Georgia asked him if he would like to give up his costume and just be a little boy. "He said, 'Yeah,' he'd like to be a little boy again." When asked if he would like some help, The Monster said he "didn't need any help, but it might be good if we helped anyway." With some coaching from me, Georgia constructed the setting for the intervention. Since The Monster was in a dark cave, Georgia gave it lighting, and then visualized a stage at one end of the cave. There were stairs at both ends of the stage and, in the center of it, a healing blue light that cast a circle of blue on the stage floor. Georgia offered an open invitation to any parts who might be listening in to join the audience. She also asked White Dragon to carry the invitation to any internal parts who were not listening in on the conversation but who might like to observe anyway. We waited for a few minutes, and then for a few minutes more. Finally, Georgia said, "Okay, *Sandy (The Snake)* is here." Georgia went on, "I asked Sandy and White Dragon to call Fluffy to see if she will come. She appears, but she's afraid. She's back in her basket. I put the basket on a chair so she could watch from there, and Sandy is gonna sit right next to her. *Princess* is here. She said she can't resist a show. *Funky Monkey* just bounced in. White Dragon is here, too."

"Let's start the show," said Georgia. "The orchestra has been warming up. The song will be a military march—something from Sousa." As I coached her, Georgia suggested to The Monster that he climb onto the stage from the stairs on the right and move slowly toward the healing blue light in the center as the orchestra continued to play and build toward a peak. Then, as The Monster stepped into the light and bathed himself in blue, the orchestra reached a crescendo. The Monster lost his fearsome features and awesome size and transformed into a little boy. The boy stepped out from the blue light on the left side of the stage to the applause of the audience and descended the stairs on the left side of the stage. He walked down the stairs to greet and be greeted by the audience. Perhaps he could say something to Fluffy to begin healing her wound? "The little boy thanked everyone for coming and told Fluffy he was sorry he hurt her. He didn't mean to be so mean to her. Somebody called, 'Let's go play!' — it was Funky Monkey." The ceremony was over. Recognizing that the theatre could be a place for parts to "hang out," Georgia put the idea before the group. Then she said, "Everyone likes the stage, but we'll first make the chairs more comfortable for now. And add a snack counter." Georgia thanked everyone for coming and asked Fluffy if she would be available for some therapy work at our next meeting. "She said that's fine."

After Georgia had left her inner world and returned her attention to the therapy room, she said, "Okay. That worked really well. They liked the idea of a clubhouse. I told the boy I'll call him *Little Boy* when I want him. I got different pictures of him, and he was dressed each time like the kids in *Little Rascals*, [a series of short films made in the 1920s and 1930s featuring the antics of a group of young children]. He wore a short-sleeved shirt tucked into shorts held up by suspenders, *Buster Brown* shoes that were dark in color. He's a cartoon boy."

Before closing for the day, I asked Georgia if she thought she might be making it all up as we went along. She replied, "No, I don't think I'm making it up as I go. I think it [her inner world] was already there. It doesn't have the feeling of me creating a drawing. I feel like I'm discovering something that's already there." She added, "Last week between sessions I was picking up on The Monster being the bossy side of me."

Happiness at Work

In session three, Georgia temporarily put aside further work with the problem of Fluffy and The Monster to bring up her dissatisfaction with her work career. She had noticed her unhappiness, especially over the last couple of months. Although she was now leaving work on time with the other employees, and thus not adding to her life the extra stress of long work hours, she observed, "I'm still not enjoying work." She was now exclusively doing high-level paralegal work and leaving it at the office when she went home for the day. She added, "If I can't be happy doing this kind of legal work I might as well be an attorney again and get paid for it." About work with law she said, "I loved law school, the school part, but I don't like the practice of law. I'm considering teaching. I've always enjoyed teaching and tutoring." We continued our discussion of teaching and of what she found attractive in the idea of teaching at various levels—grade school, high school or college—and then agreed that it might be helpful for her to consult a career counselor to get a better idea of what options she had. She said she would follow up on seeing a career counselor when she had a chance. Meanwhile, we agreed on new priorities for therapy. We would finish the work with Fluffy and The Monster and then concentrate on helping Georgia to process whatever it was that she disliked about her current work as a paralegal. Then we would work on helping her to let go of her regrets for the turns her life had taken.

Healing Fluffy

Two weeks later, after Georgia had recovered from a bout with the flu, we returned to our work with Fluffy. At first Georgia could not locate this child part, but with the aid of the helper part, White Dragon, she soon reported that both parts were present in her internal vision. We told Fluffy that we had heard The Monster's story and that we would like to hear her story of how she got hurt those many years ago. Georgia narrated the story:

> She showed me pictures of her and the Little Boy almost as if they were in a tug-of-war. There's no rope, but they lean back and forth as if they were trying to pull one. I asked if they were fighting for control over something, and she said, 'Yes.' He was being a brat and wouldn't listen to her, and she turned her back on him and started to walk away, and that's when he grabbed her arm and hurt her. And she pulled her arm free from him and ran away. She's showing me her arm, the way it looks now, and it looks better than it did when she showed it to me when we first met. His apology helped, but I think it was more just hearing his side of the story.

[Therapist: Would she like to tell her side of the story now?]

She says she just did tell her story. So I asked her if she could re-member what they were fighting over. She says the Little Boy was trying to make trouble. It was pretty close to time to go in for dinner, and if we played in the woods we couldn't get back in time for din-ner, but he didn't care. I asked if the outside me led my brothers and sisters into the woods as he wanted. She's saying that we stayed in the yard. I think she's saying that I got outvoted by my brothers and sisters. It seems that even though the Little Boy won the internal fight, he lost the external fight [i.e., The Monster won the fight for dominance over Fluffy but Georgia's siblings refused to follow him into the woods that day anyway].

Therapist: Did the internal fight result in changes in your life?
Georgia: She said that after the fight I was more bossy. She seems to be saying that after that I didn't like other people—other kids, my peers—telling me what to do.

Therapist: Does she know your college boyfriend?
Georgia: She's nodding her head.

Therapist: Does she know how the decision was made to break up with him?
Georgia: According to her it was because he wouldn't do what I wanted him to do. She says it wasn't what *she* wanted, but she doesn't know if it was what The Monster wanted. She doesn't know when he became a monster, but in her eyes, it was when he hurt her.

Therapist: Does she know she is telling us a story, a metaphor?
Georgia: I don't think she quite gets it. She pointed at her arm and said, 'It really hurt.'

Therapist: How did her life change after he hurt her?
Georgia: She says that she was sad because she lost a friend and she became very quiet.

Therapist: Does that mean that she stopped trying to get you to do what others wanted to do?

Georgia: Uh, yeah. She says she sometimes wanted me to join others, but she stopped trying to get my attention because I wouldn't listen.

Therapist: How does she feel now that you are listening to her?
Georgia: She feels better but she is still kind of shy.

It was near the end of the session, and so we arranged with Fluffy to work with us for at least one more session to ensure that her wound was entirely healed.

After Georgia released her inner world and fully returned her attention to the therapy room, I observed that the conversation was fascinating. Georgia replied, "Yeah, especially me not wanting to be like others. There was a while where if something was popular or *in* I just looked down on it. There are times when I'm bothered by being so different from other people—like much more intelligent than the people I meet and work with on a regular basis. Sometimes I don't like not fitting in. It bothers me to think of how close-minded I was when I thought I was the most open-minded be-cause I was different." We planned to continue with Fluffy at our next session.

In session five, Georgia came to our meeting with a spot of ash on her forehead, an observance of the Christian celebration of *Ash Wednesday.* This led us into a brief but relevant conversation about her experience of her church as a child. She remembered that the church was looking for altar boys and that "they were practically begging for boys to volunteer for this job in the church. I approached the priest and asked if I could be an altar boy, and became their first female altar boy. This was in 1975." Her sister and two other girls soon joined her in this role. Later, we would learn that it was the Little Boy part of her who spoke up to the priest.

Returning then to our work with Fluffy, Georgia found her quickly and reported that Fluffy the Easter Bunny was ready to heal her wound com-pletely. As the healing intervention, Georgia chose to help Fluffy process her memories in the healing pool behind the waterfall. As Fluffy immersed herself in the scented waters, Georgia described the processing of Fluffy's memories.

I just saw the argument with my brother and sisters about going into the woods, and that memory just floated away. She let the tugging between her and the Little Boy float away. Now I see the image of The Monster, the way he looked before he changed back into Little Boy; it just floated away, too. She just lifted her arm, and it's perfect, again.

Therapist: Check for memories before the tug-of-war between her and the Little Boy.
Georgia: She said, no, there weren't any problems.

Therapist: Check for disturbing memories after the tug-of-war.
Georgia: She showed me a picture of the way her arm looked when it was really ugly, but she said that's all gone now.

Therapist: Does she have her own memories of your life after she was wounded?
Georgia: No, I don't think she has memories of me growing up. I think she was hiding a lot. She says she's been paying attention since the first time we talked, when she came out of the basket, but before that she said White Dragon would tell her stories about what I was doing—kind of like news updates. I told her that I wanted her to recommend things for me now even if it's what other people are doing. She says she will do that, but she'll only recommend things now if she thinks it's a good idea. She thinks she can recommend adult things because it's adults I'm around all the time.

Therapist: Does she have anything else she wants to say before we move on to other things?
Georgia: She says she wants to thank me and [the therapist] for healing her arm.

We concluded our work with Fluffy and The Monster as Georgia recalled again how she became an altar boy at a time when only boys acted as altar boys in her church. She acknowledged that it was the Little Boy part of her who influenced her to volunteer. "It surprises me now to think how it seemed so natural to tug on the priest's sleeve and tell him girls should be doing the altar boy work. I asked him why couldn't I be an altar boy. It was about the same time I decided to be the first girl in the Naval Academy. My father went there. I changed my mind on that, later, when he pointed out that there was a lot of math and science there, and I wanted to study history."

Symbolic Wounds

Parts Psychology generally embraces clients' stories of their inner worlds without trying to interpret the symbolism that is so prevalent in the stories. Parts' names—if they have names—are linked to clients' life histories; the relationship between the two is sometimes obvious, and sometimes obscure. Exploring the symbolic connection between a part's name and the client's history can be an interesting endeavor, but it is usually not worth the effort expended when the number of sessions is limited by finances or insurance benefits. My preference is to focus upon particular problems, or blocks to a client's effective functioning. In doing this work, it is not necessary to understand the multitude of symbols found in the exploration of the inner world.

The same is true for the self-images parts present to client and therapist. Monsters are fairly common in the inner world, as are demons and witches. The *Wicked Witch of the West* from the movie, *The Wizard of Oz*, appears as a part's self-image in many clients. In most cases, we do not need to explore how parts acquired their symbolic costumes although, as with the case of Fluffy and The Monster, it can be interesting to do so. It is generally enough to know that a ferocious self-image generally indicates the presence of conflict in the system. Healing the conflict becomes our focus.

In the story of Fluffy and The Monster, we discovered Georgia's inner conflict between being a follower and being a leader. As an eldest child, she was naturally in a position to be the leader of her group of four siblings. However, she had a less dominant part of herself who would rather have her relax sometimes as she followed the less demanding path of going along with others. When The Monster inflicted the wound on Fluffy, this neglected part of herself was driven entirely into hiding; she did not appear again until Georgia experienced her adult crisis. Fluffy's wound seems to represent the inability to conform to others' popular ideas and the consequent ascendency of her drive to go her own way. The occasion of Fluffy's wounding marked a major developmental event in Georgia's life. Later, she left a relationally satisfying but intellectually undemanding corporate career for the new challenge of practicing law. Unfortunately, she found her work as an attorney to be personally unsatisfying as well as exhausting with its demands upon her time. Other parts of her personality, such as the desire to be helpful to others at her own expense, blocked her from the successes to which she was accustomed. She then began to experience significant regret for the life decisions that led her to leave her first company, break up with her college sweetheart, and pursue a career where her needs for a supportive network of associates were stifled. The conflict between Fluffy and The Monster was just one of the conflicts that set the stage for mid-life unhappiness.

Georgia did not have a monster inside her, nor even a little boy dressed as a monster. She did not have a stuffed-toy Easter Bunny or a White Dragon living within herself. She had only one body. But she did have parts, or subpersonalities, who expressed themselves as if they were real entities possessing substantial bodies of their own. These bodies symbolized different aspects of Georgia's life experiences, and they symbolized conflicts and themes that were important to her. The unconscious mind speaks to us in terms we can understand, and we can understand a bully hurting a smaller and weaker child in order to have his way. Thus, Fluffy acquired her symbolic wound. We accepted her wound as if it were an actual, external, physical wound. We treated it by healing the inner conflict it represented. The Little Boy had his own symbolic wounds, the greatest of which was the monster suit he wore. For Fluffy, the Little Boy became a Monster when he hurt her. From the Little Boy, we learned that his monster suit was acquired in response to conflict with other parts of Georgia's personality as well.

It is difficult to say exactly what is a part or subpersonality. Although it does not have a substantial body of its own, it acts as if it does. It has an influence on how we experience our actual bodies. Normal parts do not take executive control of our physical bodies, but in the extreme cases of dissociative identity disorder (multiple personality disorder), internal parts do take control of the external body. Studies have shown measurable differences in such variables as heart rate, blood pressure, and visual acuity between persons with and without executive control by subpersonalities. A part, or subpersonality, has a sense of self with its own themes for motivated action. Sometimes a part's perspective conflicts with the perspectives of other part-selves. Each has its own set of autobiographical memories that only partially overlaps with the memory sets of other parts. A part may know of life history events that are contained within the memory sets of other parts, but it does not have a felt sense of having experienced those events. A part also generally has a characteristic self representation, although that representation is not immutable. Sometimes a part's self-image is present before we do the work to discover the internal world. All of Georgia's parts appear to have had their particular self-images prior to therapy, but with other clients, parts have sometimes chosen self-images at the time we first began to work with them in therapy. That image might differ from the person in front of us by no more than a facial expression, a change in hairstyle, of a set of clothing. Finally, and this is very important for doing parts therapy, parts have a desire to continue their existence. They do not wish to disappear. The most frequent reason for a lack of cooperation by parts in therapy is the fear parts sometimes have that the work we do may cause them to disappear. When present, that fear must be addressed before we can move forward in the therapy.

Chapter 15
Summary and Conclusion

Objectives

In writing this book, my goal has been to illustrate the value of Parts Psychology in psychotherapy. Additionally, I also wanted to introduce the theory as a way of understanding the mind and the natural multiplicity of the self. Parts psychology helps patients to identify and converse with the parts of themselves (subpersonalities) that are holding on to negative emotions—and sometimes positive emotions—which then negatively influence their current behaviors and world views.

As previously noted, this book does not describe any cases of dissociative identity disorder. Each of the extended case descriptions that make up the body of the book is a study of the inner world of a person with normal personality structure. Parts are the natural building blocks of the mind, enabling humans to adapt and adjust to the normal experiences of dealing with new environments and novel social interactions. Parts appear in our lives organically, as the result of a universal developmental process, emerging as a way to deal with or manage new challenges or painful life experiences. They generally contain the memory of their creation events, as well as memories of other personally significant events, and they influence the self's thoughts and actions in those situations that somehow resemble the themed contents of their memory sets.

Much of the imagery and reported conflict between parts can be understood as metaphor. Some individuals are able to call up extremely vivid imagery, while others imagine their parts as a blob of emotion. Because of time constraints, it is generally not important to explore the origin of the imagery behind the parts as they are visualized. It is more important to facilitate internal conversation with the goal of discovering memories relevant to presenting therapeutic issues and then unburdening those particular emotionally charged memories.

When first introducing parts work to a new client, I am less concerned with imagery or conversational content than with facilitating the development of dialog between observing self and part. Thus, the precise answers to orienting questions regarding age, name, function, awareness of other parts, etc. are less important than the development of the dialog itself. Later, with communication pathways established, we can begin to explore parts dynamics and the healing of painful memories.

In general, parts work seems to be effective in helping clients focus less on day-to-day irritants — although those, too, benefit from the unburdening process — and more on the deeper past emotional experiences that shape behavior in the present.

At a minimum, parts work provides patients with a language to better describe their emotions. Parts Psychology approaches memories as the primary contents of different parts, with the memories being accessible to consciousness when the part is present with the observing self.

There are a few clients who cannot visualize their subpersonalities, yet who manage to do excellent parts work. Of these, most connect to their internal parts through body sensations. For example, a male client experienced parts sensations at various locations in his body. There were parts who spoke from the left, right, and back of his head; another manifested a sensation between his eyes and yet another from the area of the heart. These sensations appeared to be permanent connections between the client and his parts, and he communicated with them just as well as those who have internal images upon which to focus.

Although the great majority of clients are able to develop and maintain an internal image or other means of consistently connecting with an internal part, some 10 to 15 percent are unable to do parts work. Most often, this appears to be due to an aversion or antipathy to viewing the self as other than unitary. For example, several clients have cited their fears that having parts would mean they are *crazy*, or, doing parts work might *make* them crazy. A very few clients seem to lack the ability to visualize anything at all. Although fears that doing parts therapy are groundless, it is probably better to turn to more traditional helping approaches than to insist upon working with parts.

Even in these cases where the client is afraid of addressing internal parts, some of the visualization techniques described in this book can be helpful to the therapist engaged in traditional talk therapy. For example, suppose the therapy is stuck on a particular issue or experience and the client is unable to progress. A simple case might be where the client is unable to forgive a partner's insult delivered in the course of a heated argument. The client might acknowledge that the insult did not represent the partner's true feeling but still be unable to get past the sting of the insult. From a part's perspective, it is clear that a vulnerable part of the self has been hurt and the logic of the adult cannot reach it. In such a case, without ever talking about the idea of parts, the therapist might ask the client to focus on the memory of the powerful argument and insult, find an image of himself or herself in the memory scene, and then rescue the visualized self from the scene. The client might accomplish the rescue by imagining reaching out to the image of the self trapped in the memory scene, visualize taking its hand and leading it out of the memory scene and to a safe place. With the memory scene now altered, the client will no longer be stuck in the original event. A close reading of the Parts Psychology approach will provide many other ways to bring Parts Psychology techniques into the traditional talk therapy session.

About Parts

A formal definition that is consistent with all of the ways parts have presented themselves in the 13 narrative chapters follows. I use the terms part and subpersonality interchangeably. The primary content of a part, or subpersonality, is a set of autobiographical memories that are linked to each other through one or a small number of themes, such as loss of a loved one, personal embarrassment, or joyful moments of parenthood. There is at least a minimal consciousness, and sometimes full coconsciousness, with the observing self. There is a sense of personal identity and a desire to continue to exist. Most often there is a consistent self representation, but in cases where no internal visual self representation exists prior to the therapy, parts quickly adopt one. Parts vary considerably in the extent to which they have names prior to therapy. Some insist that they have always had names. Others acknowledge adopting one when they are first differentiated. Some do not have names and insist they do not want one, while some others don't

have a name but want one. The names and internal visual self representations are often metaphors, but what they represent are real phenomena of
the mind.

There are a number of different theories that attempt to account for the
creation of parts or subpersonalities. My own view, based upon work with
nearly a thousand clients and several thousand parts, is that our minds
spontaneously create new parts as we need them. Most often, parts appear
during difficult or painful times in our lives, although they may also appear
at times of pleasure, such as the birth of a woman's first child or a boy's
discovery of pornography. The key seems to be novelty. If the person already has strategies for dealing with a range of painful or pleasant experiences, no new part needs to appear. When there is something new in a
person's life, something for which existing parts have no familiarity or
adaptability, the mind will spontaneously create a new subpersonality to
deal with the challenge.

Clients report a wide range of internal images for their parts. Most often
parts present as current or younger versions of the client. Other parts may
appear as human strangers, material objects (clouds of depression or balls of
angry fire), black blobs, or cartoon characters. All such visualizations no
doubt carry symbolic meaning, whether conscious or unconscious, for the
clients who visualize them. However, discovering these meanings is not the
central focus of therapy. The goal of Parts Psychology is to heal the client
through work with the memory sets of the parts. The symbolic meanings of
parts' images may become clear through this work, but it may not. Given
that most clients have constraints on time or finances for therapy, those
resources usually can be better utilized doing direct healing through unburdening rather than aiming for insight through deciphering the symbolism.
Whatever the images that subpersonalities present of themselves, whether as
fantasy entities or as current-self copies, all clients can be equally successful
in working with unburdening them.

Although each part is connected with every other part within the larger
system, there is considerable variation in the degree to which individual
parts comprehend the larger system, as well as how they understand their
own role in the system. For example, some parts may be aware of a number
of dominant parts while others may be unaware of any other parts at all.

Some parts may understand that they protect the self in some way while others seem too immersed in their own pain to have any insight into their larger role. These latter parts may have no other autobiographical knowledge outside the moments of crisis where we find them.

The presenting age of a part is a strong indicator of the age at which it acquired consciousness and came into being. Autobiographical memories begin at this time. Sometimes, however, parts will know about events in the client's life but will not consider this knowledge to come from their own experiences. Sometimes they will say they learned about these events from other parts and sometimes they will not have an explanation, but they are sure that the events did not involve *them*. A fair analogy for this kind of knowing is the knowledge we may have for some of our own childhood events, not because we remember them, but because our parents told us about them more recently.

There are frequent exceptions to the idea that the apparent age of a subpersonality represents the beginning of autobiographical memories. An adolescent subpersonality, for example, may have early childhood memories; its appearance as a teenager my simply indicate that this time in the client's life was the part's most recent active period. Nor does a part's apparent age necessarily correspond to the *upper limit* of memories contained within its memory set. For example, a 12-year-old part may remember the client's high school or college years and may claim some of those memories as its own autobiographical experiences.

Individual subpersonalities may be entirely unaware of the client's current family life, or, if aware, may feel no familial relationship with spouses and children. Different parts may also express differing emotional values for the same family member. For example, one part may *like* the spouse; another may *love* the spouse and still another may *dislike*, even *hate*, the spouse. Parts may also know of some, but not all events from a given period of time. For example, Carson's 18-year-old part in Chapter 6 remembered parts of high school, but not the graduation. This subpersonality also knew of Carson's wife and children, but did not consider them to be his own.

Parts sometimes change their appearance over time, usually as a result of unburdening or other memory processing. After Carson's 18-year-old part began describing its memory set, Carson noted that the part looked "less crazed" than when he first identified him. In Chapter 4, Georgia's *Sword* part changed its appearance, becoming quite bright and shiny after completing its unburdening work. With child parts, unburdening commonly brings smiles to sad faces.

The Treatment Protocol

The basic protocol for parts work follows. First, find the part or parts that carry the problem emotion or behavior. This can be accomplished by asking the client to think about a person or event that causes them to become aware of the problem emotion—irritation or anger, for example. Ask the client to focus on the emotion and then to speak inwardly to the emotion, asking the emotion to give the client a picture of itself. The image that appears in the client's internal view represents the part.

Second, elicit the problem memories held by the part by asking the part to describe its earliest memories and, especially, its earliest *painful* memories. Then ask the client to rate how disturbing each individual memory is on the SUD (Subjective Units of Disturbance) scale from zero to 10, where zero represents neutrality and 10 represents the most disturbing level a memory can reach. In some cases the therapists may use a SUE (Subjective Units of Energy) scale, because the memory in question is not experienced negatively. It is important to remember that individuals experience something as *painful* or *traumatic* according to their own frameworks. Something that is considered a normal life experience by one individual may be considered traumatic by another. Something experienced as traumatic by a four-year-old part may seem quite minor from an adult perspective. It is important to respect the perceptions of each individual client, as well as his or her parts, and work to unburden those memories of their negative energy no matter how insignificant the memory might be to the adult or observing self.

Third, neutralize the energy attached to the problem memories through unburdening.

Unburdening

Unburdening involves neutralizing the usually negative, but sometimes positive, emotions or sensations that are attached to a part's memory set. This can be most efficiently accomplished through the visualization of a part releasing its problem burden of emotions through some sort of symbolic action. I often suggest that the part give up its burden to fire, wind, or water, but clients come up with many different means to disperse the disturbing energy associated with their memories.

As the part goes through the unburdening process, the SUD (or SUE) level should fall, eventually reaching zero. Zero is generally the only acceptable result of unburdening. When this proves impossible, work should be directed to the other parts in the system who are, intentionally or unintentionally, blocking this result. Repetition is often necessary to fully neutralize a memory. With each pass of the fire, wind, water, or other intervention, the therapist asks the client to ask the part to assess the remaining energy level. The process should continue until the memory is neutralized or until no further progress can be made.

Fully unburdening a client's difficult memories may take many weeks as the therapist works with the individual memories of a number of different parts. With some clients, the process can be sped up significantly by working with a large set of memories in a single unburdening intervention. Client variables, such as ease of access to internal parts, a sense of urgency, and whether the problem represents a stand-alone issue or is connected with a number of other problem issues, will also extend or shorten the time needed to heal a client.

Sometimes a part cannot immediately identify the memories that underlie a particular emotion or attitude. In such cases, the unburdening can proceed by suggesting that the part can release the problem emotion or attitude directly to the chosen intervention. What will likely happen during the unburdening is that multiple memories will flash through the client's mind as the intervention is carried out. These memories are quickly neutralized.

Working just with the part identified as the carrier of the problem is often not enough to fix the problem. This part is enmeshed in a web of relationships such that other parts may have investments in that part's destiny. Resistance should be expected from parts who fear that change may adversely affect their situations. When there is resistance of this sort, it is important to find the manager part who is resisting the work. Sometimes, requesting permission from the manager is sufficient to get the intervention moving again. On other occasions, the manager part must itself be unburdened significantly before the process can continue with the first part.

Sometimes, a part will appear to resist completing the unburdening, particularly as the SUD level drops. There are several possible reasons for this. If the SUD level drops very little during the initial unburdening intervention and the part claims no knowledge of any reason why this is so, it may be due to a younger, so far unrecognized part. The unrecognized part may be stuck in a distressing memory and may be amplifying that distress in such a way that the targeted part is unknowingly serving as a receiver. One way to locate the earlier memory or younger part is simply to ask the first part if it is aware of another part in the vicinity. Another technique is to bridge internally by asking the part to feel its distress and allow itself to float along the emotion until it connects to an earlier distressing memory or a younger distressed part. Chapter 8 provides an example of this where the client, Brandy, was having difficulty processing the Candace part's painful memories of her mother. Brandy asked Candace to look around to see if she could locate another part in distress. This allowed us to discover a seven-year-old Brandy part. As with this example, if the newly discovered part contains a significant traumatic memory, we then work to unburden the new part before continuing with the part we started with.

Another common reason for a part's resistance to unburdening is a fear of forgetting an important lesson it believes it has learned from the painful experience. In addition to assuring the part that it won't forget the lesson, the therapist can also guide the part in doing a temporary unburdening. For example, the therapist might ask the client to ask the part to place its burden into a portable container, such as a briefcase, which the part should hold in its possession. The therapist could then suggest that if the part continues to remember the lesson even with the negative emotions in a container, then perhaps they can be permanently released because the lesson is remembered without them.

A part might not have a clear explanation for its reluctance to unburden. In Chapter 3, one of Tina's parts was reluctant to allow the unburdening, but could not explain why that was so. I asked Tina to speak to the part, explaining the part's function in the larger self-system. That is, its job was to protect the self by holding the negative energy contained in the memory away from the self. By acknowledging the part's success and asking it to continue helping the self now by unburdening, the client was able to convince the part to cooperate.

The most frequent reason a part does not wish to give up its negative emotion is that it identifies so strongly with the emotion that it fears it might disappear if the emotion is unburdened. Thanking a part for the role it plays in sequestering negative emotion generally leads to greater cooperation in therapy. The part feels appreciated, even if it does not quite understand what it is being thanked for. Assuring the part that it can continue to play an important role in the system even after completing the unburdening process is also important. So, too, is developing a new role for the part and helping it to adjust to its new function in the system.

Unburdening Non-Negative Energy

Problem memories are often, but not always, painful ones. I have extended the concept of unburdening beyond work with negative emotions to include work with positive emotions or sensations, such as love and sexual arousal. Problem memories may also be memories that cannot be described as either positive or negative, just as containing a lot of energy. I use a 0-10 SUE (Subjective Units of Energy) scale to measure the energy invested in an experience when that energy is not negative. This measure works for positive memories as well as those where the part cannot classify the memory as either positive or negative.

In Chapter 4, I described the process of unburdening positive memories, which can have detrimental effects on a client's functioning similar to that of negative memories. In that case, Georgia's positive experiences of helping others in childhood were the foundation for Georgia's excess in helping others in adulthood. In Chapter 7, I helped Sam to unburden the positive energy associated with his love for Mary so that he could accept his coming divorce after Mary moved in with another man. Sam's romantic part, *Dream Sam*, had only positive memories of being with Mary and only a vague awareness of the bad times between them. This is typical of romantic parts. Our strategy was to release the positive energy from the accumulated events of the part's rather narrow memory set. This would allow other, struggling parts to unburden permanently the pain they felt over the loss. Dream Sam was reluctant to engage in the unburdening process at first. Sam reminded Dream Sam that the purpose of its existence was to help Sam and that Mary now lived with another man. She had refused even to speak to him for nearly a year; Sam needed to be released from his emotional ties to Mary. We concluded the session as Sam and Dream Sam negotiated a new role for the part: Dream Sam would help Sam select a new and appropriate partner.

We used a similar strategy of unburdening positive energy in treating Brandy's bingeing in Chapter 8. As is common with parts who are created out of positive emotion—in this case eating pleasure—the Candace part was reluctant to give up the positive energy connected to her memories. Uncommonly, however, our initial unburdening attempts failed to reduce the SUE level at all for Candace. This finding suggested the presence of another part who was somehow blocking the work. Previous experience with reluctant parts suggested that Candace should still have been able to reduce the SUE level by at least one or two. When Brandy asked, Candace identified an angry part as the one preventing her from unburdening. We moved on to work with the angry part with the eventual result that Candace was later able to successfully unburden her positive memories of binge eating.

Of course, memories can be *both* positive and negative. In the same chapter, Brandy tried to get her father's attention for a picture she had drawn while he was cleaning the pool; but he ignored her while he focused on his task. She set out to make her father feel bad about ignoring her by tearing up her picture and crying until he got out of the pool to console her. The part who carried this memory was *Monster Boy,* and it disturbed him to a level seven on the SUD scale. At the same time, however, the memory also registered a nine for him on the positive energy SUE scale. Brandy first unburdened Monster Boy of the negative energy connected to her perceived rejection by her father. Then she turned her attention to the positive energy Monster Boy felt for being able to control her father. Although the positive burden was more difficult to unburden than the negative one, Brandy was able to direct Monster Boy to do so within three minutes of beginning the intervention.

Ending a Session

It is important for the therapist to monitor the emotional state of a client near the end of a session in order to ensure that the powerful deep work with emotions does not lead to emotional overwhelm between sessions. When a part's memories have been activated during a session, but not yet unburdened, it is possible for the attached emotions to create significant problems during the coming week. For example, unresolved anger may lead to unnecessary conflict, or unresolved sadness may lead to a period of depression. The best way to guard against such emotional overwhelm is to elicit only those memories for which there is processing time available during the session. When that doesn't happen, it is helpful to visualize leaving the unprocessed emotional energy in the therapist's office. For example, the therapist might suggest that the client guide the part in visualizing the placement of its energized emotions in a file cabinet or in some other real or imagined container in the office. A client might also have his or own ideas about how best to store the potentially dangerous energy. In Chapter 8, Brandy coached her Candace part to put her remaining binge energy into a safe in her garage until time to come to Brandy's next session. In addition to this symbolic energy storage, I also recommend that the therapist request that the client transport the highly emotional part to an imagined *safe room* or *playroom* where the part can entertain itself in a secure environment until the next session.

Endnotes

[1] Noricks, J. (1981). *A Tuvalu dictionary: Volume 1, volume 2.* New Haven: Human Relations Area Files Press; Noricks, J. (1981). The meaning of Niutao *fakavalevale* (crazy) behavior: A Polynesian theory of mental disorder. *Pacific Studies, 5,* 19-33; Noricks, J. (1985). Native-speaker componential models: A method for elicitation. *Ethnology, 24,* 57-76.

[2] For example, Noricks, J. (1983). Unrestricted cognatic descent and corporateness in Niutao, a Polynesian island of Tuvalu. *American Ethnologist, 10,* 571-584; Noricks, J. (1987). Testing for cognitive validity: Componential analysis and the question of extensions. *American Anthropologist, 89,* 424-438; Noricks, J., et. al. (1987). Age, abstract thinking, and the American concept of person. *American Anthropologist, 89,* 667-675.

[3] Prince, M. (1925). The problem of personality: How many selves have we? *Pedagogical Seminary and Journal of Genetic Psychology, 32,* 266-292.

[4] American Psychiatric Association (1994). *Diagnostic and statistical manual of mental disorders (4th ed.).* Washington DC: American Psychiatric Press.

[5] Roberto Assagioli, the Italian psychiatrist whose *Psychosynthesis* framework is internationally recognized, also developed his ideas in the early 20th century. He called parts *subpersonalities.* See Assagioli, R. (1965). *Psychosynthesis: A manual of principles and techniques.* New York, NY: Penguin Books.

[6] Watkins, J.G. & Watkins, H.H. (1997). *Ego states: Theory and therapy.* New York: WW Norton.

[7] Schwartz, R.C. (1995). *Internal Family Systems therapy.* New York, NY: Guilford Press.

[8] For example, see Stone, H. & Winkelman, S. (1989). *Embracing ourselves: The voice dialogue manual*. Mill Valley, CA: Nataraj Publishing. The authors interpret parts (subpersonalities) as the local representations of Carl Jung's archetypes.

[9] Helen Watkins describes an intervention she calls, *the silent abreaction*, which has some similarity to the unburdening concept. However, it appears to apply only to the release of anger. See: Watkins, H.H. (1980). The silent abreaction. *International Journal of clinical and experimental hypnosis, XXVIII*, 101-113.

[10] American Psychiatric Association (1994). *Diagnostic and statistical manual of mental disorders (4th ed.)*. Washington DC: American Psychiatric Press.

[11] Wolpe, J. (1990). *The practice of behavior therapy (4th ed.)*. New York, NY: Pergamon Press. In bringing the SUD and SUE scales to Parts Psychology, I was influenced by Francine Shapiro's use of the SUD scale in her EMDR treatment model. See Shapiro, F. (2001). *Eye Movement Desensitization and Reprocessing: Basic principles, protocols, and procedures. Second edition*. New York, NY: The Guilford Press.

[12] Watkins, J.G. (1971). The affect bridge: A hypnoanalytic technique. *International Journal of Clinical and Experimental Hypnosis, 19*, 21-27. For the somatic bridge, see Watkins, J.G., (1992). *Hypnoanalytic techniques: Clinical hypnosis (Vol.2)*. New York, NY: Irvington.

[13] Schwartz, R.C. (1995). *Internal Family Systems therapy*. New York, NY: Guilford Press.

[14] Schwartz, R.C. (2005). *Freeing the Self: Releasing the exiles*. Workshop presented 01/01/05-01-07/05, Esalen Institute, Big Sur, California 93920.

[15] Ellenberger, H.F. (1970). *The discovery of the unconscious. The history and evolution of dynamic psychiatry*. New York, NY: BasicBooks.

[16] Asking the client to visualize the therapist intervening in the memory scene is a favored technique in ego state therapy. See Watkins, J.G. & Watkins, H.H. (1997). *Ego states: Theory and therapy*. New York, NY: WW Norton.

[17] Bernstein, B. & Putnam, F.B. (1986). Development, reliability and validity of a dissociation scale. *Journal of Nervous and Mental Disease, 175*, 727-735.

[18] Putnam, F.B. (1997). *Dissociation in children and adolescents*. New York, NY: Guilford Press.

[19] Putnam, F.B. (1989). *Diagnosis and treatment of multiple personality disorder*. New York, NY: Guilford Press.

[20] Dell, P.F. (2006). The Multidimensional Inventory of Dissociation (MID): A comprehensive measure of pathological dissociation. *Journal of Trauma & Dissociation, 7*(2), 77-106. The MID Report as generated by MID Analysis v3.6.

[21] Dell, P.F. (2006). The Multidimensional Inventory of Dissociation (MID): A comprehensive measure of pathological dissociation. *Journal of Trauma & Dissociation, 7*(2), 77-106. Maria's report stated, "A MID score of 8-14 suggests that the test-taker has a few, diagnostically insignificant, dissociative experiences. This level of dissociation is common in therapy clients who do not have a dissociative disorder" (MID Report, Version 3.6).

[22] Radloff, L.S. (1977) The CES-D scale: A self report depression scale for research in the general population. *Applied Psychological Measurement, 1*, 385-401.

Index

20878115R00217

Made in the USA
Lexington, KY
21 February 2013